T0301769

The **Impact** of
C VID-19
on World Aviation Industry

Challenges and Opportunities

The **Impact** of
CVID-19
on World Aviation Industry

Challenges and Opportunities

Editors

Paolo Rizzi
Link to Beijing Consulting Partnership, China

Cristiano Rizzi
Link to Beijing Consulting Partnership, China & Eurasian Development Solution, China

Mario Tettamanti
Link to Beijing Consulting Partnership, Switzerland–China

World Scientific

NEW JERSEY · LONDON · SINGAPORE · BEIJING · SHANGHAI · HONG KONG · TAIPEI · CHENNAI · TOKYO

Published by

World Scientific Publishing Co. Pte. Ltd.

5 Toh Tuck Link, Singapore 596224

USA office: 27 Warren Street, Suite 401-402, Hackensack, NJ 07601

UK office: 57 Shelton Street, Covent Garden, London WC2H 9HE

Library of Congress Cataloging-in-Publication Data

Names: Rizzi, Paolo, editor. | Rizzi, Cristiano, editor. | Tettamanti, Mario, editor.
Title: The impact of COVID-19 on world aviation industry : challenges and opportunities /
    editors, Paolo Rizzi, Link to Beijing Consulting Partnership, China, Cristiano Rizzi,
    Link to Beijing Consulting Partnership, China & Eurasian Development Solution, China,
    Mario Tettamanti, Link to Beijing Consulting Partnership, Switzerland–China.
Description: New Jersey : World Scientific, [2022] | Includes bibliographical references and index.
Identifiers: LCCN 2022004946 | ISBN 9789811246135 (hardcover) |
    ISBN 9789811246142 (ebook) | ISBN 9789811246159 (ebook other)
Subjects: LCSH: Airlines--History--21st century. | COVID-19 Pandemic, 2020---Influence.
Classification: LCC HE9776 .I57 2022 | DDC 387.7--dc23/eng/20220202
LC record available at https://lccn.loc.gov/2022004946

British Library Cataloguing-in-Publication Data
A catalogue record for this book is available from the British Library.

For any available supplementary material, please visit
https://www.worldscientific.com/worldscibooks/10.1142/12522#t=suppl

Desk Editors: Aanand Jayaraman/Lixi Dong

Typeset by Stallion Press
Email: enquiries@stallionpress.com

Printed in Singapore

Preface

This book is intended to explore the future of air travel and its many facets, how this world is going to be changed in light of the crisis which has severely hit this industry, and also the potentialities emerged from this unforeseen scenario, and thus the advancements toward a greener aviation. Many elements play an important role in the aviation industry and all governments around the world have introduced restrictions to travels, but the authorities directly involved in the regulation of air transportation have responded with protocols which seem to work properly. However, it is a fact that this crisis will change the industry drastically. This book tries to explain these aspects in a clear manner by introducing the new trends in aviation.

The entire world economy depends on the transportation of goods and this aspect is also considered in the book and is an integral part of the work.

The global aviation industry has been disrupted by the COVID-19 pandemic on a scale not seen in its century of operation. But while many fleets of aircraft are grounded and travel is postponed, the industry has a unique opportunity to change its path and advance toward a more green aviation industry. Thus, this new book is aimed at illustrating not only the impact of COVID-19 on the global aviation industry and its many facets but also the disruptive innovations this crisis is bringing to this industry triggering a new phase of development for air transportation. There is now a great expectation for a greener aviation industry with the use of new sustainable fuels (including hydrogen). Moreover, this industry is now advancing and pushing for the so-called "electrification mode" for new aircraft. New electric aircraft are already a reality, especially for the general aviation segment, and soon bigger electrical airplanes will allow the transportation of passengers. This is only one aspect of the changes the crisis has provoked. In fact, another leap forward is a new concept of air travel and a completely new type of aircraft, the so-called eVTOL (that is, Electric Vertical Take-off and Landing Aircraft). The entry of air mobility with the use of VTOL will be at the center of the next revolution in the air mobility.

This new reality is already taking place with the development of prototypes although the road to its full implementation is still full of challenges. VTOLS are a new breed of aircraft, they are somewhere between commercial airplanes and remotely controlled drones, configured to carry large payloads and people.

After examining the global impact of COVID-19 on the entire aviation industry and the remedies governments and commercial airlines are taking in order to allow them to resist and navigate through this thunderstorm, there is a focus on China because it represents the biggest market for the future not only in relation to the number of passengers but also for a growing new market, that is to say the general aviation market which will be fostered by new regulations. As a matter of fact, China is opening its door wider to the private aviation sector because it sees it as an enormous opportunity to stimulate its internal economy and it also represents a push for the aviation industry, in particular the general aviation sector is a new segment for China where Chinese companies have already heavily invested in buying foreign manufacturers and a sector where Chinese investors see new opportunities. The fact that this book also examines the growing importance of general aviation in China offers a unique panorama of the aviation industry and of its potentiality especially when the pandemic will be overcome.

This book also evidences the passage to a greener aviation industry, touching themes such as sustainable aviation fuels, the use of hydrogen and in the near future the use of batteries which shall lead to zero emissions. The electrification of the aircraft is not a remote scenario, but a reality which is already taking place in the general aviation sector and it has already been introduced and adopted by some small commercial airliners. All these topics are treated in sequence and linked together in this book. This is the first time all these different aspects are analyzed together offering a meaningful panorama for the future of the aviation industry. This book presents aspects of the aviation industry which usually are downplayed but which are part of an ecosystem and represent an important part of the said industry. In addition, this new manuscript introduces a very hot and promising theme, which is "Urban Air Mobility," putting it into the context of air transportation.

China without any doubt represents the new frontier in relation to the general aviation and business aviation. For China these sectors are full of new opportunities and can foster the aviation industry itself; the internal market of the Middle Kingdom will see enormous developments related to these facets thus contributing in sustaining its economy.

Cristiano Rizzi and Paolo Rizzi

About the Editors

Paolo Rizzi is an Italian professional who has been working as a project developer for EU companies for the past 8 consecutive years. Paolo possesses a two-fold qualification as a Lawyer: Incorporated as *Abogado* (Lawyer) at the "Illustre Colegio de Abogados de Salamanca" (Spain), and registered as "Established Lawyer" at the Milan BAR (Italy). Paolo has obtained a Master's degree (LL.M.) in International Business Law at Oxford Brookes University (UK). After his professional experience, Paolo obtained his Commercial Pilot License with instrument rating (on multiengine land) and became an Ultra-Light Flight Instructor with both Spanish and Italian ratings. After his experience as a flight instructor, Paolo started developing specific aviation services in the EU allowing pilots to obtain and convert their licenses in the EU, and he is now developing new services in the aviation sector in Mainland China also and has started assisting Chinese pilots to obtain EU qualifications.

The author co-ordinated the development of this work, and co-authored of Chapters 1, 2, 3, and 4 with Cristiano Rizzi.

Cristiano Rizzi, is a foreign professional who has been working "on the ground" in Mainland China for the past 12 consecutive years, and is now cooperating with Mario Tettamanti, finding investment opportunities in the EU for Chinese companies. Rizzi is incorporated at the *Illustre Colegio de Abogados de Salamanca* (Spain), registered as "Avvocato Stabilito" at the *Consiglio dell'Ordine degli Avvocati di Milano* (Italy), Rizzi holds an LL.M in Chinese Law — obtained at Peking University (Beijing, China), an LL.M. in Spanish Law, University of Valladolid

(Spain), and an LL.M in International Business Law, University of Exeter (Exeter, UK). The author co-treated the parts related to Chapters 1, 2, 3, and 4 with Paolo Rizzi, and is the sole author of Chapter 6 concerning the Chinese legal framework regulation of general aviation in China.

Mario Tettamanti is partner and CEO of "Link to China." Tettamanti holds a Ph.D. in Economics (1981), and has worked in Mainland China for 8 consecutive years. Tettamanti is an Editorialist and Chief Redactor of the Economic Section at "Corriere del Ticino" (Switzerland). He is Professor at the Centro di Studi Bancari (Lugano). Tettamanti has a vast experience in the financial field and has worked as Deputy Head of the Financial Department, "Banco di Lugano" (UBS Group), and he was also Head of the Investment Advisors Committee — the first Vice President. During the period of 1985–1987, he was responsible for Italian, French, and German clients at UBS New York, in the position of Vice President. Tettamanti also acts as a point of reference for the most important private financial group in China and is assisting several Chinese companies in finding investment opportunities in the EU. Mario Tettamanti is the sole author of Chapter 5 regarding the cost toward a greener aviation industry.

Acknowledgments

This new manuscript titled *The Impact of Covid-19 on World Aviation Industry: Challenges and Opportunities* was prepared together with my brother Cristiano, and with Mario Tettamanti who have published several books about Chinese investments and policies, and how China is moving toward a more sophisticated economy. In this new context, we have underlined China's progress in expanding its aviation industry, both in terms of the growing number of passengers, and in opening up a new segment, which is the general aviation (GA) sector that seems to have a brilliant future and is destined to sustain further Chinese economy. These two professionals helped me in exposing in an organized manner all the different topics touched in this work. All these themes are of great importance to understand the aviation industry and the consequences and opportunities emerging from the impact of COVID-19 crisis for this industry which has been severely hit, forcing it to change and evolve into a more sustainable and green aviation industry.

Thus, I would like to express my gratitude to my co-authors for helping in developing this meaningful book which in our intention is aimed at offering to the general public, but not only, a clear panorama on where this industry is heading.

With their help we have analyzed in detail the many facets of the aviation industry and an important part is dedicated to the costs of transition toward a greener aviation and the legal framework regulating the general aviation sector in China which seems to have a great future.

We have tried and we hope we have succeeded in exposing in a clear manner what is happening to the aviation sector without being too technical. The reforms China is adopting should help in expanding the aviation sector and this opportunity is to be grasped by foreign investors also.

My gratitude goes to my Family also, for always encouraging me in pursuing this objective.

Paolo Rizzi

Contents

Preface   v

About the Editors   ix

Acknowledgments   xi

Abbreviations and Acronyms   xxiii

Introduction   1

Chapter 1   The Growing Interdependence between the Aviation
             Industry and the Economic Development of Nations   5
             Paolo Rizzi and Cristiano Rizzi

1. Contribution of the Aviation Industry to the Global Economic
    Development   6
    1.1 Aviation as a major contributor to global prosperity   6
    1.2 The direct and indirect impacts on other related
         economic activities   8
    1.3 Social benefits of aviation: Brief overview   9
    1.4 Sustainable air transport development   10
    1.5 Investments for the modernization and expansion
         of aviation infrastructures and use of new technologies   14
2. The Regulatory Framework: A Basic Introduction   19
    2.1 Hierarchy of the regulating bodies   20
         2.1.1 Regional organizations   21
         2.1.2 National regulators   22

2.2 An overview about ICAO and its functions   24
    2.2.1 Triennial Assembly   24
    2.2.2 Council   24
    2.2.3 Secretariat and Secretary-General   25
    2.2.4 Air Navigation Commission   27
2.3 Airport Council International: The "voice of the airports"
    interacting with world civil aviation bodies   27
2.4 IATA: Leading the airline industry   29
    2.4.1 A bit of history: From a new trade association
        to a new strategic thrust   30
    2.4.2 Main components of the IATA organizational
        structure   31
3. Classification and Definitions Used for Civil Aviation Activities 32
  3.1 Commercial air transport services   32
    3.1.1 Scheduled   33
    3.1.2 Non-scheduled   34
    3.1.3 Cargo services   35
  3.2 General aviation   37
    3.2.1 Instructional flying   37
    3.2.2 Pleasure flying   37
    3.2.3 Business flying   38
    3.2.4 Corporate aviation   38
    3.2.5 Aerial work   38
  3.3 Airport-related matters   39
    3.3.1 Ground handling (doc 9626)   39
    3.3.2 Slot allocation   40
    3.3.3 Fixed-Based Operators (FBOs)   40
  3.4 Air navigation services   41
  3.5 Maintenance and overhaul   41
  3.6 Civil aviation manufacturing   41
  3.7 Aviation training   43

Chapter 2   The Responses of the Market Concerning the
          Impact of COVID-19 on Different Sectors
          of the Aviation Industry   47
          Paolo Rizzi and Cristiano Rizzi

1. Economic Impacts of COVID-19 on Commercial Aviation:
  Airlines Need Financial Support for Restructuring in
  Order to Overcome the Crisis   48

1.1 IATA's view on financial aid and analysis of economic
    impacts of COVID-19   48
    1.1.1 Remedies adopted by the EU   50
    1.1.2 US response: Brief introduction   53
    1.1.3 China's response   55
1.2 Commercial airlines need restructuring to survive
    the impact of COVID-19   56
    1.2.1 Massive airlines consolidation   57
    1.2.2 Giant planes: Do they still have a reason to be
          operated?   58
    1.2.3 Reduction of fleets and the role of leasing
          companies   59
1.3 How leasing companies are reacting to COVID-19   60
    1.3.1 The rapid growing importance of Chinese leasing
          companies   61
    1.3.2 China's contribution to the world's aircraft leasing
          industry   63
    1.3.3 Chinese leasing companies becoming international   63
1.4 Impact of COVID-19 on CO_2 emissions: Introduction   65
    1.4.1 Impact so far: Informative box   65
    1.4.2 Keeping emissions low after the COVID-19:
          Brief introduction   67
2. Policies of ICAO and IATA Regarding the Emissions of CO_2 68
   2.1 CORSIA — The ICAO global market-based measure   69
   2.2 Sustainable aviation fuel and CO_2 emissions   70
       2.2.1 ICAO Global Framework for Aviation and
             Alternative Fuels (GFAAF)   71
       2.2.2 ICAO work on SAF   72
       2.2.3 Business Aviation Coalition for Sustainable
             Aviation Fuel to sustain SAF   73
   2.3 ICAO stocktaking process: Brief introduction   74
   2.4 New standards set   75
       2.4.1 Technology goals and standards   76
   2.5 State Action Plans and assistance   77
   2.6 The ultimate technology to decarbonize air travel:
       The use of hydrogen   78
       2.6.1 Challenges to overcome for the use of hydrogen   79
3. Impact of COVID-19 on Airports and on Personnel Involved
   in the Aviation Industry   80

3.1 ACI world data show dramatic impact of COVID-19
on airports   80
     3.1.1 Loss of more than 4.6 billion passengers   81
3.2 How ACI intends to manage the post-COVID aviation
landscape   82
3.3 Impact of COVID-19 on personnel and pilots   84
3.4 European aviation unites in call for support for green
recovery from COVID-19   87
3.5 Impact of COVID-19 on Maintenance Repair and
Overhaul (MRO)   89
     3.5.1 Looking ahead: Planning for the future   90
4. Aviation Must Prepare for the New Normal   91
4.1 ICAO and its "Take Off" guidelines to reconnect the
world and help airlines   92
     4.1.1 The role of civil aviation and the 10 key principles
for secure and sustainable recovery   93
     4.1.2 The CART "Take off" guidelines   95
4.2 IATA guidance complementing ICAO's CART   96
4.3 Flight plan to succeed in the new normal   99
     4.3.1 Airports to implement enhanced passenger flow
management   99
     4.3.2 Increased presence of automation and robots
at airports   100
     4.3.3 Improved hygiene management   101
     4.3.4 Airport Indoor Air Quality (IAQ)   102
4.4 Cargo services survived to the COVID-19   102
4.5 COVID-19 has favored business aviation: Introduction   103

Chapter 3   The Impact of New Technologies on the Evolution
of a Greener Aviation Industry and the Emerging
of a New Urban Air Mobility (UAM)   105
Paolo Rizzi and Cristiano Rizzi

1. ICAO Sustains Innovation in Line with EU Strategy   106
1.1 Innovative fuels   108
     1.1.1 Sustainable aviation fuels   108
     1.1.2 Lower carbon aviation fuels   109
     1.1.3 Hydrogen   109
1.2 ICAO is monitoring innovation in aviation   110
     1.2.1 Electrification of large commercial aircraft   110
     1.2.2 Regional/business aircraft   112

1.2.3 General aviation (GA) and recreational aircraft 112
1.2.4 Vertical take-off and landing (VTOL) aircraft 113
1.3 Evolution in UAM: Brief introduction 113
2. Hydrogen as an Evolution of SAF 113
2.1 What benefits can hydrogen offer? 114
2.1.1 Two options for hydrogen: Fuels cells or
combustion? 115
2.1.2 The future is not so far away: The world's first
four-seater hydrogen fuel cell aircraft was
presented in December 2020 116
2.2 Five key barriers for the use of hydrogen 118
2.3 Looking to the future 121
2.3.1 Transition to hydrogen inevitable but requires
more technological advancements 122
2.4 Transition to the electric propulsion 124
3. Electrical Propulsion for the Future 125
3.1 Electrical propulsion: Not a question of if, but when 126
3.1.1 Technological obstacles 126
3.1.2 Market demand 128
3.1.3 Regulation 129
3.2 Electrical aircraft: Possible future scenarios 130
3.2.1 Scenario 1: Evolution of today trend 130
3.2.2 Scenario 2: Niche application of electrical
propulsion 131
3.2.3 Scenario 3: Small-scale evolution of electrical
propulsion 131
3.2.4 Scenario 4: Large-scale evolution
of electrical propulsion 132
3.3 Electrical propulsion: A revolution impacting on several
aspects of aviation industry 132
3.3.1 Challenges for engine manufacturer and airframer 132
3.3.2 Technological and commercial challenges 133
3.3.3 Latest development: Electric airplanes could
finally take-off with ultra-light lithium-sulfur
batteries 134
3.4 Not only GA and recreational electric aircraft 136
3.4.1 The experience of Pipistrel 136
3.4.2 EASA certifies first fully electric plane worldwide 137
3.4.3 The revolution in action: "Eviation" another
example anticipating the future 138

4. UAM: Old Players and Newcomers Conquering the
   New Frontier   139
   4.1 What is an eVTOL and the factors which will
        determine its success   140
        4.1.1 Urban air traffic management   142
        4.1.2 Safety and certifications   143
        4.1.3 Competitive service-based pricing   143
        4.1.4 Social acceptance   145
        4.1.5 Mobile networks for low-altitude connectivity   145
   4.2 Which direction will UAM take?   147
        4.2.1 Air taxis (inner-city point-to-point services)   148
        4.2.2 Airport shuttles (suburban to urban services)   148
        4.2.3 Interregional services (intercity flights)   149
   4.3 New infrastructures needed: Vertiport are on the horizon   149
   4.4 Airbus, Boeing, and other manufactures developing eVTOL   150
        4.4.1 Boeing   151
        4.4.2 Porsche and Boeing to partner on premium
               UAM markct   152
        4.4.3 Aston Martin: Innovation in personal air mobility   153
        4.4.4 Embraer Dreammaker   153
        4.4.5 Airbus is testing its CityAirbus   154
   4.5 The future of air mobility in Europe: Brief introduction   155

Chapter 4   Business Aviation, and Its "Declinations" Have
            Responded with a Positive Feat to the Global Crisis   159
            Cristiano Rizzi and Paolo Rizzi

1. *Business Aviation*: Definition and Its Growing Importance   160
   1.1 Rise in private aviation's demand during the
        COVID-19 crisis   162
   1.2 Business aviation industry: Brief introduction and
        categories of aircraft   163
        1.2.1 Very lights jets   164
        1.2.2 Light business jets   167
        1.2.3 Midsize business jets   167
        1.2.4 Super midsize business jets   167
        1.2.5 Large business jets   168
        1.2.6 Ultra large business jet (VIP airliners)   168
2. Business Aviation Industry and Its Major Manufacturers
   and the Impact of COVID-19   168

2.1 Boeing and Airbus: Two heavy weights in aerospace
    service market   170
    2.1.1 BBJ by Boeing   172
    2.1.2 Airbus and its new concept of business jet   174
2.2 Smaller players but top global jet manufacturers:
    Impact of COVID-19 on deliveries   176
    2.2.1 Gulfstream airspace corporation: A brief
        introduction of its fleet and its new flagship G700   177
    2.2.2 Bombardier Inc. — Fleet composition overview
        and performances during the pandemic   180
    2.2.3 Dassault aviation: The Falcon family and the
        newest Falcon 6X — Results and deliveries
        of business jets during the pandemic   185
    2.2.4 Embraer: Line of production and performances
        during the pandemic   190
    2.2.5 Textron aviation (Cessna Citation business jets
        and Beechcraft) — Line of production and
        perspectives despite the impact of COVID-19   193
3. Revolution in Business Aviation with the Introduction of
  Celera 500L   198
  3.1 Business aviation goes greener with the Celera
    500L keeping an eye on performances   199
  3.2 Aerodynamics and the most efficient propulsion system
    make the difference   200
  3.3 An aircraft with an incredible gliding capability
    and internal volume   201
4. The "Supersonic Renaissance"   201
  4.1 Uncertainties about compliance remain   202
  4.2 The ultimate supersonic experience by Aerion:
    An interrupted dream   204
  4.3 Spike Aerospace and its S-512 supersonic business jet   205
  4.4 Gulfstream and its pragmatic approach to supersonic speed   206
  4.5 A new supersonic airliner with "Boom" and its overture   207
  4.6 Virgin Galactic plans to go supersonic   209

Chapter 5   Toward a Green Aviation: Financial Investments
            in a Promising Sector   211
            Mario Tettamanti

1. Introduction: What is Sustainable or Green Finance?   211

1.1 The sustainable finance   213
1.2 The sustainable financial markets   213
1.3 Types of sustainable investments   214
1.4 The green financial instruments or products   216
     1.4.1 The green bonds   216
     1.4.2 The green mutual funds   217
     1.4.3 The stock market   217
     1.4.4 The ETF the so-called "green exchange-traded
            funds"   218
1.5 The urgent need for improved regulation in the green
     financial sector   219
2. The Green Finance in the Aviation Sector   219
   2.1 Measures to achieve international aviation's global goals   220
   2.2 Green alternatives: Sustainability-linked instruments
        for the aviation sector   221
   2.3 The aviation's public funding   223
        2.3.1 The network of public financing programs   224
   2.4 Private investing in green aviation   225
        2.4.1 Thanks to ESG, the private sector invest in
               green aviation   225
        2.4.2 Use of green finance can help the industry to
               obtain capital for green aviation   226
   2.5 Technology and financing in the green aviation   227
3. Transition toward a Green Aviation: Final Notes   228

Chapter 6   The Fast Economic Growth in China Will Favor the
            Development of Commercial and General Aviation   229
            Cristiano Rizzi

1. Regulatory Framework for Aviation in China and the Role
   of the CAAC   230
   1.1 Functions of CAAC and its departments   231
   1.2 Departments of the CAAC and their responsibilities:
        Brief overview   233
        1.2.1   Department of General Affairs   233
        1.2.2   Office of Aviation Safety   234
        1.2.3   Department of Policy, Law and Regulation   234
        1.2.4   Department of Development Planning   234
        1.2.5   Department of Finance   235
        1.2.6   Department of Personnel, Science & Technology
                and Education   236

	1.2.7	Department of International Affairs (Office of Hong-Kong, Macao, and Taiwan)	236
	1.2.8	Department of Transport	237
	1.2.9	Department of Flight Standards	237
	1.2.10	Department of Aircraft Airworthiness Certification	238
	1.2.11	Department of Airports	238
	1.2.12	Office of Air Traffic Regulation	239
	1.2.13	Bureau of Aviation Security	239
	1.2.14	CAAC Party Committee (Office of Ideological and Political Work)	240
	1.2.15	Group of Discipline Inspection (Bureau of Supervision Stationed in CAAC)	240
	1.2.16	National Civil Aviation Trade Union	241
	1.2.17	Bureau of Retired Officials	241
	1.3	CAAC's unique role: Final considerations	241

2. The Opening of Low-Altitude Airspace to Favor the Development of GA in China — 242
2.1 Definition of GA according to civil aviation law — 244
2.2 China to further open low-altitude airspace to boost GA — 245
2.3 The evolution of China's GA industry policy: A brief introduction — 247
2.4 Perspectives for the development of GA industry after low-altitude opening — 249
2.4.1. Industry insiders — 249

3. China Market is Responding More Quickly and Efficiently to the Crisis Caused by COVID-19 — 251
3.1 Pre-COVID-19 trend in domestic air travel and the impact of the outbreak — 251
3.2 Containing the outbreak is the starting point to reinvigorate low demand — 252
3.3 China the new frontier for business aviation and GA — 253
3.3.1 Consequences and impact of COVID-19 to the private jet market in China — 254
3.3.2 The private jet charter market and air taxi market are soaring in China — 255
3.3.3 The "air taxi" will be best mode of transportation in the future — 256
3.4 China sees an increase in GA companies — 258

4. The Aviation in Connection with the Belt and Road Initiative:
   A Brief Introduction   259
   4.1 More liberalization and common policies needed
        among the BRI countries   260
   4.2 ICAO Secretary-General calls for investments
        in air transport to enhance connectivity between
        Belt and Road countries   262
   4.3 China's air cargo market is embracing opportunities
        of Belt and Road   263
   4.4 The impact of COVID-19 on China's air cargo sector:
        Brief introduction   264

Conclusion   269
Bibliography   273
Index   285

Abbreviations and Acronyms

AAA	Authentication, Authorization, and Accounting
ABFA	Advanced Bio-fuels Association
ACI	Airport Council International
AMF	Aircraft Flight Manual
AFTF	Alternative Fuels Task Force
AIS	Aeronautical Information Services
ANSP	Air Navigation Service Provider
ATAG	Air Transport Action Group
ATC	Air Traffic Control
ATI	Air Transport Infrastructures
ATM	Air Traffic Management
AVIC	Aviation Industry Corporation of China
BRI	Belt and Road Initiative
BOC	Bank of China
CAAC	Civil Aviation Administration of China
CAAFI	Commercial Aviation Alternative Fuels Initiative
CAIGA	China Aviation Industry General Aircraft
CAEP	Committee on Aviation Environmental Protection
CNS	Communication, Navigation, and Surveillance
CANSO	Civil Air Navigation Services Organization
CC	Chicago Convention (or *Convention on International Civil Aviation*)
CORSIA	Carbon Offsetting and Reduction Scheme for International Aviation
CART	Council Aviation Recovery Task Force

CAV	Cargo Air Vehicle
CIC	China Investment Corporation
CNY	Chinese Yuan
CPC	Communist Party of China
CPCC	Communist Party Central Committee
C-UAS	Counter Unmanned Aircraft System
EASA	European Aviation Safety Agency
EBAA	European Business Aviation Association
EC	European Commission
ECA	European Cockpit Association
EU	European Union
EPD	Environmental Product Declaration
ESG	Environmental, Social and Governance
eVTOL	Electric Vertical Take-Off and Landing vehicle
FAA	Federal Aviation Administration (former CAA)
FYP	(or 5YP) Five Years Plan
E-HAPI	Electric and Hybrid Aircraft Platform for Innovation
EUR	Euro (unit of currency used in the EU)
FBO	Fixed-Based Operator
FDI	Foreign Direct Investment
GA	General Aviation
GAMA	General Aviation Manufacturers Association
GDP	Gross domestic product
GFAAF	Global Framework for Aviation and Alternative Fuels
GHG	Green House Gas
HFC	Hydrogen Fuel Cell
IATA	International Air Transportation Association
IBAC	International Business Aviation Council
ICAO	International Civil Aviation Organization
ICCAIA	International Coordinating Council of Aerospace Industries Associations
ICT	Information and communication technology
IFALPA	International Federation of Air Line Pilots' Association
IPCC	Intergovernmental Panel on Climate Change
IPRs	Intellectual Property Rights
ITU	International Telecommunication Union
LCA	Large Commercial Aircraft
LCAF	Lower Carbon Aviation Fuel

LMA	Loan Market Association
M&A	Mergers and acquisitions
MOFCOM	Ministry of Commerce (of the People's Republic of China)
MRO	Maintenance Repair and Overhaul
NBAA	National Business Aviation Association
NEXITT	New Experience Travel Technologies
NextGen	Next Generation Air Transportation System
NBSC	National Bureau of Statistics of China
NDRC	National Development and Reform Commission
ODI	Outbound Direct Investment
OECD	Organization of Economic Co-operation and Development
OEM	Original Equipment Manufacturer
OFDI	Outward Foreign Direct Investment
PPE	Personal Protective Equipment
PPP	Public-private partnership
PRC	People's Republic of China
R&D	Research and Development
RMB	Renminbi
SAF	Sustainable Aviation Fuel
SAFA	Safety Assessment of Foreign Aircraft
SEMS	Security Management system
SARPs	Standards and Recommended Practices (prepared by ICAO)
SESAR	Single European Sky Air Traffic Management Research
SES	Single European Sky
SC	State Council
SDGs	Sustainable Development Goals
SIPO	State Intellectual Property Office
SME	Small and Medium Enterprise
SOEs	State Owned Enterprises
S&T	Science & Technology
STCA	Supersonic Transport Concept Airplane
UAM	Urban Air Mobility
UATM	Urban Air Traffic Management
UAS	Unmanned Aircraft System
UN	United Nations

US	United States of America
UNEP	United Nations Environment Program
VTOL	Vertical Take-off and Landing aircraft
WCO	World Customs Organization
WMO	World Meteorological Organization

Introduction

Paolo Rizzi and Cristiano Rizzi

It seems appropriate before introducing the impact of COVID-19 on the aviation industry and in particular on air transportation, to illustrate some basic elements on how this sector is regulated. In particular, it is necessary to stress the importance of air transport for our society, and the classification of the different components forming this complicate ecosystem, in order for the general public to better understand how "air transport" is regulated and thus understand the functioning of the main regulatory bodies. Only after this preliminary introduction it will be possible to proceed with a more detailed analysis on the impact of the COVID-19 on the aviation industry.

Substantially two main international organizations contribute in disciplining this sector, namely ICAO, i.e. "International Civil Aviation Organization"[1] and IATA, i.e. "International Air Transportation Association."[2] Therefore, we have introduced some of their characteristics in order to have a plain and exhaustive panorama on how these international organizations are contributing in helping the recovery of aviation while facing this unprecedented crisis.

---

[1]The ICAO is a UN specialized agency, established by States in 1944 to manage the administration and governance of the Convention on International Civil Aviation (Chicago Convention).

[2]The IATA is the trade association for the world's airlines, representing some 290 airlines or 82% of total air traffic. IATA supports many areas of aviation activity and helps formulate industry policy on critical aviation issues.

As a matter of fact, the global aviation industry has been severely hit and disrupted by the COVID-19 pandemic on a scale not seen in its century of operation. This undoubtedly has also signaled the beginning of its transition toward a greener aviation industry, pushing all players in searching for new solutions for a safer and sustainable travel, accelerating the use of sustainable fuels and the implementation of new technologies. Speaking at the *Global Sustainable Aviation Forum*,[3] industry leaders reiterated that long-term climate action should be a priority alongside economic recovery in the coming years. Speaking about the need to focus on sustainability as part of the industry's long-term recovery from COVID-19, the Director General of Airports Council International, Luis Felipe de Oliveira, said: "The recovery of the aviation industry will be a key driver of the global economic recovery. To ensure that aviation can continue to provide the economic and social benefits, it is crucial that we pursue a green recovery and lay the foundation for a prosperous and sustainable industry for the long term. Airports are central to the interconnected and interdependent aviation ecosystem. Airports and their partners in the aviation industry need the support of appropriate regulation and government policies to facilitate a green recovery and push for real change."[4]

The crisis brought by COVID-19 will change forever not only the development path of this industry but also the modality for the public willing to travel by air. Likely, new technologies will help not only in reaching zero emissions which was already a target but also introducing a new

---

[3]Global Sustainable Aviation Forum, September 29–30, 2020 (virtual event). ATAG (Air Transport Action Group) 2020 Global Sustainable Aviation Forum — Green Recovery: The aviation industry emerging from the COVID-19 pandemic. As the aviation sector continues to reel from the sudden collapse of the air transport system, its challenges are compounded by the need to meet ambitious climate change goals going forward, while also meeting sustainability commitments. This year marks 15 years since ATAG, ACI, CANSO, IATA, IBAC, and ICCAIA first brought the aviation industry, its partners, and stakeholders together to discuss aviation and sustainability. The event is well-established as an important annual meeting of industries, governments, and environmental groups to address key factors that influence aviation's sustainability and to proactively seek solutions. On-demand access to the recordings of the 2 days is available for purchase, visit: https://web.event.com/event/d0f999af-d3c0-410f-ad79-3ffabba01661/summary? rp=00000000-0000-0000-0000-000000000000 (accessed December 5, 2021).

[4]IATA (2020), "Airlines Committed to a Green Recovery," available at: https://airlines. iata.org/news/airlines-committed-to-a-green-recovery (accessed December 5, 2021).

concept of traveling by air with the widespread of the so-called VTOL (Vertical Take-off and Landing aircrafts). This is only one of the aspects considered in this book. Commercial airlines are struggling to survive and certainly there will be a profound restructuring in the market allowing less operators than before, but hopefully with a more efficient and environmental friendly industry.

The aviation industry is composed of many facets, and it is possible to affirm that it is a sort of ecosystem in which each single player has a vital role. This is why we have introduced and treated, even if briefly, as many aspects as possible. However, an important component related to the "pure pleasure" of the flying it alone, is the ability to pilot a private aircraft, or flying "privately." This is the main reason why we decided to insert into this book a substantial part related to private business jets, which during the pandemic saw an incredible rise in its utilization, and also we decided to introduce the so-called "general aviation" with a particular focus on the China market, because this sector is on the rise. Especially in China this sector seems destined to boom, and an important reality such as Aviation Industry Corporation of China has already invested huge amount of money to acquire manufacturers to import the technology and the necessary expertise to build this new market which is only at its inception in China. Of course, China also needs to update and enhance its regulatory framework in order to accompany the take-off of general aviation but it seems dedicated authorities are already working to make it happen.

China's domestic aviation industry is now very close to 2019 levels and will likely enter the positive territory soon (in 2021). Thus, this aspect is also treated in this book. China in fact represents the next frontier in terms of volume of passengers and it is predicted to become the world's largest aviation market together with the surge of the aforementioned general aviation sector. China, the original epicenter of the outbreak, successfully contained the outbreak and has effectively suppressed flare-ups in Beijing and other provinces ever since through effective prevention works led by local governments. Air transportation in China has almost returned to normality because not only China was able to control the virus but also because there was a key piece of new technology (QR codes) and some old technology (face masks) that encouraged travelers to fly. In China each person's QR code is unique and linked to their mobile number, which is linked to their ID card. With public co-operation it has been very effective in containing even small outbreaks and in restoring the normal activities of people. It is noteworthy that mask wearing in China — and most of Asia — has been commonplace for decades. It is viewed as a common courtesy to protect others in the community. China's mask-wearing culture and other public health precautions, such as widespread temperature checking, have driven even higher levels of confidence in health and safety while traveling.

The part of the manuscript concerning China represents a substantial portion of this book not only for its dimension and further prospective growth but also because China is opening a new segment, namely general aviation which has enormous potentialities for manufacturers given the fact that the Chinese government intends to foster its economy and use general aviation as another pillar for sustaining internal economy.

https://doi.org/10.1142/9789811246142_0002

Chapter 1

The Growing Interdependence between the Aviation Industry and the Economic Development of Nations

Paolo Rizzi and Cristiano Rizzi

Aviation or in other terms "air transportation" and economic activities are deeply interconnected and interdependent. Real economy in fact drives the demand for air transportation services, and this relationship is extremely complex and bidirectional. Notably air transportation provides employment and enables certain economic activities in related sectors. The air transportation system is defined by its infrastructure capability, regulatory framework, and airline capabilities.[1]

Aviation is one of the most "global" industries: connecting people, cultures, and businesses across continents, and it is composed by several linked sectors as it will emerge from this chapter.

In consideration of the importance of aviation for economic development the UN (UN) also issued some general guidelines and formed a special Advisory Group, namely the "High-level Advisory Group on Sustainable Transport" which aims at formulating recommendations to help the world address rising congestion and pollution, particularly in

---

[1] In this sense, Mariya A. Ishutkina and R. John Hansman (2009), "Analysis of the Interaction between Air Transportation and Economic Activity: A Worldwide Perspective," Report No. ICAT-2009, available at: https://core.ac.uk/download/pdf/4407391.pdf (accessed December 7, 2021).

urban areas, and to better tap into the tremendous opportunities that sustainable transport can make possible.[2] In accordance with the recommendation made by the UN Secretary-General's Advisory Group, all stakeholders must make a genuine commitment to transforming the transport system in terms of individual travel and freight into one that is *"safe, affordable, accessible, efficient, and resilient while minimizing carbon and other emissions and environmental impacts."*

1. Contribution of the Aviation Industry to the Global Economic Development

Aviation is a key driver of the global economic development and it facilitates international trade. For instance over a third of all trade by value is sent by air, which makes aviation a key component of business worldwide. Compared to other modes of transport, air freight is fast and reliable over great distances. However, these benefits come at greater cost than other transport modes. Consequently, air freight is mostly used to deliver goods that are light, compact, perishable, and have a high unit value.[3] The development of aviation industry has impacted not only on our lives and permitted to travel all around the world in a few hours but also it has enormously contributed to global prosperity thanks to fast connectivity. A series of benefits derive from this industry and deserve to be briefly analyzed in order to clearly point out how important aviation is in this globalized world.

1.1 *Aviation as a major contributor to global prosperity*

As it will emerge more clearly from the next sections, aviation has enormously contributed to global prosperity, and it has become an integral part of our economic systems. Notably air transport facilitates world trade and

---

[2] In this sense, UN Secretary-General Ban Ki-moon (2016), "Mobilizing Sustainable Transport for Development — Analysis and Policy Recommendations from the UN Secretary-General's High-Level Advisory Group on Sustainable Transport," Foreword by Secretary-General, available at: https://sustainabledevelopment.un.org/content/documents/2375Mobilizing%20Sustainable%20Transport.pdf (accessed December 7, 2021).
[3] See, Aviation Benefits Beyond Borders, "Enable Trade," available at: https://aviationbenefits.org/economic-growth/enabling-trade/ (accessed December 7, 2021).

it contributes to the global economy by increasing access to international markets and allowing the globalization of production.

According to recent estimates by the cross-industry Air Transport Action Group (ATAG),[4] the total economic impact (direct, indirect, induced, and tourism-connected) of the global aviation industry reached US$2.7 trillion, some 3.6% of the world's gross domestic product (GDP).[5]

Recent data contained in the report prepared by the ATAG, *the air transport industry also supported a total of 65.5 million jobs globally. It provided 10.2 million direct jobs. Airlines, air navigation service providers and airports directly employed around three and a half million people. The civil aerospace sector (the manufacture of aircraft, systems and engines) employed 1.2 million people. A further 5.6 million people worked in other on-airport positions. 55.3 million indirect, induced and tourism-related jobs were supported by aviation.*[6]

These estimates do not include the intrinsic value that the speed and connectivity of air travel provides, or domestic tourism and trade, as well as foreign direct investment simulated by good air transport connections, which is crucial to developing productive assets for economic growth in the long term.

---

[4]ATAG is a highly respected not-for-profit association that represents all sectors of the air transport industry. It is the only global industry-wide body to bring together all aviation industry players so that they can speak with one voice — and it works to promote aviation's sustainable growth for the benefit of our global society. ATAG's existence is entirely dependent upon funding from its members. These include airports, airlines, airframe and engine manufacturers, air navigation service providers (ANSPs), airline pilot and air traffic controller unions, chambers of commerce, tourism and trade partners, ground transportation and communications providers. The diversity of ATAG's membership adds to its credibility and high level of influence with international decision makers. ATAG has some 40 members worldwide. Its funding members play a driving role within ATAG and devote substantive time and resources to the association. They include: Airports Council International (ACI), Airbus, ATR, Boeing, Bombardier, Civil Air Navigation Services Organization (CANSO), CFM International, Embraer, GE, Honeywell Aerospace, International Air Transport Association (IATA), Pratt & Whitney, Rolls-Royce, and Safran. More information available at: https://www.atag.org/about-us/who-we-are.html (accessed December 7, 2021).
[5]Reference: ATAG (2018), "Powering Global Economic Growth, Employment, Trade Links, Tourism And Support for Sustainable Development Through Air Transport," available at: https://www.atag.org/our-publications/latest-publications.html (accessed December 7, 2021).
[6]*Ibid.*

Just to complete this short introductory section, it is worth reporting that air transport and in particular cargo service is a driver of global trade. The small volumes of air cargo amount to big values in world trade. Here it is sufficient to report that around 90% of business to consumer e-commerce parcels are currently carried by air. The e-commerce share of scheduled international mail ton kilometers (MTKs) grew from 16% to 88% between 2010 and 2018 and is estimated to grow to 96% by 2025.[7] This was a prevision before the outbreak of the COVID-19. In any case these numbers are to be revised. Although cargo service likely is not going to be hit so heavily compared to passengers service, a reduced capacity may occur or be decided by operators to meet the new circumstances.

1.2 *The direct and indirect impacts on other related economic activities*

The aviation industry is a source of considerable economic activities, impacting directly and indirectly on other businesses and services surrounding the whole sector. These not only include airports where it is possible to buy goods tax free, but also construction companies that build airport facilities, ANSPs,[8] other transports such as trains, taxies, shuttles, buses which serve passengers from airports to their final destinations, check-in, baggage handling, catering services (for airlines), not to mention all high-skill jobs in the manufacturing sector with those companies that produce aircrafts, engines, and other vital technologies for the correct functioning of airplanes and also for airports (scanners and other security devices). These are some of the services and activities which are concerned, however there are others to be considered such aviation fuel suppliers, and suppliers of sub-components used in aircrafts, and finally also suppliers of products such as radars and satellite-based navigation systems to the air traffic management (ATM) industry.

---

[7]Estimates jointly by ICAO, Universal Postal Union (UPU), and UN Conference on Trade and Development (UNCTAD).

[8]ANSP refers to any public or private entity providing air navigation services for general air traffic. Definition Source: EUROCONTROL (2007), "Principles for Establishing the Cost-Base for *En Route* Charges and the Calculation of the Unit Rates," p. 29; ICAO, DOC 9885 Guidance on the Use of Emissions Trading for Aviation 2008, p. (ix).

Aviation's impacts on other industries do not stop here, impressively it also offers just-in-time delivery systems in the supply chains; enables international investments into and out of countries and regions; and supports innovations by encouraging effective networking and collaboration between organizations located in different parts of the globe. Good air transport links are considered to be essential factors influencing where companies choose to invest. Countries need connectivity to fully participate in the worldwide economy.[9]

Another important industry which is intrinsically connected to air transport is tourism. Tourism represents a significant contribution to the worldwide economy. The connectivity brought by air transport is in fact at the heart of tourism development, providing substantial economic benefits for all those involved in this industry. Before the impact of the COVID-19, approximately 1.4 billion tourists were crossing borders every year.[10] However, unfortunately everything has changed and it is to be seen when and how this correlated industry will recover.

1.3 *Social benefits of aviation: Brief overview*

The ability to travel all around the globe by air can be considered as one of the most important social benefits of aviation. Connecting people and accessing distant regions contribute in strengthening relations among nations, in other terms air transport greatly contributes to the so-called globalization.

Air transport enables us to travel and experience new countries and cultures more conveniently because we can reach our desired destinations in a short period of time. Going abroad for work and study, or simply for holidays is more convenient and it can be done at a very reasonable price.

What we are trying to highlight here is that air transport connectivity can make it possible to realize determined goals for the society such as promoting lifelong learning opportunities to access higher-quality education for many traveling to another country, sometimes to another corner of the globe — simply because air transport render it possible, in fact these

---

[9]In this sense, see the report titled Aviation Benefits Report, 2019, ICAO, available at: https://www.icao.int/sustainability/Documents/AVIATION-BENEFITS-2019-web.pdf (accessed December 7, 2021).

[10]World Tourism Organization (UNWTO) (2019), *World Tourism Barometer*, Vol. 17.

opportunities would not be feasible, particularly for shorter-term university exchange programs if we need to reach our destinations via other means of transport.[11]

Health also is to be included as another social benefit: *Although not directly linked to improving physical heath, air transport, with its ability to provide speedy and safe transport of people and cargo to places that are often in remote areas of the world, has a part to play.*[12] As reported in the ATAG's report a prime example of how aviation plays a role in public health is the ability to transport medical supplies and medical staff. *A prime example of how aviation contributes to public health is the rapid delivery of medical supplies and organs for transplantation worldwide. Not only are these vital medical supplies time sensitive, making other modes of transport unviable over long distances, but their destinations are often remote areas where other transport modes are limited.*[13] Aviation's unique ability to combine speed with flexibility renders it vitals to respond to emergencies or special situations in hours. Aviation provides the only possible transportation means for certain health and humanitarian aid.

1.4 *Sustainable air transport development*

Air transport undeniably is contributing to sustainable development and this was recognized by the UN: "in September 2015, world leaders gathered at the UN and adopted the *Transforming Our World: 2030 Agenda for Sustainable Development.*[14] This Agenda is a plan of action that aims to achieve sustainable development in areas of critical importance to humanity and the planet, touching upon matters related to economic, social and environmental responsible and durable progress while ensuring that no one is left behind." Notably, the principles contained in this Agenda are shared by the International Civil Aviation Organization

---

[11] See ATAG's report titled, *Aviation: Benefits Beyond Borders*. This 2018 edition of the full report is at: https://www.atag.org/our-publications/latest-publications.html (accessed December 7, 2021).

[12] *Ibid.*

[13] *Ibid.*

[14] Reference: UN, *Transforming Our World: 2030 Agenda for Sustainable Development*, available at: https://sustainabledevelopment.un.org/post2015/transformingourworld (accessed December 7, 2021).

(ICAO)[15] which has further elaborated on it and produced its own views and initiatives. Indeed ICAO *is committed to taking all necessary actions to maximize the benefits of aviation in a sustainable manner that is safe, secure, efficient, economically viable and environmentally responsible; and seek new, innovative, sustainable air transport solutions to accelerate the implementation of the ICAO No Country Left Behind (NCLB)*[16] *initiative and in support of the SDGs*[17] *of the UN Transforming our World: 2030 Agenda for Sustainable Development* (Dr. Fang Liu, Secretary General, ICAO).

Attainment of the Sustainable Development Goals (SDGs) relies on advances in sustainable air transport and mobility, which is a driver of sustainable development. Needs for assistance and capacity-building, including infrastructure, should be mapped out and prioritized in line with the SDGs. All stakeholders must make a genuine commitment to transforming the transport system, in terms of individual travel and freight, into

---

[15]The ICAO is a UN specialized agency, established by States in 1944 to manage the administration and governance of the Convention on International Civil Aviation (Chicago Convention). More information is available at: https://www.icao.int/publications/Documents/7300_cons.pdf (accessed December 7, 2021).

[16]The NCLB initiative highlights ICAO's efforts to assist States in implementing ICAO Standards and Recommended Practices (SARPs). The main goal of this work is to help ensure that SARP implementation is better harmonized globally so that all States have access to the significant socio-economic benefits of safe and reliable air transport. See: https://www.icao.int/about-icao/nclb/pages/default.aspx. These socio-economic benefits include: expanded tourism; greater access for businesses and producers to foreign supplies and markets; improved emergency transport and search and rescue (SAR) capabilities; and many other cultural and economic advantages arising from the global connectivity provided by aviation. See *Annual Report of the ICAO Council: 2015 — All Strategic Objectives: No Country Left Behind*, available at: https://www.icao.int/annual-report-2015/Pages/all-strategic-objectives-nclb-initiatives.aspx (accessed December 7, 2021).

[17]The 17 SDGs and 169 targets under the 2030 Agenda of the UN for sustainable development can be used as a compass for aligning countries' plans with their global commitments by 2030. Due to the interlinked nature of these goals and targets, a global partnership is required in order to bring together governments, the private sector, civil society, the UN system and other actors to mobilize all available resources in the pursuit of a better and more sustainable future for all. More detailed information can be found in the Agenda: UN, *Transforming Our World: 2030 Agenda for Sustainable Development*, available at: https://sustainabledevelopment.un.org/post2015/transformingourworld (accessed December 7, 2021).

one that is *safe, affordable, accessible, efficient, and resilient while minimizing carbon and other emissions and environmental impacts.*[18]

It is noteworthy that many of the SDGs are directly and indirectly connected to sustainable air transport as ICAO has highlighted.[19] Besides the aforementioned social and economic benefits, aviation contributes to the SDGs in the following ways:

- SDG 8 in particular calls on governments to promote inclusive and sustainable economic growth, employment and decent work for all. Through policy convergence between air transport and tourism, aviation directly contributes to SDG Target 8.9[20]: *devise and implement policies to promote sustainable tourism that creates jobs and promotes local culture and products by 2030.*
- SDG 9 states that building resilient infrastructure, promoting inclusive and sustainable industrialization and fostering innovation, is a prerequisite to the mobility of people and goods. Aviation is one of the most innovative industries in the world. The manufacturing sector is continually developing new technology and creates significant urban infrastructure through the construction of airports and navigational infrastructure.[21]
- SDG 11 aims at making cities inclusive, safe, resilient, and sustainable. Aviation plays a fundamental role in overcoming the social exclusion of vulnerable groups because aviation-related infrastructure is a major part of the urban and rural communities worldwide and contributes to the connectivity of populations through integrated transport links.[22]

---

[18] See UN (2016), *Mobilizing Sustainable Transport for Development*, available at: https://sustainabledevelopment.un.org/index.php?page=view&type=400&nr=2375&menu=1515 (accessed December 7, 2021).

[19] More detailed information on how ICAO supports the SDGs is available at: https://www.icao.int/about-icao/aviation-development/Pages/SDG.aspx (accessed December 7, 2021); ICAO's Strategic Objectives are strongly linked to 15 of the 17 UN SDGs. The organization is fully committed to working in close cooperation with States and other UN bodies to support related targets.

[20] SDG indicators, see https://unstats.un.org/sdgs/indicators/database/?indicator=8.9 (accessed December 7, 2021).

[21] See ATAG's report titled, *Aviation: Benefits Beyond Borders*. This 2018 edition of the full report is at: https://www.atag.org/our-publications/latest-publications.html (accessed December 7, 2021).

[22] *Ibid.*

• SDG 13 states that urgent action to combat climate change and its impacts is a key priority for every responsible citizen or organization today. According to the most recent figures from the Intergovernmental Panel on Climate Change (IPCC), aviation (domestic and international) accounts for approximately 2% of global CO_2 emissions produced by human activity; international aviation is responsible for approximately 1.3% of global CO_2 emissions.[23]

Naturally, progress toward the sustainable goals established by the UN, in particular those related to aviation, are monitored by the specialized agency ICAO of the UN. ICAO is a custodial agency responsible for collecting traffic data and sharing the information with the UN system to support the agreed global indicator (passenger and freight volumes by mode of transport) of the SDG Target 9.1[24] — Develop quality, reliable, sustainable, and resilient infrastructure with a focus on affordable and equitable access for all.[25] This global indicator helps States to take a data-driven approach to address infrastructure gaps through appropriate policy and financing interventions. Finally, it is also worthy reporting that national-level progress and challenges on implementation toward the achievement of the SDGs are reported annually by States to the UN High Level Political Forum on Sustainable Development in the form of the Voluntary National Reviews (VNRs). By including aviation within the VNR reporting, States recognize the strong link between aviation and development.[26]

---

[23] See the report by IPCC, *Change 2014: Mitigation of Climate Change*, Assessment Report, available at: https://www.ipcc.ch/report/ar5/wg3/ (accessed December 7, 2021).

[24] SDG indicators, see https://unstats.un.org/sdgs/indicators/database/?indicator=9.1.2 (accessed December 7, 2021).

[25] See in this sense, UN, Economic and Social Council (2017), "Progress towards the Sustainable Development Goals," Report of the Secretary-General, available at: https://unstats.un.org/sdgs/files/report/2017/secretary-general-sdg-report-2017--Statistical-Annex.pdf; see also: https://unstats.un.org/sdgs/indicators/database/?indicator=9.1.2 (accessed December 7, 2021).

[26] In this sense, see the report by ICAO titled *Aviation Benefits Report 2019*, available at: https://www.icao.int/sustainability/Documents/AVIATION-BENEFITS-2019-web.pdf (accessed December 7, 2021).

1.5 *Investments for the modernization and expansion of aviation infrastructures and use of new technologies*

In order for aviation to continue to growth, new investments are needed to ameliorate air transport infrastructure (ATI).[27] Investments for the modernization and expansion of quality aviation infrastructures is likely to increase. For example, the global investment needs for airport expansion and construction are estimated at US$1.8 trillion from 2015 to 2030.[28] These previsions were made about one decade ago. Though the impact of COVID-19 on investments directed to ATI is uncertain today, it certainly will resume because ATIs are essential to the development of air transport. Notably investment in aviation infrastructure "ensures that the capacity of the global aviation system can meet future demand; generate gains such as reductions in travel time and improvement of service predictability and reliability; and, at the same time, maintain public confidence that aviation is safe, secure and environmentally responsible."[29]

Concerning ATI investments, unlike other modes of transport, in general the aviation industry has been paying for a vast majority of its own infrastructures (like for example, runways, airport terminals, air traffic control), rather than being financed through taxation or public investment. Basically, infrastructure costs are covered through payments of user charges, as well as other revenue sources generated by these infrastructures in particular facilities for passengers at airports.

As stated in the report by ICAO, "build a transparent, stable and predictable investment climate, it is necessary for States to take pragmatic measures, for example, by engaging multi-stakeholders, diversifying funding sources and elevating the role of the private sector, including through private investment, business reform, private finance initiatives, public–private partnerships (PPPs) and various incentive schemes."[30] Furthermore the same report also affirms that "where private capital is

---

[27]ATI includes airports and broader infrastructures required to facilitate air travel; these include air traffic control centers (ATCs).

[28]See Organisation for Economic Co-operation and Development (OECD) (2011), *Strategic Transport Infrastructure Needs to 2030*.

[29]In this sense, see the report by ICAO titled *Aviation Benefits Report 2019*, section "Modernizing Aviation to Maximize Its Benefits," available at: https://www.icao.int/sustainability/Documents/AVIATION-BENEFITS-2019-web.pdf (accessed December 7, 2021).

[30]*Ibid.*

required, appropriate and targeted oversight delivering the right incentives needs to be put in place to guarantee capital injection into much needed infrastructure while safeguarding consumer interests and increasing efficiency in the use of infrastructure. Such policy decisions will not only affect an infrastructure operator's bottom line but also the overall services and choices that are offered to the travelling public."[31]

Modernization is a key factor for enhancing the functioning of aviation, and in fact international organizations such as the IATA[32] and ACI[33] involved in its development are pushing initiatives and attracting investments aimed at improving the efficiency of the entire sector. For instance the introduction of "New Experience Travel Technologies" (NEXTT) will shape the future of air transport.

NEXTT is a joint IATA and ACI initiative that defines a vision for the future of air transport that seeks to improve efficiency, customer experience and operational effectiveness by leveraging the latest technology and innovative processes. The NEXTT vision examines the elements that will likely transform the complete end-to-end journey over the next 20 years. Planning ahead for the seamless, multimodal door-to-door journey of the future, the focus is on three emerging concepts:

- *off-airport activities — flexibility in what can happen before and beyond the airport;*
- *advance processing — increasing use of digital identity management, automation and robotics; and*

---

[31] *Ibid.*

[32] The IATA is the trade association for the world's airlines, representing some 290 airlines or 82% of total air traffic. IATA supports many areas of aviation activity and helps formulate industry policy on critical aviation issues. More information is available at: https://www.iata.org/en/about/mission/ (accessed December 7, 2021).

[33] The ACI is the only global trade representative of the world's airports. Established in 1991, ACI represents airports' interests with governments and international organizations such as ICAO, develops standards, policies and recommended practices for airports, and provides information and training opportunities to raise standards around the world. More information is available at: https://aci.aero/about-aci/ (accessed December 7, 2021).

> - *interactive decision making — linking everything together and using predictive modelling and AI to optimize operations with trusted, real-time data.*
>
> *NEXTT includes partnerships with airlines, airports, service providers, and manufacturers to learn from individual concepts and trials, and to identify ways to integrate systems and improve operations in the most secure, effective and sustainable manner. It will help to identify areas where best practices can be defined, where further research is needed, and where regulatory development is required.*
>
> *Source*: ACI and IATA.

The *Aviation Benefits Report 2019* by ICAO highlights the importance of ATM and stresses the necessity to have it upgraded and modernized in order to respond to the dramatic traffic growth projections and the pressing need for more determined and effective climate-related stewardship. As pointed out by the report, mid-20th century technology is still being used to direct air traffic, with aircraft needing to zig-zag between ground-based radar posts throughout their journey in many regions of the world. This can be ameliorated using the latest technology. Technology in fact can help ATM to be more efficient, resulting in increased airspace capacity with the reduction of congestion and delays, improvement in safety, and reduction in aviation's environmental impact. Notably investment in ATM infrastructure requires a long-term planning horizon, considering the long lead-times for procuring new equipment such as ATCs and the latest surveillance equipment. It is the role of the States to ensure that improvements to ATM infrastructure are properly financed in collaboration with airports, airlines, and air navigation services providers.

It is worth reporting that in Europe, a collaborative project is underway called Single European Sky Air Traffic Management Research (SESAR), which is a part of the vision to consolidate fragmented European airspace into a single zone. The Single European Sky (SES) will enable far more efficient routing for civil aircraft, resulting in a 12% reduction in environmental impact alone through savings of between 8 and 14 minutes of flight time, 300 to 500 kilograms of fuel, and 948 to

1,576 kilograms of CO_2 per flight.[34] There are parallel initiatives in other regions. In the United States, the Next Generation Air Transportation System (NextGen) is the ongoing transformation from a ground-based system of air traffic control to a satellite-based system of ATM, resulting in an overall benefit-to-cost ratio of 3-to-1.[35] In the Asia and Pacific region, upgrading air navigation services would increase the overall aviation contribution to regional GDP from US\$470 billion in 2010 to US\$2,358.76 billion by the year 2030.[36]

Remote Tower Revolutionizes Air Traffic Control

In a small airport, air traffic control accounts for 30 to 40 per cent of its operating costs. Digitization of air traffic control towers provides one of the solutions to reduce operating costs without any loss of service or reduction in safety. Örnsköldsvik Airport in northern Sweden is the world's first airport with remote air traffic control.

---

[34]The implementation of the SESAR project, requires a total investment of US\$3.7 billion from 2008 to 2024. As the technological pillar of Europe's ambitious SES initiative, SESAR is the mechanism which coordinates and concentrates all EU research and development (R&D) activities in ATM, pooling together wealth experts to develop the new generation of ATM. Today, SESAR unites around 3,000 experts in Europe and beyond. More information is available at: https://www.sesarju.eu/discover-sesar (accessed December 7, 2021). The Single European Sky (SES) is an ambitious initiative launched by the European Commission in 2004 to reform the architecture of European ATM. It proposes a legislative approach to meet future capacity and safety needs at a European rather than local level. The key objectives of the SES are: (i) To restructure European airspace as a function of air traffic flows; (ii) To create additional capacity; (iii) To increase the overall efficiency of the ATM system, available at: https://www.sesarju.eu/background-ses (accessed December 7, 2021).
[35]The NextGen is an FAA-led modernization of America's air transportation system to make flying even safer, more efficient, and more predictable. NextGen is not one technology, product, or goal. The NextGen portfolio encompasses the planning and implementation of innovative new technologies and airspace procedures after thorough testing for safety. Through research, innovation, and collaboration, NextGen is setting standards around the world and further establishing the FAA's global leadership in aviation, available at: https://www.faa.gov/nextgen/ (accessed December 7, 2021).
[36]Economic Analysis of Seamless Air Traffic Management (presented to the Fourth Meeting of the ICAO Asia/Pacific Seamless ATM Planning Group (APSAPG/4)), 2013, IATA.

> *Since April 2015, air traffic services to and from the airport has been controlled from a remote tower in Sundsvall, 150 km away from the airport. This technology is much cheaper than building a tower; all that is needed are a series of cameras and sensors to record what is happening instead. A data network is used to digitally transfer images and data to Sundsvall. The data traffic can take several routes to ensure that the data arrives even if an interruption occurs.*
>
> *Developing countries can leapfrog to these latest, cheaper technologies to keep remote aerodromes open and viable, and buy surveillance "as a service" from a satellite-based surveillance supplier, rather than building costly air traffic control towers, radar and other ground-based infrastructure. Economies of scale also exist, with air traffic control at one central tower managing multiple airports.*
>
> *Source*: LSV, SaaB, and CANSO.

To conclude this section it is worth mentioning that modernization includes the use of new technologies also related to new forms of payments and related services. In particular, it is necessary to briefly mention why airlines should care about Fintech.[37] Innovation in financial technology has allowed for the development of new applications which render the experience of acquiring goods or services more smoothly and thus to bring nearer the needs of consumers with the offers of service providers especially in this case where travelers are seeking more convenient manners to book and pay for their journey. Fintech in fact is being built around consumers' needs, which is why Fintech companies have been able to

---

[37]Financial technology — more popularly known as Fintech — is a madly exciting and booming field that impacts every aspect of business and personal life, from loans and fundraising to mobile payments and asset management. Without a doubt, Fintech is a megatrend that is coming fast and revolutionizing all facets of the financial services industry. The air travel industry is preparing to embrace this trend, as the solution answers the demands of customers for 24/7 online access to services as well as the need for real-time, inexpensive, and reliable business partners. More information is available at: https://w3.accelya.com/blog/the-fintech-revolution-an-opportunity-for-airlines (accessed December 7, 2021).

deliver personalized customer experiences and establish trust in ways that traditional financial institutions haven't. Considering that airlines have experienced a surge of passengers, especially with the booming of low-cost carriers, there is a need to improve customer experience and to offer multi ways to acquire services (for example, car rentals and hotels) in the most convenient manner.

Fintech can also be employed to gather traveler data, which allows airlines to form insights and offer more customized services to their customers. Many Fintech firms have eliminated the middle man, which will undoubtedly lower transaction fees for airlines and increase their bottom lines. Fintech carries significant benefits for both airlines and their customers. Such technologies have the ability to greatly improve the customer experience while giving airlines a reliable and cost-effective financial partner.[38]

Having exposed in this first section some of the characteristics of aviation and how it impacts on the global economic development, it appears now appropriate to briefly describe the functioning of the international bodies which regulate air transport because it is clear that a more coordinated and predictable framework will help in enhancing the entire aviation industry.

2. The Regulatory Framework: A Basic Introduction

The continuous growth of air traffic and enhanced air connectivity can only be sustained with a globally harmonized regulatory framework. Modern aviation was founded upon the Convention on International Civil Aviation (the so-called "Chicago Convention" of 1944)[39] which set forth

---

[38] *Ibid.*

[39] The Chicago Convention, which is also known as international civil aviation convention was signed on December 7, 1944, by 52 States and came into force on April 4, 1947. The Convention was divided into four parts containing 22 Chapters and 96 Articles. Moreover, the Chicago Convention is a dual purpose treaty. It provides an "international civil aviation code" and also establishes the *"Constitution of the International Civil Aviation Organization"* (Mankiewiczt, 1963, p. 54). The text of the Chicago Convention is available at: https://www.icao.int/publications/Documents/7300_9ed.pdf (accessed December 7, 2021). The Chicago Convention had been amended several times including in 1947, 1954, 1961, 1962, 1968, 1971, 1974, 1977, 1980, 1984, 1989, 1990, 1995, and

the core principles permitting international transport by air and led to the creation of the ICAO. The mandate of ICAO, then (as it is today) was to help States to achieve the highest possible degree of uniformity in civil aviation standards, policies, and procedures.

2.1 *Hierarchy of the regulating bodies*

Each nation adhering to the Chicago Convention has its own regulatory body at the national level; however, since the adoption of the Convention the necessity to harmonize rules and to have in place a more predictable and unified framework to optimize the potential of air transport has emerged. The Chicago Convention gave rise to what is now the most important international organization for the regulation of air transport, namely ICAO which is a specialized UN agency that finds itself at the top of the hierarchy of the regulatory bodies. The ICAO was formed in 1944 when the Chicago Convention was signed, and initially had 52 member states. Today, 193 states[40] worldwide are members of the ICAO. The headquarters is in Montreal, Canada, and there are seven regional offices.[41]

1998 (Air Law Treaties and Conventions, 2007, p. 176). The convention was signed by Iraq on December 7, 1944, and ratified on June 2, 1947, by Iraqi Law No. 6 of 1947 (Iraqi Law No. 6 of 1947). Likewise, the current legal basis of international air transportation is the result of the Chicago Convention of 1944. The main principle of the Convention is the principle of complete control of each State over its airspace. The main aims of the Convention which were laid down in parts I and II are as follows: The first one is that the adoption of rules which governs air navigation also dictates the particular ambit of air transportation. The second purpose of the convention which was adopted in part II is the constitutional provisions related to the foundation, systematization, and the role of ICAO.

[40] See the complete list at: https://www.icao.int/MemberStates/Member%20States.English.pdf (accessed December 7, 2021).

[41] Each regional office is responsible for serving the Contracting States to which it is accredited and maintaining liaison with non-Contracting States and other territories in the areas of general responsibility, for the performance of the following: (1) **Air Navigation Functions**, including, assisting, expediting, and following up of: (i) action by States to implement regional plans and regional supplementary procedures; and (ii) implementation of ICAO standards, recommended practices, and procedures; (2) **Air Transport Functions**, including States and international organizations of ICAO air transport policies and activities, and encouraging States to file statistics, to implement Annex 9 on facilitation, to submit replies to economic study questionnaires and to submit data for revision of

2.1.1 *Regional organizations*

Below ICAO there are regional organizations. In Europe, for example, the European Aviation Safety Agency[42] (EASA) is an European Union (EU)

---

the Manual of Airport and Air Navigation Facility Tariffs; (3) **Regional Bodies**, where established, close co-operation with the regional bodies such as African Civil Aviation Commission (AFCAC), European Civil Aviation Conference (ECAC), Latin American Civil Aviation Commission (LACAC), and co-ordination of interrelated work programs to avoid duplication of effort and to ensure harmony in the development of the international air transport system as a whole; (4) **Technical Co-operation Functions**, including the Regional Scholarship Program and assistance in investigating fellowship applications; provision of advice on programing, including co-ordination within the region of requests for regional projects; briefing of newly-recruited Technical Co-operation experts; (5) **Legal**, obtaining current copies of air laws and regulations, as well as information on contemplated air legislation and regulations, from Contracting States; obtaining, on request, judicial information relating to aviation matters; (6) **Aviation Security**, encouraging, assisting, expediting, monitoring, and following up all aspects of aviation security in accordance with ICAO policy, standards, recommended practices, and procedures; (7) **General**, reporting on implementation by States of Assembly and Council Resolutions regarding aviation security; reporting on aviation accidents and incidents to enable follow-up action by ICAO as may be required; the distribution of ICAO publications and documents in accordance with headquarters policy; the holding of meetings at regional office locations, or other appropriate locations within the areas of general responsibility, the participation in press, television, and radio interviews and the provision of lectures on ICAO activities; the follow-up with Contracting States, as required, on the collection of contributions and the attendance at meetings of other international organizations, available at: https://www.icao.int/secretariat/RegionalOffice/Pages/default.aspx (accessed December 7, 2021).

[42]The EASA is the centerpiece of the EU's strategy for aviation safety. Its mission is to promote the highest common standards of safety and environmental protection in civil aviation. The Agency develops common safety and environmental rules at the European level. It monitors the implementation of standards through inspections in the member states and provides the necessary technical expertise, training, and research. The Agency works hand in hand with the national authorities which continue to carry out many operational tasks, such as certification of individual aircraft or licensing of pilots. The main tasks of the Agency currently include: (i) Rulemaking: drafting aviation safety legislation and providing technical advice to the European Commission and to the member states; (ii) Inspections, training and standardization programs to ensure uniform implementation of European aviation safety legislation in all Member States; (iii) Safety and environmental type-certification of aircraft, engines, and parts; (iv) Approval of aircraft design organizations worldwide as and of production and maintenance organizations outside the EU; (v) Authorization of

agency and applies to all of EU, very similar to how the Federal Aviation Administration[43] (FAA) is a US agency that applies to all of the US.

Notably in Europe, the EU provides legislations for its member states. Non-regulatory organizations, such as the EASA, assist the EU in developing regulations (but the EU, not EASA, is the regulatory authority).

2.1.2 *National regulators*

Below the regional level there are national regulators, commonly referred to as "civil aviation administrations" or "authorities" (CAAs).[44] Each country will have their own CAA.[45]

Generally speaking, a national regulator will be following framework regulations published by the national ministry of transport. The term ministry of transport is also sometimes applied to the departments or other government agencies administering transport in nations who do not employ ministers. The framework regulations from the ministry of transport are largely based on ICAO SARPs,[46] Procedures for Air Navigation

---

third-country (non EU) operators; (vi) Coordination of the European Community program Safety Assessment of Foreign Aircraft (SAFA) regarding the safety of foreign aircraft using Community airports; (vii) Data collection, analysis, and research to improve aviation safety. For more details on these tasks visit: https://www.easa.europa.eu/.

[43] The FAA is a governmental body of the United States with powers to regulate all aspects of civil aviation in that nation as well as over its surrounding international waters. Its powers include the construction and operation of airports, ATM, the certification of personnel and aircraft, and the protection of US assets during the launch or re-entry of commercial space vehicles. Powers over neighboring international waters were delegated to the FAA by authority of the ICAO. Created in August 1958, the FAA replaced the former Civil Aeronautics Administration (CAA) and later became an agency within the US Department of Transportation. For more information about the functioning of FAA visit: https://www.faa.gov/.

[44] CAAs are responsible for the oversight and regulation of civil aviation with a focus on aviation safety, security, airspace policy, economic regulation, efficiency, sustainability, consumer protection, and respect for the environment.

[45] A complete list of these authorities is available at: https://en.wikipedia.org/wiki/National_aviation_authority (accessed December 7, 2021).

[46] ICAO SARPs: Technical specifications adopted by the Council of ICAO in order to achieve the highest practicable degree of uniformity in regulations, standards, procedures, and organization within air navigation. Member states will conform to standards and will

Services (PANS),[47] Regional Supplementary Procedures (SUPPs),[48] and any regional regulations (such as EU regulations).

The national regulator will publish detailed regulations, which are adopted by the ANSPs, as well as airlines, pilots, air traffic controllers, maintenance companies and all related subjects (other service providers like air navigation services, such as communication, navigation and surveillance equipment, meteorological services, ATM and aeronautical information, and SAR).

The service providers work together with the national regulators to develop detailed procedures, but do not (usually) have any regulatory authority.

It is also worth mentioning that there are the International Telecommunication Union (ITU)[49] and the World Meteorological Organization (WMO),[50] both of which function on an global level and also provide services for the proper functioning of aviation-related activities.

---

endeavor to conform to recommended practices. States are invited to inform ICAO of non-compliance.

[47] PANS comprise operating practices and material too detailed for SARPs. They are suitable for application on a worldwide basis. Member states are invited to publish differences between national procedures when considered important in the interest of safety.

[48] SUPPs are supplementary procedures which are only valid within one of the ICAO regional office regions. For example, there are supplementary procedures published only valid within the European/North Atlantic region.

[49] ITU is a UN specialized agency for information and communication technologies (ICTs). It was founded in 1865 to facilitate international connectivity in communications networks, allocate global radio spectrum and satellite orbits, develop the technical standards that ensure networks and technologies seamlessly interconnect, and strive to improve access to ICTs to underserved communities worldwide. Every time you make a phone call via the mobile, access the Internet or send an email, you are benefiting from the work of ITU. More information is available at: https://www.itu.int/en/about/Pages/default.aspx (accessed December 7, 2021).

[50] WMO is a specialized agency of the UN with 193 member states and territories. WMO works to facilitate worldwide cooperation in the design and delivery of meteorological services, foster the rapid exchange of meteorological information, advance the standardization of meteorological data, build cooperation between meteorological and hydrological services, encourage research and training in meteorology, and expand the use of meteorology to benefit other sectors such as aviation, shipping, agriculture, and water management, available at: https://public.wmo.int/en (accessed December 7, 2021).

2.2 *An overview about ICAO and its functions*

This section is only aimed at illustrating the main functions of ICAO. Its primary role is to provide a set of standards which will help regulate aviation across the world. It classifies the principles and techniques of international air navigation, as well as the planning and development of international air transport to ensure safety and security. ICAO works with the Chicago Convention's 193 member states, and industry groups to reach consensus on international civil aviation SARPs as we have already exposed in the previous sections. It is necessary to underline that ICAO, through its governing bodies, also elaborates policies in support of a safe, efficient, secure, economically sustainable, and environmentally responsible civil aviation sector.

It appears appropriate to briefly explain the functions of the different governing bodies and illustrate the work of ICAO in order to have a more complete understanding of the importance of this international organization.

2.2.1 *Triennial Assembly*

"The Assembly, comprised of all Member States of ICAO, meets not less than once in three years and is convened by the Council at a suitable time and place. The Assembly has numerous powers and duties, among them to: elect the Member States to be represented on the Council; examine and take appropriate action on the reports of the Council and decide any matter reported to it by the Council; and approve the budgets of the Organization. The Assembly may refer, at its discretion, to the Council, to subsidiary commissions or to any other body any matter within its sphere of action."[51]

2.2.2 *Council*

The ICAO Council is a permanent body of the Organization responsible to the Assembly. It is composed of 36 member states elected by the Assembly for a three-years term. As one of the two governing bodies of ICAO, the Council gives continuing direction to the work of ICAO. In this

---

[51]More information about the Triennial Assembly is available at: https://www.icao.int/about-icao/assembly/Pages/default.aspx (accessed December 7, 2021).

regard, one of its major duties is to adopt international SARPs and to incorporate these as Annexes to the Chicago Convention. The Council may also amend existing Annexes as necessary.

"The Council has numerous functions, notable among which are to submit annual reports to the Assembly; carry out the directions of the Assembly; and discharge the duties and obligations which are laid on it by the Chicago Convention. It also administers the finances of ICAO, appoints and defines the duties of the Air Transport Committee, as well as the Committee on Joint Support of Air Navigation Services, the Finance Committee, the Committee on Unlawful Interference, the Technical Co-operation Committee and the Human Resources Committee. It appoints the Members of the Air Navigation Commission."[52]

The Council's objectives are to be achieved by a series of policies decided by the ICAO, and one of the most important is fostering the development of a sound and economically viable civil aviation system. This strategic objective reflects the need for ICAO's leadership in harmonizing the air transport framework focused on economic policies and supporting activities.[53]

Another key function of the Council is to appoint the Secretary-General.

2.2.3 *Secretariat and Secretary-General*

The Secretariat[54] of the ICAO is headed by the Secretary-General. The Secretariat consists of five bureaus: the Air Navigation Bureau,[55] the Air

---

[52]See: https://www.icao.int/about-icao/Council/Pages/council.aspx (accessed December 7, 2021).

[53]More strategic objectives are explained in detail at the following website: https://www.icao.int/about-icao/Council/Pages/Strategic-Objectives.aspx (accessed December 7, 2021).

[54]Reference: https://www.icao.int/secretariat/Pages/default.aspx (accessed December 7, 2021).

[55]The Air Navigation Bureau manages the Safety and Air Navigation Capacity and Efficiency strategies of ICAO in a partnership with aviation stakeholders. This work is carried out within a framework with the following elements: (i) Policy and Standardization, (ii) Safety and Infrastructure Monitoring, (iii) Safety and Infrastructure Analysis, and (iv) Safety and Infrastructure Implementation. Further information is available at: https://www.icao.int/safety/airnavigation/Pages/default.aspx (accessed December 7, 2021).

Transport Bureau,[56] the Technical Co-operation Bureau,[57] the Legal Affairs and External Relations Bureau,[58] and the Bureau of Administration and Services.[59]

---

[56] The Air Transport Bureau supports the implementation of the Strategic Objectives of ICAO in particular: Security and Facilitation; Economic Development of Air Transport; and Environmental Protection. This Bureau also contributes toward Safety. The Bureau works under the direction of the Council, Air Transport Committee, the Committee on Unlawful Interference and the Committee on Joint Support of Air Navigation Services. Secretariat support is provided to the Committee on Aviation Environmental Protection (CAEP), which is a Committee of Council. See: https://www.icao.int/secretariat/air-transport/Pages/default.aspx (accessed December 7, 2021).

[57] ICAO's Technical Co-operation Bureau provides advice and assistance in the development and implementation of projects across the full spectrum of civil aviation aimed at the safety, security, environmental protection, and sustainable development of national and international civil aviation. Its program is conducted under the broad policy guidance of the ICAO Assembly and of the Council. Subject to general guidance by the Secretary General, the Technical Co-operation Program is executed by the Technical Co-operation Bureau (TCB). See: https://www.icao.int/secretariat/TechnicalCooperation/Pages/default.aspx (accessed December 7, 2021).

[58] Legal Affairs and External Relations Bureau provides advice and assistance to the Secretary General and through him to Council and other bodies of the Organization and to ICAO member states on constitutional, administrative, and procedural matters, on problems of international law, air law, commercial law, labor law, and related matters. The Bureau is responsible for reviewing, advising on and coordinating ICAO's relations with member and non-member States, the Organizations of the UN Common System and with other international organizations. See: https://www.icao.int/secretariat/legal/Pages/default.aspx (accessed December 7, 2021).

[59] The Bureau of Administration and Services (ADB) is responsible for providing the administrative support required by the Organization and plays a leading role in its effective and efficient administrative management. ADB guides ICAO toward results-based management and a performance-oriented organizational culture to meet the needs of the member states, industries, and other customers as well as the general public. The Bureau performs its functions through: (i) Providing high-quality human resources and services as well as efficient administrative and management processes; (ii) Applying the highest standards of work ethics and conduct, and advancing human resource management to meet changing needs of the Organization; (iii) Using results-based management skills and tools to support the Organization in achieving its strategic objectives, available at https://www.icao.int/secretariat/Administration/Pages/default.aspx (accessed December 7, 2021).

The Secretary-General of ICAO is head of the Secretariat and chief executive officer of the Organization responsible for general direction of the work of the Secretariat.[60]

2.2.4 *Air Navigation Commission*

"The Air Navigation Commission (ANC) considers and recommends Standards and Recommended Practices (SARPs) and Procedures for Air Navigation Services (PANS) for adoption or approval by the ICAO Council. The Commission is composed of nineteen members who have *suitable qualifications and experience in the science and practice of aeronautics*, as outlined in the *Convention on International Civil Aviation* (Chicago Convention). Although ANC Commissioners are nominated by specific ICAO Member States, and appointed by the Council, they do not represent the interest of any particular State or Region. Rather they act independently and utilize their expertise in the interest of the entire international civil aviation community."[61]

2.3 *Airport Council International: The "voice of the airports" interacting with world civil aviation bodies*

Airport Council International (ACI)[62] is the "voice of the airports" for interacting with world bodies and advocating for the global airports industry before the media and opinion leaders. International partner organizations include the UN ICAO. ACI has continued to increase its

---

[60]The Secretary-General provides leadership to a specialized international staff working in the field of international civil aviation. The Secretary-General serves as the Secretary of the Council of ICAO and is responsible to the Council as a whole and, following established policies, carries out the duties assigned by the Council, and makes periodic reports to the Council covering the progress of the Secretariat activities. See: https://www.icao.int/secretariat/SecretaryGeneral/Pages/default.aspx (accessed December 7, 2021).

[61]Reference: https://www.icao.int/about-icao/AirNavigationCommission/Pages/default.aspx (accessed December 7, 2021).

[62]In 1991, airport operators around the world created the ACI — the first worldwide association to represent their common interests and foster cooperation with partners throughout the air transport industry. Through ACI, the airport community now speaks with a single voice on key issues and concerns and, despite regional diversity, can move forward as a united industry.

engagement with ICAO and regularly works with representatives from countries around the world and the ICAO Secretariat to advance the interests of airports.

ACI is a non-profit organization, whose prime purpose is to advance the interests of airports and to promote professional excellence in airport management and operations. By fostering co-operation among airports, world aviation organizations, and business partners, ACI makes a significant contribution by providing the traveling public with an air transport system that is safe, secure, efficient, and environmentally responsible.[63]

Airports are an invaluable asset for the communities they serve, helping them to develop their full economic potential and ensure stable growth, bolstering long-term business development and employment.

ACI defends airports positions and develops SARPs in the areas of safety, security, and environment initiatives. It also advances and protects airport interests in important policy changes on airport charges and regulation, strengthening the hand of airports in dealing with airlines.

The association also works closely with the World Customs Organization (WCO),[64] the IATA, and regional airline associations. Contacts are maintained with the International Federation of Air Line

---

[63]In this sense, Airports Council International — Celebrating 20 Years — 1991–2011, available at: (accessed December 7, 2021) https://issuu.com/aciworld/docs/aci_20th_anniversary_book/1.

[64]The WCO was established in 1952 as the Customs Co-operation Council. It is an independent intergovernmental organization whose primary mission is to enhance the effectiveness and efficiency of Customs administrations worldwide. As the only intergovernmental organization specialized in Customs matters, the WCO established its headquarters in Brussels in 1952, and currently represents 183 members across the globe at all stages of social and economic development. As the global center of Customs expertise and the voice of the international Customs community, the WCO provides an ideal forum for Customs administrations and their stakeholders to hold in-depth discussions, exchange experiences, and share best practices on a range of international Customs and trade issues. Today, the WCO represents 183 Customs administrations across the globe that collectively process approximately 98% of world trade. As the global center of Customs expertise, the WCO is the only international organization with competence in Customs matters and can rightly call itself the voice of the international Customs community. More information is available at: http://www.wcoomd.org/en/about-us/what-is-the-wco.aspx (accessed December 7, 2021).

Pilots' Associations (IFALPA),[65] the CANSO,[66] the International Air Rail Organization (IARO),[67] and the ATAG.[68]

2.4 *IATA: Leading the airline industry*

IATA represents, leads, and serves airline Industry. IATA is a trade association and its major responsibility is to serve and support aviation with global standards for airlines safety, security, efficiency, and sustainability. In fact, one of its main objectives is to cooperate with ICAO in order to accomplish these tasks. Another objective is to provide a common platform for travel agencies and tour operators in order to promote and develop international tourism.

For air carriers, IATA provides a pooled resource for scheduling, traffic and routes, standardizing services, and the creation of a worldwide public service for the air industry. For consumers, IATA sets the

---

[65] IFALPA is the global voice of pilots. An international not-for-profit organization, IFALPA represents over 100,000 pilots in nearly 100 countries. The mission of the Federation is to promote the highest level of aviation safety worldwide and to be the global advocate of the piloting profession; providing representation, services, and support to both the members and the aviation industry. More information is available at: https://www.ifalpa.org/.

[66] CANSO was founded in 1996 as more of the world's ANSPs separated from their regulatory authorities. CANSO brings the world's ANSPs' leading industry innovators and ATM specialists together to share knowledge and develop best practices, for secure and seamless airspace. More information is available at: https://www.canso.org/about-canso (accessed December 7, 2021).

[67] The IARO is a worldwide organization dedicated to spreading world-class best practice and good workable ideas among people interested in rail links to airports and air-rail intermodality. Its worldwide membership includes organizations planning, developing, building, and operating rail air links — and also people (like airlines) who have a business interest in partnerships for their success. More information is available at: https://www.iaro.com/.

[68] ATAG is a highly respected not-for-profit association that represents all sectors of air transport industry. ATAG has some 40 members worldwide. Its funding members play a driving role within ATAG and devote substantive time and resources to the association. They include: ACI, Airbus, ATR, Boeing, Bombardier, Civil Air Navigation Services Organisation (CANSO), CFM International, Embraer, GE, Honeywell Aerospace, IATA, Pratt & Whitney, Rolls-Royce, and Safran. More information is available at: https://www.atag.org/about-us/who-we-are.html (accessed December 7, 2021).

international standard for services and business practices among member airlines. As an example, the three-digit airport codes used internationally are an IATA convention. Additionally, the Association aims to foster air commerce, and it also studies problems connected with airline industry.

2.4.1 *A bit of history: From a new trade association to a new strategic thrust*

The old IATA was able to start small and grow gradually. It was also limited to a European dimension until 1939 when Pan American joined. The post-1945 IATA immediately had to handle worldwide responsibilities with a more systematic organization and a larger infrastructure. This was reflected in the 1945 Articles of Association[69] and a much more precise definition of IATA's aims than had existed before 1939.

- *To promote safe, regular and economical air transport for the benefit of the peoples of the world, to foster air commerce, and to study the problems connected therewith.*
- *To provide means for collaboration among the air transport enterprises engaged directly or indirectly in international air transport service.*
- *To cooperate with the newly created International Civil Aviation Organization (ICAO — the specialized UN agency for civil aviation) and other international organizations.*

In many ways, those tasks remained the same as in 1945. But IATA gave them new relevance and focus by redefining its mission and goals in 1994:

- *Safety & security*: *to promote safe, reliable and secure air services.*
- *Industry recognition*: *to achieve recognition of the importance of air transport worldwide social and economic development.*
- *Financial viability*: *to assist the industry to achieve adequate levels of profitability, by optimizing revenues (yield management) while minimizing costs (fuel, charges and taxation).*

---

[69]The Articles of Association of IATA are available at: https://www.iata.org/contentassets/01e197ea66384f27a9e763d151ae2d7d/articles-of-association.pdf (accessed December 7, 2021).

- **Products & services:** *provide high-quality, value for money, industry required products and services that assist the airlines in meeting the needs of the consumer.*
- **Standards & procedures:** *to develop cost-effective, environmentally-friendly, standards to facilitate the operations of international air transport.*
- **Industry support:** *to identify and articulate common industry positions and support the resolutions of key industry issues (congestion, infrastructure).*[70]

These objectives proved to be relevant and most were carried over to the new millennium, where they still form most of IATA's current mission.

2.4.2 *Main components of the IATA organizational structure*

The IATA Annual General Meeting (AGM) is the sovereign body of the association. All active members have an equal vote in its decisions. It is convened every year as the "World Air Transport Summit" in recognition of its status as the premier, industry-wide platform for the debate of critical issues at the highest level.

The IATA *Board of Governors*[71] *(BG)*, composed of elected Chief Executives of member airlines, provides year-round policy direction.

IATA *Special Committees* are established from time to time, with the approval of the Board of Governors, to advise on subjects of special concern to the industry. Other bodies such as subcommittees, boards, panels and working groups are also established from time to time with specific terms of reference.

The four IATA *Standing Committees* (Financial, Industry Affairs, Operations, and Cargo) are composed of experts nominated by individual member airlines. The IATA Industry Affairs Committee (IAC) advises the

---

[70] https://www.iata.org/en/about/history/history-trade-association-activities/ (accessed December 7, 2021).

[71] The IATA Articles of Association establish a Board of Governors ("the Board") to exercise executive committee functions, accountable to a General Meeting, and authorize the Board to adopt its rules and regulations. More information about IATA's Corporate Governance is available at: https://www.iata.org/en/about/corporate-structure/ (accessed December 7, 2021).

Board of Governors and the Director General on all commercial matters connected with international air transport and oversees the work of the Traffic Conferences.

The IATA Secretariat, a staff headed by the Director General and Chief Executive Officer, supports general and committee meetings and the various Traffic Conferences and also performs several functions for, and provides various services to, member airlines and others.[72]

3. Classification and Definitions Used for Civil Aviation Activities

The classification and definitions used to describe civil aviation activities have been elaborated by ICAO to support the process of preparing and updating the various Annexes to the Chicago Convention and related documents such as manuals and circulars.

Aviation activities can be divided into two major categories: (i) commercial air transport services, which it has its own sub-categories as it will be exposed, and (ii) general aviation which also is divided into sub-categories.

Of course aviation activities also include the following: (i) airport services; (ii) air navigation services; (iii) civil aviation manufacturing; (iv) aviation training; (v) maintenance and overhaul; (vi) regulatory functions.

Commercial and general aviation have a common goal: to transport cargo or people safely and efficiently from one destination to another. However, there are several differences between commercial and general aviation, and these differences characterize the essence of these two categories which are distinct in nature.

3.1 *Commercial air transport services*

Commercial aviation concerns scheduled flights from larger tarmac airports that involve the transportation of passengers or cargo. When you purchase a ticket to fly on a plane, your travel falls into this category.

---

[72] *Manual on the Regulation of International Air Transport*, ICAO (Doc 9626), Third Edition, 2016, Chapter 3.8, IATA p. 95, available at: https://www.icao.int/Meetings/a39/Documents/Provisional_Doc_9626.pdf (accessed December 7, 2021).

Pilots who fly commercial aircraft are held to higher medical and safety standards, and they are required to hold the appropriate license and training before they can operate large commercial planes.

According to ICAO, commercial air transport operations can be classified into scheduled and non-scheduled operations.

3.1.1 *Scheduled*

3.1.1.1 Definition of a scheduled international air service

A scheduled international air service is a series of flights that possesses all the following characteristics:

(a) *it passes through the airspace over the territory of more than one State;*
(b) *it is performed by aircraft for the transport of passengers, mail or cargo for remuneration, in such a manner that each flight is open to use by members of the public;*
(c) *it is operated, so as to serve traffic between the same two or more points, either*
  (i) *according to a published timetable, or*
  (ii) *with flights so regular or frequent that they constitute a recognizably systematic series.*[73]

This Definition typically encompasses a service:

(a) which is part of an international network of services, operating according to a published timetable;
(b) where the on-demand passenger has a reasonable chance of securing accommodation;
(c) which normally operates irrespective of short-term fluctuations in payload;

---

[73] *Policy and Guidance on the Economic Regulation of International Air Transport* ICAO (Doc 9587), Fourth Edition, 2016 Part 1, p. 20, available at: https://www.icao.int/ Meetings/a39/Documents/9587-PROVISIONAL%20VERSION.pdf (accessed December 9, 2021).

(d) where stopover and interlining facilities are offered to the user with the appropriate ticket or air waybill, subject to the relevant international agreement, if any.[74]

3.1.2 *Non-scheduled*

3.1.2.1 Non-scheduled air services

A non-scheduled air service is a commercial air transport service performed as other than a scheduled air service. A charter flight is a non-scheduled operation using a chartered aircraft. Though the terms non-scheduled and charter (i.e. a contractual arrangement between an air carrier and an entity hiring or leasing its aircraft) have come to be used interchangeably, it should be noted that not all commercial non-scheduled operations are charter flights.[75]

Unlike scheduled international air services which are regulated primarily on the basis of bilateral agreements between States, non-scheduled international air services are generally authorized on the basis of national regulation. Aviation regulators also sometimes regulate commercial non-transport operations (such as aerial crop dusting and surveying) as well as operations such as overflight and landing by private, corporate, military, and State aircraft.

ICAO in its *Manual on the Regulation of International Air Transport* defines more precisely the characteristics of "Non-scheduled air services" and it states they may be performed by all types of air carriers and may be distinguished from scheduled services by the following characteristics. They are usually operated:

- pursuant to a charter contract on a point-to-point and often plane-load basis (but several charterers may share the capacity of an aircraft);
- either on an *ad hoc* basis or on a regular but seasonal basis;
- not subject to the public service obligations that may be imposed upon scheduled air carriers such as the requirement to operate flights according to a published timetable regardless of load factor;

---

[74] *Ibid.*

[75] *Manual on the Regulation of International Air Transport*, ICAO (Doc 9626), Third Edition, 2016, Chapter 4.6, Non-Scheduled Air Services, p. 150, available at: https://www.icao.int/Meetings/a39/Documents/Provisional_Doc_9626.pdf (accessed December 9, 2021).

- with more operational flexibility with respect to choices of airports, hours of operation, and other operational and service requirements than scheduled services;
- with the financial risk for underutilized payload being assumed by the charterer rather than the aircraft operator;
- generally without the air carrier maintaining direct control over retail prices (the aircraft capacity is usually sold wholesale by the carrier to tour operators, freight forwarders, or other entities); and
- subject to seeking permission, or giving prior notification, for each flight or series of flights, to/from the country of origin or destination or both.[76]

ICAO under its classification of non-schedule services also includes *on demand services* which comprehend *air taxi* and *commercial business aviation* (the latest can be both commercial and general aviation depending on whether or not there is a charge for the service provided). On-demand, non-scheduled flights on short notice for the carriage by air of passengers, freight, or mail, or any combination thereof for remuneration are usually performed with smaller aircraft including helicopters (typically no more than 30 seats). This definition includes any positioning flights required for the provision of the service.[77]

3.1.3 *Cargo services*

3.1.3.1 Definition of air cargo

Air cargo or freight refers to any property carried on an aircraft other than mail, stores and passenger baggage (see Annex 9 to the Convention on International Civil Aviation). The term air cargo is also used in a broader sense by the airline industry to mean any property (freight, express, and mail) transported by air except baggage. An all-cargo service is an air service that carries cargo only, whether scheduled or non-scheduled.

---

[76] *Ibid.*

[77] See ICAO Working Paper titled *Review of the Classification and Definitions Used for Civil Aviation Activities*, November 2009, available at: https://www.icao.int/Meetings/STA10/Documents/Sta10_Wp007_en.pdf (accessed December 9, 2021).

In the field of international air transport, attention is often paid to passenger air services, yet air cargo is also an important component of air transport. To many States, air cargo services are important to their national development and international trade, for example, landlocked countries and States whose main export commodities are high value goods or perishables.

To freight shippers, air services render a competitive alternative to other forms of transport (rail, trucking or shipping) in meeting their shipping requirements in terms of speed, quality (much less en-route damage) and cost. As more companies adopt the philosophy of "just in time" (i.e. goods arrive when needed for production or for use rather than being stockpiled and becoming expensive inventory), aircraft will be used increasingly as, in effect, airborne extensions of warehouses in order to reduce inventory carrying cost.[78]

Air Cargo services have their own characteristics which can summarized as follows:

3.1.3.2 Distinct features of air cargo

(i) Cargo, by nature, is generally less sensitive than passengers to time between origin and destination (except express), routes, and stops. While passengers must be transported to their destinations without delay, cargo can often wait if space is not immediately available, can move on different routes and make numerous stops.

(ii) While passengers tend to make round trips, air cargo generally moves only one way. There are few routes where the volume of cargo traffic is the same or similar in both directions, but many where the volume is several times greater in one direction than the other.

(iii) Air cargo tends to use more intermodal transport, i.e. more than one form of transport, e.g. aeroplane, truck, rail, or ship between origin and destination. Special devices are often used for air cargo, such as standardized pallets (i.e. platforms on which goods are assembled and secured by nets or straps) and containers (i.e. specially designed receptacles that fit in the cargo compartments of the wide-body aircraft) — such devices are often referred to by the generic term

---

[78] *Manual on the Regulation of International Air Transport*, ICAO (Doc 9626), Third Edition, 2016, Chapter 4.5, Air Cargo, p. 147, available at: https://www.icao.int/Meetings/a39/Documents/Provisional_Doc_9626.pdf (accessed December 9, 2021).

ULDs (unit load devices). The use of these devices has not only helped enhance efficiency but has also facilitated interlining and intermodal transport.

(iv) Most scheduled international airlines regard air cargo carried in the aircraft's lower-deck compartment as an additional source of revenue, treating it as a byproduct of their passenger services. However, air cargo can assume greater importance on a route with a sufficient volume of cargo traffic to justify using a combi aircraft (which carries both passengers and cargo on the main deck) and is the sole generator of revenue with respect to an all-cargo aircraft or a freighter.[79]

3.2 *General aviation*

ICAO defines General aviation "as all civil aviation operations other than scheduled air services and non-scheduled air transport operations for remuneration or hire. For ICAO statistical purposes the general aviation activities are classified into instructional flying, business flying, pleasure flying, aerial work and other flying."[80]

3.2.1 *Instructional flying*

Instructional flying is defined as the use of an aircraft for purposes of formal flight instruction with an instructor. The flights may be performed by aero-clubs, flying school, or commercial operators.[81]

3.2.2 *Pleasure flying*

Pleasure flying is defined as the use of an aircraft for personal or recreational purposes not associated with a business or profession.[82]

---

[79] *Ibid.*

[80] See ICAO Working Paper titled *Review of the Classification and Definitions Used for Civil Aviation Activities*, November 2009, available at: https://www.icao.int/Meetings/STA10/Documents/Sta10_Wp007_en.pdf (accessed December 9, 2021).

[81] *Ibid.*

[82] *Ibid.*

3.2.3 *Business flying*

Business flying is defined as the use of an aircraft to carry personnel and/or property to meet the transport needs of officials of a business, firm, company, or corporation. These flights may be performed by a commercial pilot or by a private pilot.[83]

It must be stressed that business aviation can be either commercial or general aviation depending on whether or not there is a charge for the service.

3.2.4 *Corporate aviation*

Corporate aviation: It is the non-commercial operation or use of aircraft by a company for the carriage of passengers (company executives) or goods as an aid to the conduct of company business, flown by a professional pilot employed to fly the aircraft. Note that corporate aviation is a subset of general aviation (Annex 17, Chapter I, p. 1–1).[84]

Corporate aviation can be distinguished by the so-called *fractional ownership* which refers to the shared ownership of expansive assets such as aircraft. In general, the fractional owner pays regular fees to a company that manages the asset (operates the aircraft) on behalf of all owners. Fractional ownership has recently become very popular in business aviation since it reduces the cost of ownership while offering a greater operational flexibility and a wider airport (destination) access.[85]

3.2.5 *Aerial work*

Aerial work: It is an aircraft operation in which an aircraft is used for specialized services such as agriculture, construction, photography, surveying, observation and patrol, SAR, and aerial advertisement.

---

[83] *Ibid.*

[84] Annex 17 to the Convention on International Civil Aviation, ICAO, Ninth Edition, March 2011, available at: https://www.spilve.lv/library/law/Annex%2017.pdf (accessed December 9, 2021).

[85] ICAO Working Paper titled *Review of the Classification and Definitions Used for Civil Aviation Activities*, November 2009, available at: https://www.icao.int/Meetings/STA10/Documents/Sta10_Wp007_en.pdf (accessed December 9, 2021).

With reference to *agricultural flying*, it involves the use of an aircraft for activities such as crop dusting, chemical or fertilizer spraying, seed dissemination, prevention of frost formation, insect fighting, and animal herding. Other aerial work include: use of an aircraft for activities such as aerial photography; patrol and surveillance; prospecting; construction (i.e. aerial work in construction projects); advertising; medical, relief and rescue work.

Other flying: These are all general aviation flights other than glider and free balloon flights that cannot be included in the above four categories. Flights by pilots for maintaining their flying proficiency are also included.[86]

3.3 *Airport-related matters*

Airport-related matters include a series of airport services which are specified by ICAO in its dedicated section titled *Aerodromes, Operability and Interoperability* (AOI).[87]

3.3.1 *Ground handling (doc 9626)*

Although there is no formal, official definition, *ground handling is generally understood to broadly include services necessary for an aircraft's arrival at, and departure from, an airport but to exclude those provided by air traffic control.* The Airport Economics Manual (Doc 9562)[88] separates the ground-handling function into terminal handling (passenger check-in, baggage, and freight handling) and ramp handling

---

[86]*Ibid.*

[87]ICAO describes in detail not only the functioning of an airport-related services but also their operability and interoperability, for a complete reference visit: https://www.icao.int/safety/airnavigation/Pages/aga.aspx (accessed December 9, 2021).

[88]In this document ICAO further differentiates ground handling stating that it comprehends: *activities necessary to support the servicing of aircraft and processing of passengers (excepting government inspection services) and can include passenger check in, boarding, apron handling of aircraft, cleaning, and can also include catering, fueling, and some maintenance activities. Generally undertaken by independent contractors or airline employees, in some cases airport operators provide ground handling services*; See p. 46 of the Fourth Edition of Doc 9562 — Airport Economics Manual, 2019, available at: https://www.icao.int/Meetings/a40/Documents/PRELIMINARY_VERSION_

(aircraft handling, cleaning and servicing). Ground handling generally excludes maintenance and repair of aircraft, although in some instances the so-called line maintenance may be considered as a part of ground-handling services.

Services related to ground handling may be provided at an airport by one or more airlines, by one or more concessionaires, by the airport itself, or by a combination of any of these means.[89]

3.3.2 *Slot allocation*

An airport slot is a specific designated day and time (usually within a 15- or 30-minute period) for an aircraft to arrive at or depart from an airport.

Slots are important to air carriers not only for operational reasons (e.g. for aircraft, crew, and gate-use scheduling) but also for commercial reasons (e.g. matching departure and arrival times to time periods believed to be preferred by most travelers provides a more attractive service). The availability of slots at an airport can be limited due to various physical constraints such as the capacity limitations of the runway(s), terminal(s), boarding gates, and air traffic control facilities. Therefore, in situations where an airport becomes congested and the demand for slots exceeds available supply, some type of rationing or slot allocation mechanism, i.e. a formula for the allocation of slots among their users, will be required.[90]

3.3.3 *Fixed-Based Operators (FBOs)*

The term Fixed Base Operator (FBO) is given to a commercial enterprise that has been granted the right by an airport authority to operate on that airport and provide aviation services, such as fuel, parking and hangar space, to the General Aviation (GA) community. At a smaller airports, or ones located near a remote or small community, it is often the town or the

---

OF_DOC_9562_AIRPORT_ECONOMICS_MANUAL_FOURTH_EDITION_2019_en.pdf (accessed December 9, 2021).

[89]*Manual on the Regulation of International Air Transport*, ICAO (Doc 9626), Third Edition, 2016, Chapter 4.10, Airport-Related Matters, p. 174, Ground Handling, available at: https://www.icao.int/Meetings/a39/Documents/Provisional_Doc_9626.pdf (accessed December 9, 2021).

[90]*Ibid.*, p. 175.

airport authority which provides basic FBO services such as provision of fuel and parking. However, at larger airports serving major cities, there are often several privately owned Fixed Base Operators in competition for the business of both permanently based and transient general aviation aircraft.[91]

3.4 *Air navigation services*

Air navigation services: This term includes ATM, communications, navigation and surveillance systems (CNS), meteorological services for air navigation (MET), SAR, and aeronautical information services (AIS). These services are provided to air traffic during all phases of operations (approach, aerodrome, and *en route*).[92]

3.5 *Maintenance and overhaul*

Maintenance: The performance of tasks required to ensure the continuing airworthiness of an aircraft, including any one or combination of overhaul, inspection, replacement, defect rectification, and the embodiment of a modification or repair (Annex 8, Part I, p. 1–2).

3.6 *Civil aviation manufacturing*

Among the civil aviation activities naturally the manufacturing of aircraft represents the fundamental core of this industry.

The aircraft industry is the industry supporting aviation by building aircraft and manufacturing aircraft parts for their maintenance. This includes aircraft and parts used for civil aviation and military aviation.

Most production is done pursuant to type certificates and Defense Standards issued by a government body. This term has been largely subsumed by the more encompassing term: "aerospace industry."

[91] Sky https://www.skybrary.aero/index.php/Fixed_Base_Operator_(FBO) https://skybrary.aero/articles/fixed-base-operator-fbo (accessed December 9, 2021).
[92] ICAO Working Paper titled *Review of the Classification and Definitions Used for Civil Aviation Activities*, November 2009, available at: https://www.icao.int/Meetings/STA10/Documents/Sta10_Wp007_en.pdf (accessed December 9, 2021).

In order to make an aircraft the manufacturers have to source a number of different and unique parts to be able to construct the aircraft. There is a large network of specialized parts suppliers throughout the world that support the requirements of major manufacturers, who sometimes only provide the initial design and final assembly in their own plants.

Among the most important manufactures those that deserve to be mentioned are Airbus,[93] Boeing,[94] Bombardier,[95] and Embraer.[96] Airbus and Boeing mainly manufacture the wide-body and narrow-body jet airliners, while Bombardier and Embraer concentrate on aircrafts for

---

[93] Airbus is a commercial aircraft manufacturer, with Space and Defense as well as Helicopters Divisions. Airbus is the largest aeronautics and space company in Europe and a worldwide leader. Airbus has built on its strong European heritage to become truly international — with roughly 180 locations and 12,000 direct suppliers globally. The company has aircraft and helicopter final assembly lines across Asia, Europe, and the Americas, and has achieved a more than six-fold order book increase since 2000. More detailed information is available at: https://www.airbus.com/ (accessed December 9, 2021).

[94] Boeing is the world's largest aerospace company and leading manufacturer of commercial jetliners, defense, space and security systems, and service provider of aftermarket support. As America's biggest manufacturing exporter, the company supports airlines and US and allied government customers in more than 150 countries. Boeing products and tailored services include commercial and military aircraft, satellites, weapons, electronic and defense systems, launch systems, advanced information and communication systems, and performance-based logistics and training. More detailed information is available at: https://www.boeing.com/company/ (accessed December 9, 2021).

[95] Bombardier Aviation designs, manufactures, and supports innovative aviation products for the business, commercial and specialized aircraft markets. With this comprehensive aircraft portfolio, it holds the number one position in business and regional aircraft. Its high-performance aircraft and services set the standard of excellence in several markets, including: (i) Business aircraft — *Learjet*, *Challenger*, and *Global* aircraft families; (ii) Regional aircraft — CRJ Series; (iii) Aerostructures & Engineering Services — aircraft structures, component repair, and other services; (iv) Specialized aircraft solutions — Bombardier aircraft modified for special missions; (v) Aircraft services and training — aircraft parts, maintenance, training, technical support, and publications, and online services. More detailed information is available at: https://www.bombardier.com/en/home.html (accessed December 9, 2021).

[96] Embraer has become one of the main aircraft manufacturers in the world by focusing on specific market segments with high growth potential in commercial, defense, and executive aviation. Based in Brazil, Embraer continues to lead the industry with its innovative regional and commercial jet product lines, available at: https://embraer.com/global/en/about-us (accessed December 9, 2021).

regional airlines. As for the general aviation sector a number of other manufacturers serve the GA market with a focus on private aviation and flight training such as Cessna,[97] Cirrus Design,[98] Diamond,[99] and Piper.[100]

This is only a brief overview concerning a few manufacturers, a more detailed analysis in relation to the role and products of the most well-known manufacturers of GA aircraft and business Jet is offered in Chapter 4. These represent two distinct markets: General Aviation and Business Aviation, and of course each of these markets have its leading products.

3.7 *Aviation training*

Annex 1 to the Convention on International Civil Aviation comprehends International Standards and Recommended Practices of Flight Crew and Other Personnel as listed in the same Annex 1, Chapter I, p. 1–8.[101]

---

[97] Cessna Aircraft Company is the leading designer and manufacturer of light and mid-sized business jets, utility turboprops, and single engine aircraft as it has sold and delivered more aircraft than anyone else. More detailed information is available at: https://txtav.com/en/company (accessed December 9, 2021).

[98] The Cirrus Design Corporation, doing business as Cirrus Aircraft (formally Cirrus Design), is an aircraft manufacturer that was founded in 1984. The company is owned by a subsidiary of the Chinese government-owned AVIC. More detailed information is available at: https://cirrusaircraft.com/about/ (accessed December 9, 2021).

[99] Diamond Aircraft, headquartered in Austria with facilities in Canada and China, is among the leading aircraft manufacturer in general aviation. Founded in 1981, Diamond has pioneered many aviation firsts and achieved numerous milestones and industry expert accolades. More detailed information is available at: https://www.diamondaircraft.com/en/about-diamond/why-diamond/ (accessed December 9, 2021).

[100] Piper Aircraft, Inc. is a manufacturer of general aviation aircraft, located at the Vero Beach Municipal Airport in Vero Beach, Florida, United States which is owned since 2009 by the Government of Brunei. Throughout much of the mid-to-late 20th century, it was considered to be one of the "Big Three" in the field of general aviation manufacturing, along with Beechcraft and Cessna. https://www.piper.com/ (accessed December 9, 2021).

[101] According to Annex 1, Chapter 1, p. 1–8, (a) Flight crew include: (i) private pilot — aeroplane, airship, helicopter, or powered-lift; (ii) commercial pilot — aeroplane, airship, helicopter, or powered-lift; (iii) multi-crew pilot — aeroplane; (iv) airline transport pilot — aeroplane, helicopter, or powered-lift; (v) glider pilot; (vi) free balloon pilot; (vii) flight navigator; (viii) flight engineer; and (ix) as of November 3, 2022, remote pilot — aeroplane, airship, glider, rotorcraft, powered-lift, or free balloon. (b) Other personnel

All these personnel must receive a specific training to obtain a proper license (recognized by ICAO) in order to perform their duties and work.

Training is the acquisition of knowledge and skills provided by ICAO and/or training organizations associated with ICAO issuing a certificate of completion or a certificate of achievement with the ICAO emblem or an ICAO program emblem.

Recognition is a public statement of support, an acknowledgment of compliance. An ICAO recognition is a statement of support for the methods or practices of an aviation activity or organization or its delivery of a certain type or quality of service or product that comply with specific ICAO provisions contained in Annexes to the Convention on International Civil Aviation and related guidelines.[102]

---

include: (i) aircraft maintenance (technician/engineer/mechanic); (ii) air traffic controller; (iii) flight operations officer/flight dispatcher; (iv) aeronautical station operator.

[102] In this sense see: ICAO Civil Aviation Training Policy, May 2016, available at: https://www.icao.int/training/SiteAssets/20160525-TrainingPolicy_EN.pdf (accessed December 9, 2021).

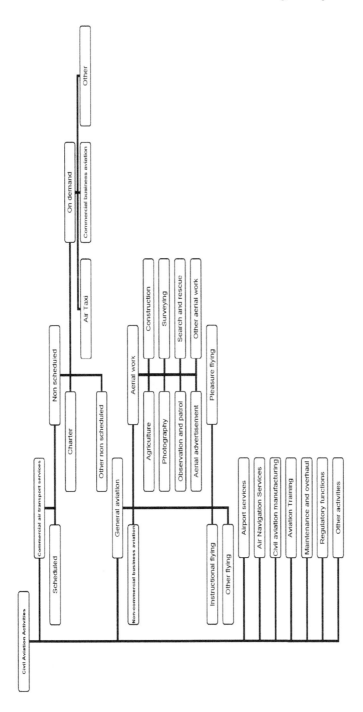

Chapter 2

The Responses of the Market Concerning the Impact of COVID-19 on Different Sectors of the Aviation Industry

Paolo Rizzi and Cristiano Rizzi

International aviation industry has been severely hit first by the COVID-19 outbreak and second by diverse national measures adopted across different countries aimed at containing the pandemic. In particular, these circumstances have drastically affected passenger transportation. According to the International Air Transport Association (IATA) airline revenues have fallen by hundreds of billions of US dollars.[1] However, only at the end of the pandemic it will be possible to quantify the loss and the damages caused by COVID-19. China, the original epicenter, was the first to ban certain domestic and international travels to prevent the spread of the virus, followed by the EU and the US. The financial implications on the global industry were relatively limited, due to the monopoly of state-backed Chinese airlines in that market. With the virus' spread to the other big aviation markets in Europe and then North America, the situation has become a global and serious issue which has put the existence of many operators at risk. Governments all around the world, and institutions

---

[1] IATA released updated analysis showing that the COVID-19 crisis will see airline passenger revenues drop by US$371 billion in 2020 and 2021, compared to 2019, available at: https://www.iata.org/en/pressroom/pr/2020-04-14-01/ (accessed December 9, 2021).

like the EU Commission[2] have shown their willingness to give a hand to this so hard-hit industry by providing financial aid, while airlines initiated restructuring to overcome and re-emerge from the crisis stronger.

1. Economic Impacts of COVID-19 on Commercial Aviation: Airlines Need Financial Support for Restructuring in Order to Overcome the Crisis

The UN aviation body International Civil Aviation Organization (ICAO) welcomed a statement from G20 countries to aid in the global recovery from COVID-19, highlighting that aviation is one of the worst-hit sectors. ICAO's Council President Salvatore Sciacchitano affirmed that international air transport is clearly suffering very acutely as personal and global mobility continues to be curtailed, and in light of its instrumental role in worldwide response in times of crisis he is greatly encouraged that relief may soon be on the way.[3] On the same page is ICAO's Secretary General, Dr. Fang Liu, who applauded the G20 statement's highlighting of the need for "bold and large-scale fiscal support," and the hope that "the magnitude and scope of this response will get the global economy back on its feet and set a strong basis for the protection of jobs and the recovery of growth."

1.1 *IATA's view on financial aid and analysis of economic impacts of COVID-19*

As IATA has put in evidence, governments must include aviation in stabilization packages. Airlines are at the core of a value chain that supports

---

[2] In this period of crisis, the European Commission has shown its willingness to help member states in the design of state aid schemes and/or individual measures to support companies facing economic difficulties due to the COVID-19 outbreak, available at: https://www.twobirds.com/en/news/articles/2020/global/state-aid-and-the-covid-19-pandemic-in-the-aviation-sector (accessed December 9, 2021).

[3] The G20 on March 26, 2020 said it will do "whatever it takes" to overcome the pandemic, and will continue to "conduct bold and large-scale fiscal support," available at: https://www.icao.int/Newsroom/Pages/ICAO-leaders-welcome-G20-calls-.aspx (accessed December 9, 2021).

some 65.5 million jobs worldwide. Each of the 2.7 million airline jobs supports 24 more jobs in the economy.

Alexandre de Juniac, IATA's Director General and CEO, affirmed that: "Financial relief for airlines today should be a critical policy measure for governments. Supporting airlines will keep vital supply chains working through the crisis. Every airline job saved will keep 24 more people employed. And it will give airlines a fighting chance of being viable businesses that are ready to lead the recovery by connecting economies when the pandemic is contained. If airlines are not ready, the economic pain of COVID-19 will be unnecessarily prolonged."[4]

IATA proposes a number of relief options for governments to consider, including:

- **Direct financial support** to passenger and cargo carriers to compensate for reduced revenues and liquidity attributable to travel restrictions imposed as a result of COVID-19.
- **Loans,** loan guarantees and support for the corporate bond market by governments or central banks. The corporate bond market is a vital source of finance for airlines, but the eligibility of corporate bonds for central bank support needs to be extended and guaranteed by governments to provide access for a wider range of companies.
- **Tax relief:** Rebates on payroll taxes paid to date in 2020 and/or an extension of payment terms for the rest of 2020, along with a temporary waiver of ticket taxes and other government-imposed levies.[5]

It is quite unlikely that the scale of the crisis will make a sharp V-shaped recovery. Realistically, it will be a U-shaped recovery with domestic travel coming back faster than the international market.[6] We

---

[4]See: Covid-19 Puts Over Half of 2020 Passenger Revenues at Risk, available at: https://www.iata.org/en/pressroom/pr/2020-04-14-01/ (accessed December 9, 2021).

[5]*Ibid.*

[6]ICAO when assessing the economic impacts on civil aviation, works with many different scenarios in order to reflect the very uncertain nature of the current situation and the rapidly changing environment. In order to explore the potential economic implication of the COVID-19 pandemic for the near future, ICAO has elaborated a report containing six different recovery paths under two indicative scenarios: (1) "V-Shaped": It follows the normal shape for recession where a brief period of contraction is followed by quick/smooth recovery — most optimistic path; (2) "U-Shaped": This indicates prolonged

could see more than half of passenger revenues disappear. That would be a US$314 billion hit (data as of April 14, 2020).[7] Several governments have stepped up with new or expanded financial relief measures but the situation remains critical.

1.1.1 *Remedies adopted by the EU*

In order to help ease the impact of the outbreak, the European Commission has put forward targeted legislation[8] to help the EU companies, and thus airlines to overcome with the crisis caused by COVID-19. Measures approved so far are designed to meet liquidity needs. Airlines are likely to

---

contraction and muted recovery with a possibility of no return to trend line of growth (L-shaped) — most pessimistic path. The actual path will eventually depend upon various factors, *inter alia*, duration and magnitude of the outbreak and containment measures, availability of government assistance, consumers' confidence, and economic conditions. See: https://www.icao.int/sustainability/Pages/Economic-Impacts-of-COVID-19.aspx (accessed May 9, 2021). For an update about the impact of COVID-19 on aviation industry visit: https://www.icao.int/sustainability/Documents/COVID-19/ICAO_Coronavirus_Econ_Impact.pdf (accessed December 9, 2021).

[7]The latest data indicate US$238–US$418 billion potential loss of gross operating revenues of airlines. The impacts depend on duration and magnitude of the outbreak and containment measures, the degree of consumer confidence for air travel, and economic conditions. Source: *Effects of Novel Coronavirus (COVID-19) on Civil Aviation: Economic Impact Analysis*, ICAO, May 20, 2020, p. 3, available at: https://www.icao.int/sustainability/Documents/COVID-19/ICAO_Coronavirus_Econ_Impact.pdf (accessed December 9, 2021).

[8]This framework includes the (i) *Temporary Framework for State Aid Measures to Support the Economy in the current COVID-19 Outbreak* (2020/C 91 I/01), March 20, 2020, and (ii) *Amendment to the Temporary Framework for State Aid Measures to Support the Economy in the Current COVID-19 Outbreak* (2020/C 112 I/01), April 4, 2020 ("first amendment"), (iii) *Amendment to the Temporary Framework for State Aid Measures to Support the Economy in the Current COVID-19 Outbreak C* (2020) 3156 final, May 8, 2020 (second amendment). Based on these horizontal rules and in close cooperation with the member states, the Commission has to-date approved an estimated €1.9 trillion in State aid to the EU economy — to provide urgently needed liquidity for companies, save jobs, enable research and development, and ensure the supply of products to fight the coronavirus outbreak. The second amendment complements the types of measures already covered by the temporary framework and existing State aid rules, by setting out criteria based on which the member states can provide recapitalizations and subordinated debt to companies in need, while protecting the level playing field in the EU. For further info visit: https://ec.europa.eu/commission/presscorner/detail/en/ip_20_838 (accessed December 9, 2021).

need fresh equity, not just credit. This will require airlines to break new ground in the crisis response. Regarding the aviation sector in particular, the Executive Vice-President Margrethe Vestager stated that "compensation can be granted to airlines under Article 107(2)(b) TFEU[9] for damages suffered due to the COVID-19 outbreak, even if they have received rescue aid in the last ten years."

Besides the financial aid the EU Commission also approved specific measures changing the landing slot rules. In order to ease the economic and environmental impact of the outbreak, the European Commission has decided to put forward very rapidly targeted legislation to temporarily alleviate airlines from their airport slot usage obligations under EU law. Announcing the measure, President of the European Commission, Ursula von der Leyen, said: "We want to make it easier for airlines to keep their airport slots, even if they do not operate flights in those slots because of declining traffic. This temporary measure helps both our industry and the environment. It will relieve pressure on the aviation industry, and in particular on smaller airline companies, and it will also decrease emissions by avoiding so-called 'ghost flights' — when airlines fly almost empty planes, simply to keep their slots." Commissioner for Transport, Adina Vălean, added: "The temporary measure will allow airlines to adjust their capacity in view of the falling demand caused by the outbreak. [...] Given the urgency, the Commission will in due course present a legislative proposal and calls on the European Parliament and the Council to swiftly adopt this measure in co-decision procedure."

In particular Regulation (EEC) No. 95/93 sets the rules on the allocation of slots at EU airports. Its Article 10 contains a "use-it-or-lose-it" rule, whereby air carriers must use at least 80% of their allocated slots within a given scheduling period in order to keep precedence in respect of the same series of slots within the corresponding scheduling period of the next year (so-called "grandfather rights"). The sanitary crisis created by the COVID-19 outbreak in early 2020 had a serious impact on air carriers leading to a significant decline in air traffic worldwide. The decline in passenger demand led to air transport companies canceling a number of flights, which resulted in slot usage below the 80% threshold imposed by the Regulation. The Commission proposed an amendment on March 13,

---

[9]The EU Commission concluded that the COVID-19 outbreak qualifies as an "exceptional occurrence" for the purpose of Article 107(2)(b) of the Treaty on the Functioning of the European Union.

2020 so as to protect the grandfathering rights of air carriers for those slots that have not been used during the period when the aviation market has been most affected by the COVID-19 outbreak. This amendment was approved on March 30, 2020. The EU thus will suspend until October 24, 2020 the airport slot requirements which oblige airlines to use at least 80% of their take-off and landing slots in order to keep them the following year. If the current serious situation persists, the measure can be extended quickly by means of a Commission delegated act.[10] This measure was extended by the EU Commission on 23.07.2021, therefore the slot use rate for the winter 2021/2022 scheduling period should be set to 50%.

European supply chains are maintained through an extensive network of freight transport services involving all modes of transport. Continued and uninterrupted air cargo services are of essential strategic importance for the EU. More specifically related to cargo airlines, the European Commission released guidance on facilitating air cargo operations during the COVID-19 outbreak on March 26, recognizing the potential need for international co-operation in the aviation industry to ensure the supply and fair distribution of products. The guidance, which relates to the maintenance and facilitation of air cargo operations (including the transport of essential goods, such as, for example, medical equipment, personal protective equipment (PPE) — particularly where delivery is time-sensitive), encourages member states to implement temporary operational and organizational measures until air traffic and travel restrictions are lifted. Such recommended measures include granting necessary authorizations and permits for transport from outside the EU, temporarily removing night curfews or slot restrictions for essential air cargo operations, and exempting asymptomatic transport personnel from travel restrictions. The Commission emphasized that these measures are targeted toward preventing shortages of essential goods and services, and it will continue to prohibit companies cartelizing or abusing their dominant position.[11]

---

[10]See: *Regulation (EU) 2020/459 amending Council Regulation (EEC) No. 95/93 on Common Rules for the Allocation of Slots at Community Airports*, available at: https://www.europeansources.info/record/regulation-eu-2020-459-amending-council-regulation-95-93-common-rules-allocation-slots-community-airports/ (accessed December 9, 2021).

[11]For more information regarding the European Commission released guidance on facilitating air cargo operations during the COVID-19 outbreak, please refer to European Commission Guidelines, available at: https://ec.europa.eu/transport/sites/transport/files/legislation/c20202010_en.pdf (accessed December 9, 2021).

1.1.2 *US response: Brief introduction*

Of significant importance is the US response to the crisis; in fact, with a bold move the US government injected US$2.1 trillion to sustain its economy.[12] Of this historic amount, US$61 billion have been assigned to support its aviation industry.

In contrast to the EU's generalist framework approach, the US has acted pragmatically in providing specific relief measures and amounts for its aviation industry as part of its "CARES Act" passed on March 27, 2020.[13]

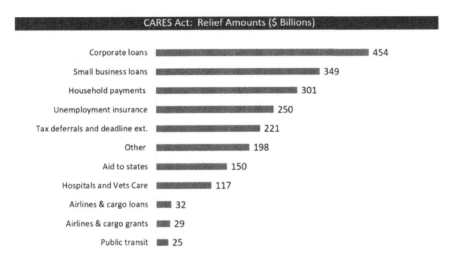

Source: Wall St. Journal

This provides US$61 billion in grants and loans as well as excise tax relief for the US aviation industry. All US carriers stand to gain from this. Thus, for example, Delta Air Lines will receive US$5.4 billion in payroll support through the Act's program and is reported to be intending to ask for US$4.6 billion for more general assistance, while American Airlines will receive US$5.8 billion in payroll support (made up of a direct grant of US$4.1 billion and a low-interest loan of US$1.7 billion), and is

---

[12] See: Coronavirus Aid, Relief, and Economic Security Act, also known as the CARES Act, available at: https://www.congress.gov/bill/116th-congress/house-bill/748 (accessed December 9, 2021).

[13] Unprecedented in size and scope, the legislation was the largest-ever economic stimulus package in the US history, amounting to 10% of total US gross domestic product.

apparently planning to apply for a separate loan of almost US$4.8 billion for other purposes. According to the *Wall Street Journal*[14] the airlines had wanted the loans to be forgiven but the treasury secretary, Steven Mnuchin, told carriers that 30% of the assistance would need to be repaid,[15] and that airlines would have to offer stock warrants — giving the government the right to buy shares in the companies — on a portion of those funds.

The US Department of Treasury posted a table listing the participants and some loan details for its airlines payroll assistance program on its website.[16] Mnuchin has approved US$25 billion in payroll assistance for 352 applicants, which included contractors, passenger and cargo carriers, the Treasury said. It must be noted that airlines are not depending on

---

[14] https://www.wsj.com/articles/treasury-airlines-reach-agreement-on-aid-11586898079?mod=hp_lead_pos3 (accessed December 9, 2021).

[15] There was widespread criticism after the last recession when the US taxpayer bailed out some of the US's largest banks and the auto industry but did not gain from their eventual recovery, this is why now the US Treasury has posed these conditions. The split between grants and loans angered industry officials who wanted 100% grants; however, the 30% of this aid can be repaid at very low interest rate.

[16] The Payroll Support Program under Division A, Title IV, Subtitle B of the CARES Act provides payroll support to passenger air carriers, cargo air carriers, and certain contractors for the continuation of payment of employee wages, salaries, and benefits. A total of up to US$25 billion is available for passenger air carriers; US$4 billion for cargo air carriers; and US$3 billion for certain contractors. As specified in Section 4113 of the CARES Act, the amount to be received by each air carrier or contractor is based on its payroll expenses from April 2019 through September 2019, subject to proration. Funds received by these air carriers and contractors must exclusively be used for the continuation of payment of employee wages, salaries, and benefits. Certain participants in the Payroll Support Program are required to provide financial instruments as appropriate compensation to the US Government for the provision of the financial assistance. After consultation with the Department of Transportation and consistent with Section 4117 of the CARES Act, Treasury determined that passenger air carriers receiving payroll support of more than US$100 million, cargo air carriers receiving more than US$50 million, and eligible contractors receiving more than US$37.5 million are required to provide financial instruments as appropriate compensation. Participants that receive payroll support of more than US$100 million are required to provide financial instruments to the US Government in the form of a 10-year senior unsecured promissory note and warrants for shares of common stock.

federal funds alone, having tapped credit markets for billions of dollars in new loans, as well as existing revolvers. Tens of thousands of employees have volunteered for time off, from unpaid short-term voluntary leave to early retirement.

1.1.3 *China's response*

China has adopted an articulated response to fight the impact of COVID-19. In particular, China has implemented a series of financial policies to sustain its economy. China's financial policies are being and will be implemented by various government agencies, banks, financial institutions, and government-controlled guarantee and re-guarantee institutions to support the resumption of operations and production. With the gradual stabilization and control of COVID-19 in China, both the central and local governments are likely going to introduce more policies in the coming months to enhance economic development as well as social stability. These financial policies include providing loans with preferential conditions through financial institutions to certain frontline companies, reducing the costs of financing guarantee services, postponing the repayment of loans, optimizing corporate bond issuance procedures, and facilitating cross-border financing, which are generally available to eligible companies regardless of whether they are controlled by PRC or foreign shareholders. Notably on March 4, 2020, Department of Finance (MOF) and Civil Aviation Administration of China (CAAC) jointly promulgated a circular on financial support policies for civil aviation and transportation enterprise (the "Airlines Support Circular"),[17] which has a validity period of January 23, 2020–June 30, 2020. According to the Airlines Support Circular, cash support will be provided to both domestic and foreign airlines that operate international flights either to or from China in an effort to help them fight against the difficulties brought about by the COVID-19 outbreak and to encourage the resumption or continuous

---

[17] Circular of MOF and CAAC on Financial Support Policies for Civil Aviation Transportation Enterprise during the Prevention and Control of COVID-19 Pandemic (财政部、民航局关于民航运输企业新冠肺炎疫情防控期间资金支持政策的通知) promulgated and effective on March 4, 2020, available at: http://www.gov.cn/zhengce/zhengceku/2020-03/05/content_5487155.htm (Chinese version, accessed December 9, 2021).

operation of their international flights. Key details of the supporting policies are summarized as follows:

- Eligibility requirements: Airlines should be either (i) domestic and foreign airlines that operate international flights in and out of Mainland China, or (ii) airlines that carry out major flight missions assigned by the State Council's Joint Prevention and Control Mechanism.
- Conditions: (i) Airlines that did not halt their operations or have resumed their international flights during the COVID-19 outbreak are eligible for the funding; (ii) funding standards are CNY 0.0176 per seat kilometer for the co-operated air routes and CNY 0.0528 per seat kilometer if the route is covered by a sole airline; (iii) for multi-city flights and fifth freedom flights, the cash support will be calculated based on the number of international flight segments involving Chinese destinations; (iv) if a second carrier operates or resumes flights on the routes which were at first identified as being operated by a sole carrier, the two carriers shall be provided with cash support according to the standards for the co-operated routes; and (v) subsidies will be given to the carriers performing major transportation tasks in accordance with the actual costs confirmed by the intermediary agency commissioned by CAAC after the COVID-19 pandemic.
- Filing and review procedures: All eligible carriers shall file their applications with CAAC and MOF before the seventh (7th) day of each month and shall provide supporting documents, including the information regarding air routes, flight frequency, aircraft type, available seat kilometers, inventory of materials, and cost and revenue data. After reviewing the application documents, domestic airlines will be reimbursed by MOF or its local counterparts and foreign airlines will be reimbursed by CAAC.[18]

1.2 *Commercial airlines need restructuring to survive the impact of COVID-19*

As a matter of fact the COVID-19 crisis has put the aviation industry under great pressure and airlines during the pandemic have grounded all, or almost all, of the planes in their fleet. Naturally in this situation

---

[18] *Ibid.*

financial aid is of extreme importance but not sufficient, and other measures are needed. Some have even used their aircrafts as freighters, however a more drastic rethinking and restructuring of their operations must be put in place to overcome the impacts of this crisis which has caused a number of operators to cease their activity. The maintenance of the aviation industry is essential for international connectivity, prosperity, and growth. For these reasons extraordinary actions need to be taken to grant the industry to survive and re-emerge stronger and to prosper. One obliged path is thus the restructuring of the entire sector and in particular the combination of activities of the major players through M&A to create synergies, and the base for a re-birth of the commercial aviation.

1.2.1 *Massive airlines consolidation*

It is clear that the increasing indebtedness of airlines will lead to bankruptcy of many companies and thus a massive consolidation will follow. This can be easily predicted especially for the two major markets, where the large majority of airlines operates, that is to say Europe and the US.

No industry's ownership is more strictly regulated than that of the airline industry. Without exceptions, a US airline cannot be controlled by a non-US person[19] nor can an EU airline be controlled by a non-EU person.[20] The COVID-19 pandemic raises questions around some of the barriers to a worldwide consolidation of airlines.

---

[19]The Civil Aeronautics Act of 1938 requires that US citizens own or control at least 75% of the voting interests of the US airlines, available at: https://libraryonline.erau.edu/online-full-text/books-online/CivilAeronauticsAct.pdf (accessed May 9, 2021). Federal laws on foreign investment in US airlines date back to the 1920s and establish the limits of allowable foreign ownership and control. The requirements were enacted in the Air Commerce Act of 1926 and the Civil Aeronautics Act of 1938, and have largely remained the same since then. Foreign ownership may comprise up to 25% of the voting stock of the US airlines, and among other control requirements, boards of directors may include up to 33% non-US citizens. GAO (US Government Accountability Office) 19-540R Airline Foreign Ownership, June 25, 2019, available at: https://www.gao.gov/assets/700/699954.pdf (accessed December 9, 2021).

[20]Under Regulation (EC) No. 1008/2008 each member state is required to withdraw the operating license of an airline if such airline is under control of a non-EU person, available at: https://eur-lex.europa.eu/legal-content/EN/TXT/PDF/?uri=OJ:L:2008:293:FULL&from=EN (accessed December 9, 2021).

Within the EU, member state airline mergers do not face merger restrictions in principle for as long as the EU ownership rules are observed. However, major airlines face antitrust scrutiny if they are interested in acquiring competing EU airlines. The EU Commission reviews airline mergers on a route-by-route basis. This means that if too many routes overlap, the expected clearance conditions may make a merger unattractive or too risky. In contrast, a merger of equals between European and US airlines or a divestiture-like transaction to a third party not being a US or an EU person, respectively, is *per se* not possible according to the existing legislation. However, interestingly, the position is different with respect to airports, aircraft producers, or service providers to airlines or airports, which can all be controlled by non-US or non-EU persons. The ownership of airlines could simply fall under the foreign direct investment rules (FDI) of the member states like other critical industries. Therefore, when it comes to M&A activity in the airline industry, consolidation is restricted by antitrust concerns and by ownership restrictions.

1.2.2 *Giant planes: Do they still have a reason to be operated?*

The drastic reduction of passengers due to COVID-19 has put into evidence the difficulties for airlines to operate giant planes (such as airbus A380)[21] because of their operational costs, thus evidencing that such giants are inadequate in this scenario where all airlines are trying to overcome this crisis concentrating in maximizing efficiency and rationalizing their fleet adopting more cost-effective aircrafts, preferring now the

---

[21] The Airbus A380 is a wide-body aircraft manufactured by Airbus. It is the world's largest passenger airliner. Airbus studies started in 1988 and the project was announced in 1990 to challenge the dominance of the Boeing 747 in the long-haul market. The A3XX project was presented in 1994; Airbus launched the €9.5 billion (US$10.7 billion) A380 program on December 19, 2000. The first prototype was unveiled in Toulouse on January 18, 2005, with its first flight on April 27, 2005. Difficulties in electrical wiring caused a two-year delay and the development cost ballooned to €18 billion. It obtained its type certificate from the EASA and the FAA on December 12, 2006. It was first delivered to Singapore Airlines on October 15, 2007 and entered service on October 25. Production peaked at 30 per year in 2012 and 2014. However, Airbus concedes that its US$25 billion investment for the aircraft cannot be recouped. On February 14, 2019, after Emirates reduced its last orders in favor of the A350 and the A330neo, Airbus announced that A380 production would end by 2021, available at: https://en.wikipedia.org/wiki/Airbus_A380 (accessed December 9, 2021).

two engines fuel-effective eco-friendly, and others capable of long range routes. Giant aircraft will be used less and less. As airlines need more flexibility, they will opt above all for medium-capacity aircraft whose profitability is achieved with fewer passengers. In this context, manufacturers such as Embraer and Bombardier could see their order books fill up faster than those of Airbus and Boeing. As an example of this reduction in the production of these giants, the consequences for Emirates, which has the largest fleet of A380s,[22] need to be considered. Its boss, Tim Clark, may well regret having said that Emirates was the only company that knew how to use this giant aircraft.[23] In any case, Emirates is looking for billions of dollars in loans to save itself.[24]

1.2.3 *Reduction of fleets and the role of leasing companies*

In order to face the consequences caused by COVID-19, and in order to find new financial resources, it has become necessary for airlines to rethink their structure also in terms of the size of their fleets. This will allow to find a part of the needed financial resources to optimize their functioning and recovery. To this extent examples have already occurred: (i) in the US, United Airlines sold 22 of its planes to the Bank of China (BOC Aviation Limited, April 2020),[25] because it was starved for revenue during the pandemic; another example is (ii) Southwest who did the same,

---

[22]As of April 2020, the Emirates mainline fleet in service consists of the following wide-body aircraft: 115 Airbus A380; 10 Boeing 777-200LR; 132 Boeing 777-300ER. For further info, visit: https://en.wikipedia.org/wiki/Emirates_fleet (accessed December 9, 2021).

[23]*Emirates' Tim Clark Slams Airlines over Poor Use Of A380*, available at: https://www.airlineratings.com/news/emirates-tim-clark-slams-airlines-poor-use-a380/ (accessed December 9, 2021).

[24]Emirates — an emblem of Dubai's meteoric rise in the last three decades from a desert outpost into a global business and tourism hub — is being particularly hard hit by the abrupt collapse in air travel as countries lock down to slow the spread of the COVID-19. The government said it would step in to shield the airline with new equity. See: https://www.bloomberg.com/news/articles/2020-04-05/emirates-airline-said-to-seek-billions-of-dollars-in-bank-loans (accessed December 9, 2021).

[25]On April 19, *Reuters* reported that United Airlines will sell and lease back 22 planes to BOC Aviation. The company plans to sell six Boeing 787-9 aircraft and 16 Boeing 737-9 MAX aircraft. However, BOC Aviation did not disclose the selling price. Notably, the

selling 10 planes to BOC Aviation.[26] This could just be the beginning. However, the move caused some concerns in the US. Unless Congress acts, most of the commercial aircraft operating in America could be owned by Chinese companies. Substantially China is exploiting two of the US's greatest strengths namely: massive economic might and openness to world commerce, providing an opportunity for China in acquiring planes at a reduced price, and in the long term competing with the US airlines which will find themselves in a more fragile situation.

It is necessary to stress that more than half of the 7,000 commercial airliners flown in the US are owned not by the US airlines but by companies that lease the aircraft to them. Airlines might initially buy the planes themselves, but they often later sell them to finance companies that lease them back to the airlines. These "sell and leaseback"[27] transactions generate capital that is routinely used to buy new aircraft and pay for a variety of infrastructure improvements. This back-and-forth arrangement, which has become embedded in the aviation system over the past 25 years, has helped keep the cost of air travel low enough for tens of millions of Americans to fly both regularly and safely.

1.3 *How leasing companies are reacting to COVID-19*

As we have introduced earlier the role of leasing companies is of critical importance for the continuity of the correct operations of airlines. In particular, in the US the CARES Act failed to address leasing companies' vulnerability. In the majority of the cases, aircrafts are owned by these lease companies and not directly by airlines, therefore when the US

---

deal will close this year. BOC Aviation stated that it will lease back the planes to the United Airlines on long-term agreements.

[26] See https://www.bocaviation.com/en/Press-Releases/2020/5/BOC-Aviation-Signs-PLB-With-SWA-For-10-B737MAX8.

[27] Many of the ultimate owners of aircraft leasing companies are US-based public employee pensions, university endowments, and other institutions whose shareholders are middle-class Americans. These days, many airplanes are parked unused on tarmacs across the country and are rarely in the air. As a result, nearly all passenger airlines have asked their lessors — the leasing companies that actually own the idled aircraft — for financial assistance. Leasing companies are being forced to restructure leases and accept delayed rent payments. See: https://www.foxbusiness.com/economy/coronavirus-china-us-aviation (accessed December 9, 2021).

airlines cannot pay their monthly rent on aircraft, leasing companies are left holding all financial responsibilities. These companies stand to lose up to 95% of their income. Because airlines have financial support from the federal government, they would not go out of business. But the companies that actually own the aircrafts will "fly into troubles." The question is: What will happen to these aircrafts if these lease companies fail? One likely scenario is that these planes will be purchased for only a portion of their remaining value by Chinese leasing companies.[28] As these leasing companies are all owned by financial institutions controlled by the State, substantially the Chinese government will result to be the owner of all these planes.

1.3.1 *The rapid growing importance of Chinese leasing companies*

In 2006, no aviation leasing companies existed in China. Today, there are more than 40 of them, and they receive the active support of the Chinese government.[29] The role of the Chinese leasing companies has grown exponentially in the last decade and now 11 of the top 50 leasing companies are Chinese. In January 2019, Chinese leasing companies owned more than 20% of global commercial aircraft by value. Notwithstanding the crisis caused by COVID-19, it seems that the Chinese share is increasing. According to a US source it seems that Chinese leasing companies manage 16% of the US passenger airline fleet, a number that could skyrocket unless the federal government steps in to assist America's aviation leasing industry. "Aircraft leasing companies aren't asking for a lot. All they need is access to CARES Act loans, which would be fully repaid. In the end,

---

[28]Top Chinese lessors see combined fleet values at over US$50 billion in 2018 — US$10 billion more than 2017. The most important Chinese leasing company is ICBC Leasing who came sixth in the global ranking. Its total fleet value in 2018 equated to over US$16 billion. See: https://www.cirium.com/thoughtcloud/cirium-awards-chinese-aircraft-lessors/ (accessed December 9, 2021).

[29]In this sense: Stephen Yates, "In coronavirus aftermath China threatens takeover of US aviation: Ex-Cheney Deputy National Security Adviser — Unless Congress acts, most of the commercial aircraft operating in America could soon be owned by Chinese companies," *FoxBusiness*, available at: https://www.foxbusiness.com/economy/coronavirus-china-us-aviation (accessed December 9, 2021).

Top 50 lessors by fleet value

2018 Rank	2017 Rank	Lessor	Total fleet value			Average Value		Managed Only	
			$m	Change	Total fleet	$m	Change	$m	% of Fleet
1	(1)	AerCap	34,690	9.5%	1,059	32.7	9.4%	1,496	4.3%
2	(2)	GECAS	24,652	-4.1%	1,232	20.0	3.3%	2,114	8.6%
3	(4)	BBAM	20,916	14.1%	498	42.0	-7.0%	13,591	65.0%
4	(3)	Avolon	19,426	3.5%	569	34.1	4.9%	1,467	7.6%
5	(5)	SMBC Aviation Capital	16,200	2.8%	421	38.5	5.3%	2,118	13.1%
6 ●	(6)	ICBC Leasing	16,148	12.7%	385	41.9	-4.2%	999	6.2%
7	(8)	Air Lease	14,796	14.5%	335	44.2	0.2%	1,764	11.9%
8	(7)	BOC Aviation	14,620	4.8%	335	43.6	0.8%	858	5.9%
9	(9)	DAE Capital	10,610	0.0%	352	30.1	0.5%	506	4.8%
10	(10)	Aviation Capital Group	9,206	24.4%	312	29.5	10.0%	1,358	14.8%
11 ●	(12)	BoComm Leasing	7,900	17.8%	196	40.3	-0.8%	68	0.9%
12 ●	(11)	CDB Aviation Lease Finance	7,390	6.1%	214	34.5	-1.4%	0	0%
13	(14)	ORIX Aviation	7,308	18.8%	238	30.7	11.3%	921	12.6%
14	(15)	Nordic Aviation Capital	6,467	8.3%	474	13.6	-3.4%	1,177	18.2%
15	(19)	Goshawk	6,467	58.2%	168	38.5	-4.9%	928	14.3%
16	(13)	Jackson Square Aviation	6,412	3.5%	157	40.8	-1.8%	0	0%
17	(16)	Aircastle	5,782	0.1%	246	23.5	-3.6%	380	6.6%
18	(22)	Amedeo	5,003	77.4%	48	104.2	-37.2%	3,480	69.5%
19 ●	(20)	China Aircraft Leasing Company	4,642	18.7%	133	34.9	-0.9%	109	2.3%
20	(17)	Macquarie AirFinance	4,635	-6.4%	197	23.5	-3.1%	29	0.6%
21	(18)	Standard Chartered Aviation Finance	4,602	-0.1%	137	33.6	-8.0%	370	8.0%
22	(21)	Arctic Aviation Assets	3,820	21.6%	82	46.6	2.3%	298	7.8%
23	(29)	Carlyle Aviation Partners	3,488	41.4%	229	15.2	-0.6%	2,877	82.5%
24	(28)	International Airfinance	2,992	20.8%	55	54.4	-16.5%	0	0%
25	(30)	ALM - Aircraft Leasing & Management	2,920	25.0%	84	34.8	8.6%	2,893	99.1%
26 ●	(24)	CMB Financial Leasing	2,856	1.6%	73	39.1	-9.6%	0	0%
27 ●	(25)	CCB Financial Leasing	2,789	-0.6%	68	41.0	-5.0%	227	8.1%
28	(23)	Doric	2,566	-9.0%	38	67.5	-6.6%	1,521	59.3%
29	(26)	ALAFCO	2,495	-6.9%	63	39.6	-1.0%	0	0%
30	(36)	Castlelake	2,493	31.4%	180	13.8	15.4%	2,487	99.8%
31 ●	(45)	AVIC International Leasing	2,425	59.4%	106	22.9	32.3%	0	0%
32	(32)	MCAP/MC Aviation Partners	2,266	1.7%	70	32.4	-1.2%	1,878	82.9%
33	(31)	Altavair	2,225	-4.8%	50	44.5	-2.7%	0	0%
34	(37)	Accipiter	2,118	14.1%	69	30.7	0.8%	0	0%
35	(34)	Deucalion Aviation Funds	2,079	-3.1%	102	20.4	-0.3%	1,067	51.3%
36	(33)	Tokyo Century	2,072	-3.7%	50	41.4	6.0%	0	0%
37	(42)	VTB-Leasing	2,053	23.5%	77	26.7	5.9%	60	2.9%
38	(39)	VEB-Leasing	1,858	5.5%	68	27.3	-6.9%	67	3.6%
39 ●	(43)	Minsheng Financial Leasing	1,821	13.9%	47	38.7	-0.6%	0	0%
40	(51)	GTLK – State Transport Leasing Company	1,818	40.1%	106	17.1	0.4%	0	0%
41 ●	(46)	SPDB Financial Leasing	1,704	14.7%	39	43.7	-5.9%	0	0%
42	(47)	GOAL - German Operating Aircraft Leasing	1,666	16.9%	54	30.9	34.2%	0	0%
43	(41)	Boeing Capital	1,635	-2.2%	195	8.4	-4.2%	11	0.6%
44	(38)	FPG Amentum	1,616	-11.1%	46	35.1	4.3%	929	57.5%
45	(49)	Banc of America Leasing Ireland	1,536	12.9%	30	51.2	16.6%	0	0%
46	(44)	Novus Aviation	1,453	-7.6%	19	76.5	-12.5%	83	5.7%
47	(53)	Sberbank Leasing	1,429	23.7%	67	21.3	10.8%	0	0%
48	(55)	Titan Aviation Leasing	1,370	36.9%	33	41.5	3.7%	0	0%
49 ●	(48)	Changjiang Leasing Company	1,331	-6.0%	65	20.5	-4.8%	0	0%
50 ●	(50)	Comsys Aviation Leasing	1,178	-11.7%	23	51.2	-4.1%	0	0%
		Total	309,932	10.7%	9,894	31.3	3.4%	48,129	15.5%

Notes: Ranking: The survey is based on the top 50 companies with a substantial operating lease business ranked by the value of their owned and/or managed fleets at December 31, 2018. Change: The change figures are based on fleets/values supplied by FlightGlobal's Flight Fleets Analyzer and Ascend Values databases for December 2017 and 2018. Operating lessors: Lessors are defined as those with an active operating lease business and a substantial investment in fleet. Companies that are solely or predominantly financiers have been excluded. Fleets and values: The survey represents a snapshot of fleets, including stored aircraft, with half-life current market values supplied by Flight Ascend Consultancy. Note the composition of fleets is constantly changing. The red points indicate the top Chinese leasing companies. Data is updated to December 2018.

Source: Flight Fleets Analyzer and Ascend Values data, end-2018. May exclude some orders placed in the final few days of 2018.

taxpayers wouldn't lose a dime, but America's essential aviation industry would be protected from a hostile takeover by China."[30]

1.3.2 *China's contribution to the world's aircraft leasing industry*

China did not get involved in aircraft leasing business in a massive way until 2007 when it allowed a few of its banking giants to form their leasing companies. Today these companies play a major role also in financing a large portion of the world's new aircraft deliveries from the manufacturers of Boeing, Airbus, and others. China's contribution to the world's aircraft leasing industry, which used to be dominated by the rich and developed countries as the aircraft leasing industry demands a huge input of capital, is now growing as per data. It seems that this trend will continue considering the difficulties the other players in the West are facing. However, Chinese leasing companies are also faced with challenges, in fact as Michael Duff, Managing Director of The Airline Analyst, a London-based consultancy in the aviation finance sector, affirmed: "The big challenge for them going forward is the re-marketing skills and capability." He also added that: "When their planes come to the end of their lease with the existing airline, they have to have a strong marketing presence globally in order to be able to re-lease the aeroplanes to other airlines."[31]

A growing number of Chinese leasing companies are contributing to the expansion of this business because they dispose of the necessary financial resources, and they are growing internationally preferring to establish their presence especially in Europe where it is more easy to flourish.

1.3.3 *Chinese leasing companies becoming international*

As an example ICBC Financial Leasing Company Ltd. (ICBC Leasing) is one of the earliest leasing companies established in China by the country's largest banking group Industrial and Commercial Bank of China. In 2010, ICBC Leasing set up an overseas arm in Dublin as Ireland is a global aircraft leasing center. Other Chinese leasing companies have established

---

[30] *Ibid.*

[31] Zhang Qi, "Interview: China is major player in global aircraft leasing market, says expert," January 23, 2019, available at: http://en.people.cn/n3/2019/0123/c90000-9540838.html (accessed December 9, 2021).

a presence in Ireland and in doing so they have contributed in consolidating Ireland's position as a global leader in the aviation sector.

It must be stressed that because of their success at home Chinese leasing companies started to look for growth in foreign markets. Their overseas ambitions also have received the government's support in the form of a decision in 2015[32] to provide subsidies to and streamline regulatory and tax frameworks governing cross-border financial leasing services. Since then, all major Chinese lessors have built up a sizable presence abroad, typically starting their international operations in Ireland or Hong Kong, or a combination of the two. These locations offer significant benefits to lessors considering and comparing various international leasing and financing platforms. Particularly Ireland, with its 72 double tax treaties,[33] is the global hub for aircraft leasing and an ideal place for Chinese firms to base their foreign business. Hong Kong is becoming a regional draw with its rule of law, low regulatory barriers, and recent tax reforms aimed at promoting aviation finance. Hong Kong also offers benefits to companies from the mainland such as geographical proximity, a shared language and business culture, and access to new growth markets such as the Greater Bay Area.[34]

There is plenty of room to grow: IATA before the crisis caused by COVID-19 had predicted global air passenger numbers to double to 8.2 billion in 2037 and the Asia-Pacific region would have accounted for over half of this growth; this scenario is still possible if airlines recoup the normal growing trend they were experiencing before the crisis.

---

[32]*China to speed up development of financial leasing industry.* According to the document, financial leasing will be an important tool in equipment investment and technology upgrades by 2020 and China will see a world-class industry with a group of leading enterprises and an effective regulation system in the future. This push in the development of the financial leasing industry has favored the aviation leasing sector also, available at: http://english.www.gov.cn/policies/latest_releases/2015/09/07/content_281475184814808.htm (accessed December 9, 2021).

[33]An interesting article concerning aviation financial industry and tax regime is available at: https://www.tmf-group.com/en/news-insights/articles/2018/december/aviation-finance-industry-in-asia/ (accessed December 9, 2021).

[34]Chinese aircraft lessors can be seen preparing for the industry's next growth phase, fueled by a continuing boom in air travel in China and across Asia-Pacific, available at: https://www.tmf-group.com/en/news-insights/articles/2019/january/chinese-next-growth-phase/ (accessed December 9, 2021).

1.4 *Impact of COVID-19 on CO₂ emissions: Introduction*

Airlines' carbon emissions could drop by more than one-third in 2020 and could stay low in the near future if air traffic cannot completely recover. In fact, traffic forecasts by the IATA suggest airlines' emissions could drop 38% in 2020 due to the impact of COVID-19.[35] Eurocontrol Data Snapshot reported that CO_2 emissions from flights declined by 57% in 2020, but with considerable variation between states.

Aviation is currently powered by oil products which generate CO_2 when burnt. According to the ICAO, the global peak body for commercial aviation (passenger and freight transport) currently accounts for around 2% of global CO_2 emissions.[36]

Emissions from global commercial aviation are not available for 2019. International Air Transport Association (IATA) estimates a 1.1% increase on 2018 CO_2 emissions for 2019.[37] We can therefore estimate 2019 commercial transport CO_2 emissions at 928 Mt CO_2, and for passenger transport specifically at 755 Mt CO_2.[38]

1.4.1 *Impact so far: Informative box*

> *COVID-19 has already had a substantial impact on air traffic and commercial aviation emissions globally. This section estimates the scale of that reduction.*

---

[35] IATA estimates a 38% decline in revenue per passenger kilometers (RPKs), which serves as a yardstick for commercial airline activity. This equals to a commensurate decline in emissions of CO_2, available at: https://www.iata.org/en/pressroom/pr/2020-03-24-01/ (accessed December 9, 2021).

[36] ICAO (2019), "Destination Green, The Next Chapter," p. 111, available at: https://www.icao.int/environmental-protection/Documents/ICAO-ENV-Report2019-F1-WEB%20(1).pdf.

[37] IATA (2019), "Economic Performance of the Airline Industry," available at: https://www.iata.org/en/iata-repository/publications/economic-reports/airline-industry-economic-performance---december-2019---report/ (accessed December 9, 2021).

[38] See: Audrey Quicke and Emily Jones, "Civil Aviation Emissions Reductions under COVID-19 in Australia and Globally and the Potential Long-Term Impacts to Emissions in the Sector," The Australia Institute, Discussion paper April 2020, available at: https://www.tai.org.au/sites/default/files/P894%20Grounded%20-%20Aviation%20Emissions%20during%20Covid-19%20%5BWEB%5D_0.pdf (accessed December 9, 2021).

Global flight tracking service, Flightradar24 provides timely and credible data on commercial air traffic. Commercial aviation includes scheduled passenger and cargo flights operated by an airline. It excludes private flights and "general aviation," such as aerial work, instructional flying, and pleasure flying.[39] Flightradar24 is releasing data on commercial aviation during the COVID-19 crisis compared with the same period in 2019.

According to Flightradar24, commercial air traffic in February 2020 was 4.3% lower than the same month in 2019,[40] and 10% lower in the period March 1–19, 2020 compared to the same period in 2019.[41]

There was a substantial acceleration in flight cancellations in mid-March, with most of the reduction happening in the week from 11 to 19 March.[42]

CO_2 emissions from global commercial aviation for February 2019 and March 2019 are estimated based on the proportion of yearly traffic in those months. ICAO calculates traffic based on Revenue Passenger Kilometers (RPK), an airline industry metric that shows the number of kilometers traveled by paying passengers:

- *Yearly RPKs occurring in February = 7.1%*
- *Yearly RPKs occurring in March = 8.1%[43]*

---

[39] Australian Government (2020) General Aviation, available at: https://www.infrastructure.gov.au/infrastructure-transport-vehicles/aviation/general-aviation.

[40] Flightradar24 (2020) Commercial air traffic down 4.3% in February 2020.

[41] Flightradar24 (2020) March commercial traffic down 10% below 2019 so far, https://www.flightradar24.com/blog/march-commercial-traffic-down-10-below-2019-so-far/.

[42] 4.9% lower over March 1 to March 11, and 7.2% lower over March 1 to March 15 according to Flightradar24 Flightradar24 (2020) Commercial air traffic now down 7.2% in March, flightradar24.com/blog/commercial-air-traffic-now-down-7-2-in-march/.

[43] ICAO (2020), Economic Development: February 2020: Air Transport Monthly Monitor, p. 1 https://www.icao.int/sustainability/Documents/MonthlyMonitor-2020/MonthlyMonitor_February2020.pdf (accessed December 9, 2021).

Note the highest traffic months are the Northern Hemisphere Summer (June to August).

Assuming the monthly share of commercial CO_2 emissions generally corresponds to RPKs this would mean CO_2 reductions in 2020 of

- *2.84 Mt CO_2 for February, and*
- *7.51 Mt CO_2 for March 1st–19th.*

This suggests that the COVID-19 pandemic has resulted in approximately 10.3 Mt CO_2 reduction in global air transport CO_2 emissions during February and March, with the remainder of March likely to show further deep falls.

Source: The Australia Institute, Discussion paper, April 2020, *Civil Aviation Emissions Reductions under COVID-19 in Australia and Globally and the Potential Long-Term Impacts to Emissions in the Sector.*

1.4.2 Keeping emissions low after the COVID-19: Brief introduction

The outbreak of COVID-19 has provoked a shock and caused almost the collapse of air transportation, but one significant collateral consequence was the reduction of emissions which in any case was an objective of the aviation industry and of its players. Naturally, the goal remains to reduce emissions once this COVID19-related side-effect wears off and we will fly again, albeit with a more limited growth trend.

Commercial aviation is responsible for about 2% of global carbon emissions. In 2009, the industry put in place an ambitious and robust carbon emissions strategy, with specific targets and a four-pillar action plan to gradually reduce emissions.

The aviation industry recognizes the need to address the global challenge of climate change and in 2009 adopted a set of ambitious targets to mitigate CO_2 emissions from air transport:

- An average improvement in fuel efficiency of 1.5% per year from 2009 to 2020.

- A cap on net aviation CO_2 emissions from 2020 (carbon-neutral growth).
- A reduction in net aviation CO_2 emissions of 50% by 2050, relative to 2005 levels.[44]

As it will be exposed in the following section both ICAO and IATA have issued specific policies addressing aviation's climate impact. The aim of these policies is to have a long-lasting impact on global CO_2 emissions.

2. Policies of ICAO and IATA Regarding the Emissions of CO_2

ICAO formulates policies, develops and updates Standards and Recommended Practices (SARPs) on aircraft emissions, and conducts outreach activities with a view to minimize the adverse effects of international civil aviation on the global climate. In particular, ICAO aims at indicating policies to reduce CO_2 emissions. All these activities are conducted by the Secretariat and the Committee on Aviation and Environmental Protection (CAEP).[45]

Notably civil aviation accounted for 2.4% of fossil CO_2 emissions in 2018,[46] and up to 5% of total global warming impact when including warming from non-CO_2 effects of combusting fuels in the upper atmosphere.[47] International aviation alone was responsible for 543 million tonnes (Mt) of CO_2 emissions in 2018,[48] more than the Indonesian

---

[44] See: IATA, Climate Change, available at: https://www.iata.org/en/policy/environment/climate-change/ (accessed December 9, 2021).

[45] CAEP is a technical committee of the ICAO Council established in 1983. CAEP assists the Council in formulating new policies and adopting new SARPs related to aircraft noise and emissions, and more generally to aviation environmental impact.

[46] B. Graver, K. Zhang, and D. Rutherford (2019), "CO_2 Emissions from Global Aviation. International Council on Clean Transportation WP2019-16," available at: www.theicct.org/publications/co2-emissions-commercial-aviation-2018 (accessed December 9, 2021).

[47] David S. Lee *et al.* (2009), Aviation and global climate change in the 21st century. *Atmos. Environ.*, 43, 3520–3537, available at: https://www.sciencedirect.com/science/article/pii/S1352231009003574 (accessed December 9, 2021).

[48] M. Muntean, D. Guizzardi, E. Schaaf, M. Crippa, E. Solazzo, J. G. J. Olivier, and E. Vignati (2018), *Fossil CO_2 Emissions of All World Countries — 2018 Report*, EUR 29433 EN, Publications Office of the European Union, Luxembourg.

economy and about 1.5% of the global total. By comparison, international aviation and domestic aviation together represent 918 Mt of CO_2, or equivalent to the combined fossil fuel emissions of Germany (6th largest country emitter) and the Netherlands (36th largest country emitter).[49]

IATA also has introduced a series of policies in order to reduce the impact of CO_2 emissions and it fosters the development of sustainable low-carbon fuels. IATA recognizes the need to address the global challenge of climate change and adopted a set of ambitious targets to mitigate CO_2 emissions from air transport in line with ICAO policies.

These initiatives have produced a significant result in terms of shared goals which are listed in the so-called Carbon Offsetting and Reduction Scheme for International Aviation (CORSIA).

2.1 *CORSIA — The ICAO global market-based measure*

In 2016, ICAO adopted CORSIA, a global carbon offsetting[50] scheme to address CO_2 emission from international aviation which consists of a market-based measure that sets a target of net CO_2 emissions of international aviation at the average of 2019–2020 levels for the years 2021–2035 (before the impact of COVID-19). CORSIA requires individual aeroplane operators to compensate for their calculated share of emissions

---

[49]M. Crippa, G. Oreggioni, D. Guizzardi, M. Muntean, E. Schaaf, E. LoVullo, E. Solazzo, F. Monforti-Ferrario, J. G. J. Olivier, and E. Vignati (2019), *Fossil CO₂ and GHG Emissions of All World Countries*, Publications Office of the European Union, Luxembourg.
[50]Offsetting allows a company to compensate for its emissions by financing a reduction in emissions elsewhere. While carbon offsetting does not require companies to reduce their emissions "in-house," it provides an environmentally effective option for sectors where the potential for further emissions reductions is limited. There are many ways to achieve CO_2 reductions that can be used as offsets, many of which bring other social, environmental or economic benefits relevant to sustainable development. Offsetting and carbon markets have been a fundamental component of emissions reduction policies and continue to be an effective mechanism to underpin action against climate change. Offsetting is also more effective than a tax, as a carbon tax merely requires companies to pay for their emissions, without any guarantees that the payment will lead to any emissions reductions.

above their 2020 baselines using eligible emissions units[51] and sustainable alternative fuels with demonstrably lower life-cycle emissions. While CORSIA is anticipated to address up to 2.5 Gt of CO_2 emissions between 2021 and 2035,[52] this is not enough to ensure that this rapidly growing industry decarbonizes at levels and timeframes required to meet the 1.5°C temperature goal of the Paris Agreement.[53]

After the adoption of these measures in 2016 it must also be remembered that the ICAO Assembly at its 40th Session in 2019 adopted Resolution A40-18: *Consolidated Statement of Continuing ICAO Policies and Practices Related to Environmental Protection — Climate Change.*[54] It reiterated the two global aspirational goals for the international aviation sector of 2% annual fuel efficiency improvement through 2050 and carbon neutral growth from 2020 onward, as established at the 37th Assembly in 2010.

2.2 *Sustainable aviation fuel and CO_2 emissions*

Sustainable aviation fuels (SAFs) are one of the elements of the ICAO basket of measures to reduce aviation emissions, which also includes

---

[51] CORSIA Eligible Emissions Units have not been designated yet. Fourteen programs are currently being screened by the Technical Advisory Body, available at: https://www.icao.int/environmental-protection/CORSIA/Pages/TAB.aspx (accessed December 9, 2021).

[52] See EDF. Cumulative Emission Reductions to be Achieved Depending on Participation in ICAO's MBM, available at: https://www.edf.org/climate/icaos-market-based-measure; and see IATA (2019), https://www.iata.org/en/programs/environment/corsia/ (accessed December 9, 2021).

[53] Paris Agreement: The Paris Agreement sets out a global framework to avoid dangerous climate change by limiting global warming to well below 2°C and pursuing efforts to limit it to 1.5°C. It also aims to strengthen countries' ability to deal with the impacts of climate change and support them in their efforts. The Paris Agreement is the first-ever universal, legally binding global climate change agreement, adopted at the Paris climate conference (COP21) in December 2015. The EU and its member states are among the close to 195 Parties to the Paris Agreement. The EU formally ratified the agreement on October 5, 2016, thus enabling its entry into force on November 4, 2016, available at: https://unfccc.int/process-and-meetings/the-paris-agreement/the-paris-agreement (accessed December 9, 2021).

[54] Resolution A40-18: Consolidated statement of continuing ICAO policies and practices related to environmental protection — Climate change. Document available at: https://www.icao.int/environmental-protection/Documents/Assembly/Resolution_A40-18_Climate_Change.pdf (accessed December 9, 2021).

technology and standards, operational improvements, and the CORSIA. In its Resolution A40-18 (see previous footnote), the ICAO Assembly acknowledged the need for SAF to be developed and deployed in an economically feasible, socially and environmentally acceptable manner, and requested States to recognize existing approaches to assess the sustainability of all alternative fuels in general, including those for use in aviation which should: achieve net Green House Gas (GHG) emissions reduction on a life-cycle basis; respect the areas of high importance for biodiversity, conservation, and benefits for people from ecosystems, in accordance with international and national regulations; contribute to local social and economic development, and competition with food and water should be avoided.[55]

2.2.1 *ICAO Global Framework for Aviation and Alternative Fuels (GFAAF)*

The ICAO Global Framework for Aviation and Alternative Fuels (GFAAF) is the online database for sharing information related to SAF. It contains links to over 600 news articles dating back to 2005, details of past and ongoing initiatives, facts, and figures, answers to frequently asked questions, and links to additional resources. It also includes a live feed of flights using SAF.[56] ICAO continues to maintain this database, which was created as an outcome of the 2009 ICAO Conference on Aviation Alternative Fuels.[57]

The first ICAO Assembly Resolution reference to SAF was registered during its 36th Session (2007). At the time, initial studies on the technical feasibility of these fuels were being conducted, and the Assembly recognized the importance of research and development in fuel efficiency and alternative fuels for aviation that will enable international air transport operations with a lower environmental impact. The Assembly also encouraged the Council to promote improved understanding of the potential use, and the related emissions impacts, of alternative fuels.

---

[55]More info on this theme available at: https://www.icao.int/environmental-protection/pages/SAF.aspx (accessed December 9, 2021).

[56]See: https://www.icao.int/environmental-protection/pages/SAF.aspx (accessed December 9, 2021).

[57]See: https://www.icao.int/Meetings/caaf2009/Pages/CAAF-General-Information.aspx (accessed December 9, 2021).

In 2009, the First ICAO Conference on Aviation and Alternative Fuels (CAAF/1),[58] held in Rio de Janeiro, Brazil in November 2009, endorsed the use of SAF as an important means of reducing aviation emissions and recommended the development of life cycle methodologies and sustainability criteria for these fuels. CAAF/1 also recommended the creation of the ICAO Global Framework for Aviation Alternative Fuels (GFAAF), a global platform where information on worldwide initiatives and actions on SAF are shared.

Since 2009, significant progress has occurred, including six certified conversion processes for SAF production, more than 180,000 flights using a blend of SAF, six airports regularly distributing SAF, reductions in production costs, and evolution on the sustainability aspects of these fuels. To follow up on these developments, the Second ICAO Conference on Aviation and Alternative Fuels[59] (CAAF/2) was held in October 2017 in Mexico City, Mexico. This second Conference endorsed the 2050 ICAO Vision for Sustainable Aviation Fuels,[60] which called on States, industry, and other stakeholders for a significant proportion of SAF use by 2050.[61]

2.2.2 *ICAO work on SAF*

The Assembly requests related to SAF are being pursued by the ICAO Secretariat and the ICAO Committee on Aviation Environmental Protection (CAEP).[62] In 2013, CAEP established the Alternative Fuels Task Force

---

[58] See: https://www.icao.int/Meetings/caaf2009/Documents/CAAF-09_SD003_en.pdf (accessed December 9, 2021).

[59] https://www.icao.int/Meetings/CAAF2/Pages/default.aspx (accessed December 9, 2021).

[60] https://www.icao.int/environmental-protection/GFAAF/Pages/ICAO-Vision.aspx (accessed December 9, 2021).

[61] ICAO Secretariat, Sustainable Aviation Fuels, Chapter Five, in *Destination Green — The Next Chapter*," available at: https://www.icao.int/environmental-protection/Documents/EnvironmentalReports/2019/ENVReport2019_pg171-173.pdf (accessed December 9, 2021).

[62] CAEP is a technical committee of the ICAO Council established in 1983. CAEP assists the Council in formulating new policies and adopting new SARPs related to aircraft noise and emissions, and more generally to aviation environmental impact. CAEP undertakes specific studies, as requested by the Council. Its scope of activities encompasses noise, local air quality (LAQ) and the basket of measures for reducing international aviation CO_2 emissions, including aircraft technology, operational improvement, SAFs, and

(AFTF)[63] to provide technical support to ICAO work on aviation fuels and the environment. Due to the valuable input that AFTF has provided to ICAO's work, in 2019 CAEP agreed to evolve AFTF into a permanent CAEP group, called the Fuels Task Group (FTG). CAEP has been focusing on the development of processes and methodologies for consideration of aviation fuels under CORSIA, including globally accepted sustainability criteria and life-cycle methodologies.

It is worth reporting that many producers are now working on biofuels. Advanced Biofuels Association[64] (ABFA) is an example of joint efforts to produce clean fuels which can be used for aviation also.

2.2.3 *Business Aviation Coalition for Sustainable Aviation Fuel to sustain SAF*

It is noteworthy that the Business Aviation Coalition[65] for Sustainable Aviation Fuel was created by a group of international aviation organizations to encourage the use of SAF by increasing the awareness of its

---

market-based measures (CORSIA). CAEP informs the Council and Assembly's decision-making with the ICAO Global Environmental Trends, which assess the present and future impact of aircraft noise and aircraft engine emissions. The Global Environmental Trends is crucial to the work of ICAO as it provides a robust single reference for sound discussion and decision-making, available at: https://www.icao.int/environmental-protection/Pages/Caep.aspx (accessed December 9, 2021).

[63] The FTG was created at the CAEP/11 meeting (2019), following a CAEP agreement to evolve the AFTF into a permanent CAEP group. FTG focus is on the work required on SAF and lower carbon aviation fuels (LCAF) as part of the Annex 16, Vol. IV maintenance, and as part of other ICAO initiatives on aviation fuels. For more info visit: https://www.icao.int/environmental-protection/Pages/CAEP-FTG.aspx (accessed December 9, 2021).

[64] The ABFA has approximately 30 member companies, representing a wide range of technologies, feedstocks, and molecules within the advanced biofuels industry. "Many of the finished products will be hydrocarbon-based molecules that are fungible and can be used seamlessly in cars, trucks, buses, planes, boats and trains. These advanced fuels are consumer ready and do not require significant changes to our current infrastructure, such as separate pumps, new flex fuel cars, or pipelines. The fuels that our member companies produce are as energy dense as their petroleum-based counterparts," available at: http://advancedbiofuelsassociation.com/section.php?sid=6 (accessed December 9, 2021).

[65] The organizations behind this coalition are the Canadian Business Aviation Association, Commercial Aviation Alternative Fuels Initiative, European Business Aviation Association, General Aviation Manufacturers Association, International Business Aviation Council,

safety and availability and the use of it by OEMs, ground handlers, and owners/operators globally. It also seeks to promote a build-out of infrastructure to increase SAF's manufacture as well as its further development. The coalition released a guide, "Fueling the Future,"[66] which details how industry leaders can introduce SAF into their operations and accelerate its adoption, at the same time reducing greenhouse gas emissions.

2.3 *ICAO stocktaking process: Brief introduction*

As indicated in the document "Sustainable Aviation Fuels: *in response to a decision from CAAF/2, ICAO is periodically reviewing the progress on SAF development and deployment through a stocktaking process, including the organization of regular workshops and seminars. The first ICAO Stocktaking Seminar toward the 2050 Vision for Sustainable Aviation Fuels (SAFS2019) was held in Montreal from April 30 to May 1, 2019. Information gathered at this Seminar shows that commercial production of SAF increased from an average of 0.29 million liters per year (2013–2015) to 6.45 million liters per year (2016–2018). Additionally, up to 6.5 Mt (8 billion liters) per year of SAF production capacity may be available by 2032. The CAAF/2 noted that progress on SAF development and deployment should be periodically reviewed through a stocktaking process, including the organization of regular workshops and seminars. Such a stocktaking process will lead to the convening of CAAF/3 no later than 2025, with a view to updating the 2050 ICAO Vision to include*

National Air Transportation Association, and the National Business Aviation Association or "NBAA."

[66]The new guide, titled, *Fueling the Future,* serves as an educational and informational resource about the practicalities of SAF development, industry adoption, and pending expansion of supply and use, primarily from the perspectives of the business aviation community. Business aviation has been working to increase the use of SAF, which can cut flight emissions by as much as 80%. The industry's efforts are led by the Business Aviation Coalition for Sustainable Aviation Fuel (SAF Coalition), which includes the Commercial Aviation Alternative Fuels Initiative (CAAFI), European Business Aviation Association (EBAA), General Aviation Manufacturers Association (GAMA), International Business Aviation Council (IBAC), National Air Transportation Association (NATA), and the National Business Aviation Association (NBAA). The SAF Coalition's work is supported by a Steering Committee that includes dozens of aviation businesses, representing every point in the SAF development-and-supply chain, available at: https://abag.org.br/wp-content/uploads/2020/08/fueling-the-future.pdf (accessed December 9, 2021).

a quantified proportion of SAF use by 2050, as well as the associated carbon reductions.[67]

SAF are only one part of the strategy adopted in order to reduce emissions, other actions include the use of more advanced technology to reduce the impact on the environment.

2.4 *New standards set*

The CO_2 standard provides an additional requirement into the design process that increases the priority of fuel efficiency in the overall aeroplane design. It is an important step forward to address the growing CO_2 emissions from the aviation sector, and will contribute to the climate change mitigation objectives of the UNFCCC Paris Agreement.[68]

To foster technology development, ICAO regularly sets technology goals, with the purpose of providing stretch yet reasonable targets for industry R&D to aim at, in co-operation with States. These ICAO technology goals are developed by panels of independent experts, which ensure transparency and involvement from all stakeholders. An Independent Expert Review specifically focused on CO_2 emissions was delivered in 2011, as registered in ICAO Doc 9963 — *Report of the Independent Experts on the Medium and Long Term Goal for Aviation Fuel Burn Reduction from Technology.*[69]

The latest set of technology goals for CO_2 emissions is detailed in the *ICAO Doc 10127 — Independent Expert Integrated Technology Goals Assessment and Review for Engines and Aircraft (2019).*[70] This was the first time that ICAO developed technology goals for noise, LAQ, and

---

[67] https://www.icao.int/environmental-protection/Documents/EnvironmentalReports/2019/ENVReport2019_pg171-173.pdf (accessed December 9, 2021).

[68] UNFCCC, 2015, COP 21 Paris Agreement, available at: https://unfccc.int/process-and-meetings/the-paris-agreement/the-paris-agreement (accessed December 9, 2021).

[69] ICAO Doc 9963 — *Report of the Independent Experts on the Medium and Long Term Goal for Aviation Fuel Burn Reduction from Technology, available at:* http://www.icscc.org.cn/upload/file/20190102/Doc.9963-EN%20Report%20of%20the%20Independent%20Experts%20on%20the%20Medium%20and%20Long%20Term%20Goals%20for%20Aviation%20Fuel%20Burn%20Reduction%20from%20Technology.pdf (accessed December 9, 2021).

[70] *ICAO Doc 10127 — Independent Expert Integrated Technology Goals Assessment and Review for Engines and Aircraft, available at:* http://www.icscc.org.cn/upload/file/20200603/20200603140731_33885.pdf (accessed December 9, 2021).

CO_2 emissions in an integrated manner, with full consideration of the interdependencies between the technologies.

2.4.1 *Technology goals and standards*

The ICAO Assembly Resolution A39-1[71] requests the Council, with the assistance and co-operation of other bodies of the Organization and of other international organizations, to continue with vigor the work related to the development of Standards, Recommended Practices and Procedures and/or guidance material dealing with the impact of aviation on the environment.

Annex 16 Volumes I,[72] II[73] and III[74] contain the environmental certi-fication standards that shall be observed by aircraft and engine designs. The development and update of the environmental certifica-tion Standards ensure that the benefits offered by technology are reflected in real reductions of aviation environmental impacts, while balancing environmental benefit with technological feasibility, eco-nomic viability, and the interdependency between environmental factors.

To foster the development of new technologies, ICAO regularly sets technology goals, with the purpose of providing targets for industry research and development, in co-operation with States. Once the State of the Art of technology reaches these goals, consideration is

---

[71] Document available at: https://www.icao.int/environmental-protection/Documents/Resolution_A39_1.PDF (accessed December 9, 2021).

[72] Annex 16 to the Convention on International Civil Aviation — Environmental Protection Volume I — Aircraft Noise, available at: https://store.icao.int/catalogsearch/result/?q=annex+16+environmental+protection+volume+1+aircraft+noise+english+printed (accessed December 9, 2021).

[73] Annex 16 to the Convention on International Civil Aviation — Environmental Protection, Volume II — Aircraft Engine Emissions, available at: https://store.icao.int/en/annex-16-environmental-protection-volume-ii-aircraft-engine-emissions (accessed December 9, 2021).

[74] Annex 16 to the Convention on International Civil Aviation — Environmental Protection, Volume III — Aeroplane CO_2 Emissions, available at: https://store.icao.int/en/annex-16-environmental-protection-volume-iii-aeroplane-co2-emissions (accessed December 9, 2021).

given to updating the ICAO Environmental Standards to ensure the latest technologies are incorporated into aircraft and engine designs.

The latest set of ICAO technology goals was developed by a panel of independent experts, which ensure transparency and involvement from all stakeholders. The results are detailed in the ICAO Doc 10127 — Independent Expert Integrated Technology Goals Assessment and Review for Engines and Aircraft. This was the first time that ICAO developed technology goals for noise, local air quality and CO$_2$ emissions in an integrated manner, with full consideration of the interdependencies between the technologies.

Source: ICAO, available at: https://www.icao.int/environmental-protection/Pages/technology-standards.aspx (accessed December 9, 2021).

2.5 *State Action Plans and assistance*

Since the beginning of ICAO's journey to progress in terms of policy development and standards setting to limit and reduce the impact of aviation on the global climate, ICAO member states demonstrated that they were interested in taking action and advancing initiatives on environmental protection. However, not all of them had the human, technical, and financial resources to do so. To overcome this challenge, ICAO launched the State Action Plan initiative in 2010 as a means to provide States with the capacity and tools to take action.[75]

This initiative enables all ICAO member states to establish a long-term strategy on climate change for the international aviation sector, involving all interested parties at national level. These parties are encouraged to work together to define a quantified baseline scenario, select appropriate emissions mitigation measures from ICAO's basket of measures, and calculate the expected results of implementing those measures.

---

[75] In this sense see ICAO at: https://www.icao.int/environmental-protection/Pages/ClimateChange_ActionPlan.aspx (accessed December 9, 2021).

In order to support its 193 member states with the development of their State Action Plans, ICAO has developed a series of guidance documents and quantification tools.[76]

2.6 The ultimate technology to decarbonize air travel: The use of hydrogen

European aerospace giant Airbus sees hydrogen power as one of the most promising technologies available to decarbonize air travel and is looking to utilize it as part of plans to roll out a zero-emission aircraft by 2035.

Airbus CEO Guillaume Faury affirmed that his company is *"committed to developing sustainable flight and believes hydrogen is one of the most viable solutions."* He also added that "hydrogen is one of the most promising technologies available to help us reach zero-emission flights by 2035." This is in line with the European Commission's hydrogen strategy[77] to reduce harming emissions for the atmosphere.

Hydrogen presents several competitive advantages relative to conventional fuels and SAFs. In particular, hydrogen removes carbon dioxide emission entirely, and it has the potential to reduce other GHG emissions.

"Two main options for hydrogen-fueled aircraft exist. In hydrogen combustion aircraft, thrust is generated through the combustion of hydrogen in a modified jet engine, which eliminates most but not all GHG emissions. Overall, the transition would require less aircraft and engine

---

[76]https://www.icao.int/environmental-protection/Pages/Tools.aspx (accessed December 9, 2021).

[77]On July 8, 2020 the European Commission unveiled plans to promote hydrogen based entirely on renewable electricity like wind and solar, but said low-carbon hydrogen derived from fossil fuels will also be supported in order to scale up production in the short term. Hydrogen is seen as a potential silver bullet to decarbonize hard-to-abate industrial sectors like steel and chemicals, which currently rely on fossil fuels and cannot easily switch to electricity. It is also seen as a long-term solution for shipping, aviation and heavy-duty road transport where electrification is not feasible at the moment. Kadri Simson, the EU's energy commissioner presented the strategy on July 8, 2020. COM (2020), "Communication from the Commission to the European Parliament, The Council, The European Economic and Social Committee and the Committee on the Regions — A Hydrogen Strategy for a Climate-Neutral Europe, 301 final, available at: https://ec.europa.eu/energy/sites/ener/files/hydrogen_strategy.pdf (accessed December 9, 2021).

redesign than hydrogen fuel cell propulsion, making it somewhat less disruptive to the current setup of the aerospace industry. Hydrogen fuel cell (HFC) aircraft could offer a 'true zero' solution for GHG emissions as the only output of fuel cells is water vapor, the impact of which can be minimized through careful aircraft operation. Studies indicate that hydrogen fuel cell aircraft would be 20–40 percent more efficient than hydrogen combustion designs. Furthermore, a fuel cell aircraft would share many attributes with electrically-propelled aircraft, such as electric motors, thereby benefiting from compatibility with the rapidly developing electric powertrain supply chain."[78]

2.6.1 *Challenges to overcome for the use of hydrogen*

Notably the use of these new technologies imply some technical issues which need to be addressed to become a real alternative. For instance in order for hydrogen technology to become a viable solution, the aviation industry needs to find the best solutions regarding critical aspects such as:

- A redesign of much of the aircraft, from the propulsion system to fuel storage.
- Advancements in light-weighting storage tanks and cryogenic cooling systems, in order to take advantage of hydrogen's high energy density.
- A significant ramp-up in "green" hydrogen and/or carbon capture and storage (CCS) to increase the share of emissions-free hydrogen production.
- Hydrogen infrastructure improvements in fuel delivery to airports and airport refueling.
- A reduction in the price of production methods for "green" hydrogen in order to compete with kerosene on a cost basis.

"Comparing hydrogen's advantages and drawbacks against other sustainable aviation technologies, it will likely be the all-important narrowbody/Middle-of-the-Market sector where hydrogen will be a strong candidate for future propulsion. In this category, OEMs

---

[78] In this sense see: Robert Thompson (2020), *Hydrogen: A Future Fuel for Aviation?*, available at: https://www.rolandberger.com/en/Publications/Hydrogen-A-future-fuel-of-aviation.html (accessed December 9, 2021).

(original equipment manufacturers) will have to prove that it is more viable than hybrid-electric solutions, and airlines will have to verify that the cost of adopting this technology is justified amid growing sustainability concerns."[79]

Naturally these technologies, when all technical shortcomings will be solved, will have an enormous impact on air transportation favoring the development of a greener and sustainable aviation industry. More elements are offered in the dedicated chapter on the impact of new technologies on aviation.

3. Impact of COVID-19 on Airports and on Personnel Involved in the Aviation Industry

It is now necessary to briefly discuss about the impact of COVID-19 on airports because they represent an integral part of this industry. Airports are essential to the economic development of the cities, countries, and regions worldwide. They directly contribute to the growth of economies, connecting people and countries, moving passengers, and transporting cargo, providing services to airlines which connect all corners of the world. The movement of goods and people also benefits governments, consumers, and industries. Given the importance of airports to the economic development of cities and entire regions, the broader impact of COVID-19 on the global economy is enormous.

3.1 *ACI world data show dramatic impact of COVID-19 on airports*

Airports Council International (ACI) World data have revealed that global passenger traffic declined by an unprecedented −94.4% year-over-year in April as a result of the unfolding COVID-19 pandemic, representing the worst decline of global passenger numbers in the history of the aviation industry. In particular, global passenger traffic experienced an overall drop of −41.8% in the first 4 months of 2020 with the 12-month rolling average for the global industry continuing to decline — it was recorded

---

[79] *Ibid.*

at −11.3% by the end of April, without signs of consistent recovery in the future months.[80]

In the face of these losses, airports in some regions are now embarking on the first steps to restart operations and make plans for a sustained, long-term recovery. To underpin this recovery, ACI World reflected that financial assistance and relief is needed to safeguard essential operations and protect millions of jobs generated by the airport industry and all sectors in the ecosystem. Airports are key generators of sustainable economic development and the impact in the communities they serve have been catastrophic.

3.1.1 *Loss of more than 4.6 billion passengers*

ACI World now estimates a reduction of more than two billion passengers at the global level in the second quarter of 2020 and more than 4.6 billion passengers for the whole of 2020.[81]

According to ACI forecast the recovery for the industry will be slow and data are impressive: "Global international and domestic markets posted unprecedented declines falling by −98.9% and −90.7%, respectively. The 12-month rolling average for the international segment was recorded at −11.4% and the domestic sector at −11.1%. All major regional markets posted declines above −95% of their global passenger traffic, except for Asia-Pacific, where the domestic segment started to show a fragile sign of recovery. Globally, Asia-Pacific recorded a −87.7% decline compared to last year. International passenger traffic almost came to a halt with all regions recording decline above −98%. Domestic passenger markets were also severely affected by the ongoing crisis. North America, the second largest domestic market in the world, was hit hard with a loss of −95% of its traffic volume. In contrast, the start of a recovery in the Chinese domestic market, as well as in other countries like Australia,

---

[80] In this sense see ACI Media Releases, *ACI World Data Shows Dramatic Impact of COVID-19 on Airports*, available at: https://aci.aero/news/2020/07/03/aci-world-data-shows-dramatic-impact-of-covid-19-on-airports/ (accessed December 9, 2021).

[81] See: *Predicted Global Impact of COVID-19 on Airport Industry Escalates*, available at: https://aci.aero/news/2020/05/05/predicted-global-impact-of-covid-19-on-airport-industry-escalates (accessed December 9, 2021).

helped Asia-Pacific to record the lowest but still very significant decline of −81.0% in April compared to the prior year."[82]

3.2 *How ACI intends to manage the post-COVID aviation landscape*

Notably the EU has suspended until October 24, 2020 the airport slot requirements which oblige airlines to use at least 80% of their take-off and landing slots in order to keep them the following year. The waiver adopted by the Council is designed to help air carriers cope with the drastic drop in air traffic caused by the Coronavirus crisis.

Waiving the "use it or lose it" rule until October is intended to mitigate the heavy economic impact on airlines and to give them certainty over the whole summer season. The waiver which expires on October 24, 2020 it was extended by the EU Commission on 23.07.2021 for the winter 2021/2022 with the slot use rate set at 50%. It will also apply retroactively from January 23 to February 29, 2020 for flights between the EU and China or Hong Kong. The start date of January 23, 2020 is when the first airport was closed by the authorities in China.

Introducing the slot waiver required an amendment to the EU slots regulation.[83] If the current serious situation persists, the measure can be extended quickly by means of a Commission delegated act.

IATA in June 2020 called for an extension of the waiver of the 80-20 use-it-or-lose-it rule for airport slots into the winter season; however, ACI Europe has warned about the potential negative consequences on air connectivity and economic recovery.

"Airlines claim they need the airport slot waiver to be extended into the winter season so as to get additional operational flexibility to plan their schedules in the recovery. But that additional operational

---

[82] In this sense see ACI Media Releases, *ACI World Data Shows Dramatic Impact of COVID-19 on Airports*, available at: https://aci.aero/news/2020/07/03/aci-world-data-shows-dramatic-impact-of-covid-19-on-airports/ (accessed December 9, 2021).

[83] Regulation of the European Parliament and of the Council Amending Council Regulation (EEC) NO95/93 on Common Rules for the Allocation of Slots at Community Airports, Brussels, March 30, 2020, available at: http://data.consilium.europa.eu/doc/document/PE-4-2020-REV-1/en/pdf. this amends Regulation 95/93 on Common Rules for the Allocation of Slots at Community Airport, available at: https://eur-lex.europa.eu/legal-content/GA/TXT/?uri=CELEX:31993R0095 (accessed December 9, 2021).

flexibility comes at a high cost to airports as it allows airlines to declare full schedules, hold on to the requested slots and cancel their flights close to their date of operation — thus leaving airports with the operational costs involved and no revenues to cover them. Crucially, by preventing reallocation to other airlines, the continued late hand-back of unused slots will impact competition and slow down the restoration of air connectivity. This means that extending the waiver for the winter season also risks coming at a high cost to the travelling public and the economy."[84]

According to Olivier Jankovec, Director General of ACI EUROPE, "There is no need to rush with a decision on this just now. The winter season is still more than 4 months away, with considerable uncertainty about the pace and shape of the recovery in demand for air transport. We urge the European Commission to follow a data-driven and evidenced-based approach to assess whether extending the waiver beyond the end of October will be the most appropriate measure to support the restoration of air connectivity. This means it will also need to consider the impact on consumers and communities — as well as the economic viability of the entire air transport eco-system, including airports."[85]

ACI Europe has evidenced that a number of airports are reporting that airlines plan to operate full programmes for the winter season — with their request for slots even exceeding those made last year for the same period. This indicates that airlines' assumptions as regards activity levels are not aligned — indeed are at odds, with their request for an extension of the airport slot waiver. According to ACI analysis, there is a danger here that airlines use the airport slot allocation system and the flexibility afforded by the waiver to ensure airport slots cannot be reallocated and keep competition at bay.[86]

Finally, on this theme it is worth reporting that ACI Europe calls upon the European Commission and EU States to abide by the following principles when considering airport slot waivers, for the benefit of all stakeholders and in order to avoid abuses:

---

[84] See: "Airports Call for Data-Driven Approach to Establishing the Post-COVID Aviation Landscape," available at: https://www.aci-europe.org/media-room/260-airports-call-for-data-driven-approach-to-establishing-the-post-covid-aviation-landscape.html (accessed December 9, 2021).

[85] *Ibid.*

[86] *Ibid.*

(i)   A data-driven and evidence-based approach is imperative.

(ii) If a waiver is deemed relevant when based on data — whether full or partial — strict conditions should be attached to avoid unintended impacts on the competitive landscape and ensure that consumers are protected from last-minute cancellations.

(iii) Slots allocated in response to new requests should not be eligible to qualify for the waiver. This is necessary to avoid the possibility of airlines building up rights for the post-COVID-19 future without necessarily using all newly allocated slots, which would block access to others who may be able to operate sooner.

(iv) Slots must not be covered by waivers when an airline publicly announces that it will cease or importantly reduce its services at an airport. Airlines that are ready and able to operate to support the recovery must not be blocked from entering airports by airlines having confirmed they will exit these markets but continue to hold slots.

This is what is happening and how ACI intends to manage the post-COVID crisis regarding the operation of airports; however, it is necessary to spend a few words about the impact of COVID on personnel and pilots being an integral part of this ecosystem.

3.3 *Impact of COVID-19 on personnel and pilots*

The impact of COVID-19 on the personnel of airlines including cabin crew and pilots has been dramatic. Historically talking, the airline industry has faced many threats, but non quite as rapid and severe as the one posed by the spread of COVID-19. Its consequences are still difficult to figure out and it is necessary to wait till the end of the crisis in order to evaluate all the damages. One of the most evident consequences of this pandemic is the drastic reduction of the number of jobs directly connected with the operation of the aircrafts.

The flying personnel, which represents an essential element for the correct and smooth operation of air transport, is the most vulnerable category and this has emerged clearly during the dramatic phases put in place to save the industry. Pilots and crew are considered expendable when it comes to deciding how to save airlines.

Different association of pilots in Europe and US have expressed their concern and proposed their solutions. For instance in Europe, nearly 1 out of 5 pilots is on a precarious contract. This means they are working through a temporary work agency, as supposedly self-employed, or on a zero-hour contract with no minimum pay guaranteed (no flight = no pay), and no access to the protections and rights that direct employees enjoy.[87] As the President of European Cockpit Association (ECA) Capt. Jon Horne pointed out, "atypical employment in aviation is merely a smokescreen for regular employment with the attached responsibilities ignored. And We have often warned that these broker agency set-ups and bogus self-employment schemes create a pool of 'disposable' workers with diminished rights and no access to labor laws." In fact, staffing agencies dismissed thousands of pilots and cabin crews leaving them without a future.

The President of ECA and its Secretary-General Philip von *Schöppenthau have sent an open letter to the European Commission evidencing the critical situation:*

Specifically, as regards the pilot profession, which is one of the most crucial components for making a swift & sustainable upswing possible after the crisis, ECA calls on the European Commission to:

1. Adopt and communicate the principle that it is a matter of public interest to preserve a functioning aviation public infrastructure:
   - to enable and support rapid repair of the wider economy when we emerge from this damaging crisis; and
   - to preserve and support the continued employment of EU citizens in the high-quality jobs provided by the aviation sector, so that our economy is ready for the eventual upswing, and for the shorter-term economic resilience it will bring.

2. Promote, and where at all possible require, that airline managements follow a socially responsible approach in the measures they take. The Commission's and airlines' priority cannot be commercial interest for the time being, but must be about preservation, survival, and seeing what they can do to contribute to the wider needs of our society.

---

[87] See: European Cockpit Association, *COVID-19: Thousands of Aircrew Redundant – No Rights for Agency & Self-Employed Pilots* — Press Release, available at: https://www. eurocockpit.be/sites/default/files/2020-04/COVID_atypical_employment_PR_20_ 0427_F.pdf (accessed December 9, 2021).

This means:

- Providing support for management and unions to work together to balance companies' needs for survival, and pilots' and workers' future. This must be an obligation, and where airlines do not take this path there should be no support provided.
- Providing support to avoid lay-offs, pay cuts, forced reduced working time, stand down and redundancy to the maximum extent possible. Any concrete or financial support should incentivise this approach.
- Measures should be temporary, and see a return to the status quo after the crisis. Any support should incentivise this approach.

3. Adopt measures that prevent delays and avoids costs in retraining or recertification when activity resumes. However, exemption measures aimed at extending the validity period of ratings, certificates and medicals, must be harmonized, preceded by a thorough risk assessment and accompanied by appropriate mitigating measures. Safety must never be compromised.

4. Develop a European unemployment reinsurance scheme and give the profession access to the European Social Fund.

5. Develop specific economic support measures to facilitate access for laid off aircrew to training simulators for the purpose of retraining to changed industry needs, and to retain their competency and skill base, remaining "current" for the duration of unemployment. That way, pilots will keep their competencies/skills base, and licenses, allowing them to reintegrate to the market when activity resumes.

6. Be aware that the extraordinary character of the situation is already being used as "cover" for opportunistic and "predatory" behaviors from certain airlines. It is inexcusable in the present situation for a company to act without solidarity at the expense of others, for example by cutting the workforce or their terms and conditions further than necessary, or favoring lower quality jobs at the expense of higher quality ones. Action should be taken to block or provide consequences for such behavior.[88]

---

[88] ECA, "Open Letter: Impact of COVID-19 on Pilot's Professions," available at: https://www.eurocockpit.be/sites/default/files/2020-03/European_Cockpit_Association_COVID-19_Commissioners_LT_20_0320F.pdf (accessed December 9, 2021).

This situation touches all airlines globally; thus, every single country shall negotiate with the respective representatives in the sector, and according to the rules of the concerned jurisdiction, find the best solutions to grant the survival of air transport. In fact, airlines are focusing on cash preservation above all; however, human resources, although now a lot of them are layoff, after the crisis there will be again a need for skilled pilots and personnel.

3.4 *European aviation unites in call for support for green recovery from COVID-19*

Europe's aviation sector is committed to contributing to the recovery of European economies in line with the Green Deal objectives,[89] and to the benefit of all. The sector therefore calls on policymakers to include smart measures to support Europe's civil aviation sector during its recovery. This requires ensuring that aviation climate action is eligible for funding under the mechanisms foreseen by the *Next Generation EU*.[90]

A combination of public and private investment is necessary to allow air transport leaders to speed up work to decarbonize the sector — in line with the EU goal of climate neutrality by 2050.

Olivier Jankovec, Director General of ACI EUROPE, said: "Benefiting from these support measures will help our sector regain its economic

---

[89] COM (2019), *The European Green Deal* — Communication from the Commission to the European Parliament, the European Council, the Council, the European Economic and Social Committee and the Committee of the Regions, 640 final, "This Communication sets out a European Green Deal for the European Union (EU) and its citizens. It resets the Commission's commitment to tackling climate and environmental-related challenges that is this generation's defining task. The atmosphere is warming and the climate is changing with each passing year. One million of the eight million species on the planet are at risk of being lost. Forests and oceans are being polluted and destroyed. The European Green Deal is a response to these challenges. It is a new growth strategy that aims to transform the EU into a fair and prosperous society, with a modern, resource-efficient and competitive economy where there are no net emissions of greenhouse gases in 2050 and where economic growth is decoupled from resource use," available at: https://ec.europa.eu/info/sites/info/files/european-green-deal-communication_en.pdf (accessed December 9, 2021).
[90] In this sense see: *Europe's Moment: Repair and Prepare for the Next Generation*, available at: https://ec.europa.eu/commission/presscorner/detail/en/ip_20_940 (accessed December 9, 2021).

viability — a prerequisite for safeguarding both air connectivity and our ability to keep investing in decarboniszation. Airports — along with our partners in the aviation eco-system — have been brought to their knees by this crisis. Our determination to pursue climate action, in line with ACI EUROPE's commitment to Net Zero carbon emissions under airports' control at the latest by 2050, remains as robust as ever — but our ability to invest has been hit hard. Aviation is one of the sectors where decarbon-iszation is particularly challenging, so including it in a joined up green recovery makes sense for all."

Specific proposals for green recovery
1. Boosting the production and uptake of Sustainable Aviation Fuels (SAFs) in Europe through a dedicated and stable set of pol-icy measures and public investment plans. Such measures would notably be welcomed within the "ReFuel EU Aviation-Sustainable Aviation Fuels" initiative and include:

- **Direct capital investment (or ownership) in SAF production facilities,** enabling the necessary de-risking required to debt finance projects as well as the execution of off-take contracts with aircraft operators;
- **Making Europe the centre of excellence for the development and production of SAFs** through the construction and funding of commercial scale SAF projects from globally approved technol-ogy pathways.

2. Implement a green incentive scheme for airlines and aircraft operators to replace older aircraft (fixed wing and helicopters) with more modern and environmentally friendly aircraft. Use public funds dedicated to the recovery to provide such incentives to aircraft operators. On average, new aircraft models are 20–25% more fuel-efficient and produce less noise compared to previous generations. Such an incentive scheme would speed up the green transition towards the EU's shorter term ambition of 2030.

3. Increase public funding and public co-funding rates for Civil Aviation Research & Innovation (Clean Aviation and SESAR):

Use resources from the recovery funds to inject additional capital beyond the amount that will be provided through the MFF and Horizon Europe, in particular. European disruptive technologies and innovative fuels, including hydrogen, can generate deep and long-term emissions reductions towards the EU's Climate Neutrality in 2050.

4. Continued investment in the European Air Traffic Management system (ATM): Enhance the benefits of the Single European Sky and temporarily provide 100% public funding for the deployment of SESAR technologies with proven sustainable and environmental benefits. Such funds should benefit all stakeholders that will need to contribute to the deployment of new technologies, including airports, airspace users and air navigation services providers.

5. Investment in sustainable airport and heliport infrastructure: Ensure funding eligibility of projects related to energy efficiency, renewable energy and electrification (e.g. improving the energy efficiency of terminal buildings, renewable energy generation on-site, supply of electrical ground power to aircraft on stand, electrification of ground vehicle fleets, etc.).

Source: ACI, available at: https://www.aci-europe.org/press-release/261-european-aviation-unites-in-call-for-support-for-green-recovery-from-covid-19.html (accessed December 9, 2021).

3.5 *Impact of COVID-19 on Maintenance Repair and Overhaul (MRO)*

Maintenance, Repair, Overhaul (MRO) in aviation is the repair, service, or inspection of an aircraft or aircraft component. It is essentially all of the maintenance activities that take place to ensure safety and airworthiness of all aircrafts by international standards. This can be identified as "a part" of an industry but naturally end intrinsically connected to the aviation industry also.

The global MRO market was worth US$69 billion in 2018,[91] representing between 10% and 20% of the direct operating cost of an airline.

---

[91] IATA Maintenance Cost Technical Group, 2019.

This volume is slated to significantly reduce in 2020 following the capacity cuts as a response to the COVID-19 crisis; nevertheless, it will keep its place as one of the most significant direct operating cost components, even for grounded aircraft.

COVID-19 pandemic has in fact impacted all major aviation markets across the world, with the number of scheduled flights down by 63% in the fourth week of June 2020 as compared to the same week last year and two-thirds of global passenger fleet still grounded as airlines are waiting for an opportunity to resume operations.

2020 Regional Airline Performance Forecast

REGION	PASSENGER DEMAND (RPKS)	PASSENGER CAPACITY (ASKS)	NET PROFIT
Global	-54.7%	-40.4%	-$84.3B
North America	-52.6%	-35.2%	-$23.1B
Europe	-56.4%	-42.9%	-$21.5B
Asia Pacific	-53.8%	-39.2%	-$29.0B
Middle East	-56.1%	-46.1%	-$4.8B
Latin America	-57.4%	-43.3%	-$4.0B
Africa	-58.5%	-50.4%	-$2.0B

Note: RPKs = revenue passenger kilometers; ASKs = available seat kilometers
Source: IATA

"This crisis in unlike anything else the industry has seen before. The International Air Transport Association (IATA) predicts that airlines will see a US$419 billions decrease in 2020 global passenger revenue compared to 2019, leading to a historic net loss of US$84 billions in 2020 and a ripple effect for the whole aviation industry, including Maintenance, Repair and Overhaul (MRO) providers, lessors, airports, manufacturers, and others."[92]

3.5.1 *Looking ahead: Planning for the future*

The fleet grounding also allows this pause to take a more strategic view of an airline's MRO organization. It could be an opportunity to implement fundamental changes and transformation, which in daily business was

[92]COVID-19: Implications for Maintenance, Repair and Overhaul Industry, ALTON Aviation Consultancy (June 2020), available at: https://altonaviation.com/wp-content/uploads/2020/06/Alton-2020-Covid-19-Implications-for-MROs.pdf (accessed December 9, 2021).

never a priority. With due consideration to the associated expenses, an MRO organization could consider:

- Supplier contracts:
  - o Approach suppliers to **renegotiate existing contracts** which probably include minimum flight hours Approach suppliers to **renegotiate existing contracts** which probably include minimum flight hours or a minimum number of engine shop visits
  - o In case an airline was looking at outsourcing and looking for new/additional supplier contracts, it could consider **issuing an RFP** and make use of lower market prices
  - o A **make vs. buy analysis** under consideration of restructured and potentially smaller fleets in the future could come to different results than in the past
- Opportunity for reorganization:
  - o Review and revise **internal processes** which have caused headaches in the past
  - o **Restructure the organization** to come out more efficiently of the crisis. This includes adapting already now to a gradual ramp-up of operations and possibly to a smaller fleet, lower workforce postcrisis while at the same time keeping the workforce and talents in-house
- New business opportunities (for an airline MRO unit)
  - o Evaluate the potential for additional revenue from entering the **third-party business** to fill in capacity gaps left by the core airline business.[93]

4. Aviation Must Prepare for the New Normal

The impact of COVID-19 on global air transport is without precedent, even worse than by the events of 9/11 and the 2008 global financial crisis put together. With unprecedented consequences, many airlines have grounded all, or almost all, of the planes in their fleet. Several are now

---

[93] In this sense: Axel Schauenburg (2020), *MRO Operations and COVID-19: Leveraging the Enforced Ground Time and Planning for the Future*, Lufthansa Consulting, April 16, 2020, available at: https://www.lhconsulting.com/fileadmin/dam/downloads/studies/20200416_Article_MRO_during_Covid-19.pdf (accessed December 9, 2021).

flying passenger aircraft as freighters. The ICAO, through the Council Aviation Recovery Task Force (CART), in order to offer solutions has resolved to partner with its member states, international and regional organizations, and industry to address this dramatic situation and to provide global guidance for a safe, secure, and sustainable restart and recovery of the aviation sector. Inevitably however, the airline industry will wear the scars caused by COVID-19 for a very long time.

4.1 *ICAO and its "Take Off" guidelines to reconnect the world and help airlines*

The ICAO Council adopted a new Report[94] and guidelines[95] aimed at restarting the international air transport system and aligning its global recovery. The Report and guidelines were produced by CART, and they were developed through broad-based consultations with countries and regional organizations, and with important advice from the World Health Organization and key aviation industry groups including the IATA, ACI World, the Civil Air Navigation Services Organization (CANSO), and the International Coordinating Council of Aerospace Industries Associations (ICCAIA). As Salvatore Sciacchitano President of ICAO Council stressed: "The world looked to the ICAO Council to provide the high-level guidance which governments and industry needed to begin restarting international transport and recovering from COVID-19." Substantially these guidelines will facilitate convergence, mutual recognition, and harmonization of aviation COVID-19 related measures across the globe, and they are intended to support the restart and recovery of global air travel in a safe, secure, and sustainable way. The CART's Report contains a detailed situational analysis and key principles supported by a series of recommendations focused around objectives for public health, aviation safety and security, and aviation economic recovery. This content is supplemented by the report's special "Take Off" document which contains

---

[94] See: CART, Report available at: https://www.icao.int/covid/cart/Documents/CART%20 Report%20Final.pdf (accessed December 9, 2021).
[95] See: ICAO CART, "Take-off: Guidance for Air Travel through the COVID-19 Public Health Crisis," available at: https://www.icao.int/covid/cart/Pages/CART-Take-off.aspx (accessed December 9, 2021).

guidelines for public health risk mitigation measures and four separate modules relating to airports, aircraft, crew, and air cargo.[96]

4.1.1 The role of civil aviation and the 10 key principles for secure and sustainable recovery

The COVID-19 pandemic has imposed an enormous human, social, and financial toll on the world and civil aviation. At the same time, civil aviation has proven its role as a worldwide enabler in overcoming hardship, through vital air cargo services and in support of global supply chains, as well as timely emergency and humanitarian response. Air passenger services had an instrumental role when repatriating hundreds of thousands of people during the early stages of this public health emergency. However, these important contributions cannot hide the fact that severely reduced air services have put a heavy strain on the global economy and on our societies. It is important to recognize aviation's role in economic growth, job creation, and global connectivity. Aviation is a sector that brings the world closer together, promotes its social and cultural richness, and provides critical access to remote regions, isolated islands, and other vulnerable States. Restoring air connectivity will be a key contribution to a successful and rapid recovery of the global economy post-COVID-19.

Ten (10) key principles for a safe, secure, and sustainable recovery

A safe, secure and sustainable restart and recovery of the global aviation sector is best supported by an internationally harmonized approach based on the following principles:

1. *Protect People: Harmonized but Flexible Measures. States and industry need to work together to put in place harmonized or mutually accepted risk-based measures to protect passengers, crew, and other staff throughout the travel experience.*

---

[96] In this sense: ICAO Council Adopts New COVID-19 Aviation Recovery "Take Off" Guidelines to Reconnect the World, available at: https://www.icao.int/Newsroom/Pages/ICAO-Council-adopts-new-COVID.aspx (accessed December 9, 2021).

2. *Work as One Aviation Team and Show Solidarity. The respective plans of ICAO, States, international and regional organizations, and the industry should complement and support each other. While national and regional needs may require different approaches, States should harmonize responses to the extent possible, in line with ICAO's standards, plans and policies.*

3. *Ensure Essential Connectivity. States and industry should maintain essential connectivity and global supply chains, especially to remote regions, isolated islands and other vulnerable States.*

4. *Actively Manage Safety. Security-and Health-related Risks. States and industry should use data-driven systemic approaches to manage the operational safety-, security-, and health-related risks in the restart and recovery phases, and adapt their measures accordingly.*

5. *Make Aviation Public Health Measures Work with Aviation Safety and Security Systems. Health measures must be carefully assessed to avoid negatively impacting aviation safety and/or security.*

6. *Strengthen Public Confidence. States and industry need to work together, harmonizing practical measures and communicating clearly, to ensure passengers are willing to travel again.*

7. *Distinguish Restart from Recovery. Restarting the industry and supporting its recovery are distinct phases which may require different approaches and temporary measures to mitigate evolving risks.*

8. *Support Financial Relief Strategies to Help the Aviation Industry. States and financial institutions, consistent with their mandates, should consider the need to provide direct and/or indirect support in various proportionate and transparent ways. In doing so, they should safeguard fair competition and not distort markets or undermine diversity or access.*

9. *Ensure Sustainability. Aviation is the business of connections, and a driver of economic and social recovery. States and industry should strive to ensure the economic and environmental sustainability of the aviation sector.*

> 10. *Learn Lessons to Improve Resilience. As the world recovers, the lessons learned have to be used to make the aviation system stronger.*

4.1.2 The CART "Take off" guidelines

With help and guidance from the civil aviation stakeholder community, ICAO recommends a phased approach to enable the safe return to high-volume domestic and international air travel for passengers and cargo. The approach introduces a core set of measures to form a baseline aviation health safety protocol to protect air passengers and aviation workers from COVID-19. These measures will enable the growth of global aviation as it recovers from the current pandemic. It is, however, important to recognize that each stage of that recovery will need a recalibration of these measures in support of the common objective which is to safely enable air travel and to incorporate new public health measures into the aviation system, as well as to support economic recovery and growth. The work of ICAO and CART must recognize the need to reduce public health risk while being sensitive to what is operationally feasible for airlines, airports, and other aviation interests. This is essential to facilitate the recovery during each of the forthcoming stages.[97]

The CART Take-off guidance includes a section on Public Health Risk Mitigation Measures, in addition to four operational modules relating to:

– Airport Guidelines;[98]
– Aircraft Guidelines;[99]

---

[97] See: Take-off: Guidance for Air Travel through the COVID-19 public Health Crisis, available at: https://www.icao.int/covid/cart/Documents/CART_Report_Take-Off_Document.pdf (accessed December 9, 2021).

[98] *Airport Guidelines*: The airport module contains specific guidance addressing elements for: Airport terminal building, cleaning, disinfecting, and hygiene, physical distancing, staff protection, access, check-in area, security screening, airside areas, gate installations, passenger transfer, disembarking, baggage claim and arrivals areas. More info at: https://www.icao.int/covid/cart/Pages/Airports-Module.aspx (accessed December 9, 2021).

[99] *Aircraft Guidelines*: The aircraft module contains specific guidance addressing boarding processes, seat assignment processes, baggage, interaction on board, environmental

- Crew Guidelines;[100]
- Cargo Guidelines.[101]

The objective of all these guidelines is to set harmonized and uniform measures aimed at reducing health risks to air travelers, aviation workers, and the general public.

"These measures, applicable to States, airport operators, airlines, and others in the air transport industry, are designed to enable a consistent and predictable travel experience. They will also contribute to the efficient, safe, secure, and sustainable transport by air of an increasing number of passengers and cargo and will minimize the risk of COVID-19 transmission between and among these groups and the general public."[102]

4.2 *IATA guidance complementing ICAO's CART*

IATA supports the ICAO Council's Aviation Recovery Task Force (CART) aimed at providing practical guidance to governments and

---

control systems, food and beverage service, lavatory access, crew protection, management of sick passengers or crew members, and cleaning and disinfection of the flight deck, cabin, and cargo compartment. More info at: https://www.icao.int/covid/cart/Pages/Aircraft-Module.aspx (accessed December 9, 2021).

[100] *Crew Guidelines*: In order to promote safe and sustainable international air travel, a closely coordinated international approach to the treatment of air crews, consistent with recognized public health standards, will be essential to alleviate burdens on critical transportation workers. These currently include screening, quarantine requirements, and immigration restrictions that apply to other travelers. The attached crew module contains specific guidance addressing the contact of a crew member with a suspected or positive COVID-19 case, reporting for duty, dedicated end-to-end crew layover best practices, crew members experiencing COVID-19 symptoms during layover, and positioning of crew. More info at: https://www.icao.int/covid/cart/Pages/Crew-Module.aspx (accessed December 9, 2021).

[101] *Cargo Guidelines*: Cargo flight crews should apply the same health and safety considerations as passenger flight crews and are collectively included in the crew section of this document. While air cargo consignments do not come into contact with the traveling public, the cargo acceptance and hand over process does include interaction with non-airport employees. The Cargo Module addresses aviation public health including physical distancing, personal sanitation, protective barriers point of transfer to the ramp and the loading and unloading, and other mitigation procedures. More info at: https://www.icao.int/covid/cart/Pages/Cargo-Module.aspx (accessed December 9, 2021).

[102] See: https://www.icao.int/covid/cart/Pages/CART-Take-off.aspx (accessed December 9, 2021).

industry operators to restart the international air transport sector and recover from COVID-19 on a coordinated way.

As we have exposed in the previous paragraphs CART's work on its Recovery Report and the accompanying "Take-Off" guidance for international aviation, has kept the health, safety, and security of the traveling public of paramount concern.

IATA's Biosafety for Air Transport: A Roadmap for Restarting Aviation[103] was the basis for IATA's contribution to *Takeoff*. In line with its Declaration for Restarting the Industry[104] and supported by scientific evidence, IATA's Review of the Current Medical Evidence[105] paper aims to facilitate industry restart strategies.

IATA announced a commitment by the airline CEOs on its Board of Governors to five principles for re-connecting the world by air transport. These principles are:

---

[103] IATA's *Biosafety for Air Transport: A Roadmap for Restarting Aviation.* There is currently no single measure that can mitigate all the biosafety risks of restarting air travel. However, we believe that implementing the above-mentioned range of measures that are already possible represents the most effective way of balancing risk mitigation with the need to unlock economies and to enable travel in the immediate term, available at: https://www.iata.org/contentassets/4cb32e19ff544df590f3b70179551013/biosecurity-air-transport.pdf.

[104] See: IATA — *Five principles for restarting aviation.* Global air transport is a vital contributor to the world economy. In 2019, 4.5 billion travelers arrived safely at their destinations by air and air cargo delivered a third of world trade by value. This activity supported 65.5 million jobs. In the fight against COVID-19 the global air transport industry has been all but grounded as governments closed borders and limited the movement of people. Without flying, the world has become poorer. Job losses in the travel and tourism sector are devastating to economies. Countless events for business or pleasure have been missed or postponed, and people have been isolated from all-important contact with family and friends. Aviation will do its part to control the further spread of COVID-19. And we are preparing to restore aviation's social and economic contributions to our world by restarting operations at the earliest possible safe moment to do so, available at: https://www.iata.org/contentassets/59f390a70d644a12bb78a7c76403d4cd/five-principles-declaration.pdf (accessed December 9, 2021).

[105] See: IATA — Restarting aviation following COVID-19, medical evidence for various strategies being discussed as on June 9, 2020 IATA Medical Advisory Group, available at: https://www.iata.org/contentassets/f1163430bba94512a583eb6d6b24aa56/covid-medical-evidence-for-strategies-200609.pdf (accessed December 9, 2021).

1. ***Aviation will always put safety and security first***: Airlines commit to work with our partners in governments, institutions and across the industry to:
   - Implement a science-based biosecurity regime that will keep our passengers and crew safe while enabling efficient operations.
   - Ensure that aviation is not a meaningful source for the spread of communicable diseases, including COVID-19.
2. ***Aviation will respond flexibly as the crisis and science evolve***: Airlines commit to work with our partners in governments, institutions and across the industry to:
   - Utilize new science and technology as it becomes available, for example, reliable, scalable and efficient solutions for COVID-19 testing or immunity passports.
   - Develop a predictable and effective approach to managing any future border closures or mobility restrictions.
   - Ensure that measures are scientifically supported, economically sustainable, operationally viable, continuously reviewed, and removed/replaced when no longer necessary.
3. ***Aviation will be a key driver of the economic recovery***: Airlines commit to work with our partners in governments, institutions and across the industry to:
   - Re-establish capacity that can meet the demands of the economic recovery as quickly as possible.
   - Ensure that affordable air transport will be available in the post-pandemic period.
4. ***Aviation will meet its environment targets***: Airlines commit to work with our partners in governments, institutions and across the industry to:
   - Achieve our long-term goal of cutting net carbon emissions to half of 2005 levels by 2050.
   - Successfully implement the Carbon Offsetting and Reduction Scheme for International Aviation (CORSIA).
5. ***Aviation will operate to global standards which are harmonized and mutually recognized by governments***: Airlines commit to work with our partners in governments, institutions and across the industry to:
   - Establish the global standards necessary for an effective re-start of aviation, particularly drawing on strong partnerships with the International Civil Aviation Organization (ICAO) and the World Health Organization (WHO).

- *Ensure that agreed measures are effectively implemented and mutually recognized by governments.*

In this sense, Alexandre de Juniac, IATA's Director General and CEO said, "*Re-starting air transport is important. Even as the pandemic continues, the foundations for an industry re-start are being laid through close collaboration of the air transport industry with ICAO, the WHO, individual governments and other parties. Much work, however, remains to be done. By committing to these principles, the leaders of the world's airlines will guide the safe, responsible and sustainable re-start of our vital economic sector. Flying is our business. And it is everyone's shared freedom.*"

4.3 Flight plan to succeed in the new normal

As ACI pointed out the role of airports in controlling and mitigating the widespread of COVID-19 plays a fundamental role. The outbreak has in fact increased awareness of how fast a virus can spread through transport networks, and of the role of airports as important gateways and guardians that can help prevent the diffusion into the wider community. Therefore, it is inevitable that airports now not only prioritize safety and security but they also need to turn their attention to biosafety too, and in particular focus on measures which can render the airports even more secure and detect threats to wider community blocking passengers with diseases. Passengers have thus to adapt to a "new normal airport experience," in order to mitigate the risk of COVID-19 contagion and its widespread.

4.3.1 Airports to implement enhanced passenger flow management

In order to manage this critical situation and render as smoothly as possible the movement of passengers, airports and ACI in particular have produced dedicated guidelines.[106] In the absence of a vaccine or "health passports," airports have implemented and enhanced passenger flow management. Just as tower control ensures safe separations between aircraft,

---

[106] See: ACI — *Airport Operational Practice — Examples for Managing COVID-19* (2020), available at: https://store.aci.aero/product/airport-operational-practice-examples-for-managing-covid-19/ (accessed December 9, 2021).

airports are now promoting "safe separations" between passengers to maintain social distancing at least where feasible, and have issued a series of advices, like for instance:

- *Regulating access to various areas, based also on active monitoring of present and expected passenger density, to minimize the potential for congestion;*
- *Have stations for people wanting to seek medical assistance related to the presence of the virus — to minimize the risk of having such passenger wandering in the airport in search of help;*
- *Implementing queue management measures. Despite best efforts put into flow management and queue reduction technologies (e.g. mandatory digital check-in, biometric id), queues will still occur in areas naturally prone to congestion, such as check-in, security check, boarding and passport control. Hence attention needs to be paid to these areas. Such measures include for instance, modified layouts or specific floor signage indicating passenger position.*[107]

4.3.2 *Increased presence of automation and robots at airports*

Airports can rely on increased automation as a means of reducing contact between staff and passengers. Automated information kiosks are already a reality in many airports, and it is likely that these will be enhanced with more Artificial Intelligence and decision-making software.

The crisis could accelerate the trend toward increased airport robotization, a trend that was already expected to peak by 2030 before the COVID-19 outbreak. Besides the intrinsic potential for cost-saving arising from increased automation, these solutions bring the added benefit of protecting both staff and passengers by reducing the need for close interaction between these social groups.[108]

---

[107] In this sense: Planning the "new normal" passenger experience: Defining effective protective measures against COVID-19, available at: https://blog.aci.aero/planning-the-new-normal-passenger-experience-defining-effective-protective-measures-against-covid-19-at-airports/ (accessed December 9, 2021).

[108] *Ibid.*

4.3.3 *Improved hygiene management*

Starting from hand hygiene whether passengers frequently wash hands, this can contribute in limiting the spread of the virus. Relevant organizations such as the World Health Organisation as well as Centers for Disease Control and Prevention (CDC) consider it as the most efficient and cost-efficient way to limit the spread of diseases. Also, hand hygiene looks intuitively easy and common sense to implement.

Dirty hands are a known travel hazard. A recent study[109] shows that on average only 20% of passengers have clean hands at airports. At the same time, a 10% increase in the level of hand cleanliness at all airports worldwide can produce a 24% reduction in the spread of a disease, while a 40% increase would lead to a 69% reduction. This further underlines the role of airports as guardians against a pandemic, as well as the importance of promoting hand hygiene, and maintaining those measures after the current concerns over COVID-19 have abated.

For instance, a recent study investigating the accumulation of viruses on airport surfaces found that plastic security trays used at security check carry more pathogens than toilet surfaces.

While this may be the case because people are more careful to limit touch in the latter environment, the key concern is that trays are picked up by many passengers during the day and provide a perfect transmission route. It suffices for one person to contaminate one tray, which in turn is picked up by several passengers, eventually taking the virus with them.

Immediate manual measures to breaking this transmission route call for more frequent cleaning of trays, increased hand hygiene at security screening, as well as changes in security instruction procedures — i.e. passengers may be asked to store personal items such as keys, belts, coins inside their luggage rather than throwing them into the tray. Self-cleaning solutions for security trays include the use of nanotechnology, and of UV-light.[110]

---

[109] https://news.mit.edu/2020/slow-epidemic-airport-handwashing-0206   (accessed December 9, 2021).

[110] In this sense: Planning the "new normal" passenger experience: Defining effective protective measures against COVID-19, available at: https://blog.aci.aero/planning-the-new-normal-passenger-experience-defining-effective-protective-measures-against-covid-19-at-airports/ (accessed December 9, 2021).

4.3.4 *Airport Indoor Air Quality (IAQ)*

Although often neglected, IAQ is an important component of passenger experience (and employee performance). Air filled with unpleasant odors and unhealthy contaminants can provide immediate discomfort to most passengers, while making passengers with a weakened immune system like the elderly, or tired travelers, more susceptible to illness — and certainly becoming ill after visiting an airport does not translate into a positive passenger experience.

While, this was already the case in the pre-COVID world, it is expected that the demand for enhanced airport IAQ will increase following the pandemic outbreak and the associated concern for the spread of the virus in indoor environments. Based on local bio-risk analysis, airports might want to consider taking measures to decrease potential airborne contamination and diffusion levels, especially in high passenger concentration areas.[111]

The measures exposed earlier if implemented correctly can reduce the spread of the virus and other infectious diseases. Airports have the opportunity to become a role model for others in the fight against COVID-19 and any future viral threats. However, they will need the support from regulators and other aviation stakeholders to achieve this. In working for achieving a more safe environment airports will need to use many of the tools at their disposal, and implement new technologies to change their procedures to achieve the right mix for the health of both the business and the passengers.

4.4 *Cargo services survived to the COVID-19*

Cargo service also was put under stress by the pandemic, but it responded better to the crisis. Many aircrafts have been converted into cargo for goods, this has allowed their use and to generate some incomes for stressed airlines. However, the impact of the COVID-19 outbreak was severe across all major freight markets except for North America, thanks to a robust domestic freight market. Globally, air freight volumes were reduced by almost a quarter in April 2020, with a drop of −22.6% compared to April 2019.

---

[111] *Ibid.*

According to the latest air cargo figures from IATA data show recent demand has outperformed pre-Covid levels and volumes are now at levels seen prior to the US–China trade frictions.

The association said it compared figures from February 2021 with those in the same period of 2019 because "comparisons between 2021 and 2020 monthly results are distorted by the extraordinary impact of Covid-19."

> In light of this, global airfreight demand in February 2021, measured in cargo tonne km (CTKs), was up 9% on February 2019 and was 1.5% higher than January 2021. Meanwhile, global capacity, measured in available cargo tonne km (ACTKs), declined by 14.9% compared with February 2019. Willie Walsh, IATA's director general, said: "Air cargo demand is not just recovering from the Covid-19 crisis, it is growing. With demand at 9% above pre-crisis levels (February 2019), one of the main challenges for air cargo is finding sufficient capacity. "This makes cargo yields a bright spot in an otherwise bleak industry situation. It also highlights the need for clarity on government plans for a safe industry restart. Understanding how passenger demand could recover will indicate how much belly capacity will be available for air cargo. Being able to efficiently plan that into air cargo operations will be a key element for overall recovery." Looking at regional performance in February 2021, North America and Africa were the strongest performers in terms of growth in airfreight demand. All regions except Latin America reported an improvement on pre-Covid levels. Volumes carried by North America-based airlines were up 17.1% on February 2019. Capacity was up 1.9%. "The region's swift recovery has been supported by improving economic activity and the rising popularity of online shopping amidst lockdown restrictions," IATA said.[112]

4.5 *COVID-19 has favored business aviation: Introduction*

COVID-19 has not only heavily hit aviation industry, especially the commercial aviation industry, but also has provoked an unexpected collateral

---

[112]Rachelle Harry, "IATA: Airfreight Demand Back to Pre-Covid Levels but Capacity Remains Tight," April 8, 2021, available at: https://www.aircargonews.net/data/iata-airfreight-demand-back-to-pre-covid-levels-but-capacity-remains-tight/ (accessed December 9, 2021).

effect: private aviation and business aviation markets did not experience such a severe downfall. On the contrary, according to data available this market rather witnessed a surge in demand of private flights. In fact many well-off travelers who hoped to minimize their public exposure and find alternatives to suspended flights, opted to fly privately. This led to the spike in urgent demands pouring in with the private jet operators.

The current situation in the world, regarding COVID-19, has thus seen private aviation companies report an increase of 400% in queries and bookings.[113] The massive explosion in the aforementioned sector is to be attributed to the travel restrictions and social distancing recommended by health authorities which affected commercial flights.

Private flights offer reduced social contact possibility and a great flexibility. In substance, flying in a private mode can be marketed as a safer alternative. With an influx in more passengers choosing to fly privately, additional new customers will be attracted to this segment of the market which consequently will be more affordable at least for travelers already choosing to fly business or first class.

While the commercial sector will continue to adjust and adapt as needed to accommodate evolving passenger needs and expectations, private aviation likely will accommodate a broader clientele range retaining the newly acquired clientele. Business aviation companies already reported a massive number of new clients who have never flown private before. Therefore, by becoming more attractive and "more popular," business aviation is set to continue its growth and support post-crisis recovery of the sector. A more detailed analysis of this sector is offered in Chapter 4.

---

[113] See: Significant Growth in Business Aviation Amid COVID-19 Outbreak, available at: https://connectedaviationtoday.com/business-aviation-begins-bouncing-back-increased-charter-travel-during-covid-19/#.Xxa9EefOPIV (accessed December 9, 2021).

Chapter 3

The Impact of New Technologies on the Evolution of a Greener Aviation Industry and the Emerging of a New Urban Air Mobility (UAM)

Paolo Rizzi and Cristiano Rizzi

COVID-19 severely hit aviation industry and air transport with a reduction of more than 90% of passengers during the peak of the pandemic. In order to return to a normal situation and even favor the development of a greener aviation industry "innovation" is the only path. In fact as the International Civil Aviation Organization (ICAO) has stressed, innovation is essential for the achievement of the ICAO's environmental goals defined in the Assembly resolution A39-1,[1] and to support the aviation's contributions to the United Nations Sustainable Development Goals (SDGs). ICAO is closely following Research and Development initiatives that may support these objectives. New innovative technologies and energy sources for aviation are under development at a fast pace, and a significant amount of work by ICAO will be required to keep pace with

---

[1]ICAO, Resolution A39-1, Consolidated Statement of Continuing ICAO Policies and Practices Related to Environmental Protection — General Provisions, Noise and Local Air Quality, available at: https://www.icao.int/environmental-protection/Documents/Resolution_A39_1.PDF (accessed December 9, 2021).

the timely environmental certification of such new technologies, as appropriate.

1. ICAO Sustains Innovation in Line with EU Strategy

Innovation in the aviation industry plays an important role in order to render it more eco-friendly and sustainable. ICAO is working on various fronts to develop a greener aviation and it is constantly monitoring new technologies for conventional types of aircraft, including innovative fuels such as Sustainable Aviation Fuels (SAF) and Lower Carbon Aviation Fuels, in terms of their potential environmental benefits, technical feasibility, and economic reasonableness. ICAO is also monitoring the evolution of new propulsion concepts such as electric, hybrid, and hydrogen by means of the Electric and Hybrid Aircraft Platform for Innovation (E-HAPI).[2]

For instance, in Europe the EU has adopted a strategy aimed to improve the environmental impact of aviation. This strategy includes a series of measures such as:

1) R&D for "greener" technology,

2) modernized air traffic management systems,

3) market-based measures.

    1. High priority was given to "the greening of air transport" in the 7th Framework Programme for RTD. The flagship will be the "Clean Sky" Joint Technology Initiative. By 2020, the aim is to reduce fuel consumption and hence CO_2 emissions by 50% per passenger kilometer, to reduce NOx emissions by 80% (in landing and take-off according to ICAO standards) and to reduce unburnt hydrocarbons and CO emissions by 50%, alongside pursuing significant noise reductions. The 7th Framework Programme has been substituted by Horizon 2020, a 6-year plan (2014–2020), for which the motto is "Smart, Green and Integrated Transport." In the line of the former programme, it will encourage resource-efficient transport

---

[2]E-HAPI (Electric and Hybrid Aircraft Platform for Innovation).

that respects the environment by making aircraft cleaner and quieter to minimize transport systems' impact on climate and the environment, by developing smart equipment, infrastructures and services.

2. The Single European Sky (SES) legislation reforms the way air traffic management is organized in Europe. This requires a modernization of air traffic management (ATM) systems in Europe. The SESAR initiative is the technological component of SES and one of the objectives is to reduce emissions by 10% per flight.

3. Aviation is included in the EU Emissions Trading System (ETS) by Directive 2008/101/EC, in line with the International Civil Aviation Organization's (ICAO) resolution A35-5 (accessed May 9, 2021) on incorporating international aviation into existing trading schemes. However, for the period 2013–2016, the legislation has been amended so that only emissions from flights within the EEA fall under the EU Emissions Trading System (ETS).[3]

Revision of the EU ETS: On July 3, 2020, the European Commission published the Roadmap for the legislative initiative aimed at amending the EU ETS regarding aviation. This initiative, planned for the second quarter of 2021, will serve to implement the Carbon Offsetting and Reduction Scheme for International Aviation (CORSIA) by the EU in a way that is consistent with the EU's 2030 climate objectives.[4] The initiative will also propose to increase the number of allowances being auctioned under the system as far as aircraft operators are concerned. This proposal will be part of the broader European Green Deal.[5]

---

[3] See: "The EU Aviation Strategy Aims to Improve the Environmental Impact of Aviation," available at: https://ec.europa.eu/transport/modes/air/environment_en (accessed December 9, 2021).

[4] The 2030 climate and energy framework includes EU-wide targets and policy objectives for the period from 2021 to 2030. Key targets for 2030: (i) At least 40% cuts in GHG emissions (from 1990 levels); (ii) At least 32% share for renewable energy; (iii) At least 32.5% improvement in energy efficiency, available at: https://ec.europa.eu/clima/policies/strategies/2030_en (accessed December 9, 2021).

[5] COM (2019), "The European Green Deal — Communication from the Commission to the European Parliament, the European Council, the Council, the European Economic And Social Committee and the Committee of the Regions, 640 final," available at: https://ec.europa.eu/info/sites/info/files/european-green-deal-communication_en.pdf (accessed December 9, 2021).

1.1 *Innovative fuels*

As we have already evidenced in the previous chapter, the aviation industry is investing in innovative fuel concepts that may provide environmental benefits. While some of them are already being produced and used regularly in aircraft operations, (e.g. SAF), others are still under research and development, such as Lower Carbon Aviation Fuels and Hydrogen.

1.1.1 *Sustainable aviation fuels*

Annex 16 Volume IV defines a "CORSIA sustainable aviation fuel" as a "renewable or waste-derived aviation fuel that meets the CORSIA Sustainability Criteria under this Volume."[6] SAF are a reality, as can be seen by the various conversion processes and feedstocks available to produce SAF, and the large number (over 200,000 flights) of commercial flights that have been flown with SAF. Indeed SAF may see 1 billion gallon output by 2025. In fact, speaking during the virtual NBAA Go Flight Operations Conference in late February (2021), Commercial Aviation Alternative Fuels Initiative (CAAFI) Executive Director Steve Csonka outlined the building block approach that the industry has taken to get to the point where the industry can now use a 50/50 jet-A and SAF blend as a true drop-in solution. In the 50/50 blend, SAF has proven to meet the necessary fuel specifications and has demonstrated that it reduces life-cycle greenhouse gas (GHG) emissions by at least 50% and on average anywhere between 60% and 80% or more. Csonka added that, "we can make those reductions greater'" later this year, noting that some producers using feedstock such as tallow and cooking oil are on track to produce SAF by year-end that reaches almost 100% reduction of GHG emissions. It is noteworthy that currently there are three major producers that combined for nearly 60 million gallons in 2020, with Neste accounting for 35 million gallons of that total; however, the total output is expected to grow more than 1000% next year, reaching 746 million gallons, and ultimately one billion gallons by 2025 with more producers joining the few companies already involved in the production of SAF. (In this sense

---

[6]See: Annex 16 to the Convention on International Civil Aviation, Environmental Protection, Volume IV, Carbon Offsetting and Reduction Scheme for International Aviation (CORSIA), First edition, October 2018, available at: https://www.icao.int/environmental-protection/CORSIA/Pages/SARPs-Annex-16-Volume-IV.aspx (accessed December 9, 2021).

K. Lynch: AIN Publications, Vol. 50, No. 4.) Major players operating in the renewable jet fuel market include Neste (Finland), Gevo (US), World Energy (US), Eni (Italy), SkyNRG (Netherlands), Fulcrum BioEnergy (US), Velocys (UK), and Aemetis, Inc.

1.1.2 *Lower carbon aviation fuels*

Annex 16 Volume IV also brings the concept of "CORSIA lower carbon aviation fuel," defined as "a fossil-based aviation fuel that meets the CORSIA Sustainability Criteria under this Volume."[7] Research is ongoing on possible technologies that may allow the production of fossil fuels with a smaller carbon footprint, such as Carbon Capture, Utilization and Storage (CCUS) and the use of renewable energy in oil refineries. More detailed information on the Lower carbon aviation fuels (LCAF) technologies were provided during the ICAO Stocktaking Seminar 2019.[8] ICAO is closely following the evolution of such technologies and investigating the development of proper methodologies to assess their potential environmental benefits.

1.1.3 *Hydrogen*

Looking to the future, it should be noted that both definitions of "CORSIA sustainable aviation fuels" and "CORSIA lower carbon fuels" are not restricted to liquid fuels such as jet-A1. In this regard, research is ongoing to evaluate hydrogen as a possible aviation fuel in the future. To date, several factors still hinder a possible use of hydrogen in commercial flights, such as on-board storage, safety concerns, the high cost of producing the fuel and the need for dedicated infrastructure at airports. Research projects are ongoing to demonstrate the feasibility of hydrogen propulsion and to overcome these challenges, in support of longer-term environmental objectives for civil aviation. In any case, while much of the discussions about how to reduce aviation's carbon footprint have focused on the availability of SAF and when and how electric aircraft may be unshackled from the limits of battery technology, hydrogen has been moving up the

---

[7] *Ibid.*

[8] See: "Aviation Climate Policy and Lower Carbon Aviation Fuel," available at: https://www.icao.int/Meetings/SAFStocktaking/Documents/ICAO%20SAF%20Stocktaking%202019%20-%20AI2-7%20Hassan%20ElHoujeiri.pdf (accessed December 9, 2021).

future propulsion agenda. A major player in aviation industry, that is, Airbus in September 2020 announced that it is actively pursuing hydrogen-powered airliners into commercial service around 2035. The broad consensus seemed to be that all-electric or hybrid-electric propulsion should be the primary focus for smaller aircraft, but that for anything with more than 20 or more seats the green priority should be making existing turbofans, turboprops, and piston engines less gas-guzzling and thus pressing for the widespread use and availability of SAF.

1.2 *ICAO is monitoring innovation in aviation*

ICAO besides sustaining innovative fuels is also fostering researches aimed at introducing a new generation of aircraft powered with electrical and hybrid engines. As a matter of fact, a consistent increase has been noted in the electrification of aircraft systems, research on electrical propulsion, and investments in electric or hybrid aircraft designs. Investments by the big players have increased constantly and the impact of COVID-19 has only pushed forward toward these innovations.

In line with the target to reach zero emissions for aviation in 2050 the major manufacturers are developing new projects for "sustainable aviation." It is worth mentioning that other players are even developing new concepts of *air mobility* based on smaller electric-powered aircraft (also called "electric urban air-taxis"). These projects are destined to revolutionize air travel as we know it today. In the following paragraphs, we are exposing some of these fascinating projects which are already becoming a reality. Currently there are no specific ICAO environmental standards in Annex 16 to cover such aircraft types. ICAO is monitoring the developments around these new aircraft, and in order for these new vehicles to enter into operation specific SARPs will be needed.

As electrification will play a major role in aviation, in the following section we have briefly introduced the impact of this novelty on the different segments of the aviation market.

1.2.1 *Electrification of large commercial aircraft*

The large commercial aircraft (LCA) category includes initiatives focused on hybrid-electric, single-aisle aircraft with seat capacities of 100–135 and targeted entry into service after 2030.

The well-documented barriers to entry in the LCA segment mean that most of the development activity in electrically-propelled LCAs has focused on the incumbents, Airbus and Boeing. Both these manufacturers are committed to decarbonizing aviation and have introduced their own projects:

Airbus in 2017 launched the E-Fan X demonstrator with the ambition to test the technologies that would help decarbonize our skies. In the test aircraft, one of the four jet engines was slated to be replaced by a 2 MW electric motor. In less than 3 years, E-Fan X successfully achieved its three main initial goals: (i) Launching and testing the possibilities — and limitations — of a serial hybrid-electric propulsion system in a demonstrator aircraft; (ii) Gaining invaluable insights to develop a more focused roadmap on how to progress on the ambitious decarbonization commitments; (iii) Laying a foundation for the future industry-wide adoption and regulatory acceptance of alternative-propulsion commercial aircraft.[9] Airbus and Rolls-Royce made the joint decision to bring the E-Fan X demonstrator to an end in April 2020. This experiment has brought many indications to further develop this new propulsion. What has emerged is that "hybrid architectures, high-voltage systems and batteries are indispensable technology bricks for several other demonstrator projects across our wider R&T portfolio to diversify power sources. We will continue to develop and mature them at our E-Aircraft System Test House." This demonstrator also allowed "exploring the possibilities — and limitations of — serial hybrid-electric propulsion also opened up inquiry into new technology pathways. Hydrogen being one of them, which is equal parts a huge opportunity as it is a new challenge."[10]

Boeing has also released a roadmap to an electrically propelled aircraft by around 2030, building on the achievements of the More Electric 787[11] and demonstrating the way in which the More Electric Aircraft

---

[9]E-Fan X, available at: https://www.airbus.com/innovation/zero-emission/electric-flight/e-fan-x.html (accessed December 9, 2021).

[10]In this sense: Grazia Vittadini, "Our Decarbonisation Journey Continues: Looking Beyond E Fan-X," available at: https://www.airbus.com/en/newsroom/stories/2020-04-our-decarbonisation-journey-continues-looking-beyond-e-fan-x (accessed December 9, 2021).

[11]See: "Electrification and E-Flight Part 4 Boeing is on the Way to a (More) Electric Future," available at: https://www.aviationpros.com/gse/gse-technology/green-alternative-energy-gse/article/12414609/electrification-and-eflight-part-4-boeing-is-on-the-way-to-a-more-electric-future (accessed December 9, 2021).

technology is complementary to, and paves the way toward, electrical propulsion.

1.2.2 *Regional/business aircraft*

The aircraft under the regional/business aircraft category claims longer flight range close to 1,000 km with increased seat capacity (around 10).

"In the next size category up are Regional and Business Aircraft with a range between 500–1,000 km that are targeting both commercial inter-city transport and business/general aviation use by corporations and high net worth individuals. Developments in this segment are evaluating both hybrid- and all-electrical propulsion and have a business case related not only to the replacement of current non-electric aircraft, but also to competing with road- or rail-based transportation, drawing on the benefits of electrical propulsion in terms of reduced noise and zero emissions."[12]

1.2.3 *General aviation (GA) and recreational aircraft*

The general aviation/recreational aircraft group consists of aircraft with MTOW from 300 to 1,000 kg. These are mostly electric-powered aircraft with a seat capacity of two. This category includes aircraft which are already produced and certified.

"The segment of General Aviation/Recreational Aircraft has been a hotbed of development activity. The up take in this segment has been enabled by existing aircraft architectures already using propellers for propulsion, either allowing a simple substitution of the power plant or allowing designers of new platforms to draw on a wealth of relevant past experience. GA incumbents have released retrofitted versions of existing aircraft, such as the electric Cessna 172 and Pipistrel's Taurus Electro or WATTsUP electric trainer. Small independents and start-ups have also entered the field through this segment, such as DigiSky with the SkySpark demonstrator."[13]

---

[12]See Roland Berger (2017), "Aircraft Electrical Propulsion — The Next Chapter of Aviation," available at: https://www.rolandberger.com/en/Publications/New-developments-in-aircraft-electrical-propulsion.html (accessed December 9, 2021).
[13]*Ibid.*

1.2.4 *Vertical take-off and landing (VTOL) aircraft*

Significant progress has also been made on the VTOL category over recent years, with seat capacities from 1 to 5, maximum take-off weights (MTOWs) between 450 and 2,200 kg and projected flight ranges from 16 to 300 km. These aircraft projects are expected to become a reality and to entry into service in the period of 2025–2030.

It must be noted that industry giants such as Airbus and Boeing are both developing their own VTOL models followed by a myriad of other smaller manufacturers considering the promising future of Urban Air Mobility (UAM). Airbus has taken a holistic approach with an UAM portfolio initiating projects within existing divisions (e.g. Airbus Helicopter and the CityAirbus, a four-seater all-electric multi-rotor VTOL aircraft for urban environments). UAM is expected to become the next segment in aviation and in order to grasp the many opportunities, dedicated authorities also need to do their part in developing new rules for the safe use of these new aircraft in urban areas as explained in the last section of this chapter.

1.3 *Evolution in UAM: Brief introduction*

Evolution in electrification of aircraft will change air mobility, in particular "Urban Air Mobility" (UAM) with the introduction of VTOL aircraft which will be used principally as air taxis. This advancement will be possible thanks to the development in electrical propulsion. In particular, this development is occurring in the traditional centers of aerospace technology, that is to say Europe and North America basically. Clearly, electrical propulsion will have an impact on entire aviation industry, but it is likely UAM is the sector to be mostly revolutionized. As a matter of fact, this technology will also be implemented for larger aircraft, but it will take time, while developing new modes of commuting with smaller aircraft is already becoming a reality (reference must be made to the last part of this chapter).

Despite most current known electrical propulsion developments are found in Europe and the US, China could play a leading role in an electrically propelled future, as it will be exposed in the section dedicated to China.

2. Hydrogen as an Evolution of SAF

Decarbonization is a major challenge for aviation. Reduction of emissions remain the main objective and today many promising technologies are putting in place and developed by major players to reach a zero impact on the climate change. Among the many sustainable aviation technologies being considered, starting from SAF to electric propulsion, hydrogen has emerged as a potential aviation fuel of the future, with fuel cells and combustion options offering differing benefits as it will briefly explained in this section.

Hydrogen propulsion therefore has the potential to be a major part of the future propulsion technology mix that aviation industry is going to adopt for a greener aviation. Being a disruptive innovation, hydrogen propulsion requires significant research and development, as well as investments, in order to be fully deployed. Naturally, this innovation must be accompanied by new regulations to ensure safe, economic H2 aircraft, and renewed infrastructures which will respond to the new advanced needs of the next generation aircraft.

2.1 *What benefits can hydrogen offer?*

Hydrogen offers several benefits over SAFs and batteries as a power storage technology. As reported by a research[14] using hydrogen reduces GHG emissions. In the case of fuel cell propulsion — an almost "true zero" hydrogen solution — the gaseous emissions are limited to water vapor, a by-product of the energy production process. Although water vapor is a GHG, its harmful effects can be minimized through careful operation. In the case of propulsion via hydrogen combustion — a "zero carbon" solution — NO_X is produced alongside water vapor. Both have radiative forcing effects, but the solution still avoids harmful carbon emissions.

Second, especially relative to SAFs, hydrogen is likely to penetrate into other industries, too, which could speed up the development of fuel cells and storage systems, promote downstream infrastructure and push down production costs. This would benefit the aviation industry, as the R&D and infrastructure development costs would be partially borne by other industries.

Third, relative to batteries, hydrogen has a gravimetric energy density three times that of kerosene (33 kWh/kg). Hydrogen remains superior to conventional fuel in terms of power density by unit weight. This is highly relevant for flight, a weight-critical application, as it offers an MTOW advantage over all other energy storage alternatives. The main drawback

---

[14]See: Roland Berger, "Hydrogen — A Future Fuel for Aviation?" *Focus*, available at: https://www.rolandberger.com/en/Publications/Hydrogen-A-future-fuel-of-aviation.html (accessed December 9, 2021).

of hydrogen is that, due to its low volumetric density, it requires four to five times the volume of conventional fuel to carry the same onboard energy. Nevertheless, hydrogen still offers advantages over battery storage in energy density, both in gravimetric (batteries currently offer 0.3 kWh/kg) and volumetric measures.

Fourth, refueling aircraft with hydrogen is likely to be quicker than recharging batteries, enabling faster turnaround times. Similarities in the refueling process between hydrogen and kerosene could ease the transition between new and old processes: hydrogen would only require different piping and potentially different temperatures of fluid. By contrast, recharging batteries entails a completely different process, requiring ultra-fast charging or rapid battery replacement options and localized energy distribution infrastructure.

Naturally, all these benefits have to be proven on the field as soon as these technologies will be effectively adopted by the industry. It is to be seen which of the two options is going to be more widely used; in fact, as exposed in the next section fuels cells and hydrogen combustions both offer different advantages and challenges.

2.1.1 *Two options for hydrogen: Fuels cells or combustion?*

When it comes to hydrogen there are two options: (i) hydrogen combustion aircraft and (ii) hydrogen fuel cell (HFC) aircraft. These represent two different propulsion systems.

In the hydrogen combustion aircraft thrust is generated through the combustion of hydrogen in a modified jet engine. This process eliminates the CO_2, CO, SO_X and the majority of soot emissions generated by conventional jet engines. NO_X and water vapor are still emitted, representing some contribution to atmospheric GHG levels.

> Conversion to hydrogen combustion would require changes to the engine, fuel storage and fuel delivery elements of conventional aircraft. Whilst this would necessitate new designs and a lengthy certification process, the transition would require much less redesign than hydrogen fuel cell or other electric aircraft options. As the result, a move to hydrogen combustion could be less disruptive to the current setup of the aerospace industry relative to alternatives.[15]

---

[15] *Ibid.*

HFC aircraft could potentially offer a "true zero" solution for GHG emissions. The only output of fuel cells is water, which eliminates CO_2, NO_X, SO_X, CO, HC, and soot emissions. However, the water produced — around nine kilograms for every one kilogram of hydrogen reacted — would have to be released, and water vapor is also a GHG with the potential to cause contrails and Aviation Induced Cloudiness (AIC). This is critical as hydrogen fuel cell aircraft can only be considered "true zero" solutions if they eliminate contrail/AIC emissions. Unlike hydrogen combustion aircraft, HFC aircraft could be designed to store some of the water produced and release it in conditions conducive to low contrail/AIC formation (though this is not yet fully understood).

> Experts also believe that hydrogen fuel cell aircraft would be more efficient than hydrogen combustion designs, needing to carry 20–40 percent less fuel, driven by two factors. First, fuel cell propulsion can provide more efficient energy conversion — around 45–50 percent due to the combination of fuel cell efficiency (55 percent) and electric powertrain efficiency (90 percent) — versus around 40 percent for hydrogen combustion efficiency. Second, by virtue of being electric, fuel cell aircraft can benefit from distributed propulsion, which could deliver an extra 20–30 percent in fuel savings, considering improvements like boundary layer ingestion and flow control technologies.[16]

2.1.2 *The future is not so far away: The world's first four-seater hydrogen fuel cell aircraft was presented in December 2020*

Advancements toward a greener aviation seem to proceed steadily. In December 2020, the world's first four-seater hydrogen fuel cell aircraft named "HY4" was presented to the public at Stuttgart airport in Germany. "The alternative drive from a battery fuel cell system was developed in the lead by Professor Josef Kallo, who conducts research at Ulm University and at the German Aerospace Center (DLR) in Stuttgart. Only recently, the latest generation of HY4 drives received a test flight permit and can therefore take off at Stuttgart airport."[17] According to the news release the HY4 is powered

---

[16] *Ibid.*

[17] "New DLR-HY4 — The First Hydrogen-Powered Aircraft Debuts at Stuttgart Airport," available at: https://fuelcellsworks.com/news/new-dlr-hy4-the-first-hydrogen-powered-aircraft-debuts-at-stuttgart-airport/ (accessed December 9, 2021).

by a hybrid system that combines battery and fuel cell technology. If the energy gained in this way — for example when taking off or climbing — is insufficient, the lithium-ion battery takes over. In the fuel cell, hydrogen and oxygen are converted into electrical energy for propeller drive. The environmentally friendly by-product is water. The Baden-Württemberg Transport Minister Winfried Herman acknowledged at the presentation at the airport scientific achievements behind HY4: "Air transport must be as soon as possible climate-friendly. With the worldwide unique hydrogen fuel cell airplaneHY4, science is presenting a promising technology for emission-free flying. With this expertise, Baden-Württemberg is a pioneer in global competition in the field of hydrogen and fuel cell technology."[18]

I: Combustion vs. fuel cells
Comparison of hydrogen propulsion options

	COMBUSTION	FUEL CELLS
Description	· A gas turbine engine burns hydrogen and oxygen (from air) to rotate a turbine · The turbine rotates a fan to generate thrust	· A fuel cell converts hydrogen and oxygen (from air) into electricity · The electricity powers a motor that spins a propeller or ducted fan to generate thrust
Efficiency	~40%	~45-50%
Environmental footprint	· Reduced environmental impact – "zero carbon" solution · Zero CO_2, CO, SO_x, HC · NO_x emissions present · Water vapor emissions: more emissions than in an engine with comparable thrust · Contrail/cirrus cloud formation: due to the high purity of liquid hydrogen, nucleation of ice crystals will be reduced, although lifetime may be increased	· Minimal environmental impact – potential for "true zero" solution · Zero CO_2, CO, NO_x, SO_x, HC, soot emissions · Water vapor emissions: more emissions than in an engine with comparable thrust · Contrail/cirrus cloud formation: due to the high purity of liquid hydrogen, nucleation of ice crystals will be reduced, although lifetime may be increased
Technological barriers	· Redesign of engines for hydrogen as a fuel · Updated aircraft design to accommodate safe, light storage of liquid hydrogen	· Development of aviation-ready, efficient, power-dense fuel cells · Improved electric motors, power electronics, cabling and other electrical components · Updated aircraft design to accommodate safe, light storage of liquid hydrogen · Full benefits require entirely new aircraft design that leverages distributed propulsion · Effective thermal management
Advantages	· "Zero carbon" solution · Propulsion system very similar to conventional aircraft · Significantly less emissions · More compatible with current aerospace supply chain, with minimal architectural and design changes	· "True zero" solution · Compatible with electric propulsion, with potential to benefit from distributed propulsion · 20-40% more efficient than hydrogen combustion
Disadvantages	· Requires a redesign of today's aircraft to accommodate the additional volume required for hydrogen fuel tanks · Still produces NO_x and water vapor emissions so contributes to global warming · Increased water vapor emissions have an unclear impact on contrails/cirrus cloud formation	· Requires drastic aircraft redesign to accommodate the distributed propulsion system, full suite of new electric subsystems and significant hydrogen storage · Increased water vapor emissions have an unclear impact on contrails/cirrus cloud formation

Source: Roland Berger

---

[18] *Ibid.*

2.2 *Five key barriers for the use of hydrogen*

Shifting to hydrogen as a fuel for aviation is not without its challenges, however. The implications for aircraft and engine design, the necessity of effective hydrogen storage solutions, the need to produce hydrogen in a sustainable fashion, the infrastructures that will be required, and the associated costs are all elements to be taken into consideration and they will have a substantial impact on the use of hydrogen as an alternative fuel. These are challenges that the aviation industry must not underestimate. In fact, the future of hydrogen depends on the direction development will take (fuel cells or combustion). Moreover, is it to be seen which segment will prevail after COVID-19, particularly in narrow-body/Middle-of-the-Market aircraft, which are likely to emerge as the battleground between hydrogen and hybrid-electric technologies.

The following is the list of five key barriers for the use of hydrogen.

---

[1] First challenge: Aircraft and engine redesign
To exploit the full benefits of hydrogen, aircraft must change substantially. This could amount to a redesign of almost all the components of the aircraft, from the propulsion system and the form of the fuselage to the fuel storage. Hydrogen combustion requires a partial redesign of the aircraft, while fuel cells require a complete redesign. Hydrogen combustion aircraft will rely on modified conventional thrust systems. Major changes will result from fuel delivery and storage, and additional fuel storage volume in the fuselage will be required given the reduced volumetric density relative to jet fuel. This will necessitate an increased fuselage size, generating additional drag, or a complete redesign of the aircraft structure, such as a move to blended wing bodies, with significant enclosed storage volume.

In addition to storage considerations, hydrogen fuel cell propulsion will require a redesign of the thrust systems to integrate distributed electrical propulsion, involving high voltage/high power electrical systems. The form and function of such aircraft will require a complete change from contemporary tube and wings architecture, and mirrors the design shift required for series hybrid or all-electric flight at the aircraft level.

---

[2] Second challenge: Hydrogen storage

Effective storage solutions are key to unlocking hydrogen's high gravimetric energy density and will need to be refined to address the issue of low volumetric energy density.

Storage in the liquid state is currently the most promising option, offering high volumetric density relative to the gaseous alternative. The drawback of liquid storage is the requirement for cryogenic cooling (below −253 degrees Celsius). Cooling uses as much as 45 percent of the stored energy content, meaning there is a significant loss of energy between energy stored and delivered for thrust (tank-to-wing efficiency). This demonstrates the trade-off that must be made between maintaining high volumetric density alongside high tank-to-wing efficiency.

Additionally, the cryogenic requirement necessitates the inclusion of cooling systems and significant insulation. This leads to complex and heavy tank designs that consequently reduce the effective gravimetric energy density of the fuel. To take full advantage of hydrogen's high energy density, significant progress must be made in light-weighting storage tanks and advancing cryogenic cooling systems.

[3] Third challenge: Sustainable Hydrogen production

A significant ramp-up in "green" hydrogen production or Carbon Capture and Storage (CCS) for "blue" hydrogen production will be necessary to produce volumes sufficient for the aviation industry in a sustainable manner. Current production is dominated by "gray" hydrogen processes, with 96 percent of hydrogen produced directly from CO_2-emitting processes such as steam methane reforming or coal gasification. The remaining four percent is generated via electrolysis, which only produces "green" hydrogen if renewables are used. Of the 70 million tons of hydrogen produced today, only around one million tons is currently "green."

Fortunately, a clear pathway to sustainable hydrogen exists. The solution in this case is likely to be driven by the energy sector as the transition to peak load renewables may produce a need for energy supply-side management and surplus energy capture, with hydrogen storage a viable solution. This source, alongside wider deployment of CCS driven by carbon taxes, may lead to growth of sustainable hydrogen production and an associated decrease in its price.

[4] Fourth challenge: Infrastructure

Hydrogen infrastructure improvements will need to move in lock-step with technology to enable exploitation of hydrogen by aviation. Two key areas here are fuel delivery to airports and airport refueling infrastructure.

One option for fuel delivery will be via existing gas networks. A good example of this is the Leeds City Gate study, which shows that it will be possible to convert existing natural gas networks for the transportation of hydrogen gas. This is promising for the basic building blocks of hydrogen infrastructure, but significant investment will be needed by all sectors involved. The long-distance transportation of hydrogen must also be considered, especially given the disconnect between where hydrogen is produced (renewable energy plants with excess capacity and hydrogen production sites) and where it will be used (airports).

At airports, there could be an additional requirement to liquefy hydrogen on site, assuming that the infrastructure will be in place to deliver hydrogen gas. This will require local electricity generation or a reliable grid connection to ensure no network disruption costs arise.

[5] Fifth challenge: Cost

Hydrogen is more expensive than kerosene on a kWh basis: excluding storage costs, average production costs are 0.14 USD/kWh for "green" hydrogen and 0.05 USD/kWh for "gray" hydrogen. The latter is on par with kerosene, but as "green" hydrogen would be necessary for "true zero" or "zero carbon" sustainable aviation, the price of these production methods must fall to compete on a cost basis.

Underlying overall production cost is "grid-to-wing" efficiency. Hydrogen production is often criticized for requiring too many power conversion steps, each of which diminish its overall production efficiency (and increase cost). For example, converting electricity into hydrogen may seem like a redundant step, to simply convert it back into electricity in a fuel cell. By contrast, employing a battery to power an aircraft would seem simpler and more efficient. However, if battery improvements plateau at a point insufficient for mid- to long-haul flight, hydrogen may remain the only "zero carbon" or "true zero" option. Furthermore, the question of production efficiencies quickly resolves into a question of cost alone: if hydrogen combustion can be cheap, does it matter how many steps it takes?

Once again, other sectors may provide the solution. As demand for hydrogen from other transportation sectors increases, and supply rises in line with renewable energy capacity, costs will likely fall. For example, projects are under development in Australia, Saudi Arabia and North Africa where "green" hydrogen is expected to cost as little as 0.07 USD/kWh in the future. Technology improvements in electrolyzers and hydrogen compression methods are also likely to contribute further to cost reduction, as the improved efficiency of such processes will reduce the energy input per ton of hydrogen produced.

More important than the decreasing cost of hydrogen may be the increasing cost of carbon. If greater emissions sanctions are imposed on aviation, such as ETS and CORSIA, the operating cost of burning jet fuel will rise. The aviation industry should therefore be careful to monitor price trends for both hydrogen and kerosene, as an inversion in the cost differential between the two fuels would improve the business case for investing in hydrogen.

Source: Roland Berger, "Hydrogen — A Future Fuel for Aviation?" *Focus*, available at: https://www.rolandberger.com/en/Publications/Hydrogen-A-future-fuel-of-aviation.html (accessed December 9, 2021).

2.3 *Looking to the future*

It is evident that the use of hydrogen represents the next step for a greener evolution of the aviation industry. Sustainable solutions include the use of SAFs to reduce emissions, which do not require substantial changes in the functionality of the existing engines. The use of hydrogen shall push for further research to improve the efficiency of this solution impacting on both engines, in case of hydrogen combustion, and the study and development of new solutions when it comes to the use of fuel cells. However, a series of other factors need to be considered which accompany the evolution of these technologies, and while the industry will experiment all alternatives, is it possible that depending on the market to be served, that is to say short range with smaller aircraft, long-haul with bigger aircraft, different technologies will be developed and used. In the first case, "all-electric" solutions likely will be used, while in the second case it is more probable that aircraft will rely on SAFs because "all-electric," hybrid-electric, or hydrogen solutions will face gravimetric and volumetric power density challenges. In between these two extremes, regional and narrow-body/Middle-of-the-Market aircraft will likely be the battleground where hydrogen will compete against hybrid electric. Regarding hydrogen technologies and hybrid-electric solutions the science however is not yet clear on whether the total impact of GHGs produced by hydrogen aircraft (water vapor emissions, contrails, AIC, and NO_X for hydrogen combustion) are better or worse than efficient hybrids. Further, hybrids do not require investment in a hydrogen supply chain, and are compatible with SAFs, unlike hydrogen aircraft.

As hydrogen combustion requires less of a technological leap than hydrogen fuel cell aircraft, this is the path the industry seems to have chosen for the near future. In fact, as stressed in the following section, hydrogen could be used as a preferential pathway to reduce emissions within the aviation sector within the next 5 years, with a complete transition to hydrogen fueled flights possible by 2050.

2.3.1 *Transition to hydrogen inevitable but requires more technological advancements*

According to a research conducted by Commonwealth Scientific and Industrial Research Organisation (CSIRO),[19] by 2035 the role of hydrogen in reducing emissions could be substantially larger, when used to supplement fuels used in existing aircraft, starting a process of transitioning away from jet fuels. However this transition, which can be completed by

---

[19]CSIRO is an Australian national science research agency. In collaboration with Boeing, CSIRO has produced a report that outlines a pathway forward for the adoption of hydrogen and hydrogen-based fuels to support decarbonization within the commercial aviation industry. The report takes a long-term view — identifying short, medium, and long-term adoption opportunities that will assist the industry in reducing emissions and prioritizing sustainability as it recovers from the impacts of COVID-19, available at: https://www.csiro.au/en/Do-business/Futures/Reports/Energy-and-Resources (accessed December 9, 2021).

2050, would require further advancements in technologies related to the use of hydrogen.

The aviation sector has set a number of goals for reducing emissions, including a 50% cut in net aviation emissions by 2050, a cap on emissions growth from 2020. However, the latter target is set to be reviewed, given the unprecedented disruption to the global aviation sector caused by COVID-19 in 2020.

The CSIRO report sees opportunities in green hydrogen being used as the basis for the production of zero emissions "electro-fuels" where hydrogen is combined with carbon dioxide to provide direct jet-fuel replacements.

The blending of smaller amounts of "electro-fuels" with conventional, fossil fuel, derived jet fuels could commence by the 2030s, and start cutting into aircraft emissions before technologies aiming for a complete transition to zero emission fuels become mature. Using an electro-fuel approach would also allow emissions reductions to be achieved using existing airline fleets, and would avoid the need to drive early retirements of aircraft that have required a significant upfront investment by airlines.

Early hydrogen adoption could take place in areas that support airport operation, including hydrogen fueled passenger transport to, from and around airports.

The report concluded that ongoing research and development would be required, both to drive down the costs of hydrogen production to make the zero emissions fuels commercially competitive, as well as to solve some of the technical challenges of hydrogen transport and storage.

"To facilitate the uptake of hydrogen planes closer to 2050, a considerable amount of research is required in the immediate term regarding changes in engine design and the development of on-aircraft infrastructure such as light-weight cryogenic storage tanks that minimize hydrogen boil-off," the report by CSIRO says.

"It is worth noting that an important player of the aviation industry such as Boeing has contributed in preparing the report by CSIRO. Indeed Boeing has made significant improvements in efficiency and reducing emissions from our products. However, we also recognize that sustainable aviation fuels are a necessary contributor to the decarboniszation of aviation and are committed to furthering their development. We expect it will take multiple solutions to decarbonize our fuel supply. With strong developments in the hydrogen industry in recent years, there is now a distinct opportunity for hydrogen technologies to contribute to the aviation sector energy transition across different elements of the value chain."[20]

While science and technology advancements will enable to support the role of hydrogen which will contribute to a more green recovery of aviation industry, the next step is a complete electric aircraft. However, the regulatory landscape will also need to be updated in order to accompany this epochal change. The following section thus introduces the scenarios and challenges deriving from the transition toward electric propulsion.

2.4 *Transition to the electric propulsion*

Although conventional fossil fuel, SAFs, and hydrogen as sources of power for propulsion are used in currently existing aircraft and they can last many more decades, undoubtedly we will assist to a slow but inevitable transition to electric propulsion. Electric power is future-proof, and potentially more efficient compared to all existing alternatives although many technological and regulatory barriers need to be overcome before any significant change can occur.

As it will be exposed in the next section battery technology remains the most significant limiting factor. In order to see a complete electrical aircraft operational, it is necessary for the current low technological maturity of batteries to evolve and become more efficient.

According to a research concerning the evolution of aviation and in particular the development of electric power, "Lithium-ion batteries are expected to remain the most attractive for aerospace use due to their relatively higher energy densities and ability to withstand a large number of cycles. Like-for-like, it would take a battery with a gravimetric density of ~500 Wh/kg for electrical propulsion to begin to become competitive with today's traditional propulsion systems; this is not expected to occur before 2030. Current indications suggest that the automotive manufacturers that are currently leading on battery development, and are by nature more interested in volumetric density, would likely be satisfied with a gravimetric density of ~350–400 Wh/kg. If so, aerospace developers may have to

---

[20] In this sense Michael Edwards, General Manager Boeing Australia, "Boeing Foreword," in *Opportunities for Hydrogen in Commercial Aviation*, available at: https://www.csiro.au/en/Do-business/Futures/Reports/Energy-and-Resources (accessed December 9, 2021).

'take up the baton' to ensure new battery technology keeps getting investment beyond this point."[21]

It is now necessary to turn our attention to the different aspects of electric propulsion in relation to the segment of the aviation which will implement electric power. Although electric power represents that the future significant technological developments must occur, the full implementation of this new propulsion depends on market demand also.

3. Electrical Propulsion for the Future

Electrical propulsion promises to completely revolutionize the industry, and consumers can look forward to cleaner, greener, cheaper, and potentially safer flights in the near future. This revolution will start from general aviation/recreational aircraft and the emerging urban mobility. These classes of aircraft are an effective segment as a "test bed" for further developments for electrification of aircraft. Current manufacturers must now concentrate on developing regional segment and serving charter operators which are potentially a strong market in the medium term for electric propulsion. These success of regional aircraft may drive a new boom in regional aviation. Large commercial operators can be expected to convert to electrical propulsion later due to the more advanced technological requirements. Notably, the new segment of urban mobility will offer new opportunities for new entrants who not only must develop smaller aircraft but they also need to decide when and how to enter this new segment of the aviation industry. Thus, investors must decide which ventures to back and governments should consider how best to facilitate economic and industrial growth as well as implement a new series of regulations to especially foster the development of UAM.

In any case, significant barriers remain to fully deploy electrical propulsion. In the next section, we will expose the major impediments which need to be tackled to pave the way for a successful implementation of electrical propulsion.

---

[21] Study by Roland Berger (2018), "Aircraft Electrical Propulsion — Onwards and Upwards," July, available at: https://www.rolandberger.com/en/Publications/Electrical-propulsion-ushers-in-new-age-of-innovation-in-aerospace.html (accessed December 9, 2021).

3.1 *Electrical propulsion: Not a question of if, but when*

It is clear that the question is when electrical propulsion will substitute existing alternatives, and not if. The reality is that the industry is already experimenting this new type of propulsion, but it takes time to ameliorate it. Aircraft electrical propulsion truly holds disruptive potential with the promise to increase fuel efficiency, reduce GHG emissions, reduce cost, and increase safety.

This disruptive innovation will become clearer as the technology matures, but other elements also need to be considered which represent obstacles to the development of electrical propulsion. The next three sections expose these obstacles in order of importance.

3.1.1 *Technological obstacles*

The first type of technological barrier is the battery performance. This is a very critical point to be addressed; in fact, "high battery storage capacity and low weight are clearly crucial to all-electric and hybrid-electric architectures, and in order to begin to allow the creation of products with commercially viable payload-range characteristics, it is generally accepted that electrical storage systems need an energy density of at least 500 Wh/kg. The highest commercial batteries today range from 150–250 Wh/kg, with Tesla's 21-70 battery having a reported energy density of 250–320 Wh/kg. Roland Berger's analysis suggests that the current trajectory of Lithium-ion battery development will bring gravimetric density to c. 400–450 Wh/kg by the mid-2020s. However, further development or new battery chemistries will need to reach the 500 Wh/kg mark, and even if batteries do reach this level, the energy storage density will still be a factor of 25 lower than the approximately 12 kWh/kg delivered by jet fuel. In addition to high energy density, high re-charging speeds and long battery life-cycles will be crucial to underpinning the economics of battery-powered aircraft."[22] In relation to the use of batteries electric aircraft developers will need to develop effective hazard containment systems not only to

---

[22] In this sense see the study by Roland Berger (2017), "Aircraft Electrical Propulsion — The Next Chapter of Aviation?," available at: https://www.rolandberger.com/en/Publications/New-developments-in-aircraft-electrical-propulsion.html   (accessed December 9, 2021).

meet airworthiness requirements but also to satisfy public safety concerns.

ROADMAP FOR LITHIUM-ION BATTERY TECHNOLOGY [WH/KG]
Projected automotive roadmaps indicate batteries will only reach the 500 Wh/kg level required for aerospace after 2025.

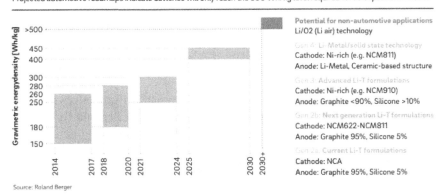

Source: Roland Berger

Source: Roland Berger (2017), "Aircraft Electrical Propulsion — The Next Chapter of Aviation?," available at: https://www.rolandberger.com/en/Publications/New-developments-in-aircraft-electrical-propulsion.html (accessed December 9, 2021).

Electrically propelled aircraft beside generating the necessary power will need electronics to convert, switch, and condition this power. According to the study mentioned earlier, to perform these functions with minimum electrical loss, power electronics will also need to operate with the minimum associated heat generation. This factor is particularly important given the multi-MW electrical power systems that will be required for regional and larger commercial aircraft and the resulting need to dump any surplus heat generated. Notably conventional aircraft can currently use fuel as a reservoir to dump surplus heat, but this option will not be available in electrically propelled aircraft.[23]

The same study affirms that an alternative way of looking at the limitations of current technology is to consider replacing the engines on an existing aircraft with an all electrical propulsion system, and seeing what characteristics that system would need to have in order to generate a comparable level of aircraft performance. The example reported in the study puts in evidence that replacing the existing turbo-prop engines on a Dornier 328 regional aircraft with electric motors and batteries of

---

[23] *Ibid.*

180 Wh/kg capacity would reduce the range from 1,200 km to just over 200 km. The study also underlines that in order to restore the range to the baseline figure of 1,200 km, the following changes would also be required: (i) Drag coefficient reduction of 20% through aerodynamics; (ii) Increase in wing span of 50% to reduce induced drag; (iii) Reduction in structural mass of 20%; (iv) Increase in battery capacity to 500 Wh/kg.

3.1.2 *Market demand*

Before electric propulsion can become widespread it is necessary to have an increased interest in the market. Indeed, the market demand for electrification is of fundamental importance for its development, and the demand is necessarily composed of the interest of operators to adopt new platforms, and the demand from passengers to fly on them. Operators must take the risk of investing and developing new electrically propelled aircraft advancing toward the target of zero emissions posed by the regulatory authorities, starting from a new segment of the market, that is to say air mobility and in particular air taxi. This must be accompanied by a surge of the demand from passengers willing to fly in a greener and in a smarter way. However, in order to reach this goal both operators and regulators should work to render this new modality safer and attractive; thus, new regulations must be implemented to standardize the use of these new platforms.

It is worth noting that passengers may also be excited, and prone, to "fly greener." However, because consumers are driven by cost, operators need to keep this factor in mind when developing this modality. For regional aviation, passengers may also be motivated by the greater convenience that can be enabled by electrical propulsion (which, being quieter, could result in more regional airports in city centers), though cost is likely to remain a key consideration. In this context, UAM represents a very promising new market at least for two reasons: (i) smaller aircraft are already existing and both seasoned players and new entrants are developing this segment, and (ii) greater convenience for commuters with traveling distances cut to a fraction of the current time. This theme is treated in the last section of this chapter analyzing the development of the so-called VTOL. However, manufacturers, airworthiness authorities, and operators alike will have to work to ensure high safety and security levels in urban air travel, while managing a carefully considered communication campaign to assure consumers of their safety and, in particular, their comfort with autonomous flight.

3.1.3 *Regulation*

A future driver for a shift to electrical propulsion can be represented by both emission regulations, and a new set of regulations impacting on the functioning of the new platforms.

In fact in general terms, international aviation has been left out of UN agreements on climate change such as the Kyoto Protocol and Paris Agreement. The industry's UN-regulator, ICAO, has so far only set up a carbon offset scheme (CORSIA) which has the potential to reduce net emissions, but these regulations only refer to existing aircraft. It is evident that technical progress in electrical propulsion is changing the industry and therefore new rules are needed to fully release the potential of electrical propulsion aviation.

As stressed in a study by Roland Berger "first as new technologies are developed in the field of electric aviation, each technology will need to have regulatory backing to be applied. For example, regulation will play a part in verifying and certifying the use of More Electric Aircraft systems, and any progression with Electrical Propulsion will require airworthiness certification, as well as broad regulatory acceptance for enabling technologies such as high-powered batteries, high voltage distribution, and boundary layer ingestion. Second, regulation will be critical to enable new platforms. Regulation and certification procedures for new architectures such as distributed fans will be required to allow the full potential of Electrical Propulsion to be realized. Third, if and when technologies and platforms progress to enable Urban Air Taxis, far-reaching regulatory changes would be required to enable entirely new aviation systems, such as for the regulation and control of urban commuter air transportation systems, as well as integration with other urban infrastructure (e.g. electricity grid, buildings, roads and automotive infrastructure) and corresponding regulatory regimes."[24]

There is no doubt that a key enabler for electric aviation is to be found in regulatory bodies, and countries that are willing to take risks to experiment with different regulatory and certification regimes, including congested cities willing to explore UAM to see which create the safest and most progressive environment for innovation.

---

[24] *Ibid.*

3.2 *Electrical aircraft: Possible future scenarios*

As noted previously, technological and market demand barriers must be overcome in order to fully deploy aircraft electrification. However another factor which can influence the development of electrification depends on how the aviation industry will respond to the COVID-19 and on which paths major players will decide to take.

The evolution of electrification may evolve in four different possible scenarios: (i) continued evolution which implies a trend of increased electrification of aircraft systems; (ii) Niche application, which represent an incremental to Scenario 1, in which technological innovation leads to some niche applications emerging for medium-range transports/business jets; (iii) Small-scale revolution which represents an incremental to Scenario 2, in which the right enabling technologies, regulatory changes, and societal acceptance all emerge to create a boom in Urban Air Taxis; (iv) Large-scale revolution: incremental to Scenario 3, in which all of aerospace is revolutionized, with the innovation of all required technologies to enable at least hybrid electric LCA, and the potential for all electric LCA.

3.2.1 *Scenario 1: Evolution of today trend*

A continuation of today's steady trend toward More Electric Aircraft systems would be sufficient to enable this scenario. However, this trend would see an increase in electric actuation and electrically powered systems. Electric actuators, such as electric-hydro-static actuators (EHAs), electro-mechanical actuators (EMA), etc., would see an increase in application in flight control system actuation, landing gear actuation, thrust reverser actuation, etc. Electrically powered systems would increasingly replace hydraulic or pneumatic systems in applications such as environmental control and ice protection, and there would be increased use of components such as metal-oxide-semiconductor field-effect transistor (MOSFETs), diodes, power modules, and hybrids to power and control pumps and air conditioning systems.[25]

---

[25] In this sense see the study by Roland Berger (2017), "Aircraft Electrical Propulsion — The Next Chapter of Aviation?," p. 23, available at: https://www.rolandberger.com/en/ Publications/New-developments-in-aircraft-electrical-propulsion.html   (accessed December 9, 2021).

3.2.2 *Scenario 2: Niche application of electrical propulsion*

This scenario is incremental to Scenario 1 and considers the adoption of some electrical propulsion in niche applications. The potential for the adoption of electrical propulsion, in particular, is greatest where a hybrid-electric or all-electric engine offers benefits over traditional jet engine.

Classes of aircraft impacted would be either all-electric or hybrid-electric, able to travel short distances (100–500 mile range) and at slow-medium speeds in an efficient manner with medium levels of battery density. Hybrid-electrical propulsion would make intermediate aircraft sizes viable, such as small-medium sized regional aircraft (up to c. 30 seats).

Several new technologies and regulatory changes would be required to enable this scenario.[26]

3.2.3 *Scenario 3: Small-scale evolution of electrical propulsion*

This scenario is incremental to Scenario 2, and would represent a sea change in how we experience urban travel with the introduction of an entirely new platform type into service. Several new technologies and regulatory changes would be required to enable this scenario as already evidenced. In particular, regulatory acceptance would have to go far beyond the aerospace industry and cover aspects of urban infrastructure such as for example buildings, roads, and the electric power grid. However, such innovation would likely be slow; in fact, cities where new platforms are going to be experimented will have to evaluate and weigh this innovation before opening up their skies. A true emergence of this trend would impact a number of non-core aerospace industries. Urban transportation, which currently consists largely of cars, trains, and buses, could significantly be disrupted with an aerial option potentially being faster, if electric then, cleaner, and over time potentially cheaper. Moreover, aerospace maintenance, repair, and overhaul would have an additional segment to service with potentially much greater volumes than existing business; further, serving this segment may need to take on a different delivery model, such as being located closer to major cities.[27]

---

[26] *Ibid.*

[27] *Ibid.*

3.2.4 *Scenario 4: Large-scale evolution of electrical propulsion*

This scenario represents a step change in electrical propulsion technology as well as large-scale adoption into service and could result in a reduction in both cost and emissions per passenger seat. Though not being strictly incremental to it, many of the technologies and regulatory changes required for Scenario 3 are subsets of those for Scenario 4. Scenario 4 would see all technological and regulatory barriers for large commercial electric aircraft lifted. In this scenario, technological advancements are necessary for all-electrical propulsion to become widespread; however, major changes must occur in existing infrastructures also. Airports would have to adapt to a ramp down in fuel distribution and a ramp up in electrical infrastructure such as charging stations and potentially localized power stations, while maintenance, repair and over-haul processes would need to be adapted.[28]

3.3 *Electrical propulsion: A revolution impacting on several aspects of aviation industry*

The taking-off of electrical propulsion will cause several changes in the aviation industry. The implications of this revolution are numerous and interest many aspects starting from the necessary changes to the aircraft including engines to the development of the different segments of the market starting from regional application to LCA passing through the GA and recreational aircraft which should be the first to experiment full elec-trical propulsion and thus to influence the new emerging UAM.

It is expected that hybrid-electric aircraft in their regional application will enter into service as early as 2032 due to the technical barriers which still need to be overcome. However, fully electrical propulsion for GA and recreational aircraft is already a reality. In summer 2020, the first European full electrical aircraft (GA) was awarded the necessary certifica-tion to fly in Europe.

3.3.1 *Challenges for engine manufacturer and airframer*

The development of an electric aircraft involves three major players, is it to say: the engine manufacturer, the airframer, and the electrical systems

---

[28] *Ibid.*

company. Clearly, all of them play a specific role and are in charge of developing and producing parts which need to be assembled and composed and functioning in synchrony to form a fully functional aircraft. These three players have separate certification requirements and departments within the regulatory authorities — and they share the resulting control and influence on the final aircraft. The question is which of the three players will have the greatest share of control and influence?

This issue has been treated in a study and experts have expressed their point of view in the following terms: "The engine maker would be a natural choice: the complexity of designing and delivering the high power-to-weight ratio aero gas turbine may necessitate that it continues to be the power systems lead, with simply an extension to existing power generation being supplied by the electrical systems provider. Alternatively, it may be discovered that the required electrical system is so complex that an electrical systems manufacturer must be the power systems lead, with better knowledge of how to optimize across multiple electrical sources and sinks — and with a gas turbine supplied in as just one component. Finally, it may also be that the airframer maintains its 'Tier 0' status with integration of the entire system being the highest value activity: indeed, the airframer may have to subsume both engine and electrical work for initial developments as new architectures are explored."[29]

Naturally, the necessary certifications by airworthiness authorities such as the FAA and EASA remain a crucial factor, and the success of the electrical propulsion will depend on technical solutions to be developed by these players and thus approved by these authorities for actual implementation. All these actors must work together and coordinate their efforts and researches to advance toward the common goal of a greener aviation. As already stressed this evolution in aviation will invest the GA and recreational segment first and then regional and commercial sectors with hybrid-electric aircraft entering into service by the early 2030s as experts predicted.

3.3.2 *Technological and commercial challenges*

Undeniably progresses are manifesting quickly and much has been made of the ongoing aircraft electrification revolution. However, still there are

---

[29] Study by Roland Berger (2018), "Aircraft Electrical Propulsion — Onwards and Upwards," July, available at: https://www.rolandberger.com/en/Publications/Electrical-propulsion-ushers-in-new-age-of-innovation-in-aerospace.html (accessed December 9, 2021).

significant technological and commercial challenges that are yet to be addressed.

Many actors claim that they are already in the position and have the capabilities to build a 10- or 11-seater electric aircraft. The reality is that there is a significant difference between producing and certifying aircraft for passenger-carrying operations: it is relatively straightforward to create an air vehicle. Being able to turn that air vehicle into an economically viable, safe, and reliable asset has a much greater level of complexity.

There are two critical conditions that an electric aircraft manufacturer need to consider: noise and the cost–benefit relationship. Firstly, manufacturers should realize that an electric motor being used does not automatically make the aircraft quieter. Around ~70 decibels is a good benchmark for an "acceptable" noise level — any regional aircraft making noise above this level will have a hard time getting a license to fly in a big city. Secondly, there's the cost–benefit relationship: the aircraft and the routes it travels must be economically viable. It must be cheap to manufacture and run, and really solve a traffic issue to be profitable.[30]

3.3.3 *Latest development: Electric airplanes could finally take-off with ultra-light lithium-sulfur batteries*

Electric aircraft are all the rage, with prototypes in development in every size from delivery drones to passenger aircraft. But the technology has yet to take off, and for one reason: lack of a suitable battery. However, a UK enterprise, namely Oxis[31] is developing a new type of ultra-light

---

[30] In this sense Neil Cloughley, Founder and Managing Director Faradair, for Roland Berger, interview available at: https://www.rolandberger.com/en/Point-of-View/Aircraft-electrical-propulsion-can-transform-regional-travel.html (accessed December 9, 2021).

[31] OXIS has developed its unique technology around sulfur-based cathode materials, highly stable electrolyte systems, and anode made of lithium metal and intercalation materials. Oxis is developing an innovative Lithium Sulfur [Li-S] battery chemistry that will revolutionize the rechargeable battery market. With a theoretical energy density five times greater than Li-ion, OXIS patented Li-S technology is lighter, safer, and maintenance free, and ready to meet the demands of tomorrow. Oxis is based on the Culham Science Centre in Oxfordshire where the original lithium-ion batteries were first developed and prototyped. Oxis has well-equipped laboratories with state-of-the-art equipment and large dry room facilities. More information about this company is available at: https://oxisenergy.com/about/ (accessed December 9, 2021).

lithium-sulfur batteries which can be a game changer and enable the taking-off of electrical propulsion earlier than expected.

The key advantage of lithium-ion batteries over their predecessors — and of lithium sulfur over lithium ion — is the great amount of energy the cells can pack into a small amount of mass. The lead-acid starter battery that cranks the internal combustion engine in a car can store about 50 watt-hours per kilogram. Typical lithium-ion designs can hold from 100 to 265 Wh/kg, depending on the other performance characteristics for which it has been optimized, such as peak power or long life. Oxis recently developed a prototype lithium-sulfur pouch cell that proved capable of 470 Wh/kg, and we expect to reach 500 Wh/kg within a year. And because the technology is still new and has room for improvement, it is not unreasonable to anticipate 600 Wh/kg by 2025.

When cell manufacturers quote energy-density figures, they usually specify the energy that is available when the cell is being discharged at constant, low power rates. In some applications such low rates are fine, but for the many envisioned electric aircraft that will take off vertically, the energy must be delivered at higher power rates. Such a high-power feature must be traded off for lower total energy-storage capacity.[32]

In order to optimize battery performance without compromising safety Oxis relies, first and foremost, on a battery management system (BMS), which is a combination of software and hardware that controls and protects the battery. It also includes algorithms for measuring the energy remaining in a battery and others for minimizing the energy wasted during charging.

Three factors will determine whether lithium-sulfur batteries ultimately succeed or fail: (i) the successful integration of the batteries into multiple aircraft types, to prove the principle; (ii) the continued refinement of the cell chemistry; (iii) the continued reduction in the unit cost. A plus here is that sulfur is about as cheap as materials get, so there is reason to hope that with volume manufacturing, the unit cost will fall below that of the lithium-ion design, as would be required for commercial success.[33]

---

[32] In this sense see Mark Crittenden (2020), "With Ultralight Lithium-Sulfur Batteries, Electric Airplanes Could Finally Take Off," available at: https://spectrum.ieee.org/aero-space/aviation/with-ultralight-lithiumsulfur-batteries-electric-airplanes-could-finally-take-off (accessed December 9, 2021).

[33] *Ibid.*

Batteries are a crucial element in the development of electrical aircraft not only for GA as exposed in the next section, but in particular for the new segment of the UAM.

3.4 *Not only GA and recreational electric aircraft*

The GA sector and recreational electric aircraft seem to be the next frontier for fully electric propulsion before this modality reach the other segments of the market (i.e. regional and commercial). Thus, it appears appropriate to introduce this theme here mentioning the latest news and briefly describing the success of the first certified fully electric aircraft.

Several manufacturers in fact are developing fully electrical aircraft for the GA sector and for recreational activities, and some of them are new entrants investing heavily in the hope to carve out a space for themselves in the market.

3.4.1 *The experience of Pipistrel*

Pipistrel is a world-leading small aircraft designer and manufacturer, specialized in energy-efficient and affordable high-performance aircraft. With more than 30 years of experience, Pipistrel has produced more than 2,200 aircraft to date, gaining significant international reputation by delivering unique, innovative products to passionate customers on all continents. First-to-fly an electric two-seater in 2007 and the winner of the NASA Green Flight Challenge in 2011 with the World's first electric four-seat aeroplane, Pipistrel has designed nine different experimental and serially produced electric aircraft. It has also developed propulsion systems, including batteries, power controllers, and electric motors, for small and GA class of aircraft for NASA and Siemens, among others.[34]

It is worth noting that in June 2020 Pipistrel obtained the first certification from EASA for its veils electro airplane.[35] The Velis Electro is a

---

[34] For more information visit: https://www.pipistrel-aircraft.com/about-us/#pipistrel-group-about (accessed December 9, 2021).

[35] See: https://www.pipistrel-aircraft.com/aircraft/electric-flight/velis-electro-easa-tc/. Slovenia-based Pipistrel is a leading small aircraft designer and manufacturer, specialized in energy-efficient and affordable high-performance aircraft. The Velis Electro (Model Virus SW 128) joins a product line-up of similar, but conventionally powered, aircraft.

two-seater aircraft intended primarily for pilot training. The aircraft is powered by the first certified electrical engine, the E-811-268MVLC, certified by EASA for Pipistrel on May 18, 2020.

3.4.2 *EASA certifies first fully electric plane worldwide*

The European Union Aviation Safety Agency announced the certification of an electric airplane, the Pipistrel Velis Electro, the first type certification worldwide of a fully electric aircraft and an important milestone in the quest for environmentally sustainable aviation. This is the first electric aircraft EASA has certified. The certification, completed in less than 3 years, was only possible in that time frame due to close co-operation between Pipistrel and EASA, with the common goal of ensuring the aircraft met the high standard of safety needed for certification. The project also brought important learnings that will support future certifications of electrically powered engines and aircraft.

"The type certification of the Pipistrel Velis Electro is the first step toward the commercial use of electric aircraft, which is needed to make emission-free aviation feasible. It is considerably quieter than other aeroplanes and produces no combustion gases at all," said Ivo Boscarol, founder and CEO of Pipistrel Aircraft. "It provides optimism, also to other electric aircraft designers, that the type certification of electric engines and aeroplanes is possible." Dominique Roland, Head of the General Aviation Department at EASA said: "For EASA, the type certification of this aircraft marks a significant dual milestone: on May 18, 2020 we type certified its engine as the first electric engine — now we have followed up with the first type certification of a plane flying that engine. This was a truly ground-breaking project which has yielded many learnings for the future certification of electric engines and aircraft, undoubtedly a growth area in coming years in line with the aims of environmental protection.

The certification project developed in two streams, firstly the typical certification activities related to the aircraft and in parallel a coordinated flight test program using a fleet of (non-certified) Alpha-Electros under EASA permit to fly. Having the ability to operate a similar aircraft meant the EASA team, which included members from the launch National Aviation Authorities (France's DGAC FR and Switzerland's FOCA), had access to operational data necessary for the certification activity, while highlighting the operational needs to enable electric aviation.

Notably during the course of these projects EASA gained first-hand experience in electric flight, learning more about batteries and their management systems, as well as electrical engine power units. This information has been used to develop the E&HPS Special Condition to further enable electric flight."[36]

3.4.3 *The revolution in action: "Eviation" another example anticipating the future*

Electrification revolution has already begun, and significant results are indicating we are steadily advancing toward a greener aviation. Certainly GA will be impacted first, followed by UAM, but it seems a newcomer is anticipating the future by introducing the fully first electrical regional aircraft by 2022. This is Eviation an Israeli company which was founded in 2016 by CEO Omer Bar-Yohay, Omri Regev, and Chairman Aviv Tzidon. Based in Kadima Tzoren (Israel), this company's vision is to change the way people travel regionally through affordable, sustainable aviation. Their mission thus is to build aircraft that create new market opportunities, challenging the limits of air travel use in a scalable, sustainable, and economically viable way. Thanks to the experience of the founders, in only 4 years they transformed this project into reality. Eviation is striving to become the first-to-market manufacturer of an all-electric propulsion aircraft, named "Alice." Alice, which targets middle-mile commutes of up to 650 miles, was unveiled at the Paris Air Show in June 2019.

The project of this Israeli company did not pass unobserved especially for the disruptive innovation which the project itself incarnates. In fact, only after 3 years from its foundation an international business group bought 70% of the equity stake in the company in order to further develop this project for regional aviation. The acquisition of Eviation by Clermont Group, headquartered in Singapore, was estimated in about US$76 million which would give Eviation a valuation of approximately US$108 million. Clermont builds industry-leading businesses in healthcare, financial

---

[36]In this sense: "EASA Certifies Electric Aircraft, First Type Certification for Fully Electric Plane World-Wide," press release available at: https://www.easa.europa.eu/news-room-and-events/press-releases/easa-certifies-electric-aircraft-first-type-certification-fully#group-easa-related-content (accessed December 9, 2021).

services, and aerospace.[37] Clermont Aerospace says it is committed to transforming Eviation's vision of electric flight into a commercial reality, and is looking forward to Alice's successful test flight and certification in the US.

Eviation seeks to provide a sustainable mobility option which radically rethinks the cost, experience, and environmental impact of regional travel. At the Air Show, Eviation also announced its first commercial contract with US regional carrier "Cape Air,"[38] and expects to begin shipping the aircraft for commercial use in 2022. Regional travel in the US although slowed down by COVID-19 is destined to growth, with an increase in consumers flying short distances between 50 and 650 miles. This growing segment offers the ideal scenario for Eviation's all-electric Alice, which aims to undercut the cost of travel by making middle-mile trips cheaper, faster, and cleaner. The shift to electric will *reduce operating costs, eliminate greenhouse gas emissions, make air travel more affordable and connect communities like never before.* Certification for "Alice" is expected in 2021, and Eviation has planned to ship the aircraft for commercial use in 2022; however, because of the impact of COVID-19 the schedule might be revised.

Electric airplanes will shape the future of the aviation and transportation industries making air travel cleaner, cheaper, and more efficient. As it is explained in the next section this trend will also impact UAM with new concept aircraft.

4. UAM: Old Players and Newcomers Conquering the New Frontier

UAM represents a new frontier in air transportation for short distances; in fact, UAM offers a new way for commuters to go to work and for the transportation of goods using electric vertical take-off and landing aircraft

---

[37] Clermont Aerospace also owns magniX, a Canadian electric engine company whose magni250 motors will power Eviation's Alice.

[38] At the Paris Air Show Eviation Aircraft announced the first commercial customer for its all-electric Alice airplane, namely Cape Air. With a fleet of 92 nine-seater airplanes, Cape Air is one of the largest regional airlines in the US, and has a double-digit purchase option for Alice. It will incorporate Eviation's Alice nine-seater planes into its existing fleet, offering flyers in the US an unparalleled flying experience.

(eVTOLs). This new reality is already taking place with the development of prototypes although the road to its full implementation is still full of challenges. VTOLS are a new breed of aircraft, they are somewhere between commercial airplanes and remotely controlled drones, configured to carry large payloads and people. UAM is estimated to open traffic lanes in the sky in the next decade, and it represents a giant leap forward in urban transportation, driven by increasing urbanization, the worsening bane of road congestion and new advances in aircraft technology and electric propulsion.

The demand for VTOL services will increase as the price becomes competitive with ground-based transportation options and consumers gain confidence that these aircraft are safe.

A growing number of players, led by aerospace, automobile, and technology companies, are working on UAM solutions. The first generation of full-scale demonstrators are flying today, and limited commercial flights are possible within the next 5 years.[39]

UAM will provide an attractive solution for congested areas where ground services cannot satisfy the growing demand for commuters. Furthermore, UAM will gradually be integrated in the existing mobility landscape, bringing a time-efficient mode of travel and a safe, enjoyable flight experience to more and more passengers at increasingly low cost.

There is no doubt that the developments on the UAM front are likely to present a key challenge to traditional GA segments in the future as the industry enters one of its most disruptive phases ever; however, some hurdles still remain both of technical and regulatory nature. But it is sure Air mobility will move forward and these obstacles will be removed to grant its success.

4.1 *What is an eVTOL and the factors which will determine its success*

We have already mentioned VTOL but here it is necessary to specify the characteristics of these aircraft and how they will influence urban mobility creating a new mode of transportation. It is possible to define *Electric*

---

[39] See: Altran (2020), "En-Route to Urban Air Mobility — On The Fast Track to Viable and Safe On-Demand Air Services," available at: https://www.altran.com/as-content/uploads/sites/27/2020/03/en-route-to-urban-air-mobility.pdf (accessed December 9, 2021).

vertical take-off and landing (eVTOL) as light commercial vehicles that can take off and land vertically like helicopters and fly forward like airplanes. Unlike helicopters, they use batteries instead of fuel for propulsion and are more maneuverable, less complex, and more efficient than helicopters. They are designed to fly at a lower altitude than commercial aircraft and will be either piloted or autonomous.[40]

Currently there are more than 100 VTOL projects under development worldwide and both seasoned players like, for example, Boeing and Airbus, and new manufacturers are competing for a stake of this new segment of the market. It is also necessary to underline that the development of these vehicles is an investment-heavy endeavor.

Much of the eVTOL investment to date has been focused on design — what the aircraft looks like, how it is powered, and how it performs — as well as how to make it as safe or safer than commercial aircraft aviation and how to create an amazing customer experience. The design criteria include:

- *Payload*: The range for air taxis is from a single-person (100 kilograms) to a nine-person-plus-baggage (960 kilograms) payload. Companies like Lilium and Joby Aviation are focused on a five-passenger eVTOL, while Volocopter and Ehang are opting for a more compact solution. EASA and FAA are recommending setting the MTOW for eVTOLs at 3,175 kilograms.[41]
- *Safety*: To fly above populated areas, eVTOLs will be required to be at least as safe as general-aviation aircraft. However, with rapid growth expected in the number of eVTOLs operating in city skies, regulators may impose more stringent safety standards than those that apply to GA.
- *Noise*: Sound pollution, both frequency and decibel level, is a serious issue for operating eVTOLs in urban environments. Uber has a set of requirements that specify eVTOLs must be 15 decibels (dB) less noisy than the existing light helicopters,[42] which is about 70 dB at 500 feet

---

[40] *Ibid.*

[41] See: European Union Aviation Safety Agency, "EASA SC-VTOL-01 Comment Response Document," available at: https://www.easa.europa.eu/sites/default/files/dfu/SC-VTOL-01%20CRD.pdf (accessed December 9, 2021).

[42] See: Uber, "Uber Air Vehicle Requirements and Missions," available at: https://s3.amazonaws.com/uber-static/elevate/Summary+Mission+and+Requirements.pdf (accessed December 9, 2021).

versus 85 dB for a typical helicopter. In comparison, the noise from a commercial jet at 25 meters is 150 dB, while a quiet rural area is 30 dB.[43]

- *Cost*: As part of the mobility-as-a-service revolution, eVTOLs will be managed by service provider and will likely not be sold to private customers. The service providers will purchase fleets of eVTOLs that will be part of an on-demand business service. This model will allow them to minimize per-vehicle product costs, and drive down the passenger cost-per-mile, which will help drive the success of the commercial eVTOL ventures.

4.1.1 Urban air traffic management

The development of UAM with the gradual widespread of VTOL will require the update and "upgrade" of existing rules for air navigation in urban areas. Existing authorities managing air traffic will certainly be involved in the drafting of new rules which will be part of the current regulation system.

As evidenced in a study by altran "unlike autonomous vehicles, eVTOLs will be regulated by air traffic management (ATM) agencies, specifically the European Union Aviation Safety Agency (EASA) and the US Federal Aviation Administration (FAA). These agencies are developing standards for innovative air traffic control (ATC) systems that can manage high-density drone and eVTOL traffic for both passenger and cargo-carrying aircraft at low altitudes in densely populated urban environments. Complicating the challenge, EASA and FAA already have their hands full managing the rapid growth of global commercial aircraft traffic, which is forecast to double over the next two decades, with the Asia-Pacific region driving the majority of the growth."[44]

It is important to stress that the European Union's EASA is still in the process of forming recommendations for urban ATM that it calls "U-Space."[45]

---

[43] See: IAC Acoustics, "Comparative Examples of Noise Levels, IAC Library," https://www.iacacoustics.com/blog-full/comparative-examples-of-noise-levels.html (accessed December 9, 2021).

[44] See: FAA, "FAA Aerospace Forecast: Fiscal 2019–2039," available at: https://www.faa.gov/data_research/aviation/aerospace_forecasts/media/FY2019-39_FAA_Aerospace_Forecast.pdf.

[45] European Union Aviation Safety Agency (2019), "Regulators and Industry Unite in Need to Address Societal Concerns on Drones," press release, available at: https://www.easa.

4.1.2 *Safety and certifications*

The most significant factor that will ultimately determine the widespread adoption of eVTOLs is human safety, and the perception by users that this mode of commuting is more convenient than ground services transportation. Both the EASA and FAA have established safety standards for aircraft that include certification of manufacturing processes, equipment testing, maintenance, and training. For this reason commercial air travel is considered as one of the safest forms of transportation. It is worth noting that "on February 3, 2020, the FAA proposed new safety standards for delivery drones, classifying them as a 'special class' of aircraft.[46] The FAA standards do not specify a timeline for implementation of the safety standards, which suggests drone deliveries to U.S consumers are likely to be years away. While aviation safety agencies around the world are drafting regulations for eVTOLs to ensure both the safety of the vehicles and the software than runs them, the expectation is that they will not be implemented until after the drone standards have been implemented."[47]

By the time eVTOLs are approved to operate, they will have better navigation sensors, enhanced connectivity, and partial autonomy that will make them at least as safe as today's commercial aircraft. It will take time for the EASA and FAA to evolve a comprehensive set of new certification standards for eVTOLs, but they are making progress.[48]

4.1.3 *Competitive service-based pricing*

It has to be considered that the price of a journey from point A to B can play a determinant role in choosing the means of transportation. The cost of the journey likely includes the price of the end-to-end trip that may

---

europa.eu/newsroom-and-events/press-releases/regulators-and-industry-unite-need-address-societal-concerns (accessed December 9, 2021).

[46] PYMTS.com, "e Safety Standards For Delivery Drones, February 3, 2020," available at: https://www.pymnts.com/news/regulation/2020/faa-to-propose-safety-standards-for-delivery-drones/ (accessed December 9, 2021).

[47] See: Altran (2020), "En-Route to Urban Air Mobility — On The Fast Track to Viable and Safe On-Demand Air Services," available at: https://www.altran.com/as-content/uploads/sites/27/2020/03/en-route-to-urban-air-mobility.pdf (accessed December 9, 2021).

[48] Mike Hirschberg (2019), "EASA Takes the First Shot at eVTOL Regulations. Did They Miss the Mark?," *Opinion, EVTOL*, available at: https://evtol.com/opinions/easa-first-shot-evtol-regulations/ (accessed December 9, 2021).

involve multiple forms of transportation, including a ride in an air taxi, so the issue of the price becomes a crucial factor when it comes to choosing the most convenient transportation service options. Thus, containing the cost of a trip in an eVTOL air taxi is vital to its widespread and success.

The nascent eVTOL industry needs to think about how air taxis will integrate with other forms of public transportation. Naturally, there is a value to saving time and increasing convenience for commuters in using eVTOL but the cost-per-mile of a journey, at least at the beginning will be higher than common transportation. As for the specific price point of an eVTOL trip, it seems there is a long way to go before an air taxi ride becomes a practical alternative for the average commuter. As pointed out in the study by Altran "if the choice is between an air taxi or driving to work, the price point of the air taxi needs to converge on the cost of driving a car, which today is about $0.50 a mile for a small sedan.[49] Uber estimates the seat price on its first generation of air taxis at $5.73 per passenger mile but believes the price will eventually drop below $0.50."[50] In the mentioned study, NASA suggests a slightly higher cost. In the near term, a 5-seat piloted eVTOL will cost about US$6.25 per passenger mile. However, in the long run, high operational efficiency, autonomy, and technology improvements will decrease the cost by about 60%, according to a 2018 NASA report.[51]

"The most likely and straightforward route to competitive pricing will be a business model that prioritizes removing costs across the design and supply chains. For example, lowering battery costs, which will be dependent on the evolution of technology, and reducing the cost of production, which will be based on economies of scale from mass production."[52]

---

[49]Ellens Edmonds (2017), "AAA Reveals True Cost of Vehicle Ownership," *AAA*, available at: https://newsroom.aaa.com/2017/08/aaa-reveals-true-cost-vehicle-ownership/?sf61705507=1 (accessed December 9, 2021).

[50]Megan Rose Dickey (2019), "Here's How Much Uber's Flying Taxi Service Will Cost," *TechCrunch*, available at: https://techcrunch.com/2018/05/08/heres-how-much-ubers-flying-taxi-service-will-cost/?guccounter=1 (accessed December 9, 2021).

[51]Executive briefing: Urban air mobility (UAM) market study, Presented to the National Aeronautics and Space Administration — Aeronautics Research Mission Directorate, October 5, 2018, NASA, available at: https://www.nasa.gov/sites/default/files/atoms/files/bah_uam_executive_briefing_181005_tagged.pdf (accessed December 9, 2021).

[52]See the study by Altran (2020), "En-Route to Urban Air Mobility — On The Fast Track to Viable and Safe On-Demand Air Services," available at: https://www.altran.com/

4.1.4 *Social acceptance*

In order for eVTOL, and thus air taxi, to become a reality, the acceptance by the general public is of paramount importance. The first step is the assurance of the technical capabilities of eVTOLs and the robustness of regulatory oversight and the safety of aircraft. Another critical issue for winning over urban residents and city planners is to allay concerns about noise, visual pollution, and privacy. Considering the large number of eVTOLs that could be flying above populated areas at any hour of the day, these issues will need to be addressed if air taxi service providers expect to build a sustainable business.[53]

In order to instill more confidence among potential users of air taxi, regulators must establish robust certification, testing, and regulatory standards so the eVTOL ecosystem members can confidently design, develop, manufacture, and operate the aircraft. Providing the aforementioned guidelines especially concerning safety, this quickly will go a long way to accelerate the time to market. Manufacturers developing eVTOL should use these standards to inform the general public of the safety of the aircraft, as there is going to be a natural suspicion about such an unfamiliar form of travel. Authorities in charge or regulating this new mode of transportation, in setting such standards, will help reduce suspicion and thus instill more confidence among travelers prone to use E-VTOL.

"A recent study of residents of Stuttgart, Germany, found that the level of knowledge about eVTOLs and the underlying technologies was an indicator of a person's perception of safety. The more knowledgeable, the more likely they are to fly in an eVTOL. As the general public becomes more technology-savvy over time, confidence in the safety of eVTOL is expected to increase."[54]

4.1.5 *Mobile networks for low-altitude connectivity*

The development of eVTOLs and its widespread use will also depend of the new 5G technology and thus the fast communication with other

---

as-content/uploads/sites/27/2020/03/en-route-to-urban-air-mobility.pdf (accessed December 9, 2021).

[53] *Ibid.*

[54] Volocopter (2019), Volocopter Launches First Urban Flight in Stuttgart, Germany," press release, available at: https://transportup.com/headlines-breaking-news/volocopter-launches-first-urban-flight-in-stuttgart-germany/ (accessed December 9, 2021).

eVTOL and the control center (reference must be made to urban ATM). The rollout of 5G communications will be important part of the deployment and use of eVTOLs. As near-real-time communications will be essential for keeping city skies safe as the volume of eVTOLs traffic grows, 5G technology will be crucial for situational awareness, and aircraft-to-aircraft, and aircraft-to-ground communication, especially in extreme weather conditions. Just as important, 5G's low latency and high bandwidth will be a must for inflight passenger applications and smart-city transportation systems applications. Air-to-ground communications is a primary focus for 5G as indicated by the 3rd Generation Partnership Project (3GPP)[55] efforts to change the specifications for aircraft. Applications include sharing weather and traffic data at an altitude between aircraft and ground control, providing more accurate forecasts of cloud formation and turbulence, real-time monitoring of aircraft for preventive maintenance, and passenger Wi-Fi and entertainment services. The study by Altran also specify that: "Another possible solution is service from constellations of small satellites that will use unlicensed spectrum for 5G communication service, including air-to-ground service. Small satellites will be part of the broader 5G umbrella and will be able to track aircraft all over the globe, including in remote areas not well covered by terrestrial antennas. However, it is not clear if small satellites can overcome the challenges of traditional satellites regarding high-latency and low speed. Presently, direct air-to-ground communication is superior to satellite service due to its lower latency and per-bit cost compared to satellites, which means air-to-ground has the potential to enable a much larger set of applications." While terrestrial applications are the focus of early 5G rollouts, several telecommunications companies are working to address the aviation 5G market to ensure secure communication and data exchange. One is AT&T, which recently announced a partnership with

---

[55]The 3GPP unites [Seven] telecommunications standard development organizations (ARIB, ATIS, CCSA, ETSI, TSDSI, TTA, TTC), known as "Organizational Partners" and provides their members with a stable environment to produce the Reports and Specifications that define 3GPP technologies. The project covers cellular telecommunications technologies, including radio access, core network and service capabilities, which provide a complete system description for mobile telecommunications. The 3GPP specifications also provide hooks for non-radio access to the core network, and for interworking with non-3GPP networks, available at: https://www.3gpp.org/about-3gpp (accessed December 9, 2021).

Uber. The relationship includes AT&T assessing and enabling LTE and 5G connectivity for low-altitude autonomous cargo drones and piloted aircraft.[56]

A concrete example

Volocopter recently announced plans for a new 5G-enabled eVTOL called the VoloCity, an urban air taxi that will carry two people a distance of 35 km at a speed of 110 km/h. The 5G capability will allow the aircraft to "see" around corners, avoid obstacles, and download flight data quickly to enhance performance and safety.[57] Volocopter has reportedly demonstrated these capabilities at trials in Dubai and Singapore. And in Benidorm, Spain, a consortium of Vodafone, the Advanced Center for Aerospace Technologies and the Polytechnic University of Valencia recently made history by testing the first drone controlled by 5G in an urban area beyond the pilot's line of sight.[58]

Source: Altran (2020), "En-Route to Urban Air Mobility — On The Fast Track to Viable and Safe On-Demand Air Services," available at: https://www.altran.com/as-content/uploads/sites/27/2020/03/en-route-to-urban-air-mobility.pdf (accessed December 9, 2021).

4.2 *Which direction will UAM take?*

It seems reasonable to affirm that UAM will develop in three different directions: (i) air taxi, (ii) airport shuttles, and (iii) interregional services. Each of these directions will have its own operational requirements. It is

---

[56] Corinne Reichert (2019), "Uber and AT&T Partner on 5G Air Taxis," *C/Net*, available at: https://www.cnet.com/news/at-t-and-uber-partner-on-5g-air-taxis/ (accessed December 9, 2021).

[57] Douglas Bloom (2019), "This Air Taxi Uses 5G to 'See' Around Corners," *World Economic Forum*, available at: https://www.weforum.org/agenda/2019/11/multicopter-helicopter-airtaxi-5g-technology-pioneers/ (accessed December 9, 2021).

[58] Cool Radio (2020), "Benidorm Hosts the World's First 5G Urban Drone Flight," available at: https://coolradiospain.com/news/benidorm-hosts-the-world-s-first-5g-urban-drone-flight-346 (accessed December 9, 2021).

also evident that manufacturers will adopt different technical solutions depending on the specific use of VTOL. For longer distances (interregional services) the configuration of the aircraft will be substantially different from those used as air taxis, due to the fact that interregional services likely will be used by more commuters.

4.2.1 *Air taxis* (*inner-city point-to-point services*)

On-demand point-to-point non-stop service from one destination to another, like conventional ground ride-hailing services, will be the first application of VTOL, and this service will be operated between any available landing pads within a defined area (in megacity). Landing pads would be spread around the city to service key points of interest, with charging facilities ideally in place at each station.

To carry one or two passengers and their light hand luggage (up to 20 kg in total) over distances of between 15 and 50 kilometers, the aircraft technology would have to be able to cope with journeys of between 35 and 70 kilometers to ensure a safety margin of roughly 20 kilometers on all flights.

Service providers would allow air taxi rides to be booked on demand. Predictive traffic management systems would enable aircraft to be dispatched based on passenger demand patterns and forecast demand at different landing pads.[59]

4.2.2 *Airport shuttles* (*suburban to urban services*)

The second application will be to serve urban areas with suburban areas, thus offering fastest transportation options between the city and airport(s). UAM landing sites should be strategically located very close to terminals and gates.

Airport shuttles would offer scheduled (rather than on-demand) flights between various landing pads and the airport. The aircraft technology would need roughly the same range as for air taxis, but would be

---

[59] In this sense: Roland Berges (2018), Urban Air Mobility — The Rise of a New Mode of Transportation," available at: https://www.rolandberger.com/en/Publications/Passenger-drones-ready-for-take-off.html (accessed December 9, 2021).

upsized to carry between two and four passengers and between 50 and 80 kg of luggage.

In this case, charging facilities would be concentrated primarily at the airport, but with some at the other landing pads as a function of distance and aircraft travel range. Passengers could book seats for fixed routes on a scheduled flight, completely eliminating the need for demand forecasts and making aircraft location and demand at each station entirely predictable.[60]

4.2.3 *Interregional services (intercity flights)*

This third application, that is intercity flights or interregional services, will be implemented to connect one city with another close by, which are too close even for regional airlines. In this case, UAM connection services between cities will render this mode of traveling more convenient for commuters and business travelers. Intercity flights would likewise be based on scheduled services. The technology would have to be able to carry 2–4 passengers and 20–40 kg of hand luggage over distances of between 50 and 250 kilometers, plus a safety margin of an extra 50 kilometers. Charging facilities would be installed at each landing pad, which would ideally facilitate direct access to key points of interest in the cities served.

As with airport shuttle and regular aviation services, flights at set times and on fixed routes could be booked in advance. Again, operational scheduling requirements would be entirely predictable.[61]

4.3 *New infrastructures needed: Vertiport are on the horizon*

VTOLs need specific and dedicated infrastructures in order to express their full potential. These new vehicles are designed to ease traffic in urban areas and thus spots have to be identified to allow customers to access the service. Likely the so-called "vertiports" will take advantage of the existing infrastructure, such as helipads, roof of public buildings in selected neuralgic node in the city.

---

[60] *Ibid.*
[61] *Ibid.*

Adapting existing infrastructures or establishing new "vertiports" is essential to operate VTOLs. Charging infrastructures and maintenance facilities must all be set up as key enablers for successful operational business models. "Failure to do so will create bottlenecks that could nip the nascent UAM market in the bud and stunt its growth. Using both ground-based facilities and rooftops for take-off and landing might appear the obvious way to go for urban aviation. However, urban aircraft need a safe landing zone that is unobstructed by buildings and/or trees, which could make this strategy hard to implement in densely populated areas."[62]

Rooftops might represent the best choice to establish "vertiports" however luxury hotels and high-end office buildings are likely to charge exorbitant fees, assuming they are willing to let passenger drones use their helipads at all, as they naturally want to avoid upsetting the wealthy guests who populate penthouse suites and the top executives who work from the upper floors of their office blocks.

On the safety front, a robust 5G cellular network will be imperative to enable communication among eVTOL aircraft, between eVTOLs and other flying objects, and between eVTOLs and control centers. Especially for on-demand services, predictive ATM will be key to ensure smooth and efficient operation of the entire eVTOL system. The control center will also take care of both route management and contingency management.[63]

4.4 *Airbus, Boeing, and other manufactures developing eVTOL*

COVID-19 has forced the industry to accelerate toward a greener aviation. Not only the major manufacturers are now committed to shaping a sustainable aviation by reducing emissions with the adoption of alternative fuels, hydrogen, and the introduction of hybrid aircraft but also contributing in making the UAM a reality. This because not only the nascent UAM is predicted to boom in the near future but also because it has the potential to become a multibillions dollars business, and the existing

---

[62]In this sense: Roland Berges (2018), Urban Air Mobility — The Rise of a New Mode of Transportation," available at: https://www.rolandberger.com/en/Publications/Passenger-drones-ready-for-take-off.html (accessed December 9, 2021).
[63]*Ibid.*

manufactures and newcomers are all interested in entering and gaining a share of this promising new market.

According to a paper prepared by Boeing,[64] the UAM market will be worth tens of billions of dollars across the value chain. The promise of UAM has led to numerous industry efforts; today, there are over 100 vehicles in various stages of development globally.[65] In addition to Original Equipment Manufacturers (OEMs), other parts of the UAM value chain will include passenger operations, unmanned aircraft systems (UAS) traffic management, operations and maintenance, infrastructure, insurance and financing. While the players and structure of the market continue to evolve, it will likely include a range of solutions operated by various operators, unlocked by business models that include ride-sharing. This growth will be facilitated by key enablers, including airspace integration, infrastructure expansion, market acceptance, seamless integration into connected mobility systems and a wide range of other ecosystem elements — many of which are yet to be imagined.

Airbus, Boeing, and other players are now focusing on developing their own solutions for UAM vehicles which will soon appear on our skies as soon as the regulatory authorities will approve their use.

4.4.1 *Boeing*

Boeing is an aviation pioneer and industry leader paying particular attention to innovation. Boeing is focusing on emerging technologies, UAS operations, and the safe introduction of these vehicles into the airspace — while preserving the flying public's confidence in air travel. With increasing urbanization and a growing global population the necessity for new, sustainable, and accessible modes of transportation especially in high density populated areas emerges. UAM presents an opportunity to provide seamless, safe, and rapid transportation to mitigate the existing and future challenges faced by these areas. Boeing NeXt is leading the safe and responsible introduction of next-generation air vehicles not only for urban areas but also for regional use.

---

[64]See: Boeing Next, "Flight Path for the Future of Mobility," available at: http://www. boeing.com/NeXt/common/docs/Boeing_Future_of_Mobility_White%20Paper.pdf (accessed December 9, 2021).

[65]ICAO is monitoring some of these projects, a short list is available at: https://www.icao. int/environmental-protection/Pages/electric-aircraft.aspx (accessed December 9, 2021).

Boeing NeXt is developing drones for the delivery of goods and VTOLs for the transportation of passengers to be used as air taxi. As for the delivery of goods Boeing has successfully completed the first outdoor flight tests of the cargo air vehicle (CAV). "In a safe and controlled environment, the electric vertical takeoff and landing (eVTOL) unmanned aerial vehicle (UAV) successfully took off, hovered, transitioned to forward flight and then landed safely. Powered by an electric propulsion system, the CAV is designed to carry a payload up to 500 pounds (227 kilograms). This opens up new possibilities for safely and efficiently transporting goods in a variety of industries."[66]

Concerning passengers transportation Boeing NeXt, which leads the company's UAM efforts, worked with Boeing subsidiary Aurora Flight Sciences to design and develop the electric vertical takeoff and landing (eVTOL) aircraft. In this case Boeing has tested, on January 2019, its autonomous passenger air vehicle (PAV) prototype. "Future flights will test forward, wing-borne flight, as well as the transition phase between vertical and forward-flight modes. This transition phase is typically the most significant engineering challenge for any high-speed VTOL aircraft. Boeing NeXt works with regulatory agencies and industry partners to lead the responsible introduction of a new mobility ecosystem and ensure a future where autonomous and piloted air vehicles safely co-exist."[67]

4.4.2 *Porsche and Boeing to partner on premium UAM market*

In October 2019, Porsche and Boeing signed a Memorandum of Understanding to explore the premium UAM market and the extension of urban traffic into airspace. With this partnership, both companies will leverage their unique market strengths and insights to study the future of premium personal UAM vehicles. Boeing, Porsche, and Boeing subsidiary Aurora Flight Sciences are also developing a concept for a fully electric vertical takeoff and landing vehicle. Engineers from both companies, as well as Porsche subsidiaries Porsche Engineering Services GmbH, and Studio F.A. Porsche, will implement and test a prototype.

---

[66]See: "Cargo Air Vehicle Completes First Outdoor Flight," available at: https://www.boeing.com/features/2019/05/cav-first-flight-05-19.page (accessed December 9, 2021).

[67]See: "Boeing Autonomous Passenger Air Vehicle Completes First Flight," available at: https://www.boeing.com/features/2019/01/pav-first-flight-01-19.page (accessed December 9, 2021).

A 2018 study by Porsche Consulting forecasts that the UAM market will pick up speed after 2025. The study also indicates that UAM solutions will transport passengers more quickly and efficiently than current conventional means of terrestrial transport, at a lower cost and with greater flexibility.[68]

4.4.3 *Aston Martin: Innovation in personal air mobility*

In parallel to the traditional large aircraft manufacturers also other players, both new comers and traditional luxury car makers, are entering this promising market of VTOL. One of these is Aston Martin.

The "Volante" Vision is a concept vehicle exploring luxury VTOL fixed-wing aircraft spearheaded by Aston Martin. "The vehicle will employ four tilting propellers up front in a double stack arrangement and two large vertical stacked propellers aft of the passenger cabin for vertical lift. The Volante has fixed wings and twin rudders for cruise mode. The motors will be hybrid-electric with emphasis on a low carbon footprint capable of cruising speeds of 460 km/h. The Volante Vision will be autonomously flown with stepped levels of pilot interaction depending on experience. It is designed to for three passengers (one forward and two rear) and the interior will have luxury trappings."[69] The Volante Vision is designed for luxury personal air or urban mobility and intercity travel.

Aston Martin has developed partnerships with Cranfield University, Cranfield Aerospace Solutions, and the Rolls-Royce company.

4.4.4 *Embraer Dreammaker*

EmbraerX, a subsidiary of the Embraer Group, another important leading aircraft manufacturer embarked in developing its eVTOL aircraft for UAM. This new aircraft includes: A human-centered design, optimal safety, high reliability, a lower noise footprint to be community friendly, simplicity in design, advanced technology, 100% electric, passenger

---

[68] See: "Porsche and Boeing to Partner on Premium Urban Air Mobility Market," available at: https://boeing.mediaroom.com/2019-10-10-Porsche-and-Boeing-to-Partner-on-Premium-Urban-Air-Mobility-Market#assets_20295_130523-117:20645 (accessed May 9, 2021).

[69] See: Electric-VTOL news, "Aston Martin Volante Vision," available at: https://www.astonmartin.com/en-gb/models/special-projects/the-aston-martin-volante-vision-concept-2019 (accessed December 9, 2021).

comfort and user experience, accessibility for anyone, low operating costs, autonomous flight, and no emissions.

When Uber signed a partnership in 2017 with EmbraerX to make an aircraft for the Uber Elevate Network, a few details were revealed: The air-taxi service that EmbraerX is working on with Uber is likely to launch in 2023. The aircraft will be an eVTOL aircraft, weight about 1 ton, with 1 pilot, and 4 passengers and baggage, be wheelchair friendly and fly at an altitude of 800–1,000 meters (2,600–3,300 feet). The batteries can be changed out in as little as 5 minutes between flights.

EmbraerX launched their white paper Flight Plan 2030[70] in May, at the Uber Elevate Summit 2019 (Washington, DC., USA). The EmbraerX Flight Plan 2030 white paper addresses one of the most critical challenges of the UAM industry: The design and management of the low-altitude urban airspace.

4.4.5 *Airbus is testing its CityAirbus*

The CityAirbus was presented on March 11, 2019 at the City of Ingolstadt to members of the German government and the public.[71] Citizens had the opportunity to ask Airbus experts questions about the vehicle and the concept of UAM. Airbus and Ingolstadt believe that a dialogue between manufacturer, authorities, and the public is a prerequisite for the successful introduction of UAM in the infrastructure of cities. Airbus and Ingolstadt are partners in the framework of the EU's EIP-SCC initiative for smart cities.[72]

---

[70] See: Harris Atech (2019), White Paper titled "Flight Plan 2030 — An Air Traffic Management Concept For Urban Air Mobility," *EmbraerX*, available at: https://daflwcl3bnxyt.cloudfront.net/m/f58fb8ea648aeb9/original/EmbraerX-White-Paper-Flight-Plan2030.pdf (accessed December 9, 2021).

[71] CityAirbus, available at: https://www.airbus.com/innovation/zero-emission/electric-flight.html#smallmediagallery-par-smallmediagallery-3 (accessed December 9, 2021).

[72] The European innovation partnership on smart cities and communities (EIP-SCC) is an initiative supported by the European Commission that brings together cities, industry, and small businesses. A smart city is a place where traditional networks and services are made more efficient with the use of digital and telecommunication technologies for the benefit of its inhabitants and business. A smart city goes beyond the use of information and communication technologies (ICTs) for better resource use and less emissions. It means smarter urban transport networks. For more information visit: https://ec.europa.eu/info/

CityAirbus marks the second full-scale eVTOL prototype from the company, after Airbus Vahana.[73] With demonstrated flight tests in both piloted and autonomous regimes, Airbus promises to be adaptable to current and future market demands in aerial mobility. If all goes well, the current prototype will continue flight testing for the remainder of the year in order to demonstrate the ability to perform safe operations without the need for an operator.

4.5 *The future of air mobility in Europe: Brief introduction*

Starting in May 2018, several European cities have been joining the UAM initiative that is part of the European Innovation Partnership in Smart Cities and Communities (EIP-SCC).[74] This partnership, which is supported by the European Commission, brings together cities and regions, citizens, industries, SMEs, investors, researchers and other smart city actors.

Under the umbrella of the UAM initiative, the setup of a number of demonstrator projects in cities across Europe will be studied and evaluated in the coming months (the latest event was organized on September 2–3, 2020),[75] which will bring urban mobility into the third dimension in

---

eu-regional-and-urban-development/topics/cities-and-urban-development/city-initiatives/smart-cities_en (accessed December 9, 2021).

[73]Vahana is a project worked on by the A^3 technological development arm of Airbus which is headquartered in Silicon Valley, CA. Built as a (now-completed) eVTOL technology demonstrator and proof-of-concept for future aircraft like the CityAirbus, Vahana uses variable-angle rotors that provide thrust vertically for takeoff and landing and swivel forward to facilitate accelerated conventional flight. https://www.airbus.com/innovation/zero-emission/electric-flight.html#smallmediagallery-par-smallmediagallery-2 (accessed December 9, 2021).

[74]Reference must be made to the European Commission and its initiative for smart cities — "Cities Using Technological Solutions to Improve the Management and Efficiency of the Urban Environment," available at: https://ec.europa.eu/info/eu-regional-and-urban-development/topics/cities-and-urban-development/city-initiatives/smart-cities_en (accessed December 9, 2021).

[75]EIP-SCC Marketplace — "General Assembly 2020, September 2–3, 2020 URBIS Fair, Brno, Czech Republic." This year's General Assembly will feature high-level speakers putting a spotlight on the challenges and opportunities cities are facing following the COVID-19 experience, discussing European efforts to deliver a sustainable urban transition, and continuing a dialogue on the upscaling and replication of Smart City solutions.

Europe. This work is aligned with ongoing and future SESAR Joint Undertaking[76] (SESAR JU) funded studies, including demonstrations, on

---

Taking into account the above and reinforced by the COVID-19 crisis, the General Assembly brings a unique opportunity to intensify the exchange of experiences and knowledge with CEE city administrations and smart city stakeholders and to engage CEE city administrations, companies and academia much better in the EIP-SCC Marketplace's community and therefore in the European Smart Cities approach. More specifically, the aims of this year's General Assembly are: (i) Demonstrate the commitment of the European Commission on a high level to the promotion of climate-neutral and smart cities and a smart city model based on European values in CEE, e.g. through the mentioned strategies such as the Green Deal, the Recovery plans, Horizon Europe, etc.; (ii) Discuss the future of the EIP-SCC Marketplace and how it will function as a hub for and synergizing with other relevant EU initiatives such as the European Energy Award, Living-in.eu, CIVITAS, Covenant of Mayors, the Horizon Europe Mission on Climate-Neutral and Smart Cities; (iii) Share best practices and good examples from the wider EIP-SCC Marketplace/SCIS context, including the Lighthouse Projects (e.g. RUGGEDISED, SPARCS, and POCITYF), adjacent initiatives such as Living-in.eu, CIVITAS, Covenant of Mayors, especially those with relevance to CEE municipalities (CEE fellow cities will be specifically engaged); (iv) Initiate a dialogue on how successful innovations and demonstrations can be adjusted to CEE contexts, and, *vice versa*, which best practices and excellent smart city innovations from CEE deserve more attention (using the General Assembly and the EIP-SCC Marketplace, its Action Clusters and Initiatives as a multiplier); (v) Enhancing the visibility of the EIP-SCC Marketplace and the Smart Cities Information System (SCIS) in CEE, informing a discussion on CEE-related barriers, explore how to develop approaches to addressing the latter, and on how to enable capacity building; (vi) Matchmaking geared toward specific needs of CEE city administrations and informing about financial and funding instruments; (vii) Promote synergies between the Lighthouse Projects' Board of Coordinators and the EIP-SCC Marketplace's Action Clusters and Initiatives. More info available at: https://www.2zeroemission.eu/mediaroom/sustainable-and-smart-mobility-strategy-european-transport-on-track-for-the-future/ (accessed December 9, 2021).

[76]As the technological pillar of Europe's ambitious Single European Sky (SES) initiative, SESAR is the mechanism which coordinates and concentrates all EU research and development (R&D) activities in ATM, pooling together a wealth experts to develop the new generation of ATM. Today, SESAR unites around 3,000 experts in Europe and beyond. In 2007, the SESAR Joint Undertaking was set up in order to manage this large scale and truly international public–private partnership. ATM is an essential part of European air transport and aviation, connecting cities and people citizens as well as boosting jobs and growth. While unseen and unnoticed by passengers, ATM plays several specific and important roles: (i) Acts as a guardian of safety; (ii) Connects European cities and Europe with the rest of the world; (iii) Addresses climate change by enabling green and efficient routes; (iv) Maximizes current infrastructure while delivering advanced information services; (v) Acts

drone traffic management in Europe moving one step closer toward the European Commission's U-space vision[77] for ensuring safe and secure access to airspace for drones. With demonstrable benefits to citizens and their approval, developing a market for drones and drone services will create jobs and growth in Europe. Particularly in urban areas, civil drones could be a way to address mobility needs such as emergency needs and traffic congestion; the latter currently costs more than €100 billion a year in the EU alone.[78]

There is no doubt that UAM in Europe, and worldwide, has a bright future; however, new dedicated regulations must be implemented to assure the smooth development of this mode of transportation, not only for goods but also especially for passengers and their safety. The next decade will be critical to the growth and acceptance of the UAM industry. During this period, standards for safety, security, and performance will be defined. Communication and data exchange standards will be created, and frameworks for airspace design and management will be decided. Technological advancements will push eVTOLs closer to full autonomy. The decisions made in the next decade will determine how UAM will be implemented in different cities and countries.[79] In the main while aviation industry is already undergoing a significant change due to COVID-19,

---

as a catalyst for Europe's competitiveness and innovative capacity. However, Europe's ATM system is based on aging technology and procedures and needs updating particularly in light of the expected traffic growth between now and 2035. This is where SESAR comes in. As one of the most innovative infrastructure projects ever launched by the European Union, SESAR's role is to define, develop and deploy what is needed to increase ATM performance and build Europe's intelligent air transport system. For more information visit: https://www.sesarju.eu/discover-sesar (accessed December 9, 2021).

[77] U-space is a set of new services relying on a high level of digitalization and automation of functions and specific procedures designed to support safe, efficient, and secure access to airspace for large numbers of drones. As such, U-space is an enabling framework designed to facilitate any kind of routine mission, in all classes of airspace and all types of environment — even the most congested — while addressing an appropriate interface with manned aviation and air traffic control. More information available at: https://www. sesarju.eu/U-space (accessed December 9, 2021).

[78] In this sense see: European Commission, "Commission Welcomes European Cities Joining the Urban Air Mobility Initiative," available at: https://transport.ec.europa.eu/transport-themes/mobility-strategy_en (accessed December 9, 2021).

[79] Harris Atech (2019), White Paper titled "Flight Plan 2030 — An Air Traffic Management Concept For Urban Air Mobility," *EmbraerX*, available at: https://daflwcl3bnxyt.

traditional airliners are losing their positions in favor of a niche segment of aviation, that is, "business aviation" which during the pandemic resisted and performed very well notwithstanding higher costs for travelers. Moreover, it seems this segment is destined to further accelerate as it will be exposed in Chapter 4.

cloudfront.net/m/f58fb8ea648aeb9/original/EmbraerX-White-Paper-Flight-Plan2030.pdf (accessed May 9, 2021).

Chapter 4

Business Aviation, and Its "Declinations" Have Responded with a Positive Feat to the Global Crisis

Cristiano Rizzi and Paolo Rizzi

COVID-19 brought all commercial airlines to their knees, but at the same time saw a niche of private airlines report a 400% increase in requests and bookings.[1] The massive explosion in this niche market can be attributed to travel restrictions and social distancing recommended by governments all around the world and to the recommendations of the World Health Organization (WHO).

The global pandemic has changed the way the world functions and deeply influenced the habits of people who usually take the plane for work and other activities.

Flying privately was chosen by many well-off travelers who hoped to minimize their public exposure and in order to find alternatives to suspended flights. This option was also chosen by those essentially traveling to or from areas of travel restrictions and flight suspensions, where private jets were the only way out. This led to the spike in urgent demands pouring in with the private jet operators. A lot of companies that were looking

---

[1] In this sense see: "Significant Growth in Business Aviation Amid COVID-19 Outbreak," April 24, 2020, available at: https://www.aviationpros.com/aircraft/maintenance-providers/mro/press-release/21135460/jet-maintenance-solutions-jet-ms-significant-growth-in-business-aviation-amid-covid19-outbreak (accessed December 9, 2021).

to pull their employees out of the infected regions also shifted to flying private.[2]

1. *Business Aviation*: Definition and Its Growing Importance

Business aviation is not precisely defined in any existing regulation, however International Civil Aviation Organization (ICAO) classifies "business aviation" under the "non-scheduled air services." This particular segment is somewhere between commercial air transport and general aviation (see Chapter 1, Section 3).

International Business Aviation Council (IBAC)[3] defines business aviation "as the sector of aviation which concerns the operation or use of aircraft by companies for the carriage of passengers or goods as an aid to the conduct of their business, flown for purposes generally considered not for public hire and piloted by individuals having, at the minimum, a valid commercial pilot license with an instrument rating."[4] However, this definition does not cover every aspect, and IBAC suggested to further specify sub-divisions of the said definition as reported in the following box:

Sub-division 1 Business Aviation — Commercial

The commercial operation or use of aircraft by companies for the carriage of passenger or goods as an aid to the conduct of their business and the availability of the aircraft for whole aircraft charter, flown by a professional pilot(s) employed to fly the aircraft.

---

[2] In this sense see: Ayushee Chaudhary, "Post COVID-19 World Likely to Witness a Rise in Flying Private," available at: http://www.sps-aviation.com/story/?id=2772&h=Post-COVID-19-world-likely-to-witness-a-rise-in-flying-private (accessed December 9, 2021).
[3] IBAC co-located at the ICAO headquarters in Montreal, Canada, provides expert advocacy and intelligence on behalf of the global business aviation community participating in various ICAO bodies whose work affects business aviation. For more information see: https://ibac.org/about-ibac.
[4] Definition of business aviation by IBAC, available at: https://ibac.org/about-ibac/resources-and-links/ibac-definitions-of-business-aviation (accessed December 9, 2021).

> *Sub-Division 2 Business Aviation — Corporate*
>
> *The non-commercial operation or use of aircraft by a company for the carriage of passengers or goods as an aid to the conduct of company business, flown by a professional pilot(s) employed to fly the aircraft.*
>
> *Sub-Division 3 Business Aviation — Owner Operated*
>
> *The non-commercial operation or use of aircraft by an individual for the carriage of passengers or goods as an aid to the conduct of his/ her business.*
>
> *Sub-Division 4 Business Aviation — Fractional Ownership*
>
> *The operation or use of aircraft operated by an entity for a group of owners who jointly hold minimum shares of aircraft operated by the entity. Fractional Ownership operations are normally non-commercial; however, the operation of the aircraft may be undertaken as a commercial operation in accordance with the AOC held by the entity.*

It is noteworthy that IBAC does not actively promote these sub-divisions of the definition of "business aviation," but they may be made available to regulatory authorities and others for specific requirements, providing that the complete definition of business aviation is also made available.[5]

The growing importance of business aviation and private air travels in general, were put in evidence by the crisis caused by COVID-19. It is likely that this segment will witness a potential long-term growth and fetch new customers. This is why it is worth introducing this theme and to give an insight of this particular segment explaining the sub-division of the aircraft used to accommodate the different needs of users.

The business aviation market is growing, while the USA still accounts for nearly two-third, European and Middle Eastern countries, China, South America, Russia, and India have recorded double-digit growth rates

---

[5] In this sense, see the document available at: https://www.ebaa.org/app/uploads/2018/01/About-business-aviation-.pdf (accessed December 9, 2021).

over the past 10 years and although the pandemic has slowed down this pace the resilience of this market is evident.

1.1 *Rise in private aviation's demand during the COVID-19 crisis*

The travel industry and air transportation in particular has changed forever because of the global COVID-19 pandemic. As noted, commercial airlines have grounded fleets, cut routes, and reduced staff due to a historic drop in demand. Booking cancellations and grounded aircraft have been the norm for months and to return to the numbers seen before the pandemic it will be necessary to wait for years; however, those passengers in need to fly are opting for private air transportation. Private aviation's demand indeed witnessed a surge during COVID-19 crisis and some of the reasons are summarized as below:

- The biggest plus point of flying private is literally the "privacy" that it offers, allowing the passenger to be sure of whom thcy arc flying with and avoid unnecessary contact.
- Even with resumed travel, company executives will not yet prefer to stay over in a place unless it is absolutely necessary. In such a scenario, flying private is the right option to optimally balance the time of visit and return from a place on one's own requirement.
- Even though commercial airlines are considering on how to make their flights more and more safe for public, that has emerged from this health crisis, the airlines and the passengers are very well aware of the potential of coronavirus spread in a confined space such as an airplane holding a large number of passengers.
- Flying private also puts the crew to less exposure and reduced contact.
- Going by the previous scenarios, the flexibility and efficiency of private air travel is likely to prove decisive for companies.
- Most of the private flights operate out of small, private aviation terminals, not mass transport hubs. Hence, further reducing the risk for passengers from coming in contact with multiple surfaces across security checks and boarding lines. The contact is reduced to mostly being by yourself once the aircraft is boarded. The passenger only comes in contact with the security agents and the crew, and some airport personnel.

- With such reduced social contact possibility and the flexibility as well as convenience, private jets can be marketed as safer alternatives and hence witness a rise in demand.
- The first-time customers can also be converted to long-term ones.
- With an influx in more passengers choosing to fly private and an addition of new customers, the private jets might come down on the costs a little, hence attracting more customers.
- The amount of flights offered commercially are most certain to see a dip in demand as the travel preference for leisure and other non-essential travel will be very low. Business travel is expected to be among the first to recover.[6]

Private aviation's demand implies the use of different categories of aircraft according to the needs of the travelers. The world of business aviation is extremely variegated and the aircraft used range from small aircraft to normal size commercial aircraft adapted by manufactures to this segment. In the following section, a brief description of the categories of aircraft which define this segment of the market is presented.

1.2 *Business aviation industry: Brief introduction and categories of aircraft*

The business aviation industry is a unique example in the entire panorama of air transport because not only it represents a growing niche market but is also seen as a valid alternative for corporations, business people, and individuals to enhance business productivity. This particular way of air travel is usually used by the wealthy to move from one place to another saving time and flying in a more safe, private, and "tailored" manner; however, with the introduction of the so called "personal jet" which is a very light jet (VLJ, i.e. the smallest private jet category) now it is not necessary to be a multimillionaire to fly in this modality.

Private-business aviation has already reported a massive number of new clients who have never flown private before. Therefore, this segment is destined to become increasingly popular for all the reasons listed in the

---

[6]In this sense: SP's aviation (2020), "Post COVID-19 World Likely to Witness a Rise in Flying Private," Issue 5–6, available at: http://www.sps-aviation.com/story/?id=2772&h= Post-COVID-19-world-likely-to-witness-a-rise-in-flying-private (accessed December 9, 2021).

previous section. No doubt private-business aviation is set to continue its growth and support post-crisis recovery.

On the market there are dozens of models available today. It is important to distinguish the different categories which take into consideration weight, range, and cabin space, in order to choose the best option according to travelers' needs.

The following categorization must be considered as a reference only, in fact manufacturers are developing new models which might differ in terms of size, performances, and range; thus, producers might further differentiate these categories.

1.2.1 *Very lights jets*

In general terms, a business jet refers to an aircraft that is specifically designed for private air travel for a small group of passengers.

VLJ is the smallest in private jet category. These aircraft typically seat 4–5 people. They are part of a new and emerging segment of the market. The VLJ offers agility to access small airports with shorter runways. It must be noted that in the US alone, it opens up over 5,000 airports for business travel. What is more, they would not overburden the operational expenditures, yet still deliver speed and travel flexibility. VLJs are typically approved for single-pilot operation. A second pilot can be confirmed upon request. The typical range is about 1,000 miles with a capability of 4–6 passengers in a limited in-cabin amenities and speeds up to 480 miles per hours.[7]

An example of VLJ which can be classified into the new category of "personal jet" is the Honda-Jet[8] with a capacity of 7–8-seat. This aircraft has a composite fuselage and an aluminum wing, and is powered by two

---

[7]The basic of private jet categories, available at: https://www.jetcraft.com/jetstream/ 2015/06/basics-private-jet-categories-2/ (accessed December 9, 2021).

[8]The Honda HA-420 HondaJet is a light business jet produced by the Honda Aircraft Company of Greensboro, North Carolina, United States. Original concepts of the aircraft started in 1997 and were completed in 1999. It took its maiden flight on December 3, 2003, received its FAA type certificate in December 2015, and was first delivered that same month. By March 2020, 150 jets had been delivered. https://en.wikipedia.org/wiki/Honda_ HA-420_HondaJet (accessed December 9, 2021).

GE Honda HF120 turbofans unusually mounted on pylons above the wing. It can reach a 420 knot (780 km/h) speed, and has a 1,400 nautical mile (2,600 kilometer) range.

1.2.1.1 Personal jet: A new dimension of private-business aviation

A completely new category in the private-business aviation, or a new dimension of it, is represented by the so-called "personal jet," perfectly interpreted by small manufacturers who try to meet the needs of new travelers and fill a gap left by the commercial airlines.

"Personal jet" can be identified as a new category of private and business aviation since the introduction of the Vision Jet[9] produced by Cirrus Aircraft,[10] because of its unique characteristics: One of the features of this new personal jet is the fact that it flies with one engine only, and it is small and simple enough to be flown by one pilot, and it is cheaper to operate than larger jets. Direct operating costs result to be under US$1,000 an hour, including fuel and maintenance costs. The single-engine entry-level aircraft is a jack-of-all-trades. With these characteristics and with a cost of around €2 million (depending on the "optionals") this aircraft is reshaping the market of VLJs, and will allow more people and travelers flying privately.

Private-business aviation has evolved with the entry of new types of aircraft and the so-called "personal jet" as interpreted by the Cirrus' family with its vision jet[11] represents the aerial equivalent of a luxury

---

[9]Vision Jet is a new VLJ developed by Cirrus. The test flying program resulted in the US Federal Aviation Administration (FAA) awarding a type certificate on October 28, 2016. Deliveries started on December 19, 2016 and by July 2020, 200 jets had been delivered.

[10]The Cirrus Design Corporation, doing business as Cirrus Aircraft (and previously branded as Cirrus Design), is an aircraft manufacturer that was founded in 1984 by Alan and Dale Klapmeier to produce the VK-30 kit aircraft. The company is owned by a subsidiary of the Chinese government-owned AVIC, and is headquartered in Duluth, Minnesota, United States. See: https://en.wikipedia.org/wiki/Cirrus_Aircraft (accessed December 9, 2021).

[11]The Vision Jet produced by Cirrus Aircraft, is one of the newest personal private jets on the market, requiring only one pilot to fly with maximum seating for seven. For further information visit: https://www.cirrusaircraft.com/aircraft/vision-jet/ (accessed December 9, 2021).

SUV which can be used to reach multiple remote destinations in a single day and be home before the end of the business day. Because of its characteristics and the relatively low cost this aircraft has attracted the interest of China which has started to shape its market for private air traveling.

1.2.1.2   China buys Cirrus aircraft: First move to advance GA and private-business aviation in China

It is worth stressing in this short section that China Aviation Industry General Aircraft (CAIGA),[12] a subsidiary of Aviation Industry Corporation of China (AVIC),[13] in June 2011 completed its acquisition of the US manufacturer Cirrus Aircraft. Sellers included private-equity firm Arcapita, which owned 60% of Cirrus, and minority shareholders (including former Cirrus Chairman and Co-founder Alan Klapmeier). The deal was concluded in summer 2011 and the buyer acquired 100% of the light aircraft manufacturer for an estimated US$210 million — minus Cirrus's outstanding debts, but US concerns about the technology transfer that stretched out the consummation of the agreement. The CAIGA officials while signing the agreement ensured that the Cirrus production plant stayed in the US and not moved to China.[14]

---

[12]CAIGA is a Chinese aircraft manufacturer headquartered in Zhuhai, Guangdong, China. CAIGA was established as a subsidiary company of the state-owned AVIC in July 2009 and it has 10 billion RMB registered capital and over 43 billion RMB of total assets. https://www.epicos.com/company/13408/china-aviation-industry-general-aircraft-co-ltd (accessed December 9, 2021).

[13]AVIC is a Chinese state-owned aerospace and defense conglomerate, it is ranked 151st in the Fortune Global 500 list as in 2019, and it has over 100 subsidiaries, 23 listed companies, and more than 450,000 employees across the globe. AVIC commits itself to commercial transportation industry, cooperating with the global partners and actively participating in the development of international programs. AVIC is a Tier I supplier of ARJ-21 and C919 and produces parts and components for aircraft manufacturers worldwide. The regional turboprop MA60 series, Y12s, and the AC series helicopters are exported. AVIC provides various services including aircraft leasing, general aviation, transportation, planning and construction. https://www.avic.com/en/aboutus/overview/index.shtml (accessed December 9, 2021).

[14]In this sense see article by Chad Trautvetter, July 27, 2011, available at: https://www.ainonline.com/aviation-news/aviation-international-news/2011-07-27/chinese-aviation-conglomerate-acquires-cirrus-aircraft (accessed December 9, 2021).

This acquisition clearly shows the interest of China on this sector. It is expected that the market for private aircraft, with an updated regulatory framework will help the inception of this new segment of the market in China along with the general aviation. This theme is treated in detail in the last two chapters of this volume.

1.2.2 *Light business jets*

This category also benefits from being able to land at smaller airports while also delivering intracontinental capabilities. The typical range is up to about 1,500 miles (or 2–3 hours flying time), thus medium-range distances. These are small aircraft, with a cabin height typically between 4 and 5 feet, and width of around 5 feet, with a capability of 5–6 passengers in a more in-cabin comforts. Cruising speed typically is 400–450 miles per hour.[15]

1.2.3 *Midsize business jets*

This category has emerged to accommodate transcontinental flight for larger groups of passengers. A business staple, the flexible midsize jet enables comfortable, in-cabin productivity during long flights. Its capability is 5–10 passengers. The typical range is 2,000–3,000 miles at a cruising speed of 430–480 per hour.[16] Midsize jets typically offer more head room — plus, there are generous amenities on board including a larger galley for greater food and beverage options.

1.2.4 *Super midsize business jets*

The super midsize category with a wide body combines speed, productivity, luxury, and ultra-range capabilities. They can climb high quickly yet comfortably, making this category a good choice for longer flights. Its capability is 8–10 passengers. The typical range is 3,400–3,600 miles non-stop (several aircraft in this class are capable of flying for well over

---

[15]"The Basic of Private Jet Categories," available at: https://www.jetcraft.com/jetstream/ 2015/06/basics-private-jet-categories-2/ (accessed December 9, 2021).
[16]*Ibid.*

five and a half hours), and the cruising speed typically is 490–590 miles per hours.[17]

1.2.5 *Large business jets*

Large business jets are purposely designed for business travel, while heavy jets (also known as "bizliners") typically are converted commercial airline aircraft. The robust cabin of these jets can be customized for luxurious and productive flight in dedicated work spaces, conference rooms/ offices, and full-service galleys. Intercontinental travel is the goal. Its capability is 10–18 passengers and the typical range is 6,000+ miles. Cruising speed typically is 480–560 miles per hour.[18]

1.2.6 *Ultra large business jet (VIP airliners)*

This category also known as Business Airliners are represented by aircraft which were usually used by commercial airlines but are "converted" to serve this very special segment of the market. The players of this segment of the market are the same big manufacturers which produce their airplanes for the majority of global airlines, thus including Airbus and Boeing as it will be better described in the next section. Business airliners are optimal solutions for groups of 20 (or more) people on medium to long-range flights where luxury or an environment for conducting business is of prime importance. There are several different types in this category including jets worthy of VIPs or heads of state. They commonly feature ultra-luxury accommodations with private dining and sleeping facilities, numerous lavatories, a gym and/or shower and meeting rooms.

2. Business Aviation Industry and Its Major Manufacturers and the Impact of COVID-19

While the COVID-19 pandemic has had a huge impact on the commercial airline industry, the trends in the private jet industry actually show

---

[17] *Ibid.*
[18] *Ibid.*

comparatively positive effects. Paradoxically, the outbreak of COVID-19 has favored this segment of the market for all the restrictions posed by authorities on commercial flights.

Business aviation comprehends an incredible variety of aircraft which are tailored depending on the needs and pockets of travelers. It is noteworthy that this segment of the market includes a variegated multitude of manufacturers, and it seems now appropriate to introduce the main producers and briefly illustrate their products. If the trend continues also after the pandemic it is possible that in the near future newcomers will appear and challenge the seasoned players. However, before introducing the major manufacturers it is worth reporting some data from this niche market:

Industry data show private aviation is coping far better than its commercial counterpart in the era of COVID-19. "Data provided by FlightAware shows the total number of flights of all types plummeted in March 2020. They have since recovered slightly but still stand at around half the numbers last year. Business flights, however, are now back to close to 2019 volume following a smaller percentage drop between March and June. FlightAware counts 'business flights' as any which are not classed as commercial or cargo services."[19] This trend is confirmed by several private jet operators and brokers who have reported an influx of business and new customers who are "first-time users." It seems these new customers are happy to pay a premium for a bespoke itinerary, involving minimal contact with the traveling public. In fact, private jet passengers are often able to drive straight on to the tarmac to board their flight, cutting out any mingling with other passengers at the airport or on board. While commercial flight numbers have halved, the number of private flights only dipped 10% between September 1 and October 15 (2020) compared with last year. According to aviation consultancy WingX,[20]

---

[19]Katherine Swindells (2020), "Private Jet Industry Trends upwards Due to COVID-19 Pandemic — Industry Data Shows Private Aviation is Coping Better Than Commercial in 2020," available at: https://www.elitetraveler.com/cars-jets-and-yachts/aviation/private-jet-trends-upwards-COVID-19-pandemic (accessed December 9, 2021).

[20]WingX is a data analytics and consulting company which provides actionable market intelligence to the global aviation industry. WINGX services include: Market Insight Reports, Online Dashboards, Customized Research, Strategic Consulting, Market Forecasts, and Surveys. WingX customers include aircraft operators, airframe, engine and

82,919 business aviation flights were operated in the first week of December, trending 24% below the same period in 2019.[21]

Business aviation is considered as a tool for corporate development and growth. The sector alone employs not only several hundreds of thousands of people working for this particular industry, but also in the world of maintenance employs operators, airport services, in the environment of the numerous airports open to business aviation. There is a ratio of 1 to 10 between airports accessible to airliners and airfields open to business aircraft, and this allows people to reach their final destinations more easily. Flying in this modality also means saving time compared to the same trips on commercial lines (travel time to the airport, check-in formalities, flight time, baggage retrieval). What is more, the cabin of a business aircraft is usually equipped with telephone, fax, broadband Internet allowing to conduct business as usual.

Business aviation offers multiple advantages due to its flexibility, such as for example, complete freedom in the choice of itinerary and of arrival and departure points; multiple stopovers on a single journey; confidentiality of travel, security. All these aspects certainly drive the business aviation which is composed of a variegated group of players offering an incredible number of solutions as exposed in the next sections.

2.1 *Boeing and Airbus: Two heavy weights in aerospace service market*

Two of the largest aerospace[22] and defense manufacturers in the world are Boeing and Airbus with revenue streams of about US$76.6 billion and €78.9 billion, respectively (2019). The list of competitors includes Gulfstream airspace corporation, Bombardier Inc., Dassault Aviation, Embraer, and Cessna; in fact, in the business jet segment they represent

---

avionics OEMs, airlines, maintenance providers, airports, fixed-based operators, Satcom providers, fuel providers, legal advisers, leasing companies, banks, regulators, investors, and private jet users.

[21] In this sense WingX, "Coronavirus Impact on Worldwide Business Aviation Activity".

[22] The global aerospace services market is worth over US$9 trillion, with key markets in the United States, France, China, and UK. Visit: https://www.statista.com/statistics/807720/global-aerospace-services-market-size-by-type/ (accessed December 9, 2021).

the major players and practically dominate almost the totality of this market.

Airbus Group serves as Europe's counterpart to the Boeing Company. During the mid-1990s, several European aerospace and defense contractors, such as DaimlerChrysler Aerospace (DASA) and Aérospatiale-Matra, were looking to take advantage of the newly formed European Union and eurozone by merging into a single entity. The resulting merger took place in July of 2000 and led to a newly formed company known as the European Aeronautic Defence and Space Company (EADS). After 14 years of operation, EADS reorganized the company into the Airbus Group, with three primary divisions in aircraft, airspace, and helicopter manufacturing.

The Boeing Company was incorporated in 1916 by William E. Boeing out of Seattle, Washington as "Pacific Aero Products Co." Boeing's background in wooden structure design is believed to have inspired his future design and assembly of airplanes. To benefit from the abundance of spruce wood in the area, Seattle remained as the primary manufacturing location.[23] Airbus Group has several manufacturing sites across Europe, while employing approximately 134,000 people globally. Boeing has become one of the largest manufacturers of commercial aircraft and an important defense contractor for many countries worldwide. Boeing's 737 aircraft series[24] have emerged as the company's bestsellers. However, the 737 MAX 8 aircraft model has come under scrutiny after a sequence of crashes. Boeing 737 gross orders[25] experienced a slump in 2019, and cancellations outpaced new orders for the 737 model family.

Both these two manufacturers are surfing the wave of the resurgence of business aviation and both have put great attention to this niche market with dedicated products. Though Boeing and Airbus are known to be two of the major commercial aircraft producers, these two giants have created their respective exclusive niche of large business jets market. Based on their line of production, these two manufacturers are in fact contributing

---

[23] https://www.statista.com/topics/3697/airbus-and-boeing/#:~:text=Two%20of%20the% 20largest%20aerospace,Corporation%20of%20China%20(Comac) (accessed December 9, 2021).

[24] Statista, available at: https://www.statista.com/statistics/273941/prices-of-boeing-aircraft-by-type/ (accessed December 9, 2021).

[25] Statista, available at: https://www.statista.com/statistics/273932/orders-of-the-boeing-737/.

in shaping a very exclusive segment of this market meeting unique needs required for an elite class of travelers.

This market represents literally another world, but it is a reality which cannot be ignored especially if we consider the development of air travel which likely will see more and more wealthy people opting for this option when it comes to choosing how to move from one place to another around the world.

2.1.1 *BBJ by Boeing*

The definition of "business jets" assumes an unique connotation when it comes to identify the Boeing Business Jets (BBJs) family. "Boeing Business Jets brings the best of commercial aviation into the realm of private air travel, offering customers a wide range of Boeing products that can be uniquely customized for the private, business or governmental sectors. The robust characteristics of these airplanes also provide an excellent value proposition when outfitted for the private market; offering larger, more personalized space, unmatched reliability and worldwide support."[26] BBJs offers a portfolio of ultra-large cabin, long-range airplanes that are perfectly suited for business and private, charter, corporate, and head-of-state operations. The product line includes the BBJ MAX family and high-performance versions of Boeing's 787 Dreamliner,[27] 777X,[28] and 747-8.[29] Since its launch in 1996, BBJs has delivered 240 jets on 262 orders.

---

[26] https://www.boeing.com/commercial/bbj/#/contact-us/sales/ (accessed May 9, 2021).

[27] Boeing's 787 Dreamliner: The airplane's unparalleled fuel efficiency and range flexibility enable carriers to profitably open new routes as well as optimize fleet and network performance. More information at: https://www.boeing.com/commercial/787/ (accessed December 9, 2021).

[28] The new Boeing 777X will be the world's largest and most efficient twin-engine jet, unmatched in every aspect of performance. With new breakthroughs in aerodynamics and engines, the 777X will deliver 10% lower fuel use and emissions and 10% lower operating costs than the competition. Visit: https://www.boeing.com/commercial/777x/ (accessed December 9, 2021).

[29] 747-8: For specification visit: https://www.boeing.com/commercial/747/ (accessed December 9, 2021).

Courtesy of Boeing Business Jets

Approximately 75% of widebody business jets sold in the last 22 years have been BBJs and include the 787, 777, and 747.[30]

The success of the BBJs was consecrated on September 5, 2020, when BBJ won the prestigious 2020 Design et al Yacht & Aviation design award competition. BBJ's entry, which Boeing built for the Dutch government, was placed first among multiple competitors in the Interior Design/VIP Completions category. The interior was designed by ALTEA Design

---

[30] For more information, visit: www.boeing.com/bbj (accessed December 9, 2021).

team and completed by the Fokker Techniek group in the Netherlands.[31] Boeing completed the project "turnkey," meaning that it not only built the airplane but also oversaw the custom interior design and the completion of its interior with customized colors and design features that reflect the Dutch history, culture, and traditions.

2.1.2 *Airbus and its new concept of business jet*

Airbus, like its US rival, has created its own world dedicated to corporate-business jets, that is the Airbus Corporate Jets (ACJ). All ACJs come from the most modern aircraft family on the market. ACJ's family business jets are all derived from Airbus' successful market-leading jetliner.[32] Since 2017, Airbus Corporate Helicopters (ACH)[33] is mirroring the successful sister brand ACJ, by providing private and executive helicopter solutions, including tailored completions and bespoke support services anywhere in the world, and ensuring a first-class ownership and transport experience.

---

[31] See: https://www.boeing.com/commercial/bbj/news/netherlands-government-bbj-is-a-winner-of-the-2020-design-et-al-award.page#/overview (accessed December 9, 2021). The airplane was delivered last year and now serves the head of state, prime minister, cabinet members, and other Dutch dignitaries in a custom outfitted jet that makes them feel at home while away.

[32] ACJ's corporate jets family includes the following models: ACJ319neo, specification available at: https://www.acj.airbus.com/en/exclusive-products/acj319neo.html; ACJ320neo, specifications are available at: https://www.acj.airbus.com/en/exclusive-products/acj 320neo.html; ACJ330neo, specifications available at: https://www.acj.airbus.com/en/ exclusive-products/acj330neo.html; ACJ350 XWB, specifications are available at: https:// www.acj.airbus.com/en/exclusive-products/acj350xwb.html; (accessed December 9, 2021).

[33] For more information on ACH visit: https://www.airbuscorporatehelicopters.com/ website/en/ref/home.html; ACH include the following models: ACH125, specifications are available at: https://www.airbuscorporatehelicopters.com/website/en/ref/ACH125_ 279.html; ACH130, specifications are available at: https://www.airbuscorporatehelicopters.com/website/en/ref/ACH130_262.html; ACH135, specifications are available at: https://www.airbuscorporatehelicopters.com/website/en/ref/ACH135_264.html; ACH145, specifications are available at: https://www.airbuscorporatehelicopters.com/website/en/ ref/ACH145_265.html; ACH160, specifications are available at: https://www.airbus corporatehelicopters.com/website/en/ref/ACH160_266.html; and ACH175, specifications are available at: https://www.airbuscorporatehelicopters.com/website/en/ref/ACH175_ 267.html (accessed December 9, 2021).

With the launch of ACH, Airbus is the only aerospace manufacturer offering both fixed and rotary wing business aviation aircraft.[34]

The European giant, on October 6, 2020 in the middle of the pandemic, launched its TwoTwenty business jet,[35] creating a whole new market segment: "The Xtra Large Bizjet."[36] This new business jet by Airbus "combines intercontinental range, unmatched personal space and comfort for all passengers. This latest technology platform offers unbeatable economics and unrivalled reliability," said Benoit Defforge, President ACJ. "Based on its compelling market appeal, we see promising demand for this aircraft in the growing business jet market." It seems Airbus succeeded in realizing a new concept of business jet: while occupying the same parking space and being able to take off from the same airports as competing business jets, the ACJ TwoTwenty will offer three times more cabin space, yet with a third less operating costs benefiting from the high performance of Airbus' latest A220 Family. The A220 Family is the quietest, cleanest, and most eco-friendly aircraft in its category, featuring a 50% reduced noise footprint compared to previous generation aircraft, and up to 25% lower fuel burn.

The ACJ TwoTwenty will have an increased range enabling the aircraft to fly up to 5,650 nautical miles/10,500 kilometers (over 12 flight hours), directly connecting city pairs like London and Los Angeles, Moscow and Jakarta, Tokyo and Dubai as well as Beijing and Melbourne, benefiting the entire A220 Program. Featuring unmatched personal space with 73 square meter/785 square feet of floor space distributed over six wide VIP living areas, the ACJ TwoTwenty offers selected interior

---

[34] More information is available at: https://www.acj.airbus.com/en/about-us.html (accessed December 9, 2021).

[35] The ACJ TwoTwenty is a clean-sheet design aircraft, based on Airbus' A220-100, featuring advanced materials and state-of-the-art technologies. The cabin will offer two times better connectivity than its competitors, a Wi-Fi system across all the cabin and latest innovations such as electro-chromatic windows and LED lighting, available at: https://www.airbus.com/newsroom/press-releases/en/2020/10/airbus-corporate-jets-launches-acj-twotwenty-business-jet.html (accessed December 9, 2021).

[36] Toulouse (France), October 6, 2020, Airbus Corporate lunches the ACJ TwoTwenty business jet. Visit: https://www.acj.airbus.com/en/exclusive-products/acj-twotwenty.html (accessed December 9, 2021). Airbus supports more than 500 airline and corporate jet customers with one of the largest support networks in the world, including tailored services for business jet needs.

arrangements and handcrafted furnishing. The cabin will allow up to 18 passengers to work, share, dine and relax at their discretion thanks to its cabin versatility and options suiting their needs and taste — all this under the tagline *"Reimagine your place in the sky..."* as Airbus slogan says. According to Airbus the ACJ TwoTwenty will provide a new value proposition to business aviation buyers. This new aircraft seems to have everything in place to beat the competitors we have as the ones described in the following sections.

2.2 Smaller players but top global jet manufacturers: Impact of COVID-19 on deliveries

Beside the two giants there are "smaller" manufacturers of business and private aircraft who play a significant role in this sector. Overall, it seems that manufacturers operating in this sector avoided the worst of the turbulence endured by their commercial counterparts during the COVID-19 crisis. According to analysts,[37] shipments in the second quarter of 2020 were down less than 25% with respect to 2019.[38] Data show that "the numbers of deliveries in the second quarter — 489 compared with 626 in 2019 — and their billed value, down from $5.58 billion in the same period in 2019 to $4.55 billion this year, show that the industry has managed to keep the revenue taps running. For the first half of the year, deliveries fell from 1,137 units in 2019 to 893, while billings were down 20.2% to $7.9 billion. Proportionally, jets — the highest-value segment by far for manufacturers — decreased the most, with 130 deliveries in the second quarter, compared with 192 last year. That follows a 15% increase in jet deliveries to 809 for the whole of 2019. Turboprop shipments were down 28 units at 81, while a total of 278 piston aircraft were handed over, compared with 325 in the second quarter of last year."[39]

---

[37] See: Murdo Morrison, "Business and General Aviation Deliveries Holding Up Despite COVID Impact," *FlightGlobal*, September 15, 2020, available at: https://www.flightglobal.com/business-aviation/business-and-general-aviation-deliveries-holding-up-despite-covid-impact/140182.article (accessed December 9, 2021).

[38] The numbers suggest this sector of the aviation industry has so far had a relatively soft landing compared with Airbus, Boeing which have seen deliveries for their passengers aircraft fell sharply as travelers stopped flying and airlines grounded their fleets. *Ibid.*

[39] *Ibid.*

As noted by analysts, while it is misleading to read too much into a single quarter's delivery totals, particularly when travel restrictions vary from country to country, among the big-jet manufacturers, Gulfstream had a solid April–June — its 32 shipments were actually one up on the same period in 2019. Canada's Bombardier, on the other hand, saw its deliveries fall from 35 to 20, while Dassault — which reports only every 6 months — notched just 16 shipments in the first half, a one-unit reduction over the same period a year earlier. Embraer too had a difficult second quarter, with 13 deliveries, compared with 25 in 2019, while Textron Aviation — which includes the Beechcraft and Cessna brands and whose numbers include small pistons to the super-midsize Citation Longitude — saw a modest drop, from 117 units to 98. Honda Aircraft, which delivered 10 HondaJets in quarter two of 2019, shipped just two of the light twins between April and June this year.[40]

2.2.1 *Gulfstream airspace corporation: A brief introduction of its fleet and its new flagship G700*

Gulfstream Aerospace Corporation[41] is an American aircraft company and a wholly owned subsidiary of General Dynamics.[42] Gulfstream designs, develops, manufactures, markets, and services business jet aircraft. Inspired by the belief that aviation could fuel business growth, Gulfstream Aerospace Corp. invented the first purpose-built business aircraft, the

---

[40] *Ibid.*

[41] https://www.gulfstream.com/en/ (accessed December 9, 2021).

[42] General Dynamics Corporation (GD) is an American aerospace and defense corporation. As of 2019, it was the fifth-largest defense contractor in the United States, and the sixth-largest in the world, by sales. The company ranked No. 92 in the 2019 Fortune 500 list of the largest United States corporations by total revenue. It is headquartered in Reston, Fairfax County, Virginia.

Formed in 1954 with the merger of submarine manufacturer Electric Boat and aircraft manufacturer Canadair, it evolved through multiple mergers and divestitures and changed markedly in the post–Cold War era of defense consolidation. General Dynamics' former Fort Worth Division, which manufactured the F-16 Fighting Falcon, was sold to the Lockheed Corporation in 1993, but GD re-entered the airframe business in 1999 with its purchase of business jet manufacturer Gulfstream Aerospace.

Gulfstream I™,[43] which first flew in 1958. Today, nearly 2,900 aircraft are in service around the world. Gulfstream's fleet includes the super-midsize Gulfstream G280™,[44] the Gulfstream G550™,[45] the high-performing Gulfstream G650ER™,[46] and an all-new aircraft family, the clean-sheet Gulfstream G500™,[47] the Gulfstream G600™,[48] and new industry flagship, the Gulfstream G700™.[49]

---

[43] The Grumman Gulfstream I (company designation G-159) is a twin-turboprop business aircraft. It first flew on August 14, 1958.

[44] Created to reimagine super-midsize performance, the G280 excels at blazing difficult trails. Certified for steep-approach operations, it makes nimble work of short runways, high-altitude airports, and low-visibility conditions. Its revolutionary wing design and engine technology result in prime fuel-efficiency — reducing operating costs and supporting environmental sustainability. More information and specifications are available at: https://www.gulfstream.com/en/aircraft/gulfstream-g280/ (accessed December 9, 2021).

[45] The G550 continues to impress with the iconic beauty and uncompromising performance that helped define modern business aviation. High-thrust Rolls-Royce engines and an outstanding maximum payload allow it to carry more of your essentials for greater distances with a low fuel burn. First introduced on the G550, the PlaneView™ flight deck remains an industry leader in safety. The G550 offers a maximum range of 6,750 nm/12,501 km at Mach 0.885. More information and specifications are available at: https://www.gulfstream.com/en/aircraft/gulfstream-g550/ (accessed December 9, 2021).

[46] The clean-sheet G650 family offers speed and range combinations that can save you significant time over the course of a year. The G650ER offers a maximum range of 7,500 nm/13,890 km at Mach 0.85 and 6,400 nm/11,853 km^2 at Mach 0.90, building upon the range of the G650, which covers 7,000 nm/12,964 km^1 at Mach 0.85 and 6,000 nm/11,112 km at Mach 0.90. More information and specifications are available at: https://www.gulfstream.com/en/aircraft/gulfstream-g650er/ (accessed December 9, 2021).

[47] Outfitted with high-thrust engines and an aerodynamic new wing, the G500 is built for effortless takeoffs and landings, enjoying access to short runways and high-altitude airports, coupled with increases in efficiency and reductions in emissions. More information and specifications are available at: https://www.gulfstream.com/en/aircraft/gulfstream-g500/ (accessed December 9, 2021).

[48] At its near-supersonic high-speed cruise of Mach 0.90, the G600 has more than enough range to connect far-flung cities like New York and Dubai, London and Beijing, or Los Angeles and Shanghai non-stop. More information and specifications are available at: https://www.gulfstream.com/en/aircraft/gulfstream-g600/ (accessed December 9, 2021).

[49] The G700™ represents the top of the line. Gulfstream G700 delivers the most spacious, innovative, and flexible cabin in the industry, plus all-new, high-thrust Rolls-Royce

Gulfstream is one of the most iconic business jet manufacturers and the company puts particular emphasis on the performances of its aircraft: "Gulfstream Aerospace Corp. today announced the next-generation Gulfstream G500™ and Gulfstream G600™ have once again demonstrated additional range capabilities through real-time operations. The newly increased range for the G500 and G600 apply to both the high-speed cruise of Mach 0.90 and the long-range cruise speed of Mach 0.85. The G500 now delivers 5,300 nautical miles/9,816 kilometers at Mach 0.85 and 4,500 nm/8,334 km at Mach 0.90. The G600's range at Mach 0.85 has improved to 6,600 nm/12,223 km and 5,600 nm/10,371 km at Mach 0.90. "The G500 and G600 have been exceeding expectations since they entered service," said Mark Burns, president, Gulfstream. "This latest demonstrated range increase provides further proof of the tremendous efficiency and versatility of these aircraft. The Gulfstream team is always looking for opportunities to improve aircraft capabilities and the customer experience, and we are pleased to deliver another performance enhancement for both existing and future customers."[50]

Gulfstream is in good company, in fact this sector comprehends another series of manufacturers which are all committed to offer the best product and conquer a greater portion of the market.

With the COVID-19 pandemic eroding orders and deliveries, Gulfstream defended itself pretty well: third-quarter (2020) aircraft deliveries at Gulfstream continued to edge closer to pre-COVID level, but were still down 15.8% from the previous year. The Savannah, Georgia-based business jet manufacturer handed over 32 aircraft (7 midsize G280s and 25 large-cabin jets) in the quarter versus 38 (9 G280s and 29 large cabins) in the same period of the previous year. In the first nine months, Gulfstream shipped 87 jets (16 G280s and 71 large cabins), compared with 103 (24 G280s and 79 large cabins) in the same period last year (2019). General Dynamics Chair and CEO Phebe Novakovic indicated that Gulfstream is expected to deliver 130 aircraft in 2020, which would

---

engines and the award-winning Symmetry Flight Deck™. The G700 offers a maximum range of 7,500 nm/13,890 km at Mach 0.925. More information and specifications are available at: https://www.gulfstream.com/en/aircraft/gulfstream-g700/ (accessed December 9, 2021).

[50] Gulfstream, press room: Gulfstream G500 and G600 Again Exceed Expectations, Savannah, Georgia, October 29, 2020, available at: https://gulfstreamnews.com/en/news/?id=6ed85935-0ee3-40fb-80bf-c58cd9472486 (accessed December 9, 2021).

put fourth-quarter shipments at 43 units — pretty much on par from the 44 handed over in the final quarter in 2019. She added that deliveries will be somewhat lower in 2021 due to G550 production ending and fewer expected G280 shipments. However, she anticipated demand picking up as the pandemic wanes, so Gulfstream could bump up large-cabin production next year (2021) if that scenario plays out.

Gulfstream's new flagship G700 program also took off. On October 23, 2020 the fifth aircraft was tested, and the first flight of T5, which will be used to test avionics and provide flight training simulator data, lasted three hours and eight minutes. Gulfstream said the twinjet, registered as N703GD, reached an altitude of 48,000 feet and exceeded the type's Mach 0.925 Mmo during the flight. The official unveiling of the G700 occurred in 2019 at NBAA-BACE, and since its first flight this new aircraft has made significant progress in the test program. During the series of test flights, the twinjet has reached Mach 0.99 and 54,000 feet, which is 3,000 feet more than its maximum cruise altitude. A stretch derivative of the ultra-long range G650 with the G500/600's symmetry flight deck, the G700 is expected to enter service in 2022.

2.2.2 Bombardier Inc. — Fleet composition overview and performances during the pandemic

Bombardier Inc. is a Canadian multinational that was founded in 1942 by Joseph-Armand Bombardier. It is a manufacturer of business jets, public transport vehicles, and trains, with the latter two businesses pending sale to Alstom.[51] Headquartered in Montreal, Canada, Bombardier has production and engineering sites in over 25 countries. The company was originally created to produce snowmobiles, but it expanded into the aviation, rail, and public transit businesses. Bombardier although has diversified its business and production, is considered as one of the top manufacturer of

---

[51]Alstom SA is a French multinational rolling stock manufacturer operating worldwide in rail transport markets, active in the fields of passenger transportation, signaling, and locomotives, with products including the AGV, TGV, Eurostar, Avelia, and New Pendolino high-speed trains, in addition to suburban, regional, and metro trains, as well as Citadis trams. Visit: www.alstom.com (accessed December 9, 2021).

private jets; the company is an industry leading aircraft manufacturer with the widest portfolio of business jets.

Bombardier Aviation manufactures and support world-class business aircraft and its line of business jets is the most comprehensive of any original equipment manufacturer (OEM), with three leading aircraft families: Learjet, Challenger, and Global (for specifications see footnotes below), spanning the light to large categories in addition to modifying these aircraft platforms for special mission purposes, from surveillance and reconnaissance to medical evacuations and dignitary transport.[52] Every detail of a Bombardier business jet is meticulously designed as stressed in its website and expert engineering and superior craftsmanship allow customers to experience productivity when they need it and comfort where they expect it. Bombardier delivers the best and elevates the exceptional private jet experience at every possible level.[53]

It is noteworthy that Bombardier Business Aircraft has over 4,700 aircraft in operation. Bombardier's line of production includes the following models: Learjet 75 Liberty,[54] the Challenger 350,[55] the Challenger 650,[56]

---

[52]Bombardier Specialized Aircraft: Bombardier Specialized Aircraft is recognized around the world for its diverse portfolio of proven and versatile aircraft platforms. Decades of experience working with special mission operators and the confidence of renowned mission systems integrators make Bombardier Specialized Aircraft the go-to provider of solutions for the most demanding missions; from urgent humanitarian assistance and head-of-state transport to securing airspace, borders, and infrastructure. More information is available at: www.specializedaircraft.bombardier.com (accessed December 9, 2021).

[53]About Bombardier Business Aircraft, available at: https://www.bombardier.com/en/aviation/business-aircraft.html (accessed December 9, 2021).

[54]The new Learjet 75 Liberty redefines the iconic Learjet brand and features the segment's first private Executive Suite. Harnessing American know-how and efficiency, the Learjet 75 Liberty offers more people the freedom to stretch out and step up into a Learjet. The Learjet 75 Liberty offers a maximum range of 2,080 nm/3,852 km at Mach 0.81. More specifications are available at: https://businessaircraft.bombardier.com/en/aircraft/learjet-75-liberty (accessed December 9, 2021).

[55]The Challenger 350 aircraft is the bestselling business jet among top corporate flight departments and charter operators worldwide. The Challenger 350 offers a maximum range of 3,200 nm/5,926 km at Mach 0.83. More specifications are available at: https://businessaircraft.bombardier.com/en/aircraft/challenger-350 (accessed December 9, 2021).

[56]The Challenger 650 is the bestselling large business jet platform of all time with over 1,000 deliveries and counting. Bombardier best-selling aircraft combines world-class

the Global 5000,[57] the GLOBAL 5500,[58] the GLOBAL 6000,[59] the GLOBAL 6500,[60] the GLOBAL 7500,[61] and the GLOBAL 8000.[62]

It is noteworthy that on June 30, 2020, Bombardier made history when it became the first business jet manufacturer to release an Environmental Product Declaration (EPD), which it did for the industry flagship Global 7500 aircraft. Third party verified in accordance with the International Standard ISO 14025, the EPD embeds environmental considerations from design to end-of-life, and from tip-to-tail, making

---

interior design with the ultimate value proposition. The Challenger 650 offers a maximum range of 4,000 nm/7,408 km at Mach 0.85. More specifications are available at: https://businessaircraft.bombardier.com/en/aircraft/challenger-650 (accessed December 9, 2021).

[57] The Global 5000 has the widest cabin in its class with more room than its nearest competitor, delivering maximum comfort and an exceptional cabin experience. The Global 5000 offers a maximum range of 5,200 nm/9,630 km at Mach 0.89. More specifications are available at: https://businessaircraft.bombardier.com/en/aircraft/global-5000 (accessed December 9, 2021).

[58] The Global 5500 introduces the Nuage seat, a revolutionary architecture and the first meaningful change in the operation design of a business aircraft seat in 30 years. The Global 5500 offers a maximum range of 5,900 nm/10,927 km at Mach 0.90. More specifications are available at: https://businessaircraft.bombardier.com/en/aircraft/global-5500 (accessed December 9, 2021).

[59] The Global 6000 aircraft perfectly blends all aspects of performance. With a class leading combination of range, speed, and reliability. The Global 6000 offers a maximum range of 6,000 nm/11,112 km at Mach 0.89. More specifications are available at: https://businessaircraft.bombardier.com/en/aircraft/global-6000 (accessed December 9, 2021).

[60] The Global 6500 and its leading-edge wing technology and new, purpose-built Rolls-Royce Pearl engines give this aircraft class-leading range, speed, and agility to connect more cities, including those its competitors cannot access. The Global 6500 offers a maximum range of 6,600 nm/12,223 km at Mach 0.90. More specifications are available at: https://businessaircraft.bombardier.com/en/aircraft/global-6500 (accessed December 9, 2021).

[61] The Global 7500 aircraft stands alone as the world's largest and longest range business jet. The Global 7500 offers a maximum range of 7,700 nm/14,260 km at Mach 0.925. More specifications are available at: https://businessaircraft.bombardier.com/en/aircraft/global-7500 (accessed December 9, 2021).

[62] The Global 8000 business jet has been crafted with an intent to maximize passenger comfort and productivity on long distance flights. The Global 8000 offers a maximum range of 7,900 nm/14,631 km at Mach 0.925. More specifications are available at: https://businessaircraft.bombardier.com/en/aircraft/global-8000 (accessed December 9, 2021).

sustainability an integral part of how we innovate.[63] Furthermore, Bombardier is taking concrete actions to make the industry more sustainable: "Bombardier is not only committed to the sustainability of its products and business operations but is also driving efforts to make the business aviation industry more responsible. Therefore, we are leading the promotion and adoption of Sustainable Aviation Fuels as we all work towards mitigating the effects of climate change."[64]

According to an article published in December 2020 by *Aviation International News*,[65] the COVID-19 pandemic took its toll on Bombardier also as deliveries fell 7 units to a total of 24 in the third quarter; furthermore, the company has taken roughly a US$2.25 billion hit on liquidity; however, the division dedicated to business aviation is predicted to ameliorate its performances. According to the same source Bombardier President and CEO Eric Martel noted the "broad and deep impact on the global economy and in our industry," but said he sees stabilization for now with more encouraging signs long term. On the positive side, Bombardier's business aircraft revenues climbed 10% in the most recent three months (that is, the third quarter of 2020) to US$1.225 billion, thanks to the delivery of 8 Global 7500s. That delivery number is anticipated to grow some 50% to about 12 in the fourth quarter, positioning the business aviation unit for further revenue expansion and near break-even on cash flow. In particular in the third quarter, Bombardier delivered 13 Globals, up from 9 a year ago (2019). But the 9-month tally of 31 Global deliveries lagged the 33 handed over in the first 9 months of 2019. As for another model, the Challenger, the 9 deliveries were down by nearly half of the 17 handed over in the third-quarter 2019. For the year so far (2020), 32 Challengers have been delivered, compared with 48 in the same period last year. Martel, however noted that Challenger sales activity strengthened in the third quarter. As for the light business jets, just two Learjets were delivered in the third quarter, down from 5 a year ago. Seven have been delivered

---

[63] Visit: https://businessaircraft.bombardier.com/en/global-7500-first-environmental-product-declaration (accessed December 9, 2021).
[64] *Ibid.*
[65] Kerry Lynch (2020), "Bombardier Debt Climbs, Deliveries Drop during COVID," *Business Aviation News*, p. 8.

through the first three quarters of the year, compared with nine a year ago (2019).

In total Bombardier delivered 70 aircraft through the first three quarters, a 20-aircraft difference from a year earlier. Martel said Bombardier in 2021 would remain at the lower delivery totals predicting between 100 and 120 business jet shipment adding that the Global 7500 will account for a significant chunk, with Martel estimating about 35 would be delivered as Bombardier works through a backlog that still stretches nearly 2 years. As Bombardier continues to work through its backlog and new sales activity has suffered under the pandemic, business aircraft backlog fell from US\$14.4 billion at the end of 2019 to US\$12.2 billion at the end of the third quarter, and the company expects deliveries will outpace orders for the near-term.

2.2.2.1 Bombardier Global 7500 EPD

It is worth reporting that "Bombardier Aviation in June 2020 achieved a first in sustainability when its Global 7500 became the first business jet to receive an Environmental Product Declaration (EPD) through The International EPD System. Verified by a third-party to international ISO standards (ISO 14025 and related — for Type III environmental declaration), the EPD discloses detailed environmental information about the Global 7500's life cycle,[66] such as CO_2 emissions, noise, water consumption, and other key environmental impact indicators. It is also worth noting that the International EPD System, which is based in Sweden, has

---

[66]Bombardier's pursuit of an EPD was incorporated throughout the development of the Global 7500. The company's eco-design team applied product innovation life-cycle processes throughout the 7500's development to ensure that ultra-long-range business jet minimized its impact on the environment from design to the aircraft's end-of-life. This involved a focus on health, safety, and environmental considerations during design, production, support, and end-of-life. In addition, this approach involved years of collaboration with the supply chain. Operational life cycles, including an evaluation of noise and fuel burn, are considered. Further, Bombardier considered recyclability and recovery rates for end-of-life, reporting that material recycling and energy recovery aggregate to 85% recoverability rate by weight for Global 7500. In this sense see: AIN Publication, Vol. 49 N. 12, December 2020, pp. 32, 34.

a library of published EPDs for products from 31 countries in an effort to foster transparency about environmental life cycles.

The Canadian airframer acknowledged the declaration as another milestone in its environmental sustainability strategy that so far has included the increased adoption of sustainable alternative fuels (SAF), a reduction of its CO2 footprint, expanded aircraft recyclability, and further sustainable sourcing."[67]

2.2.3 *Dassault aviation: The Falcon family and the newest Falcon 6X — Results and deliveries of business jets during the pandemic*

Dassault Aviation is a French aerospace company building military aircraft, business jets, and space systems.

Dassault is the designer and builder of the Falcon family of business jets, recognized for their handling qualities, operational flexibility, low fuel consumption and innovative solutions.[68]

With nearly 2,500 Falcons delivered to date, the Falcon range has been one of the market leaders in the wide cabin, long range aircraft segment for 50 years. In 2017, more than 2,100 Falcons are in service in 90 countries. 60% of the Falcons are used by companies as tools for economic development and growth. A range of six business aircraft, capable of flying from 3,350 nm (6,205 km) to 6,450 nm (11,945 km), cover a wide range of travel needs. Noteworthy Falcons benefit from the legacy and technological innovations of combat aircraft: cockpit, digital flight control system, head-up display, flight quality, aerodynamics, and much more. Moreover Falcons have fuel consumption levels that are 30 to 50% lower than competing aircraft and the lowest CO_2 emissions in the market.[69]

---

[67] Source: AIN Publication, Vol. 49 N. 12, December 2020, pp. 32, 34.

[68] More information is available at "Company Profile" available at: https://www.dassault-aviation.com/en/group/about-us/company-profile/ (accessed December 9, 2021).

[69] Visit: https://www.dassault-aviation.com/en/civil/falcon-philosophy/profile/ (accessed December 9, 2021).

Dassault's business jet line of production includes the following models: Falcon 2000S,[70] the Falcon 2000LXS,[71] the Falcon 900LX,[72] the Falcon 6X[73] which is the latest introduced in the family (presented on

---

[70]The Falcon 2000S was introduced in May 2011. This aircraft is a twin-engined. The 2000S features inboard slats, EASy II, the world's most advanced flight deck with FalconEye, Dassault's unique Combined Vision System option, along with one of the most competitive acquisition costs in its category. EASA/FAA certifications were received early April 2013. The Falcon 2000S connects business centers like Paris and Dubai, Moscow and Beijing, London and Bangor, Shannon and New York. Routes beyond the non-stop range of midsize jets — and at a lower cost per nautical mile than most aircraft in its class. The Falcon 2000S offers a maximum range of 3,350 nm/6,205 km at Mach 0.80. More specifications are available at: https://www.dassaultfalcon.com/en/Aircraft/Models/2000S/Pages/overview.aspx (accessed December 9, 2021).

[71]The Falcon 2000LXS was launched in October 2012 during the National Business Aviation (NBAA) convention in Orlando. This aircraft is a twin-engined. Compared across categories, the fuel burn advantage of the 2000LXS outperforms even smaller jets. The Falcon 2000LXS offers a maximum range of 4,300 nm/7,410 km at Mach 0.80 (maximum operating Mach 0.862). More specifications are available at: https://www.dassaultfalcon.com/en/Aircraft/Models/2000LXS/Pages/overview.aspx (accessed December 9, 2021).

[72]The Falcon 900LX was launched in October 2016 at the NBAA convention (the new version of the aircraft), the original version was launched at the European Business Aviation Convention & Exhibition (EBACE) in May 2008. This is the latest in the immensely popular Falcon 900 series. This large-cabin trijet stands alone in its class for performance, comfort, and efficiency. The Falcon 900LX offers a maximum range of 4,750 nm/8,800 km at Mach 0.87. Fuel consumption up to 40% lower than competitors shrinks operating costs and carbon footprint. More specifications are available at: https://www.dassaultfalcon.com/en/Aircraft/Models/900LX/Pages/overview.aspx (accessed December 9, 2021).

[73]The Falcon 6X was presented on December 8, 2020. This new 5,500 nm aircraft will make its first flight in early 2021 and begin deliveries in 2022. This is the most spacious, advanced and versatile twinjet in business aviation. Pratt & Whitney Canada's Pure®Power PW800 engines have been selected to power the Falcon 6X that offers the largest, quietest, and most comfortable cabin of any aircraft in its class and more cabin volume than any other Falcon ever designed. The Falcon 6X offers a maximum range of 5,500 nm/10,186 km at Mach 0.80 or 5,100 nm/9,445 km at Mach 0.85 with a maximum operating Mach 0.90. More specifications are available at: https://www.dassaultfalcon.com/en/Aircraft/Models/6X/Pages/overview.aspx (accessed December 9, 2021).

December 8, 2020), the Falcon 7X,[74] the Falcon 8X,[75] and the Falcon 10X which was announced on May 6, 2021.[76]

The Falcon 6X is however the latest introduced by Dassault and this aircraft has it all to outperform its competitors and rival with its "brothers." Dassault Aviation unveiled its first completed Falcon 6X in a virtual event on December 8, 2020 from the company's Merignac hangar in Bordeaux, France.[77] The Falcon 6X is the successor to the 5X program that was scrubbed 3 years ago following problems with the Safran Silvercrest engine chosen to power that new aircraft. Just two months after the Safran engine debacle, Dassault launched the 6X using the same fuselage as the 5X, but this time to be powered by the Pratt & Whitney Canada PW812D

---

[74] The Falcon 7X was launched in 2001. From its inception, the Falcon 7X was destined to be a revolutionary aircraft, introducing business aviation to the industry's first Digital Flight Control System. Like so many other aspects of the aircraft, its DFCS drew on Dassault's 30 years of military experience, especially its Rafale and Mirage 2000 programs. Fuel consumption is 15%–30% lower than other jets in its class. The Falcon 7X offers a maximum range of 5,950 nm/11,020 km at Mach 0.80 with a maximum operating Mach 0.90. More specifications are available at: https://www.dassaultfalcon.com/en/Aircraft/Models/7X/Pages/overview.aspx (accessed December 9, 2021).

[75] The Falcon 8X was announced at the European Business Aviation Convention & Exhibition in May, 2014. Dassault delivered the first Falcon 8X on October 5, 2016 to Greek business aviation operator Amjet Executive. This aircraft is a trijet and it offers a maximum range of 6,450 nm/11,945 km at Mach 0.80 with a maximum operating Mach 0.90. The 8X is up to 20% more fuel-efficient than any other aircraft in the ultra-long range segment. Much of the credit goes to the three highly efficient Pratt & Whitney PW307D engines which power the Falcon 8X. More specifications are available at: https://www.dassaultfalcon.com/en/Aircraft/Models/8X/Pages/overview.aspx (accessed December 9, 2021).

[76] Dassault Aviation launched the project for Falcon 10X on May 6, 2021 — Dassault Aviation today announced an all-new Falcon jet that will deliver a level of comfort, versatility, and technology unmatched by any purpose-built business jet. Featuring a range of 7,500 nautical miles, the Falcon 10X will fly non-stop from New York to Shanghai, Los Angeles to Sydney, Hong Kong to New York or Paris to Santiago. Top speed will be Mach 0.925. The Falcon 10X will enter service at the end of 2025. Dassault Aviation Launches Falcon 10X, featuring Industry's (globenewswire.com) (accessed June 8, 2021).

[77] Full presentation is available at: https://www.dassault-aviation.tv/en/theme_0/1931/Falcon_6X_rollout.html (accessed December 9, 2021).

engine. Pratt & Whitney President Maria Della Posta said during the presentation that "the new engine will require 40 percent less scheduled maintenance activity and 20 percent fewer inspections than previous engines." The aircraft will employ the same digital flight control system used in other recent Falcon aircraft, as well as the FalconEye combined vision system.[78] The 6X has a maximum range of 5,500 nautical miles (10,186 kilometer) and a maximum speed of Mach 0.90. It's also capable of flying Mach 0.85 for non-stop flights up to 5,100 nautical miles (9,445 kilometer).[79] At a cruise speed of Mach 0.80, New York to Buenos Aries or to Honolulu is possible with eight passengers and a crew of three. The 6X is capable of cruising as high as 51,000 feet. Dassault Aviation CEO Eric Trappier told O'Brien the "key goals of the new design were comfort and efficiency. With a range of 5,500 nm, trips like Los Angeles to Moscow nonstop are now possible." At 40 feet 4 inches long, 78 inches tall and 102 inches wide, the 6X cabin is the largest of any long-range business jet, besting even that of Dassault's Falcon 8X. The 6X program remains on track for first flight in 2021 and certification and entry into service will follow in 2022.

Notwithstanding the pandemic, Dassault Aviation delivered 16 Falcons in the first half of 2020, one fewer than a year ago, but at the end of the year the company succeeded in delivering 34 business jets, down from its original guidance of 40. While it has been able to keep development on the Falcon 6X going during the COVID-19 crisis (Dassault has presented it on December 8, 2020).[80] Meanwhile, the Falcon 6X is on track to begin flight testing early next year, with service entry in 2022.[81] According to Dassault Chairman and CEO Eric Trappier, the company has not experienced any order cancellations for Falcons in the first half of 2020, but some customers have delayed deliveries to next year. In the

---

[78] The Falcon 6X features the business jet world's first combined Vision System FalconEye. It provides flight crews unprecedented situational awareness in all weather conditions, day or night. FalconEye adds a significant margin of safety for all airport operations, but especially at challenging airfields with difficult surroundings.

[79] See: https://www.dassaultfalcon.com/en/Aircraft/Models/6X/Pages/overview.aspx (accessed December 9, 2021).

[80] Presentation of the roll out is available at: Falcon: Falcon 6X rollout (dassault-aviation. tv) (accessed December 9, 2021).

[81] See: https://www.ainonline.com/aviation-news/business-aviation/2020-07-23/1h-falcon-deliveries-flat-will-be-down-2020 (accessed December 9, 2021).

first six months of 2020, Dassault took in net orders for five Falcons, two fewer than in the same period last year. At the end of June, the company's backlog for Falcons stood at 42 aircraft, down from 53 at the end of 2019.

In 2020, 34 Falcon were delivered, while 30 deliveries had been guided, versus 40 in 2019. In 2020, 15 Falcon were ordered, compared to 40 in 2019. Order intake totaled €1,917 million, versus €2,308 million in 2019. This includes the "AVSIMAR" contract with France, for the development and acquisition of seven Falcon 2000LXS Albatros for the marine surveillance aircraft and associated support.

"The COVID-19 outbreak, triggering an unprecedented global sanitary crisis, very restrictive travel restrictions and strong uncertainties about the worldwide economy, directly affected our order intakes level."[82] The entire industry has been severely affected, which has disrupted and long lastingly weakened the sector.

Dassault Aviation pays particular attention to the safeguard of the environment and with its management policies contributes to the Sustainable Development Goals contained in the 2030 Agenda for Sustainable Development.[83]

As a final note on May 6, 2021 Dassault has presented its Falcon 10X featuring a range of 7,500 nautical miles at a top speed of Mach 0.925 which now represent the top of its line, Csopra note

---

[82] This information is available at: https://www.globenewswire.com/news-release/2021/01/06/2154429/0/en/Dassault-Aviation-Deliveries-order-intakes-and-backlog-in-number-of-new-aircraft-as-of-December-31st-2020.html (accessed December 9, 2021). The 2020 Annual Financial Report is available at: AFR_2020_VA.pdf (dassault-aviation.com) (accessed June 7, 2021).

[83] The *2030 Agenda for Sustainable Development* was adopted in September 2015 by the UN members at the United Nations headquarters in New York as the organization celebrated its 70th anniversary. The 2030 Agenda for Sustainable Development contains the 17 Sustainable Development Goals (SDGs), and one of the main themes is greener development and climate change. Dassault Aviation Group contributes to the scope of this initiative adopting sustainable practices and in its Financial Report are listed the activities connected to these Goals. See 2020 Annual Financial Report, p. 42. https://www.dassault-aviation.com/wp-content/blogs.dir/2/files/2021/06/AFR_2020_VA.pdf (accessed December 7, 2021).

2.2.4   *Embraer: Line of production and performances during the pandemic*

Empresa Brasileira de Aeronáutica (Embraer) was created with help from the national government as a government-owned corporation in 1969. Its first President, Ozires Silva, was a government appointee, and the company initially only produced a turboprop passenger aircraft, the Embraer EMB 110 Bandeirante. Embraer has evolved into a global company headquartered in Brazil with businesses in commercial and executive aviation, defense and security. The company designs, develops, manufactures, and markets aircraft and systems, providing customer support and services. The company is the third largest producer of civil aircraft, after Boeing and Airbus.[84] Embraer is also involved in the development of its eVTOL for future Urban Air Mobility (UAM).[85]

In 2002, a dedicated subsidiary, *Embraer Executive Jets*, was created in order to concentrate in one division the production of business jets. In 2016, Embraer delivered its 1,000th executive jet and had a market share of 17% by volume, though it lacked an ultra-long-range large cabin jet. In October 2018 Embraer announced two new business jets — the Praetor 500 in the midsize cabin category — and the Praetor 600 in the super midsize category.

---

[84] Since it was founded in 1969, Embraer has delivered more than 8,000 aircraft. Embraer is the leading manufacturer of commercial jets up to 150 seats. The company maintains industrial units, offices, service and parts distribution centers, among other activities, across the Americas, Africa, Asia, and Europe. More information is available at: https://embraer.com/global/en/about-us (accessed December 9, 2021).

[85] Embraer created EmbraerX as a subsidiary in charge of developing their eVTOL aircraft for UAM. On June 11, 2019 in Washington DC, EmbraerX unveiled a new electric flying vehicle concept during Uber Elevate Summit 2019. EmbraerX is also engaged in a variety of tailored solutions for the ecosystem, including a new business platform, named Beacon, designed to foster collaboration and synchronize aviation services companies and professionals in a streamlined and more agile way, to keep aircraft flying. More information is available at: https://embraerx.embraer.com/global/en/news?slug=1206601-embraerx-unveils-new-flying-vehicle-concept-for-future-urban-air-mobility (accessed December 9, 2021).

The complete line of production (light business jets, midsize, and super midsize business jets) include the following models: Phenom 100EV,[86] Phenom 300E,[87] Preator 500,[88] and Preator 600.[89]

---

[86] The Phenom 100EV aircraft was presented on July 27, 2016 by Embraer Executive Jets and it is an evolution of its entry-level Phenom 100 business jet. The Phenom 100EV features modified Pratt & Whitney Canada PW617F1-E engines, with 1,730 pounds of thrust, reaching a 405 knots true air speed as high speed cruise and up to 15% more thrust at hot-and-high airports, which equates to more range and a faster time to climb. The aircraft has a four-occupant range of 1,178 nautical miles (2,182 kilometer), with a maximum operating Mach 0.70 with NBAA IFR reserves (100 nautical miles). More specifications are available at: https://executive.embraer.com/global/en/phenom-100ev (accessed December 9, 2021).

[87] The Phenom 300E aircraft was launched — and debuted — at the 2017 National Business Aviation Association's Business Aviation Conference and Exhibition (NBAA-BACE), in October 2017. The new aircraft is designated "E" for "Enhanced" in reference to its entirely redesigned cabin and the addition of the industry-leading nice® HD CMS/IFE (Cabin Management System/InFlight Entertainment) by Lufthansa Technik. The Phenom 300, the new model's successful predecessor, has been the bestselling and most delivered light business jet for the last 6 years. The Phenom 300E performs among the top light jets, with a high speed cruise of 453 knots (maximum operating Mach 0.80) and a six-occupant range of 1,971 nautical miles (3,650 kilometer) with NBAA IFR reserves. More specifications are available at: https://executive.embraer.com/global/en/phenom-300e (accessed December 9, 2021).

[88] The Praetor 500 and the Praetor 600, both of which have received FAA, EASA, and ANAC certifications less than 1 year after they were first announced at NBAA-BACE 2018, are the most technologically advanced aircraft in their categories. The Praetor 500 surpassed certification goals, achieving an intercontinental range of 3,340 nautical miles (6,186 kilometers) with a high speed cruise of 466 knots (maximum operating Mach 0.83) with four passengers and NBAA IFR Reserves. The Praetor 500 is the farthest- and fastest-flying midsize jet, capable of true North America corner-to-corner, non-stop flights, such as Miami to Seattle or Los Angeles to New York. More specifications are available at: https://executive.embraer.com/global/en/praetor-500 (accessed Dec/. 9, 2021).

[89] The Praetor 600 is the farthest-flying super-midsize jet in the world, capable of non-stop flights from Paris to New York or São Paulo to Miami. With four passengers and NBAA IFR Reserves, the Praetor 600 has intercontinental range of 4,018 nautical miles (7,441 kilometer) with a high speed cruise of 466 Knots (maximum operating Mach 0.83). More specifications are available at: https://executive.embraer.com/global/en/praetor-600 (accessed December 9, 2021).

Launched in 2008 the program for two mid-size and super-midsize business jets, i.e. the Legacy 500[90] and Legacy 450[91] saw their entry into the market in 2014 and 2015, respectively. The Legacy 500 and Legacy 450 executive jets were commercially launched by Embraer at 2012's European Business Aircraft Conference and Exhibition (EBACE), in Geneva, Switzerland. Legacy 650E was later added to these models.[92]

The Lineage 1000E[93] completes Embraer's executive business jet line. This aircraft is advertised as an "ultra-large" business jet with comfortable seating for 19. The lineage is the top of the line of Embraer's executive business jet, and its first version as a business jet was launched in 2006.

---

[90]The Legacy 500 is capable of flying at 45,000 feet and is powered by two Honeywell HTF7500E engines, the greenest in their class. Taking off from airfields as short as 4,084 feet, the Legacy 500 has a range of 3,125 nautical miles (5,788 kilometers) with four passengers, including NBAA IFR fuel reserves, which enables it to fly non-stop from Los Angeles to Honolulu, or Teterboro to London, at a maximum operating Mach 0.83. More specifications are available at: https://executive.embraer.com/global/en/legacy-500 (accessed December 9, 2021).

[91]The Legacy 450 is a mid-light business jet with a best-in-class 6-foot-tall flat-floor cabin. The Legacy 450 is powered by two advanced, fuel-efficient Honeywell HTF 7500E turbofan engines, the greenest in their class. With four passengers and NBAA IFR Reserves, the Legacy 450 is capable of flying 2,900 nautical miles (5,371 kilometers), which enables non-stop flights from San Francisco to Honolulu, São Paulo to Bogotá, Moscow to Mumbai, New Delhi to Singapore, Singapore to Beijing, Beijing to Kuala Lumpur, or Hong Kong to Alice Springs, at a maximum operating Mach 0.83. More specifications are available at: https://executive.embraer.com/global/en/legacy-450 (accessed December 9, 2021).

[92]The Legacy 650E, a large business jet, is the new version of the Legacy 650, and was unveiled on October 31, 2016 in Orlando, Florida. The aircraft has a range of 3,900 nautical miles (7,223 kilometers) with NBAA IFR fuel reserves, with a maximum operating Mach 0.80. More specifications are available at: https://executive.embraer.com/global/en/legacy-650e (accessed December 9, 2021).

[93]The Lineage 1000E, the new version of the Lineage 1000, is based on the Embraer 190 airliner, with added fuel tanks in the lower deck cargo hold space, nearly doubling the jet's range. The ultra-large Lineage 1000E was introduced in 2013 during its press conference at the NBAA Business Aviation Convention & Exhibition (2013). The range of the Lineage 1000E, with eight passengers aboard, was extended from 4,400 nm to 4,600 nautical miles (8,519 kilometer), *en route* speed at ach 0.78 and a maximum operating Mach 0.82. More specifications are available at: https://executive.embraer.com/global/en/lineage-1000e (accessed December 9, 2021).

According to *Aviation International News*, Embraer's business jet deliveries slipped by six aircraft in the third quarter (2020), this is based on numbers released in November 10 by the Brazilian aircraft manufacturer. It emerges that the total for the third quarter includes 19 light jets (3 Phenom 100s and 16 Phenom 300s) and two large jets (two Preator 500s) versus 15 Phenom light jets (one 100 and fourteen 300s) and 12 large jets (four Legacy 450s, one Legacy 500, and seven Preator 600s) in the same quarter in 2019. As of now (December 2020), Embraer's business jet deliveries have declined more sharply by 20 aircraft. The total for the first nine months in 2020 was 43 business aircraft — 33 light jets (5 Phenom 100s, and 28 Phenom 300s) and 10 large jets (1 Legacy 650, 4 Preator 500s, and 5 Preator 600s). This is compared with the previous year's nine months period in which Embraer delivered a total of 63 aircraft — 42 Phenom light jets (seven 100s and thirty-five 300s) and 21 large jets (2 Legacy 650s, 5 Legacy 450s, 6 Legacy 500s, and 8 Preator 600s). Highlights of the last quarter of 2020 were the deliveries of Phenom 100EV and Phenom 300E to two different Brazilian customers that helped it reach the milestone of the 250th Embraer Phenom in operation in Latin America.[94]

2.2.5 *Textron aviation (Cessna Citation business jets and Beechcraft) — Line of production and perspectives despite the impact of COVID-19*

Textron Aviation Inc.[95] is the general aviation business unit of the conglomerate Textron[96] that was formed in March 2014 following the

---

[94] In this sense: Jerry Siebenmark (2020), "Third-Quarter Deliveries Slide at Embraer," *Aviation International News*, December.

[95] More detailed information about this company is available at: https://www.textron.com/ About/Our-Businesses/Textron-Aviation (accessed December 9, 2021).

[96] "Textron Inc. (NYSE: TXT) is one of the world's best known multi-industry companies, recognized for its powerful brands such as Bell, Cessna, Beechcraft, E-Z-GO, Arctic Cat and many more. The company leverages its global network of aircraft, defense, industrial and finance businesses to provide customers with innovative products and services. What began as a small New England business in 1923 has grown into a $13.6 billion company, with a worldwide presence supported by 35,000 people in more than 25 countries. Throughout its history, Textron has been the source of ground-breaking technologies and numerous industry-firsts. Many major steps in the evolution of aircraft, rotorcraft, armored

acquisition of Beech Holdings which included the Beechcraft[97] and Hawker Aircraft[98] businesses. The new business unit includes the Textron-owned Cessna.[99] Thus, currently Textron Aviation sells Beechcraft and Cessna branded aircraft.

The Cessna family business jet includes the following model: CitationM2,[100] Citation CJ3+,[101] Citation CJ4,[102] Citation XLS+,[103]

---

vehicles, electrical vehicles and automotive systems have emerged from our product development labs." See: https://www.textron.com/About/Company (accessed December 9, 2021). While no longer selling new Hawker airplanes, Textron Aviation still supports the existing Hawker aircraft fleet through its service centers.

[97] See: Beechcraft Aircraft | Turboprop and Piston Models (txtav.com) (accessed December 9, 2021).

[98] For reference see: Hawker Aircraft — Wikipedia (accessed December 9, 2021).

[99] The internationally known Cessna brand consists of business jets, turboprops, and piston-engine aircraft. Visit: https://cessna.txtav.com/ (accessed December 9, 2021).

[100] CitationM2 jet is perfect for corporate, charter or private use, delivers fast, efficient trips with a maximum range of 1,550 nautical miles (2871 kilometer) at a maximum cruise speed of 404 knots true airspeed (748 kilometer per hour). More specifications are available at: https://cessna.txtav.com/en/citation/m2 (accessed May 9, 2021) https://cessna.txtav.com/citation/m2-gen2 (accessed December 9, 2021).

[101] Citation CJ3+ jet offers the ultimate cabin for light-jet travel. From initial design, the seats were crafted with passenger's comfort in mind. The Citation CJ3+ aircraft is another light jet with a maximum range of 2,040 nautical miles (3,778 kilometer) at a maximum cruise speed of 416 knots true airspeed (770 kilometer per hour). More specifications are available at: https://cessna.txtav.com/en/citation/cj3 (accessed December 9, 2021).

[102] Citation CJ4 according to the company is at the top of the single-pilot class, the CESSNA CITATION CJ4 jet redefines versatility for a light jet. The CJ4 aircraft has added speed, range, and cabin size over its predecessor without incurring midsize jet operating costs. The Citation CJ4 aircraft has a maximum range of 2,165 nautical miles (4,010 kilometer) at a maximum cruise speed of 451 knots true airspeed (835 kilometer per hour). More specifications are available at: https://cessna.txtav.com/en/citation/cj4 (accessed May 9, 2021) https://cessna.txtav.com/citation/cj4-gen2 (accessed December 9, 2021).

[103] Citation XLS+ according to the company is the bestselling model of the bestselling brand. The CESSNA CITATION XLS+ aircraft combines transcontinental range and remarkable efficiency in a beautiful midsize jet. The XLS+ aircraft has a maximum range of 2,100 nautical miles (3,889 kilometer) at a maximum cruise speed of 441 knots true airspeed (817 kilometer per hour). More specifications are available at: https://cessna.txtav.com/en/citation/xls (accessed May 9, 2021) https://cessna.txtav.com/citation/cj4-gen2 (accessed December 9, 2021).

Citation Latitude,[104] Citation Sovereign+,[105] and Citation Longitude.[106] It is to be noted that Textron Aviation on March 31, 2021 announced that it has handed over the 1,000th Cessna Citation 560XL series business jet. Only two other manufacturers have accomplished this target of delivering more than 1,000 copies of business jet models, namely Bombardier Challenger 600–650 family at 1,122 aircraft, the Citation 550 family at 1,185 aircraft, and the Hawker 750–900 family at 1,102 aircraft.[107]

Textron Aviation's portfolio besides business jets includes turbo-props[108] and high-performance pistons aircraft.[109] The all line is well

---

[104]Citation Latitude jet offers a wide, flat-floor with a 6-foot stand-up cabin at a midsize price. Coupled with a range to take you 2,700 nautical miles (5,000 kilometer), you can fly non-stop from Los Angeles to New York or Geneva to Dubai at a maximum cruise speed of 446 knots true airspeed (826 kilometer per hour). More specifications are available at: https://cessna.txtav.com/en/citation/latitude (accessed December 9, 2021).

[105]Citation Sovereign+ is the successor to the Citation Sovereign model. The Sovereign+ features upgraded engines, which provide a longer range of 3,200 nautical miles (5,926 kilometer), and winglets as a standard offering versus an option on the original Sovereign. Max cruise speed: 460 knots true airspeed (852 kilometer per hour). The Sovereign+ also has improved take-off and landing capability. More specifications are available at: https://cessna.txtav.com/en/citation/sovereign (accessed May 9, 2021).

[106]Citation Longitude is Textron Aviation's largest aircraft. Textron Aviation's work is all the more impressive as the company took the fuselage from its Cessna Citation Latitude, stretched it and strengthened it. Part of the strengthening was focused on the rear fuselage, which unlike the Latitude, has a high-sweep T-tail. The result is an aircraft that can carry a maximum of 12 passengers, three more than can be accommodated in the Latitude. The maximum range of the Longitude is 3,500 nautical miles (6,482 kilometer) at a max cruise speed of 483 knots true airspeed (895 kilometer per hour). More specifications are available at: https://cessna.txtav.com/en/citation/longitude (accessed December 9, 2021).

[107]After the 2013 bankruptcy of Hawker Beechcraft, the surviving company, Beechcraft, discontinued its business jet range, including the 800 series, although the designs are still supported for parts.

[108]Turboprops are a hybrid of jet engines and the more traditional piston engine propeller that you see on smaller, lightweight airplanes. Reciprocating engine propeller airplanes are relatively efficient at low altitudes and airspeeds, and they are more economical for the average types of general aviation flights. Turboprops fill the efficiency gap between reciprocating and pure jet engines, being most efficient at mid-altitudes and airspeeds. For more information about the differences between these two types of engines see: https://airplaneacademy.com/piston-vs-turboprop-performance-efficiency-and-safety/ (accessed December 9, 2021).

[109]Piston airplanes have one or more piston-powered engines connected to the propeller(s), which provide thrust to move the aircraft on the ground and through the air. Piston-powered

represented by the two brands owned by Textron, i.e. Cessna and Beechcraft. The King Air series (all twin turboprop) by Beechcraft offers flexible, reconfigurable interiors, making them equally adept at accommodating passengers, cargo, air ambulance, or other missions, and includes the following models: the King Air C90GTx,[110] the King Air 260,[111] the King Air 360,[112] and the King Air 360ER.[113] On the other side, the turboprop family by Cessna includes: Cessna Skycourier (twin turboprop),[114] Cessna Caravan (single engine turboprop),[115]

---

aircraft most commonly use 100 octane low-leaded fuel and fly at altitudes below 15,000 feet. The inside of a typical piston aircraft seats 1–6 passengers and is configured similar to the interior of a small car. Piston aircraft used for business typically fly relatively short missions of 300–400 miles, using very small general aviation airports that are often without air traffic control towers. In this sense see definition by National Business Aviation Association, available at: https://nbaa.org/business-aviation/business-aircraft/piston-engine-aircraft/ (accessed December 9, 2021).

[110]The King Air C90GTx is capable of a maximum range of 1,260 nautical miles (2,334 kilometer), maximum cruise speed of 272 knots true airspeed (504 kilometer per hour), and maximum occupants of 8. More specifications are available at: https://beechcraft.txtav.com/king-air (accessed December 9, 2021).

[111]The King Air 260 is capable of a maximum range of 1,720 nautical miles (3,185 kilometer), maximum cruise speed of 310 knots true airspeed (574 kilometer per hour), and maximum occupants of 9. More specifications available at: https://beechcraft.txtav.com/en/king-air-260 (accessed December 9, 2021).

[112]The King Air 360 is capable of a maximum range of 1,806 nautical miles (3,345 kilometer), maximum cruise speed of 312 knots true airspeed (578 kilometer per hour), and maximum occupants of 11. More specifications are available at: https://beechcraft.txtav.com/en/king-air-360 (accessed December 9, 2021).

[113]The King Air 360ER is capable of a maximum range of 2,692 nautical miles (4,986 kilometer), maximum cruise speed of 303 knots true airspeed (561 kilometer per hour), and maximum occupants of 15. More specifications are available at: https://beechcraft.txtav.com/en/king-air-360er (accessed December 9, 2021).

[114]The Cessna Skycourier is capable of a maximum range of 900 nautical miles (1,667 kilometer), maximum cruise speed of 200 knots true airspeed (370 kilometer per hour). The Cessna SkyCourier has two configurations: It can accommodate a maximum of 19 passenger otherwise it offers a freight configuration carrying three LD3 shipping containers. More specifications are available at: https://cessna.txtav.com/en/turboprop/skycourier (accessed December 9, 2021).

[115]The Cessna Caravan is capable of a maximum range of 1,070 nautical miles (1,982 kilometer), maximum cruise speed of 186 knots true airspeed (344 kilometer per hour). The Cessna Caravan can accommodate a maximum of 10–14 passengers. More

Cessna Caravan EX (single engine turboprop),[116] and the Cessna Denali (single engine turboprop).[117]

As for the pistons "class" aircraft, which fall more specifically into the General Aviation, we have to include the Baron G58 (twin engine),[118] and the Bonanza G36[119] (by Beechcraft), and the Cessna Skyhawk,[120] Cessna Skyline,[121] and Cessna Turbo Stationair HD.[122]

---

specifications are available at: https://cessna.txtav.com/en/turboprop/caravan (accessed December 9, 2021).

[116] The Cessna Caravan EX is capable of a maximum range of 912 nautical miles (1,689 kilometer), maximum cruise speed of 185 knots true airspeed (343 kilometer per hour). The Cessna Caravan can accommodate a maximum of 10–14 passengers. More specifications are available at: https://cessna.txtav.com/en/turboprop/grand-caravan-ex (accessed December 9, 2021).

[117] The Cessna Denali is capable of a maximum range of 1,600 nautical miles (2,963 kilometer), maximum cruise speed of 285 knots true airspeed (528 kilometer per hour). The Cessna Denali interior configurations include a 6-seat executive interior complete with a refreshment center or a 9-seat commuter configuration. More specifications are available at: https://cessna.txtav.com/en/turboprop/denali (accessed December 9, 2021).

[118] Baron G58 is capable of a maximum range of 1,480 nautical miles (2,741 kilometer), maximum speed cruise of 202 knots true airspeed (374 kilometer per hour), and maximum occupants of 6. More specifications are available at: https://beechcraft.txtav.com/en/baron-g58 (accessed December 9, 2021).

[119] Bonanza G36 is capable of a maximum range of 920 nautical miles (1,704 kilometer), maximum cruise speed of 176 knots true airspeed (326 kilometer per hour), and maximum occupants of 6. More specifications are available at: https://beechcraft.txtav.com/en/bonanza-g36 (accessed December 9, 2021).

[120] The Cessna Skyhawk is capable of a maximum range of 640 nautical miles (1,185 kilometer), maximum speed cruise of 124 knots true airspeed (230 kilometer per hour), and maximum occupants of 4. The Skyhawk is ideally designed for instructors, students, and observers alike. The Skyhawk offers a three-seat training configuration or a standard four-seat configuration. More specifications are available at: https://cessna.txtav.com/en/piston/cessna-skyhawk (accessed December 9, 2021).

[121] The Cessna Skyline is capable of a maximum range of 915 nautical miles (1,695 kilometer), maximum speed cruise of 145 knots true airspeed (269 kilometer per hour), and maximum occupants of 4. More specifications are available at: https://cessna.txtav.com/en/piston/cessna-skylane (accessed December 9, 2021).

[122] The Cessna Turbo Stationair HD is capable of a maximum range of 703 nautical miles (1,302 kilometer), maximum speed cruise of 161 knots true airspeed (298 kilometer per hour), and maximum occupants of 6. More specifications are available at: https://cessna.txtav.com/en/piston/cessna-turbo-stationair-hd (accessed December 9, 2021).

As it has emerged from this short description Textron Aviation offers the most complete gamma of aircraft ranging from exclusive business jets to elegant general aviation solutions. Textron Inc. CEO Scott Donnelly while commenting the financial results in November 2020 affirmed that "while the pandemic impacted volume in the quarter we did see aircraft utilization levels continue to recover and we are encouraged by new order flow," he added that a "nice pickup in light and midsize jet activity," as well as "pretty strong order activity" for the Beechcraft King Air, increased its backlog in the third quarter by US$400 million to US$1.8 billion. During the quarter, Textron Aviation delivered 25 Cessna Citations and 21 commercial turboprops. That was lower than the 45 jets and 39 turboprops the company delivered in the same quarter last year (2019). For the first 9 months of the year, Textron Aviation recorded a loss of US$92 million on revenue of US$2.4 billion, compared with US$315 million in profit on revenue of US$3.45 billion in the same period a year ago. Financial results notwithstanding, Donnelly said increased utilization, a robust used market, and new users of business jets are driving optimism for a "decent recovery coming out of" the pandemic. "Just as you are seeing more people opting to use business aviation for personal reasons, you are going to see more people choose to use business aviation for business reasons," he explained.[123]

The world of business aviation, as we have seen, is extremely variegated and what is more is evolving rapidly. Newcomers can play a decisive role in further shaping it, and pushing it forward especially if new technologies will contribute to reducing the overall costs to operate innovative aircraft, and rendering this industry greener. The case of Celera 500L is of extreme interest because as explained in the following section it really has the potential to innovate this sector offering private services at very convenient rates and attracting new customers willing to fly in this modality.

3. Revolution in Business Aviation with the Introduction of Celera 500L

The Celera 500L represents a real game changer, a new concept of aircraft which not only reinvents conventional aircraft architecture but

---

[123] In this sense see: Jerry Siebnmark (2020), "Textron Boss Encouraged by Light, Midsize Jet Activity," *Aviation International News*, p. 12.

also drastically reduces aviation's carbon footprint maintaining the comfort and performances of very light business jets, at a fraction of their costs.

According to Otto Aviation "the Celera 500L is the most fuel efficient, commercially viable aircraft in existence. Otto Aviation's goal is to create a private aircraft that allows for direct flights between any city pair in the U.S. at speeds and cost comparable to commercial air travel. This takes a complete reinvention of how we fly and an unprecedented look at what private aviation can be."[124] The founder of Otto Aviation, William Otto, worked for decades in the aviation industry investigating many aspects related to the functioning of an aircraft, and his experience led him to create an aircraft which reassembles all the knowledge accumulated by the founder and his team resulting in the synthesis here expressed by the Celera 500L. This new innovative aircraft represents the answer to the increasing demand for private flying at the cost comparable to commercial airfare to assure passengers with security lines, avoid flight delays and cancellation, and other burdensome issues like connections which make public air transportation inconvenient. The solutions adopted by this innovative aircraft not only allow to travel in a private modality at a fraction of the cost of business jets but are also environmentally more sustainable.

3.1 *Business aviation goes greener with the Celera 500L keeping an eye on performances*

The extraordinary capabilities of the Celera 500L are mainly due to the technologies applied to this innovative aircraft. In particular, its efficiency which includes 5–7 times reduction in operational costs, 8 times lower fuel consumption, cruise speeds equivalent to similar-sized jet aircraft, is due to the laminar flow. The Celera 500L's extensive use of laminar shapes for wings, fuselage, and tail-sections makes this possible as indicated by Otto Aviation. The Shape of this aircraft makes the difference: The odd shapes of the fuselage and wings create uninterrupted airflow, reducing drag by up to 60% compared to a similarly sized business

---

[124] In this sense: Otto Aviation, more information at: www.ottoaviation.com (accessed May 9, 2021).

aircraft. This laminar-flow design is what underpins the Celera's fuel efficiency, speed, and range.

But what is laminar flow? Using the same words Otto Aviation used in its website, "Laminar flow is the minimum drag solution for aircraft surfaces, and features smooth layers of airflow with little to no mixing of adjacent layers. The design of the Celera fuselage takes advantage of an optimum length-to-width ratio to maximize laminar flow. These benefits will not scale for large jet transports and are therefore well suited for an aircraft like the Celera."

3.2 *Aerodynamics and the most efficient propulsion system make the difference*

The Celera 500L was created with the clear intent to rival with very light business jets beating them on operational costs and offering a greener option, and in order to achieve these targets the attention was posed in particular to its aerodynamics which inevitably impact on the propulsion system augmenting its efficiency and consequently the performances of this aircraft. In particular, the high-aspect ratio wings increase the Celera's laminar flow. Unusually long wingtips provide both aerodynamic efficiency and lateral stability. Designed to fly above weather and other air traffic, the Celera doubles its airspeed as it climbs between 15,000 and 50,000 feet.

The Celera 500L's aerodynamic airframe requires significantly less horsepower to achieve take-off and cruise speeds, allowing for a more fuel-efficient power plant to be utilized. In fact, its Apex Twin was designed specifically for this aircraft: The Red A03 lightweight aluminum piston engine is a liquid-cooled V-12, with each twin six-cylinder bank capable of independent operation. The engine is certified to operate on Jet AI and biodiesel fuel — which means 50% lower fuel burn compared to turbine engines in the same category, and it is capable of 550+ takeoff horsepower and best-in-class fuel efficiency. It is controlled via fully redundant electronic engine control unit with single power control lever reducing pilot workload.[125]

---

[125] Type certification approval granted via EASA (TC.E.150) and FAA (E00092EN). See: https://www.ottoaviation.com/technology (accessed December 9, 2021).

3.3 *An aircraft with an incredible gliding capability and internal volume*

The particular design of Celera 500L and its particular aerodynamics contribute to its characteristics and performances. In fact, this aircraft has a glide ratio of 22:1 (typical GA aircraft of similar size have a glide ratio of < 9:1). At an altitude of 30,000 feet the Celera 500L can glide up to 125 miles with no engine power. This is roughly 3x better than the typical aircraft.[126] The push-propeller design avoids creating turbulent airflow across the fuselage, adding to the aircraft's efficiency, while the ventral fin below provides strike protection.

It is undeniable that this innovative aircraft represents something unique capable of revolutionizing the business aviation sector with its dramatically reduced operating costs and bringing the comfort and convenience of high-end private aviation to the masses.

The aircraft's rounded shape allowed interior designers to install six spacious seats and the six-foot-two-inch headroom of a midsize jet, while placing the engine behind the cabin and using a rear prop makes for a much quieter in-flight experience. Its 448 cubic feet of volume beats competitors like Beechcraft's King Air 350, with 416 cubic feet, and the Citation CJ3 with just 311 cubic feet.

The convenience of using this new type of aircraft emerges from every angle; however, the sector of business aviation not only is growing greener but it is also exploring and expanding in other directions. People flying in a private mode with a higher capability of expenditure might be interested in alternatives offering not only cost-effective solutions but also high emotional experiences flying at supersonic velocity on board of a new generation aircraft.

4. The "Supersonic Renaissance"

Business aviation is expanding and in doing so some brave, visionary manufactures are exploring a new frontier which is not so new because the supersonic experience was first introduced and then abandoned years ago with the Concorde,[127] but they are planning to reintroduce it with a

---

[126] See: https://www.ottoaviation.com/performance (accessed December 9, 2021).

[127] The first supersonic passenger-carrying commercial airplane, the Concorde, was built jointly by aircraft manufacturers in Great Britain and France. It made its first transatlantic

completely new concept of supersonic aircraft with a lower impact and thus aimed at remaining in the boundaries of a greener aviation. This is the case of Overture and other players such as Spike Aerospace and even Virgin Galactic as exposed in the following sections. There is no doubt that there will be a next generation of quieter supersonic airplanes and to get there, the contenders not only need to design for speed and comfort but they also must address multiple technical challenges as, for example, fuel efficiency, CO_2 emissions, noise levels on takeoff and landing plus the ultimate dilemma: the sonic boom.

It seems the technology to help overcome these obstacles is now available and several manufacturers are now exploring this frontier and the reason is because the market is there.

It is evident that the primary advantage of a supersonic business aircraft would be halving the time to fly between major international destinations, such as New York–London, making it feasible for same-day transoceanic round trips. However, still some hurdles remain in particular regarding the compliance with existing regulations.

4.1 *Uncertainties about compliance remain*

When supersonic air transportation was introduced in the 1970s, there was not much attention to the environment, but now the situation has changed and technology has advanced; thus, it is natural that dedicated authorities pay more attention to the impact of supersonic flights and aviation in general. Therefore, new regulations in particular have been drafted to guide the development of new supersonic aircraft, however uncertainties about compliance remain.

It is worth noting that FAA regulations prohibit civil aircraft from operating at speeds exceeding Mach 1 over land in the United States, and the new FAA proposal[128] would not remove that prohibition, but

---

crossing on September 26, 1973, and entered regular service in 1976. British Airways and Air France stopped flying the Concorde in 2003. The Concorde had a maximum cruising speed of 2,179 kilometer (1,354 miles) per hour, or Mach 2.04. More information is available at: https://www.britannica.com/technology/supersonic-flight (accessed December 9, 2021).

[128] See: "Special Flight Authorizations for Supersonic," a proposed rule by the FAA on June 28, 2019, available at: https://www.federalregister.gov/documents/2019/06/28/2019-13079/special-flight-authorizations-for-supersonic-aircraft (accessed December 9, 2021).

instead establish procedures and noise levels for subsonic operation of some supersonic aircraft during landing and takeoff. "The FAA wants to amend noise certification regulation in 14 CFR, parts 21 and 36, to allow new supersonic airplanes, and to add subsonic landing and takeoff (LTO) cycle standards for supersonic airplanes that have a maximum takeoff weight no greater than 150,000 pounds and a maximum operating cruise speed up to Mach 1.8." There is a renewed interest in the development of supersonic aircraft, and the proposed regulations would facilitate the continued development of airplanes by specifying the noise limits for the designs, providing the means to certificate the airplanes for subsonic operation in the United States. FAA said that its proposal is based in part on the Supersonic Transport Concept Airplane (STCA) studies performed by the National Aeronautics And Space Administration (NASA), information provided to the FAA by the US industry, and ongoing work by the International Civil Aviation Organization (ICAO) Committee on Aviation Environmental Protection (CAEP).[129] This action proposes to add new supersonic airplanes to the applicability of noise certification regulations, according to the Notice of Proposed Rulemaking.[130]

---

[129] CAEP is a technical committee of the ICAO Council established in 1983. CAEP assists the Council in formulating new policies and adopting new Standards and Recommended Practices (SARPs) related to aircraft noise and emissions, and more generally to aviation environmental impact. CAEP undertakes specific studies, as requested by the Council. Its scope of activities encompasses noise, local air quality (LAQ), and the basket of measures for reducing international aviation CO_2 emissions, including aircraft technology, operational improvement, sustainable aviation fuels, and market-based measures (CORSIA). CAEP informs the Council and Assembly's decision-making with the ICAO Global Environmental Trends, which assess the present and future impact of aircraft noise and aircraft engine emissions. The Global Environmental Trends is crucial to the work of ICAO as it provides a robust single reference for sound discussion and decision-making. More information is available at: https://www.icao.int/ENVIRONMENTAL-PROTECTION/Pages/CAEP.aspx (accessed December 9, 2021).

[130] See the document by the FAA which specifically deals with this issue: 14 CFR Parts 21 and 36, "Noise Certification of Supersonic Airplanes." The document is available at: https://www.federalregister.gov/documents/2020/04/13/2020-07039/noise-certification-of-supersonic-airplanes (accessed December 9, 2021).

4.2 *The ultimate supersonic experience by Aerion: An interrupted dream*

Aerion,[131] a new visionary aviation company was targeting 2026 for initial handover of its Mach 1.4, 8–10 passenger AS2 business jet, but its plans were abruptly interrupted in May 2021 when the company in a brief statement exposed its difficulties in securing new funds to proceed with the project.

Only a few months before the debacle of Aerion, Tom Vice, Chairman, President, and CEO of Aerion Corporation had said in an interview in January 2021 that Aerion had already secured a domestic and international order backlog of US$6.5 billion and it had planned to deliver 300 aircraft over 10 years of production. The AS2's first flight was supposed to take off in 2024 and the company intended to take the plane to market in 2026.[132] Also this new supersonic aircraft was billed to serve with sustainability, in fact it was designed to run on 100% sustainable aviation fuels to deliver a net carbon reduction of 80%. Another development was announced, that is, the AS3, which was promoted to go "beyond supersonic," would be transporting up to 50 passengers between Los Angeles and Tokyo in less than three hours, and conceptualization and design tasks were already underway for this next-generation jet. It is noteworthy that one of the AS2's most innovative features was its "boomless cruise" which would have allowed the plane to fly supersonically over land without the boom striking the ground. Instead, the noise gets refracted back up into the atmosphere. However, despite all these technological advances, and according to the latest news due to its US$11.2 billion in sales backlog, Aerion had to shut down its activities because "the present financial climate has proved too challenging for Aerion to garner the capitals needed to begin production of its AS2 supersonic business jet," as told in a statement to announce the halt to its activities.

---

[131] Aerion Corporation was founded in 2003 by Texas billionaire Robert Bass as a startup working to commercialize supersonic aviation technology. Projects include the 8–12 passenger AS2 supersonic business jet. In November 2015, Aerion set a target to achieve FAA certification in 2021 and enter service in 2023, but in November 2017 amended the in-service date to 2025. The first flight was expected in 2024 and enter into service in 2026.
[132] Maureen O'Hare and Paul Sillers (2021), "Concorde Successor AS2 Takes Leap Forward with Vast New Florida HQ," *CNN*, available at: https://edition.cnn.com/travel/article/as2-supersonic-jet-florida-hq/index.html (accessed December 9, 2021).

"The Aerion Corporation has assembled a world-class team of employees and partners, and we are very proud of our collective efforts to realize a shared vision of revolutionizing global mobility with sustainable supersonic flight. Since our company's formation our team has created disruptive new innovations plus leading-edge technologies and intellectual property […] However, in the current financial environment, it has proven hugely challenging to close on the scheduled and necessary large new capital requirements to finalize the transition of the AS2® into production. Given these conditions the Aerion Corporation is now taking the appropriate steps in consideration of this ongoing financial environment." — Aerion Supersonic via statement.

Aerion has secured concrete advancements in technology for supersonic flight and for sure its experience and achievements shall serve to realize its dreams of flying at a supersonic speed in a sustainable fashion. No doubt Aerion has been one of the key names when it comes to those leading the new wave of supersonic travel and certainly this update had left certain jet operators alarmed. However, this new supersonic renaissance is not over. In fact, there are several other contenders across the aviation industry which will continue their adventure, so it is highly likely that passengers will be flying supersonic speeds soon.

4.3 *Spike Aerospace and its S-512 supersonic business jet*

Another contender in the race for supersonic business jet is Spike Aerospace.[133] This company too is working on sonic booms-mitigation technologies like Aerion and Boom for its Overture. As this represents a serious issue for all contenders they are working to minimize the supersonic "boom" in order to obtain the necessary certification.

The Spike S-512 supersonic business jet is projected to fly at Mach 1.6 (1,100 mph) and able to transport between 12 and 18 passengers. According to the manufacturer, the Spike S-512 supersonic business jet will be the first aircraft aerodynamically designed to offer proprietary quiet supersonic flight technology (depending how fast the company will

---

[133] Spike Aerospace, Inc. is a leading global collaboration of world-class aerospace firms in development of the world's first quiet supersonic jet, the Spike S-512. This revolutionary luxury aircraft, with proprietary Quiet Supersonic Flight technology, will cut flights times in half. See: https://www.spikeaerospace.com/about-spike-aerospace/ (accessed December 9, 2021).

develop and finalize this project, considering the other contenders are also working on it). This will enable it to operate at its full cruising speed without producing a loud, disturbing sonic boom on the ground.

The Spike S-512 supersonic business jet is a program currently under development which the company hopes to begin delivering starting from 2025. In consideration of its speed the S-512 will be the fastest civilian aircraft available on the market.

4.4 *Gulfstream and its pragmatic approach to supersonic speed*

It is not a secret that Gulfstream Aerospace with its latest ultra-long-range models skirting the sound barrier in flight test, has continued its research on supersonic possibilities. However, company President Mark Burns cautions that it could be 10 years before such a supersonic business jet actually reaches the market. Gulfstream's approach is more pragmatic and the company is working to further enhance the performance of its aircraft. For instance Gulfstream has reported that the G650 model and G700 model both have reached Mach 0.99 in flight test, and when asked if the company was ready to take the leap into supersonic, Burns told reporters that "we certainly look into supersonic flight in our [research and development] center." He added that the company has continued to invest in the future product line and "we're always looking out to what the future may hold." Having said that, he conceded supersonic flight presents "a tremendous hurdle for anyone to clear." Noting that Gulfstream has certified more than 11 aircraft during his tenure with the company, Burns said, "I know the difficulties associated with certifying new and novel technology. So there's a lot to be learned. There's a lot to be done before that type of airplane can be certified." One of the key obstacles is on the environmental front, he said.[134]

However supersonic flight is not limited to business jet, in fact others contenders are developing projects to host a larger number of passengers, and this is the case of Boom aerospace with its Overture, and Virgin

---

[134] See: Kerry Lynch (2020), "Supersonic Remains in Distance for Gulfstream" *AINonline*, November 24, available at: https://www.ainonline.com/aviation-news/business-aviation/2020-11-24/supersonic-remains-distance-gulfstream (accessed December 9, 2021).

Galactic which are developing their own programs as we have introduced in the following sections.

4.5 *A new supersonic airliner with "Boom" and its overture*

Boom is company testing the XB-1, a one-third scale supersonic demonstrator of its "Overture" concept — an airliner that would carry 55–75 passengers at Mach 2.2. "We've done about 66 million core hours of computing," Founder and Chief Executive Blake Scholl affirmed. Thus, he said, Boom has been able to test hundreds of iterations of aircraft design, a regime that in a wind tunnel would "be financially and time-wise just absolutely impractical." This is necessary to bring into reality that Overture is the first airliner in a new era of enduring supersonic flight. Overture is building on Concorde's legacy through faster, more efficient, and sustainable technology.

Another aspect the company is working on is fuel efficiency and it appears Overture's fleet will be able to run on 100% sustainable aviation fuels. They are also working to minimize community noise impacts, and Overture will blend in with the quietest of today's long-haul fleet. According to the company, an aircraft's fuel efficiency directly translates to how sustainably it operates. They are applying lessons from XB-1 to ensure Overture's design is maximized for sustainable performance.[135]

In particular, concerning this aspect it is important to stress the co-operation between Boom Supersonic and leading industrial technology company, Rolls-Royce. On July 30, 2020 they announced an engagement agreement to explore the pairing of a Rolls-Royce propulsion system with Boom's flagship supersonic passenger aircraft, Overture. "The goal of the new agreement is to work together to identify the propulsion system that would complement Boom's Overture airframe. The engagement will involve teams from Boom and Rolls-Royce collaborating in engine-airframe matching activities for Boom's flagship supersonic passenger aircraft, Overture. The teams will also examine certain key aspects of the propulsion system. The teams will investigate whether an existing engine

---

[135] See: https://boomsupersonic.com/sustainability (accessed December 9, 2021).

architecture can be adapted for supersonic flight, while Boom's internal team continues to develop the airframe configuration."[136]

"We've had a series of valuable collaborations and co-locations with Rolls-Royce over the past years to lay the groundwork for this next phase of development," said Blake Scholl, Boom Founder and CEO. "We look forward to building on the progress and rapport that we've already built with our collaboration as we work to refine Overture's design and bring sustainable supersonic transport to passenger travel," he added. The priorities of this engagement are informed by Boom and Rolls-Royce's shared commitment to sustainability. Both companies recognize that supersonic passenger travel has to be compatible with a net-zero carbon future, and the two teams will work together to address sustainability in Overture design and operations. Overcoming the technological challenges of supersonic flight provides a unique opportunity to accelerate innovation sustainably.[137] "We share a strong interest in supersonic flight and in sustainability strategies for aviation with Boom," said Simon Carlisle, Director of Strategy, Rolls-Royce. "We're now building on our valuable experience in this space as well as our previous work together to further match and refine our engine technology for Boom's Overture." As a result of this collaboration, Boom and Rolls-Royce expect to make significant progress toward finalizing Overture's aircraft configuration and propulsion system.[138]

Whether supersonic travel will become commonplace any time soon remains open for broader debate, also considering the many hurdles to be overcome, but the supersonic start-ups speak confidently about the opportunity. In any case, the authors of this book agree with what Scholl (CEO of Boom) said: *Supersonic travel is truly inevitable. It's only a matter of time.*

---

[136]"Boom and Rolls-Royce Announce Collaboration to Advance Overture Program," https://blog.boomsupersonic.com/boom-and-rolls-royce-announce-collaboration-to-advance-overture-program-ed6663e4a369 (accessed December 9, 2021).

[137]"Boom Supersonic and Rolls-Royce Agree on New Collaboration for Supersonic Overture Engine Program Design," available at: https://boomsupersonic.com/news/show/boom-supersonic-and-rolls-royce (accessed December 9, 2021).

[138]*Ibid.*

4.6 *Virgin Galactic plans to go supersonic*

Virgin Galactic,[139] entrepreneur Richard Branson's aerospace company, seems to be included in the crowded field of aspirants to reintroduce commercial supersonic flight. Virgin Galactic announced in summer 2020 a plan that it is working with the British engine manufacturer Rolls-Royce to develop an aircraft that can travel at three times the speed of sound. Richard Branson's Virgin Group envisions a flight at 60,000 feet, around twice the cruise altitude of ordinary subsonic jetliners. But at M3, Virgin Galactic's 9–19 seater would move nearly a Mach number faster than Boom's 55–75 seater "Overture" — also bearing a striking resemblance to Concorde and proposed to match its speed at M2.2 — and nearly three times as fast as Aerion's AS2 business jet. The other proposed supersonic project is from Spike Aerospace, whose S-512 business jet targets M1.6.[140] It is worth reporting that Virgin Galactic affirmed it completed its Mission Concept Review (MCR) and received authorization from the US FAA Center for Emerging Concepts and Innovation. The MCR describes a plane that can travel more than 3,700 kilometers per hour at altitudes higher than 18,000 meters, literally to the edge of space. Virgin Galactic signed what it called "a space act" agreement with the US space agency, NASA, to encourage commercial orbital space flight to the International Space Station, and to collaborate on high speed technology for lower orbit

---

[139]"Virgin Galactic Holdings, Inc, a vertically integrated aerospace and space travel company, which includes its manufacturer of advanced air and space vehicles, The Spaceship Company ('TSC'), announced today the first stage design scope for the build of its high speed aircraft design, and the signing of a non-binding Memorandum of Understanding (MOU) with Rolls-Royce to collaborate in designing and developing engine propulsion technology for high speed commercial aircraft. This follows the successful completion of its Mission Concept Review ('MCR') program milestone and authorization from the Federal Aviation Administration's ('FAA') Center for Emerging Concepts and Innovation to work with Virgin Galactic to outline a certification framework. This marks an exciting step forward in Virgin Galactic's development of a new generation of high speed aircraft, in partnership with industry and government leaders, with a focus on customer experience and environmental sustainability." For more information visit: https://www.virgingalactic.com/articles/virgin-galactic-unveils-mach-3-aircraft-design-for-high-speed-travel-and-signs-memorandum-of-understanding-with-rolls-royce/ (accessed December 9, 2021).
[140]https://www.flightglobal.com/air-transport/supersonic-skies-looking-crowded-with-entry-from-virgin-galactic/139603.article (accessed December 9, 2021).

travel. The company says it is also working on developing "sustainable" aviation fuel for the aircraft.[141]

To conclude this part of the book it is necessary to underline that flying privately will continue to attract more travelers considered the many options the market offers. In particular, as it has emerged from the latest sections, the market dynamics for business jets are likely to witness major transformation with the Renaissance of supersonic aircraft, and the era of supersonic business jets is likely to become a reality toward the mid-2020s with a number of industry OEMs, led by Gulfstream and Aerion and new entrants, working on the development of supersonic business jets with an active pursuit of R&D toward the development of a range of supersonic flight technologies capable of enabling feasible supersonic flights while meeting regulatory requirements simultaneously.

It is now necessary to turn our attention on another important aspect, that is the costs of transiting not only business aviation but the entire industry toward a greener aviation industry.

---

[141] In this sense see: VOA News (2020), "Virgin Galactic Plans to Build Next Generation Supersonic Commercial Aircraft," August 4, available at: https://www.voanews.com/science-health/virgin-galactic-plans-build-next-generation-supersonic-commercial-aircraft (accessed December 9, 2021).

Chapter 5

Toward a Green Aviation: Financial Investments in a Promising Sector

Mario Tettamanti

1. Introduction: What is Sustainable or Green Finance?

Sustainable finance has gained phenomenal momentum. In 2019, a record total of US$257.7 billion of green bonds were issued globally, representing 51% growth from 2018. Despite the pandemic, this momentum has continued through 2020, with issuances of US$69.4 billion in Q3, the highest ever recorded in any third quarter period. Equity markets have seen similar trends, with Morningstar[1] recording inflows of US$54.6 billion into sustainable funds in Q2 2020.

Sustainable finance, also known as responsible finance or ethical investment, or green finance, is closely related to impact investing, which

---

[1] https://www.investopedia.com/terms/m/morningstarinc.asp (accessed December 14, 2021).

Morningstar is a Chicago-based investment research firm that compiles and analyzes fund, stock, and general market data. They also provide an extensive line of internet, software, and print-based products for individual investors, financial advisers, and institutional clients. The research reaches all corners of the world, including North America, Europe, Australia, and Asia. Among its many offerings, Morningstar's comprehensive, one-page mutual and exchange-traded fund (ETF) reports are widely used by investors to determine the investment quality of the more than 2,000 funds. The Motley Fool, for instance, uses them as a chief information source.

seeks to have a positive and tangible impact on the economy. Sustainable finance refers to any form of financial service integrating environmental, social and governance (ESG) criteria into the business or investment decisions for the lasting benefit of both clients and society at large. Sustainable finance consists in choosing which assets to operate on not only on the basis of possible profits but also considering their possible social impact.[2]

Activities that fall under the heading of sustainable finance, to name just a few, include sustainable funds, green bonds, impact investing, microfinance, active ownership, credits for sustainable projects, and development of the whole financial system in a more sustainable way. Sustainable finance encompasses all activities by financial service providers that aim to reduce harm to the environment and climate, to promote social engagement and to encourage sustainable corporate governance. The Paris Agreement[3] and the EU Action Plan[4] derived from it set out concrete sustainability goals for the financial sector and thus represent a cornerstone of sustainable finance. Sustainable finance means that in the future, capital will flow toward more sustainable investments, environmental risks will be taken into greater account and transparency will be encouraged. In this way, the financial services sector is meant to

---

[2]https://www.lgt.ch/en/lp_investing-sustainably/ (accessed December 14, 2021). The criteria of the ESG sustainability rating (E stands for environment, S for social, and G for governance) have become established key assessment indicators and give you more transparency in your investment decisions.

[3]https://unfccc.int/process-and-meetings/the-paris-agreement/the-paris-agreement (accessed December 14, 2021).

The Paris Agreement is a legally binding international treaty on climate change. It was adopted by 196 parties at COP21 in Paris, on December 12, 2015 and entered into force on November 4, 2016. Its goal is to limit global warming to well below 2°C, preferably to 1.5°C, compared to pre-industrial levels. To achieve this long-term temperature goal, countries aim to reach global peaking of greenhouse gas emissions as soon as possible to achieve a climate neutral world by mid-century. The Paris Agreement is a landmark in the multilateral climate change process because, for the first time, a binding agreement brings all nations into a common cause to undertake ambitious efforts to combat climate change and adapt to its effects.

[4]https://www.greenfinanceplatform.org/policies-and-regulations/european-commissions-action-plan-financing-sustainable-growth and https://www.pwc.de/en/sustainability/sustainable-finance.html (accessed December 14, 2021). PWC, a strategic advantage for the benefit of the environment, society, and economy alike.

support the transformation of the overall economy and guide it toward sustainability.

1.1 *The sustainable finance*

Sustainable finance refers to the process of taking ESG considerations into account when making investment decisions in the financial sector, leading to more long-term investments in sustainable economic activities and projects. Environmental considerations might include climate change mitigation and adaptation, as well as the environment more broadly, for instance the preservation of biodiversity, pollution prevention, and the circular economy. Social considerations could refer to issues of inequality, inclusiveness, labor relations, investment in human capital and communities, as well as human rights issues. The governance of public and private institutions — including management structures, employee relations, and executive remuneration — plays a fundamental role in ensuring the inclusion of social and environmental considerations in the decision-making process.

In the EU's policy context, sustainable finance is understood as finance to support economic growth while reducing pressures on the environment and taking into account social and governance aspects. Sustainable finance also encompasses transparency when it comes to risks related to ESG factors that may have an impact on the financial system, and the mitigation of such risks through the appropriate governance of financial and corporate actors.

1.2 *The sustainable financial markets*

The sustainable financial markets represent an emerging opportunity for both the private sector investment and project developers. Filling this gap to finance the preservation of the world's precious ecosystems will require billions of dollars in additional capital, and private investment capital may be the main source of such funds. This highlights the need for intelligent development finance that goes well beyond filling financial gaps and that can be used strategically to leverage private resources. The private sector is seeking new opportunities to invest capital in ways that could possibly generate market-rate financial returns and an environmental impact. Already, pioneering investors have put together financial solutions that combine real assets, like tropical forests, with cash flows from operations in fields such as sustainable timber, agriculture, and ecotourism. Scarce public funding can play a significant role in helping to unlock private sector investments required to fill the existing funding gaps.

Attracting investments in conservation is challenging because potential investors perceive high financial risks and low returns. Credit enhancements — whereby a company attempts to improve its debt or credit worthiness — can encourage the flow of capital to bankable projects by reducing risk or increasing returns. Impact investors — those interested in environmental and social impact — are using a broad range of tools for credit enhancements, some of which is catalytic first-loss capital.[5]

1.3 *Types of sustainable investments*[6]

Investing in sustainable companies and financial products seems to be a trend destined to grow and integrate into other investment processes and products. What characterizes this type of investment is the conscious choice to invest in a company or fund considered attentive to social issues. Investors usually choose companies that in the context of social justice, environmental sustainability, energy and clean technologies are similar. Sustainable finance also consists in avoiding those industries with a possible negative impact on society or are harmful to the environment, such as those producing alcohol, tobacco, oil and gas, fast food, or gambling.[7]

---

[5] https://thegiin.org/assets/documents/pub/CatalyticFirstLossCapital.pdf (accessed June 14, 2021). The Global Impact Investing Network (GIIN®) is a non-profit organization dedicated to increasing the scale and effectiveness of impact investing. The GIIN builds critical infrastructure and supports activities, education, and research that help accelerate the development of a coherent impact investing industry. For more information, see www. thegiin.org. (accessed December 14, 2021).

[6] https://corporatefinanceinstitute.com/resources/knowledge/trading-investing/sustainable-investing/ (accessed December 14, 2021) and https://www.sustainablefinance.ch/upload/cms/user/201712_Handbook_on_Sustainable_Investments_CFA.pdf (accessed June 14, 2021).

Handbook on sustainable investments. The CFA Institute Research Foundation is a not-for-profit organization established to promote the development and dissemination of relevant research for investment practitioners worldwide.

[7] https://www.un.org/en/climatechange/paris-agreement (accessed December 14, 2021). Climate change is a global emergency that goes beyond national borders. It is an issue that

The new trend in finance is green. The need to adopt a sustainable footprint has, in fact, also extended to banks and investors who are showing a growing activism and interest in sustainable finance, a trend confirmed by the fact that the financial industry is moving toward an increasingly systematic integration of sustainable investing in investment processes and products.

The international debate has increasingly shifted attention to the crucial issue of environmental protection, focusing interest on the transition to a green economy. From the Sustainable Development Goals (SDGs) to COP21 in Paris a path started in the past years has been sealed toward an economic development model based on decarbonization.

In this context, finance has acquired an increasingly active role through the mobilization of capital directed toward sustainable projects. Initially it was not easy for investors and financial markets to assimilate the opportunities of green business, considering the lack of available data on the climate risk of companies and on the returns of green investments.

Over the last decade, there has been an acceleration of the financial commitment in a green key, to the point that the term green finance is coined to indicate a financial system focused on supporting investments and policies that aim to protect the environment and climate. This system

---

requires coordinated solutions at all levels and international cooperation to help countries move toward a low-carbon economy. To tackle climate change and its negative impacts, 196 countries adopted the Paris Agreement at the COP21 in Paris on December 12, 2015. Entered into force less than a year later, the deal aims to substantially reduce global greenhouse gas emissions and to limit the global temperature increase in this century to 2°C while pursuing means to limit the increase even further to 1.5°C. Today, 189 countries have joined the Paris Agreement. The agreement includes commitments from all countries to reduce their emissions and work together to adapt to the impacts of climate change and calls on countries to strengthen their commitments over time. The Agreement provides a pathway for developed nations to assist developing nations in their climate mitigation and adaptation efforts while creating a framework for the transparent monitoring and reporting of countries' climate goals. The Paris Agreement provides a durable framework guiding the global effort for decades to come. The aim is to raise countries' climate ambition over time. To promote this, the agreement establishes two review processes, each on a 5-year cycle. The Paris Agreement marks the beginning of a shift toward a low-carbon world — there is much more to do. Implementation of the Agreement is essential for the achievement of the SDGs as it provides a roadmap for climate actions that will reduce emissions and build climate resilience.

not only includes the financing of specific projects of a public or private nature but also includes support for public policies for the benefit of the environment. Among the issues at the center of the interest of green investors are clean energy, the protection of biodiversity, energy efficiency, sustainable transport, water management, adaptation and mitigation of climate effects.

1.4 *The green financial instruments or products*

1.4.1 *The green bonds*

In 2007, the first green bond, essentially a bond to support investments that benefit the environment and the climate was launched. The operation is similar to that of a normal debt security: the entity that issues the bond receives capital while the investors enjoy a fixed return in the form of interest. The difference is that green bonds explicitly provide for the allocation of proceeds for environmental purposes.[8]

The green bond market has grown exponentially over the past few years. The demand for green, social, or sustainability bonds has also been triggered by more awareness among the investors looking for companies with an easier transition to the green economy, and by end customers who are more willing to buy sustainable products. The green bond market has seen surge in support from institutional investors, retail investors, governments, treasuries, and from central banks, who are interested in buying green bonds. These investors are eager to invest in a credible green bond. Learn how a second-party opinion makes a green bond credible. While the large multilateral development banks have issued these financing mechanisms until 2012, other entities will enter the market in the following years. The first corporate green bonds are launched by the private sector, municipal by local governments, and city by different cities. Green bonds

---

[8] https://www.sustainalytics.com/esg-research/resource/corporate-esg-blog/about-green-bond-principles (accessed December 14, 2021).

The green bond market aims to enable and mobilize debt markets to fund projects that contribute to environmental sustainability. Green bonds facilitates capital-raising and investments for new and existing projects which have environmental benefits and can mitigate risks associated with climate change. With over 1,500 green bonds issued in 2018, valued at more than US$175 billion, the green bond market is growing at a fast pace. It is estimated that by 2019, green bond issuance will surpass US$210 billion.

can be corporate if issued by the private sector, municipal if by local governments and city if by different cities. In recent years, the market has experienced constant growth and the need has emerged to adopt control and monitoring tools to protect investors regarding the green nature of the projects financed. In 2009, the Climate Bonds Initiative (CBI) was established, which monitors its size every year. Certification tools are also added that aim to standardize the characteristics of green bonds, such as the Climate Bonds Standard by the CBI and the Green Bond Principles (GBP), developed by the International Capital Markets Association (ICMA).

1.4.2 *The green mutual funds*[9]

In recent years, we have seen the development of green funds that aim to invest in the field of sustainability, with a strong exposure of pension funds and insurance; not only that, starting from 2014 various banks and rating companies have launched benchmarks to assess the performance of green bonds (Bank of America Merrill Lynch Green Bond Index, Barclays MSCI Green Bond Index, S&P Green Bond Index, Solactive Green Bond Index).

1.4.3 *The stock market*

The stock exchanges have also launched lists dedicated to green bonds including London, Oslo and Stockholm; in 2016, the Luxembourg Stock

---

[9]https://economictimes.indiatimes.com/definition/mutual-fund (accessed December 14, 2021).

A mutual fund is a professionally managed investment scheme, usually run by an asset management company that brings together a group of people and invests their money in stocks, bonds, and other securities. As an investor, you can buy mutual fund "units," which basically represent your share of holdings in a particular scheme. These units can be purchased or redeemed as needed at the fund's current net asset value (NAV). These NAVs keep fluctuating, according to the fund's holdings. So, each investor participates proportionally in the gain or loss of the fund. All the mutual funds are registered with SEBI. They function within the provisions of strict regulation created to protect the interests of the investor. The biggest advantage of investing through a mutual fund is that it gives small investors access to professionally managed, diversified portfolios of equities, bonds, and other securities, which would be quite difficult to create with a small amount of capital.

Exchange established the Luxembourg Green Exchange (LGX), a platform reserved entirely for green products, with such success that the listing was then extended to stocks that support social and sustainable projects. The biggest challenge for green investments remains transparency, to allow investors to correctly assess the real impacts of each loan. Ultimately, green finance is increasingly active and can take on the role that everyone expects as an irreplaceable ally in achieving the climate objectives set out in Paris in 2015; however, several aspects still need to be improved, such as the uniformity of standards and certification criteria. The game is played on credibility: investors need greater transparency on the allocation of funds to correctly assess the real impacts of each loan, thus avoiding the risk of greenwashing.

1.4.4 *The ETF the so-called "green exchange-traded funds"*

Today's investors have access to a growing number of green ETFs, which allows them to incorporate environmentally friendly strategies into their investment decisions. ETFs are investment funds that trade on a stock exchange. Investors have a wide variety of ETFs from which to choose, from those that track a major market index to ETFs that track a basket of foreign currencies. Another type of ETF is the green ETF, which focuses on companies that support or are directly involved with environmentally responsible technologies, such as the development of alternative energy or the manufacture of green technology equipment and devices.[10,11]

---

[10] https://www.investopedia.com/terms/e/etf.asp (accessed December 14, 2021).

An exchange traded fund (ETF) is a type of security that tracks an index, sector, commodity, or other asset, but which can be purchased or sold on a stock exchange the same as a regular stock. An ETF can be structured to track anything from the price of an individual commodity to a large and diverse collection of securities. ETFs can even be structured to track specific investment strategies.

[11] https://bussolafinanziaria.it/etf-energie-rinnovabili/ (accessed December 14, 2021).

Green economy/green energy ETFs are exchange-traded funds that invest mainly in shares of companies involved in the production of alternative energy, such as solar and wind. However, equity ETFs are not the only possible solution to invest in the green economy: Recently, there are also the so-called green bond ETFs, or funds that track the performance of an index composed of "green" bonds (intended to finance projects from positive impact on the environment).

1.5 *The urgent need for improved regulation in the green financial sector*

The environmental value of green finance is only as robust as the classification, measurement, and transparency of the physical impacts. Without these, the use of green finance remains exposed to accusations of greenwashing, and efforts to improve them will be crucial over the immediate years. The EU Taxonomy Regulation[12] is a classification system, establishing a list of environmentally sustainable economic activities. The EU platform on sustainable finance has laid out a set of global criteria to determine which financial products can be marketed as "green" to investors. The Taxonomy Regulation establishes six environmental objectives: (1) Climate change mitigation; (2) Climate change adaptation; (3) The sustainable use and protection of water and marine resources; (4) The transition to a circular economy[13]; (5) Pollution prevention and control; (6) The protection and restoration of biodiversity and ecosystems.

2. The Green Finance in the Aviation Sector

Green finance in the last few years has gained phenomenal momentum. In 2019, a record total of US$257.7 billion of green bonds were issued globally, representing 51% growth from 2018. Despite the pandemic, this momentum has continued through 2020, with issuances of US$69.4 billion in Q3 — the highest ever recorded in any third quarter period. Equity markets have seen similar trends, with Morningstar recording inflows of US$54.6 billion into sustainable funds in Q2 2020.[14]

---

[12] https://ec.europa.eu/info/business-economy-euro/banking-and-finance/sustainable-finance/eu-taxonomy-sustainable-activities_en (accessed December 14, 2021).

[13] Circular economy: Solutions for a sustainable future (solarimpulse.com) (accessed December 14, 2021).

The circular economy refers to an economic model whose objective is to produce goods and services in a sustainable way, by limiting the consumption and waste of resources (raw materials, water, energy) as well as the production of waste. It is breaking with the model of the linear economy, based on a take-make-consume-throw away pattern, by proposing to transform waste into recycled raw material.

[14] Brodies LLP (2020), "Will Greener Financing Options Take Off in the Aviation Sector?," available at: https://brodies.com/insights/banking-and-finance/will-greener-financing-options-take-off-in-the-aviation-sector/ (accessed December 14, 2021).

The aviation industry progressed ahead of other sectors in agreeing to sustainability goals. The initial commitments to carbon-neutral growth from 2020 were established by the International Civil Aviation Organization (ICAO) in 2010 — a full 6 years before the Paris Agreement was signed at COP21.

Since then, companies and organizations across aviation have only ratcheted up their commitments. Thirteen airlines in OneWorld and over 500 airports in ACI Europe have committed to net zero carbon emission by 2050, and many other companies are targeting similar decarbonization trajectories.

Beyond the constant efforts to improve fuel efficiency and reduce emissions through fleet renewals, improved operations and infrastructure, other initiatives are gaining momentum. Ground equipment is becoming electrified, sustainable aviation fuels are moving from trials to commercial production, and electric propulsion is becoming a practical reality.

Accelerating these efforts to achieve the targets that airlines and airports are committing to will require vast capital. The Energy Transitions Commission (ETC) estimates the abatement cost for aviation as approximately US$170 per metric ton of CO_2. When applied to the sector's 2019 emissions, this suggests an industry cost of over US$155 billion, equivalent to over 7 years of total industry profits.

The ICAO and its member states are working together to develop State Action Plans to reduce CO_2 emissions from international aviation. The development and completion of State Action Plans on CO_2 emissions reduction activities from international aviation requires the establishment of a structured cooperation process among national aviation stakeholders which aims to provide the State authority with the information it needs to set up a long-term strategy for the mitigation of international aviation CO_2 emissions.

The voluntary submission of an action plan to ICAO provides the opportunity for States to showcase policies and actions, including tailor-made measures that are selected on the basis of their respective national capacities and circumstances.

2.1 *Measures to achieve international aviation's global goals*

To achieve international aviation's global aspirational goals, a comprehensive approach, consisting of a basket of measures has been identified, namely:

- Aircraft-related technology development — purchase of new aircraft and new equipment to retrofit existing aircraft with more fuel-efficient technology.
- Alternative fuels — investments in the development and deployment of sustainable aviation fuels.
- Improved air traffic management and infrastructure use — improved use of communication, navigation and surveillance/air transport management (CNS/ATM) to reduce fuel burn.
- Economic/market-based measures — researching and building awareness of low cost, market-based measures to reducing emissions such as emission trading, levies, and off-setting.

All of these measures, in addition to contributing to carbon neutral growth, advance the social and economic development associated with the UN SDGs. Fine modulo.

2.2 Green alternatives: Sustainability-linked instruments for the aviation sector

Sustainability data affects a firm's cost of capital in the form of sustainability-linked bonds and loans. These forms of borrowing are gaining popularity in the sustainable finance world because they can lower the cost of debt for companies who are engaged in sustainability. Banks and investors incentivize sustainability because companies that engage in sustainability are linked to financial out-performance, lower credit risk, better innovation, and good management. Sustainability-linked loans provide funds for general business purpose with interest rates that are linked to the borrower's sustainability performance. On the other hand, sustainability-linked bonds provide funds for a particular project or initiative that is committed to advancing sustainability.[15]

Sustainability-linked instruments are a potential alternative that could be utilized by airlines. These provide much more flexibility in how the proceeds are used, based on a two-way pricing mechanism. If the airlines

---

[15] https://majorsustainability.smeal.psu.edu/finance/concepts/sustainability-linked-financial-instruments/. Finance and sustainability-linked financial instruments, PENN State (accessed December 14, 2021).

achieve pre-determined ESG targets, the coupon payments decrease; if they fall short, they increase.

That aviation as an inherently carbon-emitting industry has evoked strong views from some and that currently it should not be considered for ESG-accredited financing on any terms. Conversely, the benefits of genuine ESG financing accreditation should perhaps be better viewed as an incentive for the industry to improve its environmental impact. In this way, ESG incentives in financing and investment create an opportunity for aviation industry players to strive to improve the *status quo*, and align with the principle of environmental sustainability over the long term.

The continued importance of sustainability for aviation will accelerate the requirement for capital to develop new technologies, infrastructure, and fuels. Airports can already make use of green finance for sustainable infrastructure projects, and specialist in this field expect their use to increase as the industry focuses on a green recovery from COVID-19. Airlines face greater challenges. While the current definition of green bonds eludes airlines, transition bonds and ESG-linked instruments may provide alternatives.

The expansion of the EU taxonomy to cover aviation will go a long way to legitimize the sectors' use of green finance, as will work by other organizations (such as rating agencies) to further assess and define green directives.

The use of green finance in aviation will need to tread a narrow path to ensure the reputational benefits are backed up with tangible progress toward sustainability targets, or risk miring the benefits with accusations of greenwashing. As the classifications are refined and accepted by the wider investment community, we will see accelerated use of green finance in aviation, helping fuel the necessary investments to decarbonize the sector.

While ESG factors may previously have been background considerations for credit committees, they are increasingly key determinants of capital allocation. The application of ESG to aircraft financing transactions is thus becoming more prevalent as participants are keen to avail themselves of green credentials — although there remain accusations of "greenwashing" in some quarters. In this chapter, we review the current position and future outlook.[16]

---

[16] https://www.icao.int/environmental-protection/Documents/ICAO_UNDP_GEF_FinancingLowCarbonAirportGuidance.pdf (accessed December 14, 2021).

With the support of GEF and UNDP, ICAO is working with SIDS and developing States to strengthen their national capacities and improve national processes and mechanisms for the reduction of aviation emissions by:

- improving the understanding of the costs and environmental benefits associated with implementation of various mitigation measures for international aviation emissions;
- enhancing policy framework through a series of policy instruments, including the development of guidance documents;
- sharing knowledge and resources through an integrated environmental portal, as well as other awareness-raising initiatives; and
- developing Pilot Projects, such as the installation of solar technology at airports, thus equipping developing states and SIDS with tools to carry on similar projects and multiplying their environmental benefit.

2.3 *The aviation's public funding*

The reduction of emissions and the need to use renewable energy has prompted designers, builders, and management companies to rethink the ecosystem that revolves around airports: from terminals, to runways, from transport to connections.[17] Airports are the ideal place for experimenting with new solutions, both design and procedural. Multidisciplinarity, innovation, and sustainability are primary directions for making the process more efficient, with direct effects on architectural and engineering solutions. Experts talk about territorial integration and environmental responsibility, trying to set their work on principles of flexibility and resilience in the long term. Swedavia AB, a major airport operator in Sweden, issued a US$118 million green bond with a 5.25-year maturity in 2019 to fund projects addressing climate change and sustainability. This used a framework developed by SEB and Swedbank, which aligns with the 2018 GBP defined by the International Capital Market Association.

---

[17]Financing aviation, emission reduction.

This framework has also been used by subsequent issuances, most recently for the issuance of a US$910 million green bond by the Royal Schiphol Group, specifically to finance clean transportation and sustainable buildings at Amsterdam and other airports it operates around the Netherlands. However, while the 2018 GBP defines eligible green project categories ranging from green buildings to clean transportation and renewable energy, it does not cover aviation assets and is therefore only useful for a limited number of opportunities.

2.3.1 *The network of public financing programs*

There exists a complex network of public financing programs that direct funding for climate mitigation and adaptation projects. These programs are building capacity by informing existing government institutions about climate challenges and opportunities, providing information on new regulatory and legal frameworks, and connecting staff with other stakeholders that can help advance climate programs.

This guidance document provides an overview of climate programs that may be available to ICAO member states to help them implement their State Action Plans. It is important for States to become aware of these programs, what type of funding is available, and how to begin the process of applying for funding as part of a broader national climate development program. This guidance document shows that:

- Project financing can be complex and may require that the National Action Plan Team coordinate with other national stakeholders in order to access specific information and expertise.
- Financial instruments long used in international development have been modified to benefit climate financing. They provide great opportunity for developing States, but depend on close co-operation with international agencies like the World Bank Group.
- Public financing to reform the energy sector and incentivize low carbon energy, which must be developed within the State, are critical to attracting private investment.
- State Action Plans developed using ICAO Doc 9988 can be a good starting point for financing projects to reduce international aviation emissions.

- Using internationally approved plans and methodologies as the basis to assess potential CO_2 benefits from projects can highly facilitate the approval of green financing for selected aviation projects.[18,19]

2.4 *Private investing in green aviation*

Lenders contend that borrowers with better ESG credentials are likely to have better corporate governance and are therefore a lower credit risk. This perhaps seems obvious given the "governance" aspect of ESG, but given the increasing focus on climate change many believe that companies with better ESG credentials will be inherently better placed and more robust as organizations in the future global business world. Banks are increasingly developing financial modeling on this relationship between ESG and financial performance.

2.4.1 *Thanks to ESG, the private sector invest in green aviation*

Until recently, there was often a perception that any investment in aviation (let alone an aircraft finance transaction) could not be ESG compliant because of environmental concerns regarding the industry's contribution to carbon emissions. However, attitudes seem to be shifting as there have now been a number of green or sustainability-linked financings involving airlines, lessors, and airports within the past year.[20]

With regulatory changes and increased public focus on environmental matters driving change in the aviation industry and certain capital providers available and looking to finance that change in new markets, there is scope for the right projects to receive financing at the right price. While

---

[18]Herbert Smith Freehills, "ESG in Aviation Finance," available at: hsfnotes.com (accessed June 14, 2021).

[19]https://www.icao.int/SAM/Documents/2014-ENV/04_Summary%20of%20Guidance%20Changes.pdf. ICAO Doc 9988, Guidance on the Development of States' Action Plans on CO2 Emissions Reduction Activities, was made available to all Action Plan focal points in advance of the hands-on training workshops in 2011 (in English, accessed December 14, 2021).

[20]Norton Rose Fulbright, "Green and Sustainable Financing Products for Airlines," available at: https://www.nortonrosefulbright.com/en-gb/knowledge/publications/de2464c2/green-and-sustainable-financing-products-for-airlines (accessed December 14, 2021).

the industry must be alert to accusations of greenwashing, there are a number of developments which deserve being labeled as Green Loan Principles or Sustainability-Linked Loan Principles financings. If this mixture of regulatory impetus and technological and financial ingenuity leads to a greener and more sustainable aviation industry, we will all benefit.

In December 2019, Deutsche Bank closed the first green commercial aircraft financing with lessor Aviation in respect of an ATR 72-600 aircraft on lease to Braathens, the Swedish regional airline. The ESG certification of the loan was linked to the Loan Market Association's (LMA) Green Loan Principle, with the primary ESG element being the replacement of the airline's fleet of older regional jets with more fuel-efficient turboprops (thereby reducing the airline's overall environmental impact). Although this was the first reported ESG transaction in the aircraft finance space, there have also been a number of other reported ESG financings within the wider aviation sector. The ESG credentials of the Sydney airport transaction were based on the LMA's Sustainability-Linked Loan Principles, whereas the ANA and Etihad deals were linked to the UN SDGs. Furthermore, it was recently reported that major lessor Avolon might look to offer more attractive lease rates to airlines with higher ESG ratings. Whether this will materialize into meaningful industry-wide practice remains to be seen; however, it is clear that lessors and other industry participants are under increasing pressure from investors and other stakeholders to place more emphasis on ESG strategy.

2.4.2 Use of green finance can help the industry to obtain capital for green aviation

The green finance offers an assortment of reputational, diversification, and potential yield benefits. Despite this, aviation has seen very little use of green finance. This is a supply problem, with considerable latent demand from sustainable investors keen to diversify their portfolios. However, many of the current classification systems have traditionally required the projects funded by the capital to align with the Paris Agreement, which is complicated by the unclear decarbonization trajectory for aviation.

As a result, most green finance issuances in aviation have been by airports, using existing frameworks to issue debt to fund cleaner buildings, electric vehicles, and climate change adaption.

Borrowers are facing significant reputational, political, and regulatory pressure to improve their ESG credentials, bolstered by the recent trend toward shareholder activism across markets globally. Sustainable financing will form part of an enhanced and more visible ESG strategy. Moreover, end-users are becoming more conscious of the environmental provenance of the products and services they wish to buy. Aviation faces particular pressure in this regard, with the industry needing to respond to "flight-shaming." Accordingly, many major airlines have committed to a radical overhaul of their ESG policies.

Banks (and other financiers such as sovereign wealth funds and pension funds) are also facing mounting pressure to justify their capital flows in terms of ESG criteria (one of the key aims of the Paris Agreement in 2015). Following France, Australia, and Singapore, UK regulators announced in early July that banks would soon be subject to climate stress tests. In terms of reputational considerations, a number of major financial institutions have been subject to widespread public and political criticism for their involvement in "dirty" industries such as coal and gas.

Some banks have sought to self-regulate by imposing environmental disclosure and enhanced performance via voluntary industry schemes. For example, many have already signed up to the United Nations Principles for Sustainable Investment and the Task Force on Climate-related Financial Disclosures. Further, in June 2019, 11 banks were holding C$ 100 billion of shipping loans set up the Poseidon Principles, whereby they have committed to ensuring the environmental viability of shipping debt. An analogous scheme is yet to be seen among aviation financiers but might be developed in the coming years.

2.5 *Technology and financing in the green aviation*

Private and public funding for the aviation sector focuses mainly on the search for less polluting fuels and on "normal" interventions in airports. However, it must be said that smaller public and private funding allow researchers in the sector to experiment with new ways. Differently from what occurs in rail and road transport (in particular in cars), at the moment the possible interventions in the aviation sector (engines and especially batteries) are currently very complicated. The exciting development of electric aviation technologies might usher in a revolution in this regard, but this remains a long-term project, with commercial electric flights not expected for many years (largely due to limitations in existing battery technology).

Technology is advancing and surely manufacturers will succeed in introducing new aircrafts at zero impact. However, to transit the entire aviation sector into a more "sustainable" and greener modality more investments are needed and naturally where the market growths are faster it is more likely a surge of investments with manufacturers themselves investing more resources in new technologies.

3. Transition toward a Green Aviation: Final Notes

The aviation sector shall re-emerge from the current crisis much greener to be sustainable in the future. This trend is already evident with the introduction of sustainable fuels (SAF) which is attracting the attention of operators and investors. Naturally new technologies, including electric-powered aircraft, will help to cut carbon emissions and attract investments which will be fostered by dedicated institutions to transit the entire sector toward a green aviation. What has emerged from this crisis is that climate action is a priority alongside economic recovery and aviation plays a key role in both economic recovery and in reducing CO_2 emission to reduce its impact on environment. Investments are needed to shape the air transportation of the future and financial instruments are available to help this transition.

As emerged from the previous chapters, the prospect of new technologies such as radical aircraft designs, electric and hydrogen-powered aircraft are expected to be used from around 2035–2040 for short-haul flights. Not to be forgotten electric air taxis or eVTOLs which for sure will revolutionize urban air transportation. In this scenario green finance will also play an important role to innovate the aviation sector, thus is not surprising the great interests toward these type of investments.

https://doi.org/10.1142/9789811246142_0007

Chapter 6

The Fast Economic Growth in China Will Favor the Development of Commercial and General Aviation

Cristiano Rizzi

This chapter is aimed at illustrating the potentialities of General Aviation (GA) in China in consideration of a gradual opening of the sky which is now controlled in great part by the Chinese military and basically because the airspace classification system does not treat GA air activities separately. For this reason there is a need to update the legal framework regulating GA in China in consideration of the benefits this sector can bring to the Middle Kingdom which include a further expansion of its internal economy. Today China, notwithstanding the damages caused by COVID-19, represents the world's second largest aviation market and it is projected to soon become the largest if we take into consideration the fastest recovery pace in comparison with the rest of the world and the fact that China is adopting new policies to favor the development of sectors, like aviation, and in particular GA. However, in order to allow Chinese aviation to fully express its potentiality there are three critical components which need the attention of the Chinese policymakers, which include the infrastructures (airports), the development of airlines, and enhancement of air traffic management. These three components are developing at different pace thus limiting the efforts of China to accommodate the grooving market demand for air travel. The interaction of these three components with the Civil Aviation Administration of China (CAAC)[1] is of paramount importance to combine the rapidly expanding ground aviation infrastructure and a highly constrained airspace amid increasing demand for air travel. The CAAC is the authority in charge of the regulatory framework regulating aviation which has to follow the directives and priorities of the central government.

1. Regulatory Framework for Aviation in China and the Role of the CAAC

Directly under the State Council, the General Administration of Civil Aviation of China is a ministry-level organ, which is responsible for the national civil aviation affairs. CAAC's mission is to "enforce the unified supervision and regulation on the civil aviation activities of the whole country, and in accordance with laws and State Council's decisions, to issue regulations and decisions concerning civil aviation activities within its jurisdiction." This organ is in charge of developing civil aviation in China and in order to accomplish its many tasks during the years of its existence it has undergone several changes and its role has evolved with the evolving of China.

China's civil aviation rapid growth occurred after the "Reform and Opening Up" policy in 1978,[2] which transformed the country's closed economy to one that is open and marked-oriented. Since then, aviation has been China's fastest-growing mode of transport and before the COVID-19 crisis it was already the world's second largest aviation market trailing only to the US. Although the crisis has slowed this unprecedented growth there is no doubt China's aviation will surpass the US market soon considering not only its strong demand for air transport but also the robust economic recovery. Since the inception of the opening-up policy the volume of passengers have grown from 2 million in 1978 to 500 million

---

[1]The CAAC, formerly the General Administration of Civil Aviation of China, is the aviation authority under the Ministry of Transport of the People's Republic of China and it oversees all aspects of civil aviation in China. For more information visit: http://www.caac.gov.cn/en/GYMH/ZYZN/ (accessed December 9, 2021).

[2]From December 18 to December 22, 1978, the 3rd Plenary Session of the 11th Central Committee of the CPC was held in Beijing. The conference marked the beginning of the so-called "Reform and Opening Up" policy.

in 2016.[3] It is noteworthy that between 1980 and 2016, the numbers of domestic and international routes increased from 159 and 18 to 3055 and 739, respectively, not including Hong Kong, Taiwan, and Macao air routes.[4] It is also worth stressing that during this period China's aviation system witnessed several institutional reforms with the reorganization and reshaping of the CAAC which assumed an incredible number of functions. As will be exposed in the following section more in detail CAAC substantially oversees all aspects of civil aviation in China including the following: (i) Develop industry development strategy and mid and long-term plans; (ii) Assume regulatory responsibilities for flight and ground safety; (iii) Make civil aviation airspace planning and establish and manage civil air routes; (iv) Oversee and manage security measures for civil aviation; (v) Oversee and manage construction and safety operations of civil airports; (vi) Regulate the market for air transport and GA; (vii) Develop civil aviation pricing policies and oversee the implementation; (viii) Provide guidance on human resources development, R&D, and training; (ix) Develop standards for and investigate civil aircraft accidents.[5] The CAAC is in a unique position to facilitate the growth of aviation because it is in charge of coordinating all these aspects.

1.1 *Functions of CAAC and its departments*

The CAAC is the aviation administrative and regulatory body in China and as the regulator and leading body over multiple components of the aviation system, acts as a central planner of China's aviation system. Thus, CAAC plays a bigger role in respect to traditional Air Navigation Service Provider (ANSP). For instance CAAC not only provides air traffic management for civil aviation but also controls the ground infrastructure, in fact the CAAC develops mid and long-term plans for civil aviation, specifically where and how new airports are to be developed.

---

[3]CAAC (2017), *Statistical Bulletin of Civil Aviation Industry Development of 2016*.

[4]CAAC (2016), *2016 Statistical Data on Civil Aviation of China*, China Civil Aviation Publishing House (Zhong Guo Min Hang Chu Ban She), Beijing; CAAC (2017), *Statistical Bulletin of Civil Aviation Industry Development of 2016*.

[5]These nine points represent CAAC's responsibilities pertaining to the three critical components of capacity: Namely airports, airlines, and air traffic management, see: Civil Aviation Administration of China, "Main Functions," available at: http://www.caac.gov.cn/en/GYMH/ZYZN/ (accessed December 9, 2021).

Besides these fundamental functions CAAC specifically is responsible for the development and managing of the following specific components which is composed of the aviation system and can be summarized as follows:

Assume regulatory responsibilities for civil aviation's flight safety and ground safety. Conduct certification, supervision and inspection of civil aircraft operators, airman training organizations, civil aeronautical products, and maintenance service providers; regulate the transport of dangerous goods by air; conduct nationality registration, and operational evaluation and examination of civil aircraft; provide oversight and management of flight procedures and minimum operations standards for airports; oversee and manage civil airman's qualification and civil aviation hygiene

— Conduct air traffic management for civil aviation. Make civil aviation airspace planning; establish and manage civil air routes; oversee and manage communications, navigation surveillance, aeronautical information, and aviation meteorology.

— Assume the regulatory responsibility for civil aviation security. Oversee and manage the security measures for civil aviation; deal with aircraft hijacking, bombing, and other acts of unlawful interference; conduct civil aviation safety examination; and oversee and manage the security, and firefighting and rescue operations at airports.

— Develop standards for civil aircraft accidents and incidents, and investigate and deal with civil aircraft accidents as required. Organize and coordinate emergency response to civil aviation incidents; organize and coordinate major air transport operations and general aviation tasks; facilitate national defense mobilization.

— Oversee and manage the construction and safe operation of civil airports. Give approval to the site selection, overall planning, and engineering design for civil airports, and manage the licensing of airport use; manage environmental protection, land use, and obstacle clearance protection for civil airports; oversee and manage civil aviation engineering and construction quality.

— Regulate the market for air transport and general aviation. Oversee and inspect the standards and quality of civil aviation transport service; uphold the rights and interests of air travel consumers; conduct licensing management of air transport and general aviation activities.

— Develop civil aviation pricing policies, and oversee the implementation; make recommendations for civil aviation fiscal and taxation policies. Assume the responsibility for the investment and management of civil aviation construction projects, and examine (approve) the application for the purchase and lease of civil aircraft, as provided in the mandate. Monitor financial results and operations of civil aviation; and take statistical responsibilities for the industry.

— Direct the development and application of major civil aviation scientific and technological projects; advance IT development. Provide guidance on civil aviation human resources development, R&D, education and training, and energy-saving and emission-reduction.

— Conduct international co-operation and exchange in the field of civil aviation; safeguard China's interests and rights in aviation; conduct exchange and co-operation with counterparts in Hong Kong, Macau and Taiwan regions.

— Manage CAAC regional administrations, and aviation security agencies and air marshal corps directly under jurisdiction.

— Perform other tasks assigned by the State Council and the Ministry of Transport.[6]

Of course, all these functions are coordinated by the different Departments which compose the CAAC and which are briefly described in the next section.

1.2 *Departments of the CAAC and their responsibilities: Brief overview*

This section briefly exposes the responsibilities of every single department composing the CAAC in order to better identify the ambit of each single office which complements the regulation on civil aviation in China.

1.2.1 *Department of General Affairs*

The Department of General Affairs assist CAAC executives in dealing with day-to-day administrative affairs. This department is in charge of the functioning of the CAAC, that is, it is responsible for the administrative

---

[6] *Ibid.*

work of the CAAC organs, and supervises and inspects the implementation of major decisions and affairs. Furthermore, this department deals with the advice, proposals, and queries concerning civil aviation from the NPC and CPPCC.[7]

1.2.2 *Office of Aviation Safety*

The Office of Aviation Safety conducts and coordinates the system safety management for civil aviation. Thus, its main function is to draft laws, regulations, policies, standards, and safety plans governing the management of civil aviation safety, and the investigation of civil aircraft accidents and incidents. Another important task is to coordinate for ICAO's safety audits and international exchange and co-operation in aviation safety.[8]

1.2.3 *Department of Policy, Law and Regulation*

The Department of Policy, Law and Regulation is responsible for legislation concerning the civil aviation industry, and drafts the bills on the enactment, amendment, and annulment of civil aviation-related laws, provisions, and regulations. This department organizes and coordinates the research on the guideline, policies, and major issues concerning the development of the civil aviation industry; makes policies and recommendations; it is in charge of drafting comprehensive policies for the development of the civil aviation industry in general.[9]

1.2.4 *Department of Development Planning*

The Department of Development Planning studies and formulates development strategies, mid and long-term plan for the civil aviation industry,

---

[7]For more details visit: CAAC's website at Department of General Affairs: http://www.caac. gov.cn/en/GYMH/BMJS/201602/t20160217_28415.html (accessed December 9, 2021).

[8]For more details visit CAAC's website at Office of Aviation Safety: http://www.caac.gov. cn/en/GYMH/BMJS/201602/t20160217_28416.html (accessed December 9, 2021).

[9]For more details visit CAAC's website at Department of Policy, Law and Regulation: http://www.caac.gov.cn/en/GYMH/BMJS/201602/t20160217_28417.html (accessed December 9, 2021).

and *ad hoc* planning proposals concerning cross-modal transport. Moreover, it studies and develops *ad hoc* plans concerning airport layout, aircraft fleet, civil aviation infrastructure development, and energy efficiency and emission reduction, as well as cross-regional civil aviation development plan; oversees their implementation. It also draws up laws, regulations, policies, and standards governing civil aviation planning, investment, foreign investment, statistics, prices, charges (excluding administrative charges), and energy efficiency and emission reduction, and oversees their implementation. Another important function is to manage civil aviation construction projects, process the approval of major civil aviation infrastructure development projects, such as civil airport construction, as well as the application for state investment projects; examines and approves feasibility study reports for such projects.[10]

1.2.5 *Department of Finance*

The Department of Finance is responsible for budgeting and final accounting for civil aviation entities; manages the use of civil aviation budget and financial accounting. It also makes recommendations on economic control, fiscal and taxation, and financing policies for civil aviation. It drafts the rules and management methodology governing finance and financial accounting for directly affiliated entities, and oversees and coordinates the implementation. Furthermore, it manages the financial information of the civil aviation industry; periodically analyzes and monitors the financial operation and performance of the industry, and studies and formulate coping measures. It manages the state-owned assets held by entities directly affiliated with the CAAC. It budgets the state-owned capital for directly affiliated enterprises and withholds returns on state-owned capital and remits it to the fiscal authorities.[11]

---

[10]For more details visit CAAC's website at Department of Development Planning: http://www.caac.gov.cn/en/GYMH/BMJS/201602/t20160217_28418.html (accessed December 9, 2021).

[11]For more details visit CAAC's website at Department of Finance: http://www.caac.gov.cn/en/GYMH/BMJS/201602/t20160217_28419.html (accessed December 9, 2021).

1.2.6 *Department of Personnel, Science & Technology and Education*

The Department of Personnel, Science & Technology and Education drafts specifications governing the work of directly affiliated entities concerning personnel, labor, education, and science & technology, and oversees the implementation. It is also responsible for drafting the professional criteria for special types of civil aviation work, and conducting professional skills certification of the civil aviation industry. It introduces the employment qualification system for special types of civil aviation work, and conducts supervision and inspection.

Other functions include overseeing the education offered by directly affiliated colleges and schools; developing and implementing the development plan for civil aviation colleges and schools; formulating the annual enrollment plan for directly affiliated colleges and schools.

Also this department manages the development of science and technology by the industry; develops and implements the civil aviation science and technology development plan and the annual science and technology projects plan; oversees the research and application of major science and technology projects; directs the certification of civil aviation-related scientific and technological research findings and academic exchange; directs the rewarding and commercialization of civil aviation-related scientific and technological research findings; manages cooperation projects in civil aviation-related science and technology.[12]

1.2.7 *Department of International Affairs (Office of Hong-Kong, Macao, and Taiwan)*

The Department of International Affairs drafts guidelines and policies for the development of international civil aviation ties and also harmonizes China's multilateral relations and co-operation with international organizations in the field of civil aviation; oversees the engagement in the multilateral meetings and events of the International Civil Aviation Organization; coordinates and facilitates the implementation of resolutions, standards, and recommended practices of relevant international organizations.

---

[12]For more details visit CAAC's website at Department of Personnel, Science & Technology and Education: http://www.caac.gov.cn/en/GYMH/BMJS/201602/t20160217_28420.html (accessed December 9, 2021).

Another important task is to manage the foreign-related work of CAAC departments and directly affiliated entities. Manage co-operation and exchange in civil aviation concerning Hong Kong, Macao, and Taiwan, and study, coordinate and handle major civil aviation-related issues concerning Hong Kong, Macao, and Taiwan.[13]

1.2.8 *Department of Transport*

The Department of Transport is responsible for overseeing and managing the civil aviation transport market and service quality; maintains the order of the civil aviation transport market.

This department drafts laws, regulations, policies, and standards governing civil aviation transport, GA, and market administration, management of the transport of dangerous goods by air, transport service quality management, and the protection of rights and interests of civil aviation consumers, and oversees the execution. It directs and oversees the efforts of air transport associations at sales agency management and self-discipline of the air transport business; coordinates and oversees the air transport service business of international organizations, such as the associations of the international air transport industry in China.[14]

1.2.9 *Department of Flight Standards*

The Department of Flight Standards conducts the operation certification and continuous oversight and examination of civil aviation operators; manages the issue, modification, and revocation of operation certificates and operation specifications for civil aviation operators. It drafts and oversees the implementation of laws, regulations, policies, standards, procedures, and technical specifications governing civil aviation-related flight operations, aircraft maintenance, and aviation hygiene and sanitation. It also conducts the certification and continuous oversight and inspection of civil aircraft maintenance service providers; it is responsible for the issue,

---

[13]For more details visit CAAC's website at Department of International Affairs: http://www.caac.gov.cn/en/GYMH/BMJS/201602/t20160217_28421.html (accessed December 9, 2021).
[14]For more details visit CAAC's website at Department of Transport: http://www.caac.gov.cn/en/GYMH/BMJS/201602/t20160217_28422.html (accessed December 9, 2021).

modification, and revocation of licenses for maintenance service providers.[15]

1.2.10 *Department of Aircraft Airworthiness Certification*

The Department of Aircraft Airworthiness Certification is responsible for type certification and supplemental type certification, type validation, and supplemental type validation of civil aviation products. Oversees work of the Type Certification Board (TCB); reviews and approves the civil aircraft flight manual (AFM). The department is also responsible for production certification of civil aviation products. It oversees the production of foreign civil aviation products by domestic manufacturers subject to the agreement between CAAC and foreign airworthiness authorities. Furthermore, it is responsible for type and production certification, and airworthiness certification of aviation materials, parts and components, and airborne equipment. It is responsible for certification of civil aircraft modifications, and engineering review and approval of major special overhaul programs and programs for maintenance beyond manual limits.

Another function is to draft laws, regulations, policies, and standards governing the management of airworthiness certification for civil aircraft nationality registration, civil aviation products (including aircraft, engines, and propellers, the same as below) and aviation materials, parts and components, airborne equipment, civil jet fuel, and chemical products, as well as those concerning environmental protection, and oversee the implementation.[16]

1.2.11 *Department of Airports*

The Department of Airports reviews the site of new civil airports to be built and the name of airports; reviews the master plans for civil airports, and oversees the implementation.

---

[15]For more details visit CAAC's website at Department of Flight Standards: http://www.caac.gov.cn/en/GYMH/BMJS/201602/t20160217_28423.html (accessed December 9, 2021).

[16]For more details visit CAAC's website at Department of Aircraft Airworthiness Certifications: http://www.caac.gov.cn/en/GYMH/BMJS/201602/t20160217_28424.html (accessed December 9, 2021).

It also manages the licensing of civil airports; issues and revokes the license for civil airports, and conducts oversight. Another important task is to draft laws, regulations, policies, standards, and quotas governing the construction, safety, and operational management of civil airports (including the civil portions of military and civilian combined airports, the same as below), and to oversee the implementation.[17]

1.2.12 *Office of Air Traffic Regulation*

The Office of Air Traffic Regulation develops the plan for development of civil aviation air traffic management, and oversees the implementation. It drafts laws, regulations, policies, standards, and technical specifications governing air traffic management for civil aviation, and oversees the implementation. It proposes resource allocation policies for time slots, airspace capacity, and oversees and checks the execution. The office also manages qualifications of air traffic controllers, aeronautical information personnel, aeronautical telecommunication personnel, and aeronautical meteorologists.[18]

1.2.13 *Bureau of Aviation Security*

The Bureau of Aviation Security conducts certification of security-related operational qualifications of civil airports and airlines; reviews aviation security plans of civil aviation enterprises and public institutions; oversees the implementation. It also oversees and manages work concerning civil aviation security; it plans and directs development of industry security management system (SEMS); conducts evaluation of threats to civil aviation security; issues situation analysis reports (circulars) and preventive measures and directives.

Another function is to draw laws, regulations, policies, and standards governing civil aviation security; to develop civil aviation security plans; to oversee the implementation.[19]

---

[17] For more details visit CAAC's website at Department of Airports: http://www.caac.gov.cn/en/GYMH/BMJS/201602/t20160217_28425.html (accessed December 9, 2021).

[18] For more details visit CAAC's website at Office of Air Traffic Regulation: http://www.caac.gov.cn/en/GYMH/BMJS/201602/t20160217_28426.html (accessed December 9, 2021).

[19] For more details visit CAAC's website at Bureau of Aviation Security: http://www.caac.gov.cn/en/GYMH/BMJS/201602/t20160217_28427.html (accessed December 9, 2021).

1.2.14   *CAAC Party Committee (Office of Ideological and Political Work)*

The CAAC Party Committee urges and oversees compliance by the Party group of CAAC agencies and directly affiliated entities with decisions, instructions, and work arrangements of the CAAC Party Leadership Group.

It is responsible for ideological and political development for leadership of CAAC agencies and its directly affiliated entities. It organizes and directs the study of Marxism–Leninism, Mao Zedong Thought, Deng Xiaoping Theory, the Important Thought of Three Represents, the Scientific Outlook on Development, and the lines, principles, and policies of the Party for CAAC agencies and its directly affiliated entities.[20]

1.2.15   *Group of Discipline Inspection (Bureau of Supervision Stationed in CAAC)*

The Group of Discipline Inspection oversees and inspects compliance by the leadership of CAAC, Party Committee (Party Leadership Group) of directly affiliated entities, administrative leadership and members with the political discipline of the Party and democratic centralism, their selection and appointment of officials, and their execution of the Responsibility Mechanism of Party Conduct and Incorruptness Development, and performance in incorruptness and diligence; oversees and inspects compliance with the Party and political discipline by officials of CAAC agencies at and above the division level, and other officials at departmental and bureau levels appointed by CAAC Party Leadership Group, as well as their use of power. It also oversees and inspects execution of the lines, principles, policies, and decisions of the Party, compliances with the state laws and regulations, and implementation of the decisions and instructions of the State Council, as well as the resolutions of CAAC Party Leadership Group by the Party group of CAAC agencies and directly affiliated entities.[21]

---

[20] For more details visit CAAC's website at CAAC Party Committee: http://www.caac.gov.cn/en/GYMH/BMJS/201602/t20160217_28428.html (accessed December 9, 2021).

[21] For more details visit CAAC's website at CAAC Group of Discipline Inspection: http://www.caac.gov.cn/en/GYMH/BMJS/201602/t20160217_28429.html (accessed December 9, 2021).

1.2.16 *National Civil Aviation Trade Union*

The National Civil Aviation Trade Union supports and leads implementation by all civil aviation trade unions of the Party's lines, principles, and policies, as well as the tasks and decisions identified by the National Committee and Standing Committee of China Civil Aviation Trade Union. It also engages in the development of policies, measures, and mechanisms concerning labor relations and employee interests. It conducts survey and research of major issues on employees' legitimate rights and interests. It is responsible for oversight and inspection of labor protection, and engages in investigation and handling of serious accidents involving employee injuries and deaths. It protects legitimate rights and interests of employees by the law.[22]

1.2.17 *Bureau of Retired Officials*

The Bureau of Retired Officials is responsible for the management of retired officials of CAAC agencies; it organizes activities for retired officials to read and learn documents and engages in political activities; and enables retired officials to contribute to the development of socialism with Chinese characteristics, carry out guidelines and polices concerning retired officials by the CPC Central Committee and the State Council.[23]

1.3 *CAAC's unique role: Final considerations*

CAAC plays a unique role in the regulation of China's aviation system. In fact, it has to address and manage a myriad of issues which are all connected, and in orchestrating all these aspects it must assure the smooth development of aviation and all its related activities including GA which appears to have a brilliant future in China. However, in order to favor the expansion of GA in China CAAC has to work and draft new guidelines to help utilize the existing airspace more effectively, allowing the blossoming of a niche air market which will complement commercial airlines.

---

[22]For more details visit CAAC's website at National Civil Aviation Trade Union: http://www.caac.gov.cn/en/GYMH/BMJS/201602/t20160217_28430.html (accessed December 9, 2021).

[23]For more details visit CAAC's website at Bureau of Retired Officials: http://www.caac.gov.cn/en/GYMH/BMJS/201602/t20160217_28431.html (accessed December 9, 2021).

Opening up the sky in China is essential for the aviation system to accommodate the growing market demand in both directions. The CAAC needs to continue to work with the military to gradually open up the airspace for civil aviation and GA activities. This effort evidently demands officials and policymakers to recognize the benefits of opening up the sky for the entire aviation industry and in general for China's economy; thus, the necessity of expanding aviation infrastructures (including those for the development of the GA) which will surely increase China's air capacity and offer new opportunities to expand its economy further.

It is also responsible for managing the combination of airspace capacity, airport capacity (including new infrastructures for the development of the GA), and of airline service capacity. The CAAC is thus in a unique position to address the challenges and to drive the orderly growth of both China's civil and general aviation.

2. The Opening of Low-Altitude Airspace to Favor the Development of GA in China

In China, airspace is tightly controlled by the Chinese military and the airspace classification system does not treat GA air activities separately. Strict military control over roughly 70% of all Chinese airspace is the largest single factor limiting the growth of this industry. For this reason, GA is still underdeveloped in China though there is a great potential for it in dependence of when the authorities in charge (CAAC and the military) will find a compromise to opening low-altitude airspace for GA activities. Another factor limiting the development of this particular sector of aviation is the ongoing government austerity programs that make the optics of GA ownership challenging for some potential buyers.

Despite these challenges, China is *de facto* a growing market for business aircraft, helicopters, and other GA aircraft. According to the figures contained in the latest CAAC's *Statistical Bulletin of Civil Aviation Industry Development in 2019*[24] by the end of 2019, there were a total of 2,707 registered GA aircraft, including 849 aircraft for training. Moreover, in 2019, 44 GA airports were newly certified, adding the

---

[24]CAAC (2020), "Statistical Bulletin of Civil Aviation Industry Development in 2019," available at: http://www.caac.gov.cn/en/HYYJ/NDBG/202011/t20201123_205329.html (accessed December 9, 2021).

number of certified GA airports to 246. By the end of 2019, there were a total of 67,953 valid pilot licenses in China's civil aviation industry, up 6,461 year on year, including 1,173 Sport Pilot Licenses (SPLs), 4,352 Private Pilot Licenses (PPLs), 35,329 Commercial Pilot Licenses (CPLs), 193 Multi-crew Pilot Licenses (MPLs) and 26,906 Airline Transport Pilot Licenses (ATPLs).[25] It is worth noting that a number of Chinese pilot trainees travel to the Unites States or third countries for flight training as well, and this is to be considered carefully. In fact, a revised legal framework not only would favor the development of GA but would also increment business opportunities and inject further investment in a sector which is destined to further sustain China's economy. Although the size of the GA fleet and flight hours are still relatively small, the potential importance of this industry to the Chinese economy in the long term has led aircraft OEMs and Chinese government officials to devote significant resources toward growing GA capacity. The latest updated information available states that *by August 2020, the number of certified GA airports reached 299. Despite the impact of the epidemic, GA airports have maintained a high growth rate of 22% — compared to the end of 2019.*[26]

Although the number of GA airports has increased rapidly during the 13th Five-Year Plan period (2016–2020), there is still a big gap compared to the US. However, as an industry that lags behind the pace of economic and social development, insiders said they hope the industry can achieve breakthrough development. With the push of the Chinese central government, surely there will be an increase of GA activities in China.

The interest China has put on the aviation sector and in particular on GA to further stimulate its economy is evident. Thus, China calls for accelerating the development of the GA sector, and delegates the approval of new airports to the provincial governments, and encourages private investment in building airports.

---

[25] *Ibid.*

[26] Asianskymedia (2020), "In addition to those certified, there are also 189 non-certified GA runway airports, heliports, helicopter take-off and landing platforms used for medical rescue, as well as various elevated heliports. Additionally, there are currently 76 GA airports under construction. It is estimated that by the end of 2020, the total number of will reach 500, completing the target set in the '13th Five-Year Plan'." In this sense: Asianskymedia (2020), "Overview of China's GA Infrastructure," *China GA Report*, available at: https://www.asianskymedia.com/news/2020/11/3/infrastructure-overview-1-ga-airport (accessed December 9, 2021).

2.1 *Definition of GA according to civil aviation law*

China's GA industry has seen stable development over the past 5 years from 2015 to 2020, with official data (see CAAC's Bulletins) showing that the average annual growth of business volume was 13.7%. Now that it has emerged that China intends to favor the development of GA, it is necessary to specify that the definition of GA is to be found in the Civil Aviation Law of the People's Republic of China.[27]

Chapter X of the aforementioned law specifically deals with GA from Articles 145–150, and it is evident that these general principles need to be further elaborated by the authority in charge of developing and regulating all the aspects related to aviation in China, namely the CAAC which was already examined in the previous sections. It is worth reporting here the definition of GA as it has been stated in the Law: "'General aviation" means civil aviation operations other than public air transport with civil aircraft, including aerial work in the fields of industry, agriculture, forestry, fishery and building industry, and flight operations in the fields of medical and health work, emergency and disaster relief, meteorological service, ocean monitoring, scientific experiment, education and training, culture and sports."[28] Then Article 146 states: "The operation of general aviation shall satisfy the following conditions: (1) The availability of civil aircraft suitable to the general aviation activities to be operated and conforming to the requirements of ensuring flight safety; (2) The availability of necessary airmen who have been issued licenses according to law; (3) Other conditions conforming to the provisions of laws and administrative rules and regulations. The operation of general aviation for commercial purposes is limited to corporate enterprise."

It is interesting to note that the Civil Aviation Law also has inserted an article which is aimed at safeguarding the environment while fostering the development of GA. Article 149 in fact states that: "In organizing and carrying out aerial work, effective measures shall be taken to ensure flight

---

[27]The "Civil Aviation Law of the People's Republic of China" was adopted at the 16th Meeting of the Standing Committee of the Eighth National People's Congress of the People's Republic of China on October 30, 1995 and promulgated by Order No. 56 of the President of the People's Republic of China on October 30, 1995, and entered into force on March 1, 1996.

[28]See Article 145, Chapter X — General Aviation, Civil Aviation Law.

safety, protect environment and ecological balance and prevent damage to be caused to environment, residents, crops or livestock."[29]

These are the extracts of the articles contained in the Civil Aviation Law concerning GA, but it is evident that only with the opening of low-air altitude China will effectively allow the development of this sector of aviation. Therefore, it appears now necessary to offer some more details about the planned reform to favor GA in China.

2.2 *China to further open low-altitude airspace to boost GA*

The low-altitude airspace represents a unique resource for China. It is possible to affirm that it is a strategic resource which not only relates to national security but also has a huge market potential considering the growing number of wealthy Chinese willing to explore this sector. The sector of GA in China is extremely promising and a myriad of manufacturers are eager to enter this market. Opening up low-altitude airspace means that through the reform of the management of low airspace, some aircraft will be lifted from the blockade ban and restrictions on certain activities related to GA will be removed, allowing the spring of this segment of the aviation in China too. For instance in the US, where large areas of low altitude are free to fly GA has flourished and millions of people have flight licenses and a huge aviation industry has been cultivated. Ensuring the safety of low-altitude airspace is of great significance to the development of GA and China's national economy considering the huge amount of money that could be injected into this particular sector. In order to lift some of the restrictions the State Council and the Central Military Commission issued in August 2010 the Opinions on Deepening the Reform of the Low-altitude Airspace Management System[30] which

---

[29] See Article 149, Chapter X — General Aviation, Civil Aviation Law.

[30] Opinions of the State Council and the Central Military Commission on Deepening the Reform of China's Low-altitude Airspace Management (No. 25 [2010] of the State Council (2010), "Fully comprehending the great significance of deepening the reform of low-altitude airspace management:

  1. The reform of low-altitude airspace management is a necessary requirement for economic and social development. In recent years, China's general aviation has seen rapid

marked the starting point for the liberalization of low altitude airspace and thus the beginning of GA in China.

In 2014 and 2016, the State Council issued policies to further stimulate the market by opening up the airspace below 3,000 meters with the trial cities including Shenyang, Guangzhou, and Changchun. Thus, China's interest in expanding this sector is evident though a lot remains to be done especially by the CAAC to enhance the regulatory framework with specific reference to GA.

Chinese Premier Li Keqiang delivered a government work report in March 2019, noting that the government will increase investment in infrastructure such as civil and GA. It was for the first time GA was noted in the work report. In September 2019, the State Council noted in a document that the government will promote the construction of GA airports, promote the development of low-altitude flight tourism, cultivate a dynamic GA market, and deepen reform of the airspace management system.[31] These however remain programmatic objectives, it is in fact necessary to implement specific regulations in order to allow the development of GA. A further intervention of the Chinese dedicated authorities

---

development, the average annual growth of the total flight has reached over 10%, the industry scale has been on the rise, the application fields have continuously expanded, there have been more flight types, and flight demands have been increasingly stronger. With the sustained and rapid economic growth and continuous improvement of people's living standards, the average annual growth of China's general aviation is expected to reach 15% or higher in the next 10 years, and increasing demands for low-altitude airspace will put forward higher requirements for the management and services of low-altitude airspace. Deepening the reform of low-altitude airspace management in good time will be conducive to fully developing and utilizing low-altitude airspace resources and promoting the development of the general aviation, aviation manufacturing and integrated transport system; be conducive to stimulating domestic demands, increasing employment and fostering new economic growth points; be conducive to providing an aviation human resource reserve and basic environment support for the national defense construction; and be of great strategic significance for building a moderately prosperous society in all respects and accelerating the socialist modernization construction," available at: http://www.lawinfochina.com/display.aspx?lib=law&id=8659&CGid= (accessed December 9, 2021).

In 2010, the Central Military Commission of the PRC designed and approved Low-altitude Airspace Management Reform Guidance, which allowed a gradual opening of low-altitude airspace which however has not completely been achieved yet.

[31] Global Times, "General Aviation Industry toward Development," available at: https://www.globaltimes.cn/page/202103/1217333.shtml (accessed December 9, 2021).

to unleash the potential of this sector of the aviation industry in China is therefore desirable.

2.3 *The evolution of China's GA industry policy: A brief introduction*

It is evident that the GA industry in China has undergone different stages of development according to the characteristics of the evolving features of China's economic system at the different stages it has gone through. This evolutionary trend is expected to continue, thus China's GA industry policy will gradually be expanded and improved. These changes naturally have included a series of industrial development planning policies touching different areas of the entire China's economy transiting its economy toward a more market economy.

From 1992 to 2001, it was a period when the socialist market economic system was initially established. At this stage, the Chinese general aviation industry has embarked on a systematic development path around two aspects of "improving the general aviation development environment and enhancing general aviation operations service capabilities." Early stage of the development of a dedicated policy: From the initial perfection of the socialist market economic system to the overall advancement of structural reforms (2002–present).

From 2002 to 2015, it was the initial stage of perfecting the socialist market economic system. At this stage, the State Council and the Central Military Commission promulgated the opportunity to implement the "Opinions on Deepening the Management Reform of China's Low-altitude Airspace." China's general aviation industry has focused on improving the development environment of general aviation and the scale of development and quality of development has taken a new stage. At the national level, the government has actively adopted fiscal policies and prudent monetary policies to accelerate the strategic restructuring of the general aviation industry and effectively enhanced the coordination, sustainability, and endogenous power of the development of the general aviation industry; As far as the civil aviation authority and other industry authorities are concerned, the general aviation industry policy has mainly started from industrial guidelines and management methods, special industrial development planning, industrial development guidance, industrial restructuring measures, industrial control measures, and special funds for industrial development. Form a systematic industrial policy system.[32]

Starting from the "Thirteenth Five-Year Plan" (2016–2020) the attention of the policy makers toward this industry has emerged more clearly and it seems now China is interested in making GA a new engine for promoting national economic development.

> At the national level, the government will actively promote a proactive and steady planning policy that promotes the development of the general aviation industry from the top level macro perspective, so as to comprehensively solve the current unbalanced and inadequate status of general aviation industry development; For civil aviation bureaus and other industry authorities, it is bound to strengthen the general theoretical research on general aviation industry policies, strengthen supervision from the three perspectives of policy formulation, policy implementation, and policy outcomes to ensure the general and scientific nature of general aviation industry policies. Really become a guarantee to promote the development of the general aviation industry.[33]

In particular on May 17, 2016, the General Office of the State Council announced a guideline to boost China's GA industry, named *the Guiding Opinions to Promote the Development of the General Aviation Industry (Guo Ban Fa [2016] No. 38)* (Guideline). The Guideline marked the first time the State Council, the highest administrative organ, making plans to boost the development of China's GA industry.[34] The Guideline describes

---

[32] In this sense see the paper by Zhang Liang and Hu Chengwei (2018), "Analysis of Supply Quality of General Aviation Industry Policy in China," in Advances in Social Science, Education and Humanities Research (ASSEHR), Vol. 206, *2018 International Conference on Advances in Social Sciences and Sustainable Development*, available at: https://www. atlantis-press.com/proceedings/asssd-18/25894460 (accessed December 9, 2021).
[33] *Ibid.*
[34] Closely following the Guideline, the European multinational aerospace manufacturer Airbus was reported to have signed a contract with a Chinese consortium, planning to set up an assembly line to build H135 helicopters in the West Coast New Area of Qingdao on June 13, 2016. This is the first time that Airbus has its final assembly line established outside of Europe and Airbus predicts that China will soon fly past the United States as the world's largest civil helicopter market.

the status of China's GA industry as of 2015 stating: "the scale of the GA industry was small, the infrastructure construction remained comparatively backward, the reform of the administration of low-altitude airspace progressed slowly, the GA industry lack the capability of independent R&D and manufacture, and there was still a big gap between the weak services and the consumer demands."[35]

These legislative interventions posed the basis for a steady development of the GA in China and in fact its prospective is very bright as exposed in the following section.

2.4 Perspectives for the development of GA industry after low-altitude opening

As it has emerged in the previous sections, China's GA industry is still at its early stages compared to Western countries. Although the aviation industry is destined to become an important component of China's economy and in particular civil aviation on the whole is recouping faster here than in the rest of the world, intervention of authorities is of basic importance to promote the huge demand for air mobility transport and encourage GA which includes the widespread of helicopter and business jets (and thus not only light aircraft). In particular, China is now betting on the GA to further stimulate its economy. So far, it must be stressed that the development of China's GA industry is not keeping pace with its overall economic advancement. This is the reason why new dedicated regulations and an updated framework are one of the priorities Chinese dedicated authorities, in particular the CAAC, need to address.

2.4.1. *Industry insiders*

It is worth reporting a few comments by insiders about the Chinese market to have a better idea of the opportunities and challenges the GA in China is facing:

Deng Chunpeng, General Manager of Sunward — a Changsha-based private company producing light manned aircraft and UAV said, "The biggest challenge for us is not about aircraft-related technology, but

---

[35] https://www.natlawreview.com/article/china-state-council-issues-guideline-to-boost-general-aviation-industry (accessed December 9, 2021).

getting the license from Civil Aviation Administration of China (CAAC)."
He added, "Technical problems from airframe design, to the development,
manufacturing, and production of engine, components, materials have all
been solved.... But the licenses including Production Certificate (PC) and
Type Certificate (TC) will take years to get."[36] And again Xia Jin, Deputy
Director of Aeronautical Information Engineering Department, China
Shipbuilding Industry Corporation said on GA, "China has a huge market
demand of general aircraft, but it's up to the national policy that the industry can develop even faster to meet that demand."[37]

As of August 2020, Asian Sky Group (ASG) reports that 110 airports
in China were categorized as Class A GA airports, defined as being open
to the public and capable of conducting commercial passenger operations.
A total of 189 Class B GA airports, which are closed to the public and
cannot be used for commercial passengers, were reported. Counting the
189 uncertified airfields listed by CAAC and ASG, China is expected to
reach the benchmark set in its 13th Five-Year Plan, which called for
500 operational GA airports by the end of 2020.[38]

Regarding the opportunities and attractive prospects for the development of GA industry brought about by the low-altitude opening, and the
changed attitude toward this sector by the authorities, there is no doubt
that the size of the Chinese private aircraft in the near future will increase
substantially and it is also possible for China to surpass the United States
and other Western countries if further incentives and an updated framework will favor the development of GA in China. This will be possible
together with new investments interesting the whole aviation industry. In
fact, China is set to further open its domestic civil aviation industry cap-
ping foreign investment access limits in only certain areas including public air transport, GA, and civil airports. This opening up is in line with the
Foreign Investment Law implemented on January 1, 2020, which will
guarantee greater market access and stronger protection for foreign
investors.

---

[36] Pan Zhaoyi (2019), "A Look at China's General Aviation Industry," available at: https://news.cgtn.com/news/2019-10-19/A-look-at-China-s-general-aviation-industry-KV0GS-b49PO/index.html (accessed December 9, 2021).

[37] *Ibid.*

[38] A. Kate O'Connor (2020), "China Adds More Than 50 GA Airports in 2020," *Vweb*, available at: https://www.avweb.com/aviation-news/china-adds-more-than-50-ga-airports-in-2020/ (accessed December 9, 2021).

3.   China Market is Responding More Quickly and Efficiently to the Crisis Caused by COVID-19

In recent years, the rapid expansion of China's commercial airlines has benefited from a rapid economic development and of course China's demographic characteristics. Thus, with a growing number of people are traveling using this means of transportation. Naturally, the impact of COVID-19 caused a deceleration of this trend bringing even dramatic consequences on airlines, but there is no doubt, and there are evidences already, the aviation industry in China not only will return to its pre-COVID-19 track, although it will take some time to fully recover to the level before the outbreak, but it is also destined to become stronger with the new focus on it by policymakers and by the CAAC, and what is more is its market is set to become the most important on the planet considering China's plans for its economy and especially with the further evolution of the GA.

In the following section, it is interesting to introduce the measures Chinese airlines have introduced in order to stimulate a depressed demand because of the pandemic, and the strategies adopted to gradually return to normality and then proceed with a new phase of fast development.

3.1 *Pre-COVID-19 trend in domestic air travel and the impact of the outbreak*

As a matter of fact, China's domestic air travel industry has been booming, both since the country started opening up and as regulations were gradually phased out to allow for greater competition. Air travel industry was favored also by a rise in disposable household income and thus the greater number of Chinese people traveling across their own country and other foreign destinations. According to Boeing's annual commercial market outlook, China's domestic air travel industry is projected to grow steadily until 2038, eventually becoming the world's largest domestic aviation market.[39]

This was before the impact of COVID-19, in fact as a result of the containment of the outbreak and of the different measures imposed to curb the spread of the coronavirus, China aviation market fell by over 80% in the first half of 2020. However, China's aviation industry has been

---

[39]See: Boeing, "Commercial Market Outlook 2020–2039," available at: https://www.boeing.com/commercial/market/commercial-market-outlook/ (accessed December 9, 2021).

recovering faster than most countries emerging from the COVID lockdowns, underpinned by a steady recovery in the domestic travel market after the epidemic was largely brought under control, according to the numbers at the beginning of 2021 with Chinese travelers having returned to fly thanks also to the incentives introduced by many carriers and the policies adopted by the CAAC to reinvigorate the market.

To boost cash flows, many Chinese airlines have recently rolled out discount passes that would allow passengers unlimited domestic travel with few restrictions:

> The Civil Aviation Administration of China (CAAC) has said that its industry expects to see passenger trips recovering to around 90% of the pre-epidemic level this year. The volume of air transportation for cargo and mail are also expected to rebound back to pre-epidemic level.
>
> The latest data published by CAAC shows that the country's civil aviation industry handled about 23.95 mln passenger trips alone in February 2021, a huge jump of 187.1% YoY. The transport volume of air cargo and mail increased from 54.7% YoY to 459,000 tons.
>
> Despite the wake of COVID-19, China's civil aviation industry handled 420 mln passenger trips in 2020 (63.3% of that in 2019), but it still holds the position of the world's second largest in terms of passenger trips for 15th consecutive year.[40]

It seems that the CAAC said it will continue to assist the civil aviation industry, implementing further tax, fee cuts, and favorable financing policies to further improve the industry as COVID-19 is the biggest uncertainty faced by the civil aviators.

3.2 *Containing the outbreak is the starting point to reinvigorate low demand*

It is evident that there is explicit government support for China's airline system, not only because the major airlines are state owned but

---

[40]China Knowledge, "China's Air Passenger Trips Expected To Recover To Pre-COVID-19 Level," available at: https://www.chinaknowledge.com/News/DetailNews?id=91389 (accessed December 9, 2021).

also because for China to further stimulate its economy it needs the contribution of this industry. Naturally, this support has helped to oil the wheels of the recovery in China, though to see the numbers grow to the level of pre-COVID will take some more time.

China entered and is emerging from COVID-19 first. As a result, China is further along the pandemic pathway and is learning and adapting fast. For airlines and travel industries outside China looking at the measures introduced by the authorities in charge and by airlines to stimulate the demand for air travel could be emulated to drive recovery amid the pandemic, however it is all to bring back to effectively containing and suppressing the virus.

Contributing to the recovery was not only the use of new technology such as QR codes but also some old technologies such as face masks that encouraged travelers to fly. Wearing a mask in China — and most of Asia — has been commonplace for decades. It is viewed as a common courtesy to protect others in the community.

> China has also rolled out QR code technology on people's phones, which tracks their location and travel routes, including if the person has been to a high-risk area. It is compulsory in the sense that if people want to enter any government buildings, offices, malls or restaurants, it is a requirement to have a QR code scanned first before entering. Each person's QR code is unique and linked to their mobile number, which is linked to their ID card. With public co-operation it has been very effective in containing even small outbreaks.[41]

3.3 *China the new frontier for business aviation and GA*

One of the new focuses of Chinese policymakers is to reinvigorate civil aviation and foster GA to let it become another driver for Chinese economy. Efforts to enhance China's aviation industry are underway; however, China is not yet in the position to meet its internal demand for aircraft and it needs to rely on imports. According to the unladen weight, China Customs divides the imported aircraft into four categories: small, medium,

---

[41]APEX (2020), "How China's Aviation is Recovering from COVID-19," available at: https://apex.aero/articles/2020-11-04-how-chinas-aviation-industry-is-recovering-from-covid-19 (accessed December 9, 2021).

large, and super large. Among them, the import volume of small aircraft is always the highest.[42] The interest of China toward foreign manufacturers of this category of aircraft is evident and it began as noted before (see Section 1.2.1.2) with the acquisition of Cirrus by Avic in 2011. Here it is sufficient to remind that Cirrus Aircraft is owned by China Aviation Industry General Aircraft (Caiga), which is part of Aviation Industry Corporation of China (Avic). There is no doubt that with the development of China's GA market, the number of small aircraft imported into the Chinese market would continue to rise though China is enhancing its production capacity for this category of aircraft also.

3.3.1 *Consequences and impact of COVID-19 to the private jet market in China*

Under the impact of COVID-19 in China, domestic and foreign airlines suspended their flights. Under this circumstance, more flexible and safer private jet became the first or even the only option for many Chinese people who wanted to return home during the lockdowns all around the globe, creating an unprecedented demand in the history of China's business aviation which is likely to continue after the pandemic is over. In fact, many wealthy Chinese students who were stuck abroad during COVID-19 chose private jets to come back to China and the price of private jet charter rose dramatically. For instance, the price of chartering a private jet with 14 seats rocketed by 30% from 1.35 million RMB to 1.74 million RMB in March (2020).[43] Some student paid an astonishing 180,000 RMB for a ticket home.

It is a good news for China's private jet market as the propagation of COVID-19 promoted the demand of private jet and people have become more familiar with it. On April 9, 2020, a new Gulfstream G650 landed in Liaoning, as the first private jet delivered to China after the outbreak of COVID-19. Although the number of certain buyers of private jet in China are not many, potential customers increase in terms of purchase consultation. Therefore, the Vice President of OHFLYER, Haiyang Wang,

---

[42] https://www.prnewswire.com/news-releases/china-aircraft-imports-report-2020-impact-of-the-pandemic-and-forecasts-to-2024-301127867.html (accessed December 9, 2021).
[43] 公务航空的后疫情时代-中国民航网 (caacnews.com.cn) (accessed December 9, 2021). This article is in Chinese.

said that the demand of private jet in China will definitely be higher than before COVID-19.[44]

3.3.2 *The private jet charter market and air taxi market are soaring in China*

In China, the consequences of the restrictions inducted by COVID-19 favored private flights. During the most acute phase of the pandemic the number of charter flights surged dramatically and it is likely this trend will continue and that private jet charter market will promote China's GA development. This also must be considered that more wealthy people will opt for this modality of flying because of its convenience and *status symbol*. This aspect is of particular importance, like supercars or luxury watches, social status is an important purchasing impetus for Chinese consumers. Operators saw a soar in China's demand for charted private jets:

> JetSolution, an aviation group based in Hong Kong, is profiting from plane charter service. The company recently bought Embraer Legacy 600 (carrying 13 passengers) to execute flights. The plane features a luxurious interior with large leather chairs and sofa beds and can fly up to seven hours without refueling. Besides, passengers can choose from a selection of fine wines and top-class cuisine. On another hand, Airports in China are beginning to catch up with the trend. More than 300 airports now accept private jets, with the number expected to increase to about 500 by 2020. This is good news, since the construction and improvement of airports and infrastructures will promote the development of China's aviation industry.[45]

Naturally, all this attention for charted private jets is also favoring another business segment, that is, "air taxi" which is briefly examined in the following section.

---

[44]"The Demand of Private Jet Increased under the Impact of COVID-19," available at: CAACNews.com.

[45]https://daxueconsulting.com/china-market-research-on-private-jets (accessed December 9, 2021).

3.3.3 *The "air taxi" will be best mode of transportation in the future*

In addition to the charter of private jets, "the air taxi" will be an excellent choice for people to travel in the future in China. Here it seems appropriate to spend a few words to introduce this theme: "The drones market in China has soared in recent years: In 2016, the Ehang 184, invented by China, was unveiled in Las Vegas. The invention of the flying machine marks another breakthrough for robots in the field of urban transportation. The latest drone of Ehang, the Ehang 216,[46] is powered by 16 electric rotors and can fly along a pre-planned route at over 80 mph. The aircraft weighs about 600 pounds and can carry another 500 to 600 pounds of cargo or passengers."[47] Ehang is one of the dozens of companies convinced that "flying cars" (we are referring to VTOL) will become a viable mode of urban transportation in the future. And recently, Ehang received approval from Chinese regulators to launch a commercial air mobility service in Guangzhou. AI in China's transportation industry is developing dramatically and "the air taxi" could eventually become the best choice for passengers in the near future due to congestion caused by explosive growth of urbanization in China.

As of January 2020, EHang has reported that for the EHang 216 aircraft, over 2,000 passenger flight tests have taken place including flying in

---

[46]EHang is a significant player in the quadcopter drone market. The company hopes to extend its unmanned electric VTOL technology to manned applications. The EHang 216 is based on the EHang 184, yet it has eight arms instead of four. This allows for the vehicle to seat two passengers instead of just one. The single seat version is referred to as the EHang 116. In the summer of 2020, EHang was issued a Special Flight Operations Certificate for its 216 Logistics cargo drone. The EHang 216 Autonomous Aerial Vehicle (AAV) was first announced in February 2018. Manned and unmanned flight testing was conducted in China in 2017, and a manned flight test with Dutch Prince Pieter Christian took place at the Amsterdam Arena in April 2018. In April 2019, EHang advertising states "Welcome to the Urban Air Mobility Project" and that their starting point will be Austria. Their vision: "To establish a human-focused, sustainable way for people to get about in the future. We seek to create shortcuts — so transport is no longer restricted by roads. Shortcuts that will allow nature to reconquer areas now occupied by concrete and traffic jams. Shortcuts that offer each person more freedom to move in urban space," available at: https://evtol.news/ehang-216/ (accessed December 9, 2021).
[47]*Ibid.*

winds up to 70 km/h (44 mph), in fog and with low visibility situations which have been around 50 m (164 ft). EHang is also seeking U.S. Federal Aviation Administration (FAA) approval for their aircraft and their first U.S. flight test took place in January 2020. In January 2021, it was announced that EHang has joined the European Air Mobility Urban — Large Experimental Demonstrations[48] (AMU-LED) project which will be conducting flight tests using its eVTOL aircraft in the Netherlands, Spain and the United Kingdom. The initiative will be conducting tests from 2020 through 2023 to prove that integrating eVTOL aircraft is practical and possible. The companies involved in this Urban Air Mobility (UAM) testing include Airbus, AirHub, Altitude Angel, ANRA Technologies, Boeing Research & Technology-Europe, FADA-CATEC, Cranfield University, EHang, ENAIRE, Gemeente Amsterdam, INECO, ITG, Jeppesen, NLR, Space53 and Tecnalia.

On February 11, 2021, eVTOL Magazine reported,[49] "Chinese developer EHang, which claims to be providing limited services on mainland China and is a participant in numerous European airspace study projects,[50] has seen its stock rise almost ten-fold since October, valuing the company at almost $6 billion at the time of this writing."[51]

---

[48] SESAR Joint Undertaking Air Mobility Urban-Large experimental Demonstrations (AMU-LED), "The revolution of urban air mobility (UAM) covers new concepts of operations, business cases, applicable regulations, and stakeholders and end users. This new business sector needs to be secured, invented, refined, structured and industrialized while staying sustainable and interoperable within the U-space framework. In the near future, safe, secure, green and acceptable UAM solutions will bring seamless freight, emergency, security and mobility services. Operators, regulators, traffic management, end users, public and airborne industry must collaborate to ensure UAM vehicle airworthiness and viable operations," available at: https://www.sesarju.eu/node/3744 (accessed December 9, 2021).

[49] It is also stated that: "Stocks for public eVTOL and urban air mobility companies, following the high level of interest in Tesla and other electric vehicle developers seen last year, have skyrocketed in recent months," available at: https://evtol.com/news/joby-announce-billion-spac-deal-lilium-others-follow-banner-month-evtol-industry/ (accessed December 9, 2021).

[50] The Chinese eVTOL developer EHang will play a significant role in two European projects that aim to demonstrate the application of UAM to emergency medical services. See: "EHang to Demo Medical Air Mobility in Two European Projects," available at: https://evtol.com/news/ehang-medical-air-mobility-european-projects/ (accessed December 9, 2021).

[51] https://evtol.news/ehang-216/ (accessed December 9, 2021).

As a consequence of this growing interest, in China the number in GA companies is also increasing. The next section briefly examines this trend and offers some interesting data.

3.4 *China sees an increase in GA companies*

According to the CAAC together with the growing interest toward the private aviation sector, China is witnessing an increase in GA companies despite of the impact of COVID-19: China has seen steady growth in its general-aviation sector in recent years, with the fleet growing to 2,844 general aircraft by the end of 2020. As of the end of 2020, the number of conventional GA companies in the country had risen to 523.

Aside from the sustainable development of the conventional business and aircraft, China's GA sector has also seen a boom in new forms of business, according to the CAAC. It is also interesting to note that China's growing GA sector has also seen rapid expansion in aerial tours and parachuting. "By the end of last year, there were more than 100 air routes for low-altitude tourism, providing aerial-tour services at about 50 tourist attractions nationwide, data from the CAAC shows. Vowing to further inject vitality into the general-aviation sector, a strategically emerging industry of the country, the CAAC said it will promote supervision of the sector and give full play to its nationwide route network. To ensure the sustainable development of the sector, the CAAC will also draft tailored regulations on certification and operation, the administration added. As of the end of 2020, China's total number of certified civil transport airports and general airports reached 241 and 313, respectively."[52]

It is evident that all this interest will help boost China with the development of GA which is destined to help in sustaining internal expenditure for new services related to air transportation, in a private firm also, thereby creating an impact on China's economy. Naturally, with the new opportunities opening in this market it is likely new investments in this sector will surge dramatically and of course foreign investors are welcome to explore China's market together with local operators (to smooth the

---

[52]"China's Booming General-Aviation Sector Boasts 2,800 Aircraft: CAAC," available at: http://www.china.org.cn/business/2021-03/02/content_77264515.htm?f=pad&a=true (accessed December 9, 2021).

business initiative) to fully take advantage of the "*overture*" of China in this sector.

4. The Aviation in Connection with the Belt and Road Initiative: A Brief Introduction

It seems now appropriate to introduce a theme of great importance for China namely the Belt and Road Initiative (BRI)[53] which is aimed at better connecting China with the EU because of its implications for the aviation industry. In fact, routes to connect China and the EU are already planned and under development both via land and via sea, however an "Air Silk Road" is taking shape along the BRI. The CAAC officials in September 2020 affirmed, "that CAAC pledged to implement a more transparent opening strategy, supporting the building of BRI free trade zones and ports, while pushing for reforms of global civil aviation governance, and seek a greater degree of opening-up of the nation's civil aviation sector."[54]

As a matter of fact, in parallel with the global economy, the aviation industry's center of gravity is moving east leaded by China. According to the latest Airports Council International's (ACI) "World's Airport Economics Report," while the main hubs are located at the crossroads of Asia in the Gulf, the future growth in air transport demand will come from emerging and developing economies, from the Asia-Pacific region. While the most recent figures confirm the growing trend of the aviation sector in Asia, the BRI aims mainly at developing six economic corridors, four of which are land routes. But as a plan focusing on connectivity and co-operation, the BRI will still provide growth opportunities to both commercial and cargo

---

[53]President Xi Jinping launched the BRI in 2013 when he made a speech titled *Promote People to People Friendship and Create a Better Future* at Kazakhstan's University during his visit. Now this initiative involves more than 130 countries, aimed not only at improving connection infrastructures but also trade relationships. The initiative aims at developing overland and maritime infrastructures, attracting both public and private investments to create a broad web of connections between Asia, Europe, the Middle East, and Africa. A detailed analysis of the BRI is contained in the book titled: Yu Xugang, Cristiano Rizzi, Mario Tettamanti, Fabio E. Ziccardi, and Guo Li (2018), *China's Belt and Road — The Initiative and Its Financial Focus*, World Scientific.

[54]In this sense: Global Times (2021), "China to Further Open Civil Aviation," available at: https://www.globaltimes.cn/page/202102/1215446.shtml (accessed December 9, 2021).

aviation and an "Air Silk Road" is taking shape along the initiative, broadening the network of land and maritime connections.

4.1 *More liberalization and common policies needed among the BRI countries*

In 2015, the CAAC proposed that all BRI countries, including China itself, should adopt a more flexible policy with the view of introducing a progressive approach to liberalization and competition in the international market.

According to the CAAC China has signed bilateral intergovernmental air transport agreements with 125 countries and regions, 62 of which lie along the Belt and Road (as of 2018). The country also signed the first regional air transport agreement with the Association of Southeast Asian Nations (ASEAN).[55] The objective of the CAAC is to support interconnection and intercommunication and facilitate trade and cultural exchanges with these countries, but of course China is seeking to reinforce its trade relations not only with them but with all countries involved in the development of the BRI. More common policies are in any case needed among China and its trade partners in order to enhance not only their trade relations but also to promote infrastructure connectivity. According to Liu Fang, Secretary-General of the International Civil Aviation Organization, the BRI is in line with the organization's goals and the United Nations 2030 Sustainable Development Plan,[56] *The Belt and*

---

[55]"Air Transport Agreement Between the Governments of the Member States of the Association of Southeast Asian Nations and the Government of the People's Republic of China," full text of the Agreement available at: https://www.icao.int/sustainability/ Documents/Compendium_FairCompetition/ASEAN/AirTransportAgreement_ASEAN-China.pdf (accessed December 9, 2021).

[56]The 2030 Agenda for Sustainable Development, adopted by all United Nations member states in 2015, provides a shared blueprint for peace and prosperity for people and the planet, now and into the future. At its heart are the 17 SDGs, which are an urgent call for action by all countries — developed and developing — in a global partnership. They recognize that ending poverty and other deprivations must go hand-in-hand with strategies that improve health and education, reduce inequality, and spur economic growth — all while tackling climate change and working to preserve our oceans and forests, https://sdgs. un.org/goals (accessed December 9, 2021).

Road Initiative may reshape the map of the global economy and become the largest platform of regional co-operation, creating a positive environment for trade and boosting the economy, Liu added.[57]

In this context, we can also insert the agreements signed in 2019 between China and the EU, namely the agreement on civil aviation safety and a horizontal aviation agreement[58] to strengthen their aviation co-operation which are part of this framework. The agreements followed up on the EU–China Summit of April 9, and will serve to boost the competitiveness of the EU's aeronautical sector and enhance overall EU–China aviation relations. Commissioner for Transport Violeta Bulc said: "China is one of the European Union's most important strategic partners and we attach a lot of importance to our excellent relations on transport matters. We are mutually interested in better connecting Europe and Asia and making it easier to move goods, services and people between Europe and China. That applies to aviation, too. Today's agreements will boost the European Union's trade in aircraft and related products, and ensure the highest levels of air safety."

The main objective of the bilateral civil aviation safety agreement (BASA) is to support worldwide trade in aircraft and related products.

---

[57] China Daily, "Air Network Planned for Belt, Road Connectivity," available at: https://www.chinadaily.com.cn/china/2017-05/17/content_29377998.htm (accessed December 9, 2021).

[58] The BASA signed on May 20, 2019, will remove unnecessary duplication of evaluation and certification activities for aeronautical products by the civil aviation authorities, and therefore reduce costs for the aviation sector and facilitate market access of European aeronautical companies to the very important Chinese market. The BASA will also promote cooperation between the EU and China toward a high level of civil aviation safety and environmental compatibility. With the horizontal aviation agreement China recognizes the principle of EU designation. This means that all EU airlines will have the legal possibility to fly to China from any EU member state with a bilateral air services agreement with China. Up until now, only airlines owned and controlled by a given member state or its nationals could fly between that member state and China. Therefore, the horizontal agreement will bring bilateral air services agreements between China and EU member states into conformity with EU law — a renewed legal certainty which will be beneficial to airlines on both sides. See: https://ec.europa.eu/commission/presscorner/detail/en/IP_19_2650 (accessed December 9, 2021).

4.2 *ICAO Secretary-General calls for investments in air transport to enhance connectivity between Belt and Road countries*

The theme of connectivity especially for China in connection to the BRI has become a priority and not only effort are concentrated to developing infrastructure along the land and sea roads but also aviation has become an increasingly important component of the wider BRI strategy, as China markets its aviation capabilities, from airport construction and technology to air services. This particular theme was highlighted by Liu Fang, Secretary-General Secretary of ICAO who also stressed how liberalized air transport and increased air traffic routes are currently helping many developing States move closer to the 17 SDGs adopted under the UN's Agenda 2030. Dr. Liu who participated at the second BRI Forum held in Beijing in 2019,[59] highlighted to the large number of Ministers of Transport and Infrastructure and heads of international organizations present that "a very direct relationship exists between States' investments in aviation development and their eventual realization of increased economic growth." She went on to emphasize how air transport growth holds further economic potential, but that to benefit from it countries need both the capacity in place to accommodate higher numbers of flights, in addition to the skilled personnel needed to manage them. "A key call to action I would therefore propose today is that countries firmly commit to investments in modernized aviation infrastructure and skilled human resources development, and in a manner which aligns these critical air transport objectives with their overall national development strategies," Dr. Liu underscored. The Secretary-General also informed her audience that ICAO was one of the many UN agencies that developed agreements with China to leverage the synergies between UN SDGs and the BRI, pursuant to the first belt and Road Forum in 2017. She highlighted the training and assistance programs which the UN aviation agency has already begun undertaking with support from China's South–South Co-operation

---

[59]ICAO Secretary-General, Dr. Fang Liu, attended the second Belt and Road Forum for International Cooperation in Beijing, and has highlighted the critical role air transport plays in forging new travel and trade routes between Belt and Road countries and other states. Full article available at: https://www.icao.int/Newsroom/Pages/ICAO-Secretary-General-calls-for-investments-in-air-transport-to-enhance-connectivity-between-Belt-and-Road-countries.aspx (accessed December 9, 2021).

Assistance Fund to build these needed capacities in developing Belt and Road States and countries in other regions. Dr. Liu concluded her intervention by stressing the important role that new technologies and other innovations will play in accelerating these development trends, noting that similar dynamics were already well underway in the aviation domain. "Today there are entirely new types of aircraft and operations being innovated to serve your States and economies, from low-flying drones to hypersonic transports," Dr. Liu commented. "Aviation has a significant role to play in how you connect to the world, and I firmly believe it will play a key role in making the Belt and Road initiative a truly global success story."

4.3 *China's air cargo market is embracing opportunities of Belt and Road*

Although it is evident that the great part of goods will take the land or sea road to reach Europe (the final destination of the BRI) and aviation is unlikely to be a dominant feature in the BRI, however it is becoming increasingly relevant and for some specific, urgently needed, and perishable and valuable type of goods, air cargo is the answer. This is also why investments will surge concerning airports along the two Belts — Land and Maritime — that are receiving support from Chinese construction firms and institutional investors, favored by Chinese authorities.

Chinese firms continue to enhance their presence in selected areas of these belts but not in others, and this is understandable considering that the new interest of China is now focused on the EU if we take into consideration the resistances of the US in letting Chinese investments invade the US after the trade tensions experienced in the recent past and the difficulties in finding a win–win compromise.

The majority of Chinese investments are attracted fundamentally by Western Europe, because it offers a more attractive investment environment (especially with the new bilateral investment agreement signed on December 2020 by China and the EU),[60] and then by opportunities in the

---

[60] On Wednesday December 30, 2020 China and the EU finally signed the new Bilateral Investment Agreement. This investment agreement forms part of a new relationship between China and the EU. The European Union and China agreed to an investment deal that will give European companies greater access to Chinese markets. The agreement has

east of that continent where cargo rather than passenger facilities can be erected to take advantage of a comprehensive road network. Accordingly, some small airports there have been courted by several Chinese operators/ investors. It is therefore clear how important is this sector for China and for its further development: "In the air cargo sector, with airports like Shanghai and Beijing already operating at full capacity, the BRI is also boosting prospects of other hubs and regions, including Western China. Xi'an's Xianyang International Airport (XIY), in one of the main hubs of the ancient Silk Road, is multiplying efforts to ensure it is prepared to accommodate additional international freighter flights, in particular by planning to develop a 600,000-square-meter space east of the airport into a 'Belt and Road' air cargo hub. But other airports than those in the main cities might still be preferable to remote gateways like Xi'an. Zhengzhou Airport (CGO) for example is one of China's fastest growing airports and has already emerged as a popular hub for cargo handling. In recent years, the Henan provincial government has tried to increase traffic by establishing a free trade zone (Zhengzhou Airport Economic Zone) and improve customs clearance processes."[61]

This brief analysis would not be complete without introducing the effect of COVID-19 on the air cargo sector in China which is in any case showing a better resilience compared to the passenger traffic. Thus the next section only exposes the most salient aspects of the impact of the pandemic on China's air cargo sector.

4.4 *The impact of COVID-19 on China's air cargo sector: Brief introduction*

The COVID-19 pandemic has a different influence on Chinese airlines' passenger traffic and their freight traffic, as also noted all around the

---

been nearly 7 years in the making and is likely to take at least another year to enter into force. A more detailed analysis on the business relations between China and the EU is available in the book titled: Xugang Yu, Mario Tettamanti, and Cristiano Rizzi (2021), *China–US Trade Frictions Shaping New Equilibriums with the EU and the US — Toward a New Multilateralism or Tripolarism*, World Scientific.

[61] In this sense see article by Manuela Mirkos, "An 'Air Silk Road' is Taking Shape along the Belt and Road Initiative," available at: https://www.infrastructure-channel.com/article/-/ content/an-air-silk-road-is-taking-shape-along-the-belt-and-road-initiative (accessed December 9, 2021).

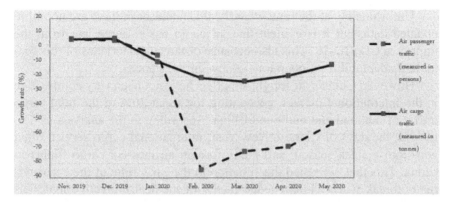

Figure 1:   Comparing Chinese airlines' air passenger traffic and air cargo traffic by year-on-year growth rate, November 2019–May 2020.

Source: Monthly statistics of major transport production indexes of China's civil aviation, CAAC.

world. Since epidemic prevention measures in aviation were mainly targeted at air passengers, air cargo has suffered a less severe depression as indicated by the data from the CAAC. Figure 1 compares the trend of passenger traffic and cargo traffic handled by Chinese airlines before and after the COVID-19 outbreak: "It can be expected that air cargo can go out of this recession more easily than passenger transport: by the end of May 2020, air passenger traffic has yet recovered to half of last year's level, but air cargo traffic had been very close to last year's level. In fact, air cargo finished by dedicated freighter aircraft in May grew by 21.8% than the same period of last year.[62] However, due to the spike in COVID-19 cases in Beijing, June 11,[63] Chinese airlines' passenger traffic cannot be expected to overrun half of last year's level by August."[64]

---

[62]China News (2020), "The Decline of Main Production Indicators of Civil Aviation Narrowed in May" (accessed December 3, 2021).

[63]CNN (2020), "Beijing's New Outbreak is a Reminder to the World that Coronavirus Can Return at Any Time," https://cnnphilippines.com/world/2020/6/19/Beijing-new-coronavirus-outbreak-.html (accessed December 3, 2021).

[64]Tao Li, "A SWOT (Strengths, Weaknesses, Opportunities, and Threats) Analysis of China's Air Cargo Sector in the Context of COVID-19 Pandemic," available at: https://www.ncbi.nlm.nih.gov/pmc/articles/PMC7402658/ (accessed December 1, 2021).

Unfortunately at the time we write this manuscript there are not more updated data, but it is evident that air cargo has suffered less from the impact of COVID-19. This also because of the characteristics of this sector and adaptability of operators to new circumstances.

However, China's air freight suppliers have not been very competitive in the international market, accounting for about 30% of the total cargo traffic of inbound and outbound China. According to the analysis by Tao Li[65] "in the days of Chinese New Year, international cargo service often goes into a slack season, and many foreign airlines cut cargo flights to China. This fact worsened the situation in the early time of the coronavirus outbreak when China needed plenty of medical protective materials from abroad. Consequently, many air passengers returning to China were called to carry the materials collected from other countries as their luggage.[66] Later, as the epicenter moved away and China became a significant supplier of epidemic prevention materials, many Chinese airlines were inspired to open up international cargo flights by converting passenger aircraft to cargo aircraft.[67] This measure may lessen the deficiency of international cargo capacity in China."

In the same analysis it is stated that "the experience of China's air cargo industry during the 2003 SARS period tells that the current dilemma may be temporary. However, COVID-19 is more infectious and spread more broadly, and accordingly, it is likely to have a more extensive impact on China's air freight industry than SARS. Chinese airlines now face more intense competition in the air cargo market than in 2003, and the epidemic control requirements bring about additional costs of fulfilling these requirements. Many enterprises face a tight financial chain."[68]

---

[65] "A SWOT analysis of China's Air Cargo Sector in the Context of COVID-19 Pandemic," available at: https://www.ncbi.nlm.nih.gov/pmc/articles/PMC7402658/#fn10 (accessed December 9, 2021).

[66] The Website of Overseas Chinese (2020), "Overseas Chinese Supported the Coronavirus Fight: 2 Tonnes of Medical Materials were Carried to China 'Bodily'," available at: http://www.chinaqw.com/hqhr/2020/01-29/244331.shtml (accessed December 9, 2021).

[67] China's Civil Aviation Online (2020), "The Booming Air Cargo Industry: The Orders of Passenger to Cargo Conversion are Scheduled to 5 Years Later," (accessed December 9, 2021).

[68] See: "A SWOT Analysis of China's Air Cargo Sector in the Context of COVID-19 Pandemic," available at: https://www.ncbi.nlm.nih.gov/pmc/articles/PMC7402658/#fn10 (accessed December 9, 2021).

The importance of air cargo for China is evident, and the government support with dedicated policies is crucial in order to combine and coordinate its development in the ambit of the BRI which is aimed at better connecting China especially with the EU and reinforcing their trade relations. Though the land and sea routes will predominate the exchange and passage of goods, a new Air Silk Road is emerging and will be coupled with a new wave of investments to enhance and build new infrastructures including airports to better serve and connect China with its major trading partner, namely the EU in consideration of the BRI and the new bilateral investment agreement which not only is aimed at reinforcing trade relations but also at creating a more predictable investment environment and a better understanding of the characteristics of these two markets, China and the EU, and thus hopefully an intensification of collaboration in other areas such as a greener aviation and sustainable development.

Conclusion

Aviation is an integral part of transportation systems around the world and its contribution to the entire global economy is evident. COVID-19 tipped the aviation industry into an unprecedented crisis. Many of the air operators will no longer exist after the crisis and the others will have no choice but reorganizing and forging new alliances and rationalizing their offer. In any case, it will take years for air travel to return to 2019 levels. However, the pandemic has also revitalized the drive to significantly reduce commercial aircraft CO_2 emissions. COVID-19 has in fact generated an acceleration toward a more sustainable aviation or in other terms the "greening of aviation." Aviation is responsible for approximately 12% of CO_2 emissions from all transport sources, compared to 74% from road transport. The industry has already made significant progress in cutting emissions over several decades. In fact, the newest aircraft in service today are over 80% more fuel efficient per seat and kilometer than the first jets in the 1960s, this was possible thanks to massive investments in research and development. But far more needs to be done for the industry to meet its pledge of cutting greenhouse gas emissions by half by 2050, compared with a baseline of 2005's levels. It must also be stressed that policymakers have been prompted to place the development of zero-emission planes at the heart of the industry's support packages, and manufacturers are working to produce new greener prototypes (including electric aircrafts) which could enter into service in about a decade. The reduction of emissions during the pandemic was due primarily because of the reduction in flights globally resulting from the closure of national borders, but this effect is only temporary. This is why there is a need to continue with the research and innovation together with the use of sustainable fuels. With flight numbers likely to take 2 to 3 years to recover, aviation seems already set on a more sustainable path.

The cost to transit the aviation industry toward a more sustainable and green aviation is huge, but there are also great opportunities for new investments, in particular for the electrification of aircraft, hydrogen, and the spread of sustainable aviation fuels. Investment in the aviation sector is posed to become a green investment. As exposed in Chapter 5, aviation is advancing not only toward a more sustainable mode but also related investment shall be guided by sustainable finance. There is no doubt that new capitals to sustain the transition toward a greener aviation will come and will be derived from more sustainable financial markets. In this context in fact, finance has acquired an increasingly active role through the mobilization of capital directed toward sustainable projects, and aviation sector, and in particular urban air mobility with its eVTOL, is already heading toward a more sustainable air transportation with interesting projects to be developed in the following years.

There is another important fact to highlight, not only the COVID-19 pandemic hit the aviation industry in a devastating manner almost annihilating the entire sector, but also an unexpected consequence was the growing of a niche segment, that is the business sector, and in general of "private flights." This modality of air travel has gained in popularity during the crisis caused by the pandemic and it is predicted that more wealthy people will opt for this choice because it offers several advantages in respect to the traditional commercial flights (e.g. flexibility and security are the most evident). More personal solutions, with the surge of business jets and the development of the so-called *general aviation*, will be offered to the public. This segment of the market will be especially pronounced in China where this sector is only at the beginning. As a matter of fact, low-altitude airspace resources have been the bottleneck and a key factor restricting the development of general aviation in this country. In China, airspace is tightly controlled by the Chinese military and the airspace classification system does not treat GA air activities separately. Strict military control over roughly 70% of all Chinese airspace is limiting the growth of this sector. However, China is now putting more emphasis on this industry with the intent to create another drive for its economy. China is a growing market for business aircraft, helicopters, and other general aviation aircrafts. Although the size of the GA fleet and flight hours are still relatively small, the potential importance of this industry to the Chinese economy in the long term has led aircraft OEMs and Chinese government officials to devote significant resources toward the growing GA capacity. China has many remote areas where GA can be a cost-effective solution. China has also invested in a GA industry structure that includes equipment manu‑ facturing, operation, maintenance, airport construction, air traffic control services, and financial services. From whatever angle we look, China has a promising GA future ahead. The government has been very supportive — the CAAC has a clear understanding of what the country needs, and are committed to seeing the development and maturity of GA through.

There is no doubt that the recovery of the aviation industry with the gradual reopening of all routes, will be a key driver of the global eco‑ nomic recovery. In order to ensure that aviation can continue to provide the economic and social benefits, it is also crucial to pursue a "greener aviation recovery" which was already a target with the introduction of "sustainable fuels" and hydrogen. This green trend will also lay the foun‑ dation for a more sustainable industry, and will accompany the develop‑ ment of a new modality for the public willing to travel by air. In fact, new technologies will help not only in reaching zero emissions but also in introducing a new concept of traveling by air with the widespread of the so-called VTOL (Vertical Take-Off and Landing aircrafts) and the devel‑ opment of the so-called Urban Air Mobility. Urban Air Mobility repre‑ sents the future of transport and it will be coupled and integrated into the more ample air transport system which is slowly returning into normality and is on the path to a greener future.

Bibliography

Textbooks

Alastair Blanshard and Mekahl Vohra (2020), "The Opportunity for Green Finance in the Aviation Sector," December 21, available at: www.icf.com/insight/transportation/opportunity-green-finance-aviation-sector.

Norton Rose Fullbright, "Green and Sustainable Financing Products for Airplanes," available at: https://www.nortonrosefulbright.com/en-us/knowledge/publications/de2464c2/green-and-sustainable-financing-products-for-airlines.

Yu Xugang, Cristiano Rizzi, Mario Tettamanti, Fabio E. Ziccardi, and Guo Li (2018), *China's Belt and Road — The Initiative and Its financial Focus*, World Scientific.

Yu Xugang, Mario Tettamanti, and Cristiano Rizzi (2020), *China's Continued Reforms in a New Era — Their Impact on Chinese Foreign Direct Investments and RMB Internationalization*, World Scientific.

Yu Xugang, Mario Tettamanti, and Cristiano Rizzi (2021), *China–US Trade Frictions Shaping New Equilibriums with the EU and the US — Towards a New Multilateralism or Tripolarism*, World Scientific.

Zhang Hong *et al.* (2015), *China's Outward Foreign Direct Investment: Theories and Strategies*, Enrich Professional Publishing, Inc.

Other Sources

Official documents, reports, analysis, and articles

"A SWOT Analysis of China's Air Cargo Sector in the Context of COVID-19 Pandemic," available at: https://www.ncbi.nlm.nih.gov/pmc/articles/PMC74 02658/#fn10 (accessed December 9, 2021).

ACI (2020), "Airport Operational Practice — Examples for managing COVID-19," available at: https://store.aci.aero/product/airport-operational-practice-examples-for-managing-covid-19/ (accessed December 9, 2021).

ACI Insights, "Planning the 'New Normal' Passenger Experience: Defining Effective Protective Measures against COVID-19," available at: https://blog.aci.aero/planning-the-new-normal-passenger-experience-defining-effective-protective-measures-against-covid-19-at-airports/ (accessed December 9, 2021).

"ACI World Data Shows Dramatic Impact of COVID-19 on Airports," available at: https://aci.aero/news/2020/07/03/aci-world-data-shows-dramatic-impact-of-covid-19-on-airports/ (accessed December 9, 2021).

Air Transport Action Group (ATAG) (2018), "Powering Global Economic Growth, Employment, Trade Links, Tourism and Support for Sustainable Development through Air Transport," available at: https://www.atag.org/our-publications/latest-publications.html (accessed December 7, 2021).

"Air Transport Agreement Between the Governments of the Member States of the Association of Southeast Asian Nations and the Government of the People's Republic of China," available at: https://asean.org/storage/images/archive/transport/Air%20Transport%20Agreement%20between%20ASEAN+China.pdf (accessed December 9, 2021).

"Airports Call for Data-Driven Approach to Establishing the Post-COVID Aviation Landscape," available at: https://www.aci-europe.org/media-room/260-airports-call-for-data-driven-approach-to-establishing-the-post-covid-aviation-landscape.html (accessed December 9, 2021).

Altran (2020), "En-Route to Urban Air Mobility — On the Fast Track to Viable and Safe On-demand Air Services," available at: https://www.altran.com/as-content/uploads/sites/27/2020/03/en-route-to-urban-air-mobility.pdf (accessed December 9, 2021).

Analysis and Policy Recommendations from the United Nations Secretary-General's High-Level Advisory Group on Sustainable Transport (2016), "Mobilizing Sustainable Transport for Development," Foreword by Secretary-General, available at: https://sustainabledevelopment.un.org/content/documents/2375Mobilizing%20Sustainable%20Transport.pdf (accessed December 7, 2021).

"Annual Report of the ICAO Council: 2015 — All Strategic Objectives: No Country Left Behind," available at: https://www.icao.int/annual-report-2015/Pages/all-strategic-objectives-nclb-initiatives.aspx (accessed December 7, 2021).

Aviation Benefits Beyond Borders, "Enable Trade," available at: https://aviation-benefits.org/economic-growth/enabling-trade/ (accessed December 7, 2021).

Axel Schauenburg (2020), "MRO Operations and Covid-19: Leveraging the Enforced Ground Time and Planning for the Future," Lufthansa Consulting, April 16, available at: https://www.lhconsulting.com/fileadmin/dam/downloads/studies/20200416_Article_MRO_during_Covid-19.pdf.

Bart Noëth (2020), "BOC Aviation Signs Sale-and-Leaseback Agreement with Southwest Airlines for 10 Boeing 737 MAX 8 Aircraft," available at: https://www.aviation24.be/aircraft-leasing-companies/boc-aviation/boc-aviation-signs-sale-and-leaseback-agreement-with-southwest-airlines-for-10-boeing-737-max-8-aircraft/ (accessed December 9, 2021).

Bowen Zhang and Jinru Mao (2019), "A Review of Research Literature on Management Reform and Low-altitude Opening of Low Air Space in Recent Years," *International Conference on Social Science, Economics and Management Research*, SSEMR.

Brodies LLP, "Will Greener Financing Options Take Off in the Aviation Sector?," available at: https://brodies.com/insights/banking.

China Daily, "Air Network Planned for Belt, Road Connectivity," available at: https://www.chinadaily.com.cn/china/2017-05/17/content_29377998.htm (accessed December 9, 2021).

China Knowledge (2021), "China's Air Passenger Trips Expected to Recover to Pre-COVID-19 Level," available at: https://www.chinaknowledge.com/News/DetailNews?id=91389 (Accessed December 9, 2021).

"China to Speed Up Development of Financial Leasing Industry," available at: http://english.www.gov.cn/policies/latest_releases/2015/09/07/content_281475184814808.htm (accessed December 9, 2021).

China's State Council Information Office (2018), "China and the World Trade Organization," *White Paper*, June 28, available at: http://english.gov.cn/archive/white_paper/2018/06/28/content_281476201898696.htm (accessed February 22, 2019).

Circular of MOF and CAAC on Financial Support Policies for Civil Aviation Transportation Enterprise during the Prevention and Control of COVID-19 Pandemic (财政部、民航局关于民航运输企业新冠肺炎疫情防控期间资金支持政策的通知) promulgated and effective on March 4, 2020, available at: http://www.caac.gov.cn/en/XWZX/202003/P020200303084661994193605.pdf.

Civil Aviation Administration of China, *"Statistical Bulletin of Civil Aviation Industry Development of 2019,"* Statistical Bulletin of Civil Aviation Industry Development in 2019 (caac.gov.cn) (accessed December, 9, 2021).

COM (2013), "EU Commission Staff Working Document — Impact Assessment Report on the EU–China Investment Relations," 297 final, and SWD (2013) 184 final.

COM (2019), "The European Green Deal — Communication from the Commission to the European Parliament, the European Council, the Council, the European Economic and Social Committee and the Committee of the Regions," 640 final, available at: https://ec.europa.eu/info/sites/info/files/european-green-deal-communication_en.pdf (accessed December 9, 2021).

COM (2020), "Communication from the Commission to the European Parliament, the Council, the European Economic and Social Committee and the Committee on the Regions — A Hydrogen Strategy for a Climate-Neutral Europe," 301 final, available at: https://ec.europa.eu/energy/sites/ener/files/hydrogen_strategy.pdf (accessed December 9, 2021).

Convention on International Civil Aviation (Chicago Convention). See: https://www.icao.int/publications/Documents/7300_cons.pdf (accessed December 7, 2021).

Coronavirus Aid, Relief, and Economic Security Act, also known as the CARES Act, available at: https://www.congress.gov/bill/116th-congress/house-bill/748 (accessed December 9, 2021).

Council Aviation Recovery Task Force (CART), "Report," available at: https://www.icao.int/covid/cart/Documents/CART%20Report%20Final.pdf (accessed December 9, 2021).

"EASA Certifies Electric Aircraft, First Type Certification for Fully Electric Plane World-Wide," press release available at: https://www.easa.europa.eu/newsroom-and-events/press-releases/easa-certifies-electric-aircraft-first-type-certification-fully#group-easa-related-content (accessed December 9, 2021).

European Union Aviation Safety Agency, "EASA SC-VTOL-01 Comment Response Document," available at: https://www.easa.europa.eu/sites/default/files/dfu/SC-VTOL-01%20CRD.pdf (accessed December 9, 2021).

FAA, "Aerospace Forecast: Fiscal 2019–2039," available at: https://www.faa.gov/data_research/aviation/aerospace_forecasts/media/FY2019-39_FAA_Aerospace_Forecast.pdf (accessed December 9, 2021).

Federal Register (2019), "Special Flight Authorizations for Supersonic," available at: https://www.federalregister.gov/documents/2019/06/28/2019-13079/special-flight-authorizations-for-supersonic-aircraft (accessed December 9, 2021).

Global Sustainable Aviation Forum (2020), "Green Recovery — The Aviation Industry Emerging from the COVID-19 Pandemic," available at: https://web.event.com/event/d0f999af-d3c0-410f-ad79-3ffabba01661/summary?rp=00000000-0000-0000-0000-000000000000 (last accessed December 5, 2021).

"Handbook on Sustainable Investments," available at: https://www.sustainablefinance.ch/upload/cms/user/201712_Handbook_on_Sustainable_Investments_CFA.pdf. The CFA Institute Research Foundation is a not-for-profit organization established to promote the development and dissemination of relevant research for investment practitioners worldwide.

IATA (2020), "Airlines Committed to a Green Recovery," available at: https://airlines.iata.org/news/airlines-committed-to-a-green-recovery (accessed December 5, 2021).

IATA, "Biosafety for Air Transport: A Roadmap for Restarting Aviation," available at: https://www.iata.org/contentassets/5c8786230ff34e2da406c72a520 30e95/roadmap-safely-restarting-aviation.pdf (accessed December 9, 2021).

IATA, "Climate Change," available at: https://www.iata.org/en/policy/environment/climate-change/ (accessed June 19, 2020).

IATA, "International Air Transport Association. IATA Forecasts Passenger Demand to Double Over 20 Years," available at: https://www.iata.org/pressroom/pr/Pages/2016-10-18-02.aspx (accessed December 9, 2021).

ICAO (2009), "Review Of The Classification And Definitions Used for Civil Aviations Activities, *Working Paper*, November, available at: https://www.icao.int/Meetings/STA10/Documents/Sta10_Wp007_en.pdf (accessed December 9, 2021).

ICAO (2011), "Annex 17 to the Convention on International Civil Aviation," Ninth Edition, March, available at: https://www.spilve.lv/library/law/Annex%2017.pdf (accessed December 9, 2021).

ICAO (2016), "Manual on the Regulation of International Air Transport," (Doc 9626), Third Edition, available at: https://www.icao.int/Meetings/a39/Documents/Provisional_Doc_9626.pdf (accessed December 9, 2021).

ICAO (2016), "Policy and Guidance Material on the Economic Regulation of International Air Transport," (Doc 9587), Fourth Edition, Part 1, p. 20, available at: https://www.icao.int/Meetings/a39/Documents/9587-PROVISIONAL%20 VERSION.pdf (accessed December 9, 2021).

ICAO (2017), "Annex 16 to the Convention on International Civil Aviation — Environmental Protection, Volume III — Aeroplane CO2 Emissions," available at: https://store.icao.int/en/annex-16-environmental-protection-volume-iii-aeroplane-co2-emissions (accessed December 9, 2021).

ICAO (2017), "Financing Aviation, Emission Reduction," this report was produced within the framework of the joint ICAO–UNDP–GEF assistance project Transforming the Global Aviation Sector: Emissions Reductions from International Aviation.

ICAO (2018), "Annex 16 to the Convention on International Civil Aviation, Environmental Protection, Volume IV, Carbon Offsetting and Reduction Scheme for International Aviation (CORSIA)," First Edition, October, available at: https://www.icao.int/environmental-protection/CORSIA/Pages/SARPs-Annex-16-Volume-IV.aspx (accessed December 9, 2021).

ICAO (2019), "Aviation Benefits Report," available at: https://www.icao.int/sustainability/Documents/AVIATION-BENEFITS-2019-web.pdf (accessed December 7, 2021).

"ICAO Council Adopts New COVID-19 Aviation Recovery "Take Off" Guidelines to Reconnect the World," available at: https://www.icao.int/Newsroom/Pages/ICAO-Council-adopts-new-COVID.aspx (accessed December 9, 2021).

ICAO Council Aviation Recovery Task Force (CART), "Take-off: Guidance for Air Travel through the COVID-19 Public Health Crisis," available at: https://www.icao.int/covid/cart/Pages/CART-Take-off.aspx (accessed December 9, 2021).

ICAO, "China Action Plan to Reduce CO2 Emissions from International Aviation," available at: https://www.icao.int/environmental-protection/Lists/ActionPlan/Attachments/5/China_en.pdf.

ICAO, "Financing Aviation Emission Reduction," available at: https://www.icao.int/environmental-protection/Documents/ICAO_UNDP_GEF_Financing LowCarbonAirportGuidance.pdf (accessed June 14, 2021).

ICAO, "Independent Expert Integrated Technology Goals Assessment and Review for Engines and Aircraft," (Doc 10127), available at: http://www.icscc.org.cn/upload/file/20200603/20200603140731_33885.pdf.

International Air Transport Association (IATA) (2016), "Manual on the Regulation of International Air Transport," ICAO (Doc 9626), Third Edition, Chapter 3.8, p. 95, available at: https://www.icao.int/Meetings/a39/Documents/Provisional_Doc_9626.pdf (accessed December 7, 2021).

IPCC, "Change 2014: Mitigation of Climate Change," *Assessment Report*, available at: https://www.ipcc.ch/report/ar5/wg3/ (accessed December 7, 2021).

Jianfa Hu (2015), "Research Progress in Visualized aeronautical Chart for Early Warning of Low-Altitude Flight," *International Conference on Logistics Engineering, Management and Computer Science*, LEMCS.

JiaoeWang, Haoran Yang, and Han Wang (2019), *The Evolution of China's International Aviation Markets from a Policy Perspective on Air Passenger Flows*, MDPI.

Kate O'Connor (2020), "China Adds More Than 50 GA Airports in 2020," December 29, *A Vweb*, available at: https://www.avweb.com/aviation-news/china-adds-more-than-50-ga-airports-in-2020/ (accessed December 9, 2021).

M. Muntean, D. Guizzardi, E. Schaaf, M. Crippa, E. Solazzo, J. G. J. Olivier, and E. Vignati (2018), "Fossil CO2 Emissions of All World Countries — 2018 Report," EUR 29433 EN, Publications Office of the European Union, Luxembourg.

Manuela Mirkos, "An 'Air Silk Road' is Taking Shape along the Belt and Road Initiative," available at: https://www.infrastructure-channel.com/article/-/content/an-air-silk-road-is-taking-shape-along-the-belt-and-road-initiative (accessed December 9, 2021).

Mariya A. Ishutkina and R. John Hansman (2009), "Analysis of the Interaction Between Air Transportation and Economic Activity: A Worldwide Perspective," Report No. ICAT-2009.

Mark Crittenden (2020), "With Ultralight Lithium-Sulfur Batteries, Electric Airplanes Could Finally Take Off," available at: https://spectrum.ieee.org/aerospace/aviation/with-ultralight-lithiumsulfur-batteries-electric-airplanes-could-finally-take-off (accessed December 9, 2021).

Pan Zhaoyi (2019), "A Look at China's General Aviation Industry," October 19, available at: https://news.cgtn.com/news/2019-10-19/A-look-at-China-s-general-aviation-industry-KV0GSb49PO/index.html (accessed December 9, 2021).

Paris Convention on Climate Change, "Paris Agreement," https://unfccc.int/process-and-meetings/the-paris-agreement/the-paris-agreement (accessed July 2, 2020).

PENN State, "Finance and Sustainability-Linked Financial Instruments," available at: https://majorsustainability.smeal.psu.edu/finance/concepts/sustainability-linked-financial-instruments/ (accessed June 14, 2021).

"Porsche and Boeing to Partner on Premium Urban Air Mobility Market," available at: https://boeing.mediaroom.com/2019-10-10-Porsche-and-Boeing-to-Partner-on-Premium-Urban-Air-Mobility-Market#assets_20295_130523-117:20645 (accessed December 9, 2021).

Rachelle Harry (2021), "IATA: Airfreight Demand Back to Pre-Covid Levels but Capacity Remains Tight," available at: https://www.aircargonews.net/data/iata-airfreight-demand-back-to-pre-covid-levels-but-capacity-remains-tight/ (accessed December 9, 2021).

Regulation of the European Parliament and of the Council Amending Council Regulation (EEC) NO95/93 on Common Rules for the Allocation of Slots at Community Airports, Brussels, March 30, 2020, available at: http://data.consilium.europa.eu/doc/document/PE-4-2020-REV-1/en/pdf this emends Regulation 95/93 on common rules for the allocation of slots at Community airport, available at: https://eur-lex.europa.eu/LexUriServ/LexUriServ.do?uri=CONSLEG:1993R0095:20090630:EN:PDF (accessed December 9, 2021).

Report of the Secretary-General (2017), "Progress towards the Sustainable Development Goals," available at: https://unstats.un.org/sdgs/files/report/2017/secretary-general-sdg-report-2017--Statistical-Annex.pdf; https://unstats.un.org/sdgs/indicators/database/?indicator=9.1.2 (accessed December 7, 2021).

"Resolution A40-18: Consolidated Statement of Continuing ICAO Policies and Practices Related to Environmental Protection — Climate Change," available at: https://www.icao.int/environmental-protection/Documents/Assembly/Resolution_A40-18_Climate_Change.pdf (accessed December 9, 2021).

Robert Thompson, "Hydrogen: A Future Fuel for Aviation?," available at: https://www.rolandberger.com/en/Publications/Hydrogen-A-future-fuel-of-aviation.html (accessed December 9, 2021).

Roland Berger (2018), "Aircraft Electrical Propulsion — Onwards and Upwards," available at: https://www.rolandberger.com/en/Publications/Electrical-propulsion-ushers-in-new-age-of-innovation-in-aerospace.html (accessed December 9, 2021).

Roland Berger, "Hydrogen — A Future Fuel for Aviation?," available at: https://www.rolandberger.com/en/Publications/Hydrogen-A-future-fuel-of-aviation.html (accessed December 9, 2021).

Ross Garnaut, Ligang Song, and Cai Fang (2018), "China's 40 Years of Reform and Development 1978–2018," ANU Press, The Australian National University.

Soochow Securities (2016), *General Aviation: The Low-Altitude Reform has Entered a Deepening Stage.*

The new EU framework for the screening of foreign direct investments has officially entered into force on April 10, 2019. The new framework is based on proposal tabled by the European Commission in September 2017 and will be instrumental in safeguarding Europe's security and public order in relation to foreign direct investments into the Union. Regulation (EU) 2019/452 of the European Parliament and of the Council of March 19, 2019, available at: https://eur-lex.europa.eu/eli/reg/2019/452/oj (accessed December 9, 2021).

U.S.–China Economic And Security Review Commission, "A 'China Model?' Beijing's Promotion of Alternative Global Norms And Standards, Hearing Before the One Hundred Sixteenth Congress, Second Session, March 13, 2020.

Uber, "Uber Air Vehicle Requirements and Missions," available at: https://s3.amazonaws.com/uber-static/elevate/Summary+Mission+and+Requirements.pdf (accessed December 9, 2021).

UNFCC, "The Paris Agreement," The Paris Agreement is a legally binding international treaty on climate change. It was adopted by 196 Parties at COP21 in Paris, on December 12, 2015 and entered into force on November 4, 2016, available at: https://unfccc.int/process-and-meetings/the-paris-agreement/the-paris-agreement (accessed June 14, 2021).

United Nations, "Transforming our World: 2030 Agenda for Sustainable Development," available at: https://sustainabledevelopment.un.org/post2015/transformingourworld (accessed December 7, 2021).

Xiaoxia Dong and Megan S. Ryerson (2019), "Increasing Civil Aviation Capacity in China Requires Harmonizing the Physical and Human Components of Capacity: A Review and Investigation," *Transportation Research Interdisciplinary Perspective*, 1, 100005.

Zhang Liang and Hu Chengwei (2018), "Analysis of Supply Quality of General Aviation Industry Policy in China," in Advances in Social Science, Education and Humanities Research (ASSEHR), Vol. 206, *2018 International Conference on Advances in Social Sciences and Sustainable Development,* available at: https://www.atlantis-press.com/proceedings/asssd-18/25894460 (accessed December 9, 2021).

Zhang Qi (2019), "Interview: China is Major Player in Global Aircraft Leasing Market, Says Expert," January 23, available at: http://en.people.cn/n3/2019/0123/c90000-9540838.html (accessed December 9, 2021).

Internet Useful Websites — Institutional Organizations (Aviation and Others)

Air Transport Action Group — ATAG, https://www.atag.org/

Airport Council International — ACI, https://aci.aero/

Airports Council International — ACI, https://aci.aero/

Belt and Road Portal, https://eng.yidaiyilu.gov.cn/info

China Aviation Administration of China — CAAC, http://www.caac.gov.cn/index.html

China Council for the Promotion of International Trade — CCPIT, www.ccpit.org/

China Foreign Investment Registration, www.wzj.gov.cn

China Internet Information Center, www.china.org.cn

Civil Air Navigation Services Organization — CANSO, https://www.canso.org/about-canso

DG Trade of the European Commission, http://europa.eu.int/comm/trade/index_en.htm

EU Delegation in China, www.delchn.cec.eu.int/

European Aviation Safety Agency — EASA, https://www.easa.europa.eu/

European Chamber of Commerce in China — EUCCC, www.euccc.com.cn/

European Commission: Trade policies, http://ec.europa.eu/trade/policy/countries-and-regions/countries/china/

Federal Aviation Administration — FAA, https://www.faa.gov/

International Air Transportation Association — IATA, https://www.iata.org/

International Business Aviation Council — IBAC, https://ibac.org/about-ibac

International Civil Aviation Organization — ICAO, https://www.icao.int/

International Federation of Air Line Pilots' Associations — IFALPA, https://www.ifalpa.org/

International Monetary Fund, http://www.imf.org/en/About

Ministry of Commerce, www.mofcom.gov.cn

Ministry of Labor and Social Security, www.molss.gov.cn

National Development and Reform Commission People's Republic of China — NDRC, http://en.ndrc.gov.cn/mfndrc/default.htm

People's Bank of China, www.pbc.gov.cn

State Administration for Industry and Commerce, www.saic.gov.cn

State Administration of Taxation, www.chinatax.gov.cn
World Customs Organization — WCO, http://www.wcoomd.org/en/about-us/what-is-the-wco.aspx
World Meteorological Organization — WMO, https://public.wmo.int/en
World Trade Organization — WTO, http://wto.org

Main Business and Commercial Aircraft Manufacturers

Aerion Corporation, https://aerionsupersonic.com/
Airbus, https://www.airbus.com/
Aviation Industry Corporation of China — AVIC, https://www.avic.com/en/
Beechcraft, Beechcraft Aircraft | Turboprop and Piston Models (txtav.com)
Boeing, https://www.boeing.com/company/
Bombardier Aviation, https://www.bombardier.com/en/home.html
Cessna Aircraft,
Dassault Aviation, https://www.dassault-aviation.com/en/group/about-us/company-profile/
Embraer, https://embraer.com/global/en/about-us
Gulfstream, https://www.gulfstream.com/en
https://txtav.com/en/company
Textron Aviation Inc., https://www.textron.com/About/Our-Businesses/Textron-Aviation

Cirrus Design Corporation: The company is owned by a subsidiary of the Chinese government-owned AVIC. https://cirrusaircraft.com/about/

Diamond Aircraft: Headquartered in Austria with facilities in Canada and China, is among the leading aircraft manufacturer in General Aviation. Founded in 1981, Diamond has pioneered many aviation firsts and achieved numerous milestones and industry expert accolades. https://www.diamondaircraft.com/en/about-diamond/why-diamond/

Piper Aircraft, Inc.: It is a manufacturer of general aviation aircraft, located at the Vero Beach Municipal Airport in Vero Beach, Florida, United States which is owned since 2009 by the Government of Brunei. Throughout much of the mid-to-late 20th century, it was considered to be one of the "Big Three" in the field of general aviation manufacturing, along with Beechcraft and Cessna. https://www.piper.com/

Otto Aviation (CELERA 500L), https://www.ottoaviation.com

Other Internet Sources

EU Smart Cities, https://eu-smartcities.eu/

Index

A

2030 Agenda for Sustainable Development, 10
ability to transport medical supplies, 10
accessing distant regions, 9
a concept vehicle exploring luxury VTOL, 153
acquisition of Cirrus by Avic, 254
actively manage safety, 94
active ownership, 212
adoption of electrical propulsion, 131
adoption of eVTOLs, 143
advancements in technology for supersonic flight, 205
advancing toward a greener aviation, 138
Aerial work, 38
Aerion, 204
Aerodromes, Operability and Interoperability (AOI), 39
aeronautical information services (AIS), 41
African Civil Aviation Commission (AFCAC), 21
agricultural flying, 39
airborne contamination, 102
Airbus, 42, 150, 170, 175

airbus A380, 58
Airbus group, 171
Airbus Helicopter, 113
air cargo, 8, 35–36
aircraft and engine redesign, 118
aircraft guidelines, 95
aircraft industry, 41
aircraft-related technology development, 221
aircraft's rounded shape, 201
air freight, 6, 102
airline mergers, 58
airlines, 96
airlines support circular, 55
Air Mobility Urban-Large experimental Demonstrations, 257
Air Navigation Bureau, 25
Air Navigation Commission (ANC), 25, 27
air navigation services, 32, 41
air passenger services, 93
Airport Council International (ACI), 15, 27–28, 30
airport facilities, 8
airport guidelines, 95
Airport Indoor Air Quality (IAQ), 102
airport operational practice, 99

airport operators, 96
airport-related matters, 39
airport robotization, 100
airport services, 32
airport shuttles (suburban to urban services), 147–148
airport slots, 51
airport slot waiver, 83
Air Silk Road, 259
airspace integration, 151
air taxi, 35, 147–148, 154, 255
air traffic management (ATM), 8, 16, 232
air traffic services, 18
air transport, 9, 10
air transport action group (ATAG), 7, 26, 29
air transportation system, 5
air transport bureau, 26
air transport committee, 25
air transport connectivity, 9
air transport infrastructure (ATI), 14
air travelers, 96
alternative fuels, 221
alternative fuels task force (AFTF), 72
ancient Silk Road, 264
antitrust scrutiny, 58
Articles of Association of IATA, 30
artificial intelligence, 100
ATM industry, 8
ATM infrastructure, 16
aviation, 9, 19
aviation activities, 41
aviation fuel suppliers, 8
aviation industry, 5, 8, 14
Aviation Industry Corporation of China (AVIC), 254
aviation infrastructure, 14
aviation leasing companies, 61
aviation's public funding, 223

aviation's role in economic growth, 93
aviation training, 32, 43
aviation workers, 96

B
baggage handling, 8
Baron G58, 197
baseline aviation health safety protocol, 95
battery performance, 126
BBJ by Boeing, 172
Beechcraft, 43, 194
Beech Holdings, 194
Belt and Road air cargo hub, 264
Belt and Road Initiative (BRI), 259
best-in-class fuel efficiency, 200
better navigation sensors, 143
bio-risk analysis, 102
biosafety, 99
bizliners, 168
blocking passengers with diseases, 99
BOC Aviation Limited, 59–60
Boeing, 42, 150, 170
Boeing Company, 171
Bombardier Global 7500 EPD, 184
Bombardier Inc., 42, 170, 180
Bonanza G36, 197
boom aerospace, 206
boomless cruise, 204
border financial leasing services, 64
building capacity, 224
Bureau of Administration and Services, 26
Bureau of Aviation Security, 239
Bureau of Retired Officials, 241
Bureau of Supervision Stationed in CAAC, 240
business aviation, 43, 104, 159–160
business aviation coalition for sustainable aviation fuel to sustain SAF, 73

business aviation — commercial, 160
business aviation — corporate, 161
business aviation — fractional
   ownership, 161
business aviation goes greener, 199
business aviation industry, 163, 168
business aviation is expanding, 201
business aviation market is growing,
   161
business aviation — owner operated,
   161
business flights, 169
business flying, 38

C
CAAC party committee, 240
capital for green aviation, 226
capital injection, 15
Carbon Offsetting and Reduction
   Scheme for International Aviation
   (CORSIA), 69, 107
CARES Act, 53, 54
Cargo flight crews, 96
Cargo guidelines, 96
Cargo services, 35
Cargo services survived to the
   COVID-19, 102
Cargo tonne km (CTKs), 103
CART "take off" guidelines, 95
catering services, 8
Celera 500L, 198
Centers for Disease Control and
   Prevention (CDC), 101
certification of manufacturing
   processes, 143
certification requirements, 133
Cessna Aircraft Company, 43, 170
Cessna Caravan, 196
Cessna Caravan EX, 197
Cessna Citation business jets and
   Beechcraft, 193
Cessna Denali, 197

Cessna family business jet, 194
Cessna Skycourier, 196
Cessna Skyhawk, 197
Cessna Skyline, 197
Challenger, 181
Challenger 350, 181
Challenger 650, 181
check-in, 8
Chicago convention, 19–20, 24–25,
   32
China Aviation Industry General
   Aircraft (CAIGA), 254
China's aviation system, 231
China's financial policies, 55
China's private jet market, 254
circular economy, 213
Cirrus Design Corporation, 43
Citation CJ3+, 194
Citation CJ4, 194
Citation Latitude, 195
Citation Longitude, 195
CitationM2, 194
Citation Sovereign+, 195
Citation XLS+, 194
CityAirbus, 113, 154
Civil Air Navigation Services
   Organization (CANSO), 29
civil aviation activities, 32
civil aviation administration of China
   (CAAC), 55–56, 230–231
civil aviation administrations
   (CAAs), 22
civil aviation airspace planning, 232
Civil Aviation Law of the People's
   Republic of China, 244
civil aviation manufacturing, 32, 41
Class A GA airports, 250
clean energy, 216
Climate Bonds Initiative (CBI), 217
Climate Bonds Standard, 217
climate change, 13
collecting traffic data, 13

commercial aircraft manufacturer, 42
commercial air transport services, 32
Commercial Aviation Alternative Fuels Initiative (CAAFI), 108
commercial business aviation, 35
Committee on Aviation Environmental Protection (CAEP), 26, 72
Committee on Joint Support of Air Navigation Services, 25
Committee on Unlawful Interference, 25
communications, navigation and surveillance systems (CNS), 41
company executives, 162
comparable level of aircraft performance, 127
connecting people, 9
containing the outbreak, 252
convention on International Civil Aviation, 19
Coronavirus Aid, Relief, and Economic Security Act, 53
corporate aviation, 38
CORSIA lower carbon fuels, 109
CORSIA sustainable aviation fuel, 108–109
council, 24
Council Aviation Recovery Task Force (CART), 92
COVID-19 caused a deceleration, 251
COVID-19 outbreak, 47
COVID-19 pandemic, 56
COVID lockdowns, 252
credits for sustainable projects, 212
Crew Guidelines, 96
cruise mode, 153
cryogenic cooling, 119
cut routes, 162

cutting emissions, 269
cutting greenhouse gas emissions by half by 2050, 269

D
damages caused by COVID-19, 47
Dassault aviation, 170, 185
decision-making software, 100
decline in air traffic worldwide, 51
delivery drones, 143
Department of Aircraft Airworthiness Certification, 238
Department of Airports, 238
Department of Development Planning, 234
Department of Finance, 55, 235
Department of Flight Standards, 237
Department of General Affairs, 233
Department of International Affairs, 236
Department of Personnel, Science & Technology and Education, 236
Department of Policy, Law and Regulation, 234
Department of Transport, 237
develop a greener aviation, 106
Develop civil aviation pricing policies, 233
development in electrical propulsion, 113
development of airlines, 229
development of eVTOLs, 145
development of sustainable low-carbon fuels, 69
development of zero-emission planes, 269
Diamond, 43
difficulties in securing new funds, 204
digitization of air traffic control, 17
direct financial support, 49

direct investment rules, 58
disruptive innovation, 114
distinguish restart from recovery, 94
diversifying funding sources, 14
drastic reduction of passengers due to COVID-19, 58

E

ease traffic in urban, 149
ecarbonization trajectory for aviation, 226
economic development of nations, 5
economic impacts of COVID-19 on commercial aviation, 48–49
economic/market-based measures, 221
effective hydrogen storage solutions, 118
effect of COVID-19 on the air cargo sector in China, 264
Ehang 184, 256
Ehang 216, 256
electrical aircraft, 130
electrically-propelled LCAs, 111
electrical propulsion, 126, 129
electrical propulsion for the future, 125
electrical propulsion in niche applications, 131
electrical propulsion system, 127
Electric and Hybrid Aircraft Platform, 106
electric aviation, 129
electric urban air-taxis, 110
electric vertical take-off and landing aircraft (eVTOLs), 139
Embraer, 42, 153, 170, 190
Embraer Executive Jets, 190
EmbraerX, 153–154
emission regulations, 129
Empresa Brasileira de Aeronáutica, 190

encourage sustainable corporate governance, 212
energy and clean technologies, 214
energy efficiency, 216
Energy Transitions Commission (ETC), 220
enhanced air connectivity, 19
enhancement of air traffic management, 229
enhance overall EU–China aviation relations, 261
ensure essential connectivity, 94
ensure sustainability, 94
environmental product declaration (EPD), 182, 184
environmental protection, 215
environmental sustainability, 214
equity markets, 211
ethical investment, 211
EU Action Plan, 212
EU Emissions Trading System (ETS), 107
EU ownership rules, 58
European Aviation Safety Agency (EASA), 21–22
European Civil Aviation Conference (ECAC), 21
European Cockpit Association (ECA), 85
European Commission and its initiative for smart cities, 155
European Green Deal, 107
European Innovation Partnership in Smart Cities and Communities (EIP-SCC), 155
EU's strategy for aviation safety, 21
Eviation, 138
evolution in UAM, 113
evolution of a Greener Aviation, 105
evolution of China's GA industry policy, 247
evolution of new propulsion, 106

eVTOL, 141, 270
eVTOL aircraft, 154
eVTOL industry, 144
eVTOLs in urban environments, 141
eVTOLs operating in city skics, 141
exchange-traded fund (ETF), 218
explosive growth of urbanization in
    China, 256
extension of urban traffic into
    airspace, 152

F
2,500 Falcons delivered to date, 185
FAA regulations, 202
Falcon 6X, 186
Falcon 7X, 187
Falcon 8X, 187
Falcon 10X, 187
Falcon 900LX, 186
Falcon 2000LXS, 186
Falcon 2000S, 186
Falcon family and the newest, 185
Federal Aviation Administration
    (FAA), 22
financial institutions, 19
financial sector, 213
financial service providers, 212
financial technology, 18
financial viability, 30
Fintech, 18, 19
first application of VTOL, 148
First ICAO Conference on Aviation
    and Alternative Fuels (CAAF/1), 72
five principles for restarting aviation,
    97
fixed-based operators (FBOs), 40
fleet renewals, 220
fly greener, 128
flying personnel, 84
flying private, 162
Flying privately was chosen by many
    well-off travelers, 159

fractional ownership, 38
freedom in the choice of itinerary,
    170
frequently wash hands, 101
fuel cell propulsion, 114
fuel-effective eco-friendly, 59
fuel efficiency, 202
fueling the future, 74
Fuels Task Group (FTG), 73
funding for climate mitigation, 224
future of air mobility in Europe, 155
future of Urban Air Mobility (UAM),
    113

G
GA and recreational aircraft, 112
GA in China is extremely promising,
    245
game changer, 198
general aviation (GA), 32, 37, 40, 43,
    197, 270
general aviation business, 193
general aviation sector, 43
general public, 96
ghost flights, 51
giant aircraft, 59
giant planes, 58
Global 5000, 182
GLOBAL 5500, 182
GLOBAL 6000, 182
GLOBAL 6500, 182
GLOBAL 7500, 182
GLOBAL 8000, 182
global connectivity, 93
global economic development, 6, 19
global economy, 7
globalization of production, 7
globalized world, 6
global pandemic has changed the way
    the world functions, 159
global prosperity, 6
global trade, 8

governance of public and private institutions, 213
greater convenience for commuters, 128
great flexibility, 104
green bond market has grown exponentially, 216
Green Bond Principles, 217
green bonds, 211–212
Green Deal, 156
greener aviation, 114
greener aviation industry, 210
greener aviation recovery, 271
greener future, 271
green exchange-traded funds, 218
Green Finance, 211
Green Finance in the Aviation Sector, 219
green financial instruments, 216
greening of air transport, 106
greening of aviation, 269
green investors, 216
Green Loan Principles, 226
green mutual funds, 217
green recovery, 222
ground handling, 39
Group of Discipline Inspection, 240
guideline to boost China's GA, 248
Gulfstream, 206
Gulfstream airspace corporation, 170, 177
Gulfstream G280, 178
Gulfstream G550, 178
Gulfstream G600, 178
Gulfstream G650ER, 178

H
hand hygiene, 101
harmonized regulatory framework, 19
Hawker Aircraft, 194
health, 10
health authorities, 104

health passports, 99
high re-charging speeds, 126
Horizon Europe, 156
human rights, 213
human safety, 143
HY4, 116
hybrid-electric, 110
hybrid-electric propulsion, 110
hydrogen, 109
hydrogen as an evolution of SAF, 113
hydrogen combustion aircraft, 115
hydrogen fuel cell (HFC) aircraft, 115
hydrogen propulsion, 109
hydrogen reduces GHG emissions, 114
hydrogen storage, 119

I
IATA Annual General Meeting, 31
IATA Articles of Association, 31
IATA Board of Governors, 31
IATA guidance complementing ICAO's CART, 96
IATA Industry Affairs Committee, 31
IATA's Biosafety for Air Transport, 97
IATA Special Committees, 31
IATA Standing Committees, 31
ICAO Council's Aviation Recovery Task Force, 96
ICAO Global Framework for Aviation and Alternative Fuels (GFAAF), 71
ICAO, Resolution A39-1, 105
ICAO SARPs, 22
ICAO's Technical Co-operation Bureau, 26
ICAO Sustains Innovation in Line with EU Strategy, 106
ICBC Financial Leasing Company Ltd, 63

ICBC leasing, 63
immigration restrictions, 96
immune system, 102
impact investing, 212
impact of COVID-19, 14
impact of COVID-19 on airports, 80
impact of COVID-19 on
    CO_2 emissions, 65
impact of COVID-19 on different
    sectors of the aviation industry,
    47
impact of COVID-19 on global air
    transport, 91
impact of COVID-19 on Maintenance
    Repair and Overhaul (MRO), 89
impact of COVID-19 on personnel
    and pilots, 84
impact of new technologies, 105
implementing queue management
    measures, 100
improved air traffic management and
    infrastructure use, 221
improved hygiene management,
    101
improved operations and
    infrastructure, 220
improve fuel efficiency, 220
In 2016, ICAO adopted CORSIA,
    69
including electric aircrafts, 269
inclusiveness, 213
increased airspace capacity, 16
increased automation, 100
increased hand hygiene, 101
incredible gliding capability, 201
industry recognition, 30
industry support, 31
inflight passenger applications, 146
infrastructure capability, 5
infrastructure expansion, 151
infrastructures, 229
ingle European Sky (SES), 156

innovation in aviation, 110
innovative fuels, 108
instructional flying, 37
integration into connected mobility
    systems, 151
intercity flights, 149
international air navigation, 24
International Air Rail Organization
    (IARO), 29
International Air Transport
    Association (IATA), 15, 29–30, 47
international air transport sector, 97
international aviation industry, 47
International Business Aviation
    Council (IBAC), 160
International Civil Aviation
    Organization (ICAO), 10–11, 13,
    16, 20
International Civil Aviation
    Organization (ICAO) Committee
    on Aviation Environmental
    Protection (CAEP), 203
International Federation of Air Line
    Pilots' Associations (IFALPA), 29
international ISO standards, 184
International Telecommunication
    Union (ITU), 23
Interregional services (intercity
    flights), 147, 149
introduction of hybrid aircraft, 150
investment decisions, 213
investment in human capital, 213
investment in sustainable airport and
    heliport infrastructure, 89
investments for the modernization
    and expansion of aviation
    infrastructures, 14

J
50/50 jet-A and SAF blend as a true
    drop-in solution, 108
job creation, 93

K

10 key principles for secure and
  sustainable recovery, 93
King Air 260, 196
King Air 360, 196
King Air 360ER, 196
King Air C90GTx, 196

L

labor relations, 213
laminar flow, 199
landing slots, 52
large business jets, 168
large commercial aircraft (LCA), 110
Latin American Civil Aviation
  Commission (LACAC), 21
Learjet, 181
Learjet 75 Liberty, 181
Legacy 450, 192
Legacy 500, 192
Legal Affairs and External Relations
  Bureau, 26
lessons to improve resilience, 95
liberalization of low altitude airspace,
  246
life-cycle greenhouse gas (GHG)
  emissions, 108
light business jets, 167
limiting global warming, 70
Lineage 1000E, 192
loans, 49
loans with preferential conditions, 55
long battery life-cycles, 126
long-term investments, 213
low-altitude airspace, 245
lower carbon aviation fuels, 106,
  109
lower carbon aviation fuels and
  hydrogen, 108
lower environmental impact, 71
lower impact, 202
Luxembourg Green Exchange, 218

M

M&A, 57
mail ton kilometers (MTKs), 8
maintenance and overhaul, 32, 41
Maintenance Repair and Overhaul
  (MRO), 91
Manual on the Regulation of
  International Air Transport, 32, 34,
  36
market acceptance, 151
market-based measures, 106
market demand, 128
massive airlines consolidation, 57
massive consolidation, 57
measures to achieve international
  aviation's global goals, 220
Meteorological Organization (WMO),
  23
meteorological services for air
  navigation (MET), 41
microfinance, 212
Midsize business jets, 167
minimize the risk of
  COVID-19 transmission, 96
mobile networks for low-altitude
  connectivity, 145
modernization of air traffic
  management (ATM), 107
modernized air traffic management
  systems, 106
modernized aviation infrastructure,
  262
modes of transport, 14
more frequent cleaning of trays,
  101
more sustainable air transportation,
  270
more sustainable industry, 271
multiple stopovers on a single
  journey, 170
multi-rotor VTOL aircraft, 113
multi-stakeholders, 14

N

nanotechnology, 101

NASA Green Flight Challenge, 136

nascent UAM market, 150

National Aeronautics and Space
    Administration (NASA), 203

National Civil Aviation Trade Union,
    241

national security, 245

needed infrastructure, 15

new concept of aircraft, 198

new concepts of air mobility, 110

New Experience Travel Technologies
    (NEXTT), 15–16

new FAA proposal, 202

new industry flagship, the Gulfstream
    G700, 178

Next Generation Air Transportation
    System (NextGen), 17

Next Generation EU, 87

next generation of quieter supersonic
    airplanes, 202

New Experience Travel Technologies
    (NEXTT), 15–16

Niche application of electrical
    propulsion, 131

No Country Left Behind (NCLB), 11

non-scheduled air service, 34

non-schedule services, 35

non-stop service, 148

O

objective of all these guidelines, 96

off-airport activities, 15

offering a greener option, 200

Office of Air Traffic Regulation,
    239

Office of Aviation Safety, 234

Office of Ideological and Political
    Work, 240

on-demand business service, 142

on-demand point-to-point, 148

on demand services, 35

opening of low-air altitude, 245

Opening of Low-Altitude Airspace to
    Favor the Development of GA in
    China, 242

Original Equipment Manufacturers
    (OEMs), 181

other manufactures developing
    eVTOL, 150

overture, 202, 206

P

Paris Agreement, 70, 212

passenger flow management, 99

Payroll Support Program, 54

personal jet, 163, 165

Phenom 100EV, 191

Phenom 300E, 191

Pilots' Associations, 29

Piper Aircraft, 43

Planning the "new normal" passenger
    experience, 100

pleasure flying, 37

policies of ICAO and IATA regarding
    the emissions of CO_2, 68

policies to reduce CO_2 emissions,
    68

pollution prevention, 213

Porsche and Boeing, 152

potentialities of General Aviation
    (GA) in China, 229

potential long-term growth, 161

power storage technology, 114

pragmatic approach to supersonic
    speed, 206

Preator 500, 191

Preator 600, 191

premium personal UAM vehicles,
    152

premium UAM market, 152

preservation of biodiversity, 213

prioritize safety and security, 99

private airlines, 159
private aviation, 104
private aviation companies, 104
private flights offer reduced social
    contact, 104
private investing in green aviation,
    225
private investment, 14
private jet operators, 159
private sector, 14
private sector invest in green
    aviation, 225
Procedures for Air Navigation
    Services (PANS), 22–23, 27
produce new greener prototypes, 269
products & services, 31
promote inclusive and sustainable
    economic growth, 12
promoting hand hygiene, 101
promoting inclusive and sustainable
    industrialization, 12
proposed rule by the FAA on June
    28, 2019, 202
protection of biodiversity, 216
protect people, 93
providing practical guidance to
    governments, 96
public financing programs, 224
public health emergency, 93
public–private partnerships, 14

Q
QR code technology, 253
quarantine requirements, 96
quiet supersonic flight technology,
    205

R
rapid battery replacement options,
    115
rationalizing their offer, 269
R&D for "greener" technology, 106

re-birth of the commercial aviation,
    57
recognized public health standards,
    96
recover from COVID-19, 97
recovery plans, 156
recreational electric aircraft, 136
reduced contact, 162
reduced staff, 162
reduce emissions, 220
reducing contact, 100
reducing emissions, 150
reducing health risks, 96
reduction of fleets, 59
regional/business aircraft, 112
Regional Supplementary Procedures
    (SUPPs), 23
regulate the market for air transport
    and GA, 231– 232
regulating access to various areas,
    100
regulation, 129
Regulation (EEC) No. 95/93, 51
regulatory framework for aviation in
    China, 230
regulatory functions, 32
reintroduce commercial supersonic
    flight, 209
reinvigorate civil aviation and foster
    GA, 253
remedies adopted by the EU, 50
Remote Tower Revolutionizes Air
    Traffic Control, 17
renaissance of supersonic aircraft,
    210
responsible finance, 211
restructuring of the entire sector, 57
returns of green investments, 215
review of the classification and
    definitions used for civil Aviation
    Activities, 35, 37
revision of the EU ETS, 107

revolution in business aviation, 198
ride in an air taxi, 144
rise in private aviation's demand
    during the COVID-19 crisis, 162
roadmap for restarting aviation, 97
role of airports, 99
role of civil aviation, 93
role of leasing companies, 59
rooftops for take-off and landing, 150

S
S-512 supersonic business jet, 205
safe environment airports, 102
safeguarding consumer interests and
    increasing efficiency, 15
safety and certifications, 143
Safety Assessment of Foreign
    Aircraft (SAFA), 22
safety & security, 30
safety standards, 143
same-day transoceanic round trips,
    202
satellite-based navigation systems, 8
satellite-based system of ATM, 17
scheduled international air service, 33
screening, 96
seat kilometer, 56
second largest aviation market, 230
Secretariat and Secretary-General, 25
Secretary-General of ICAO, 27
selected neuralgic node in the city,
    149
self-cleaning solutions for security
    trays, 101
sell and leaseback, 60
serve urban areas with suburban
    areas, 148
shift to electrical propulsion, 129
single-aisle aircraft, 110
Single European Sky Air Traffic
    Management Research (SESAR),
    16–17, 156

Single European Sky (SES), 16, 107
skilled human resources
    development, 262
slot allocation, 40
slots, 40
smaller electric-powered aircraft, 110
smart-city transportation systems
    applications, 146
social acceptance, 145
social benefit, 9–10
social benefits of aviation, 9
social considerations, 213
social exclusion, 12
social impact, 212
social justice, 214
sonic booms-mitigation technologies,
    205
space act agreement, 209
special class of aircraft, 143
special flight authorizations for
    Supersonic, 202
specific use of VTOL, 148
Spike Aerospace, 202, 205
stabilization packages, 48
Standards and Recommended
    Practices (SARPs), 11, 25, 27–28
standards & procedures, 31
strategic resource, 245
strengthening relations, 9
Strengthen Public Confidence, 94
super midsize business jets, 167
supersonic air transportation, 202
Supersonic Renaissance, 201
Supersonic Transport Concept
    Airplane (STCA), 203
supersonic travel, 208
supply chains, 9
sustainability, 213
sustainability-linked instruments for
    the aviation sector, 221
sustainable air transport development,
    10

sustainable alternative fuels, 70
sustainable aviation, 110, 150
sustainable aviation fuel and
   CO_2 emissions, 70
sustainable aviation fuels (SAFs), 70,
   106, 108, 210
sustainable aviation technologies, 114
sustainable development, 10
sustainable development goals
   (SDGs), 11–13
sustainable economic activities, 213
sustainable finance, 211–213
sustainable financial markets, 213
sustainable funds, 212
sustainable hydrogen production, 119
sustainable mobility, 139
sustainable products, 216
sustainable supersonic transport, 208
sustainable transport, 6, 216
sustainable transport by air, 96

T
5G technology, 145
tax relief, 49
tax relief for the US aviation industry,
   53
Technical Co-operation Bureau, 26
Technical Co-operation Committee
   and the Human Resources
   Committee, 25
technological obstacles, 126
technology and financing in the green
   aviation, 227
technology remains the most
   significant limiting factor, 124
territorial integration and
   environmental responsibility, 223
Textron Aviation Inc., 193
The Bureau of Administration and
   Services, 26
The European Green Deal, 87
The green bonds, 216

The impact of COVID-19 on China's
   air cargo sector, 264
three leading aircraft families, 181
times lower fuel consumption, 199
toward a Green Aviation, 211
traffic growth projections, 16
transition to a green economy, 215
transition to electric propulsion,
   124
transport Bureau, 26
transport links, 9
transport modes, 6
transport networks, 99
transport system, 11
travel all around the globe by air, 9
travel industry and air transportation,
   162
treatment of air crews, 96
Triennial Assembly, 24
twin rudders, 153
Two options for hydrogen: Fuels cells
   or combustion?, 115
TwoTwenty business jet, 175

U
UAM industry, 157
UAM represents the future of
   transport, 271
Uber, 154
Uber is likely to launch in 2023, 154
ultra-fast charging, 115
ultra large business jet (VIP
   airliners), 168
UN agreements on climate change,
   129
UN High Level Political Forum on
   Sustainable Development, 13
uninterrupted air cargo services, 52
uninterrupted airflow, 199
unit load devices (ULD), 37
urban aircraft need a safe landing
   zone, 150

urban air mobility (UAM), 105, 113, 270
urban air taxis, 129
urban air traffic management, 142
USA still accounts for nearly two-third, 161
US Department of Treasury, 54
use of green finance, 226
use of hydrogen, 78
U-space, 142, 157, 257
US space agency, NASA, 209
UV-light, 101

V
valuable type of goods, 263
vertical take-off and landing (VTOL) aircraft, 113, 128
Vertiport are on the horizon, 149
vertiports, 149
very light jet, 163–164
Virgin Galactic, 202, 209
Virgin Group envisions a flight at 60,000 feet, 209
VLJ, the smallest private jet category, 163–164
Volante, 153

VTOL category, 113
VTOLS are a new breed of aircraft, 140
VTOLs need specific and dedicated infrastructures, 149

W
waste-derived aviation fuel, 108
work as one aviation team and show solidarity, 94
world aviation organizations, 28
World Customs Organization, 28
World Health Organisation, 101
World Meteorological Organization (WMO), 23
world's first four-seater hydrogen fuel cell aircraft, 116
world trade, 8

X
XB-1, 207

Z
zero emissions for aviation in 2050, 110

Printed in the United States
by Baker & Taylor Publisher Services